Black Performance and Cultural Criticism

Valerie Lee and E. Patrick Johnson, Series Editors

Mutha' is half a word

Intersections of Folklore, Vernacular, Myth, and Queerness in Black Female Culture

L. H. Stallings

The Ohio State University Press
Columbus

Copyright © 2007 by The Ohio State University.
All rights reserved.

Library of Congress Cataloging-in-Publication Data
Horton-Stallings, LaMonda.
Mutha' is half a word : intersections of folklore, vernacular, myth, and queerness in black female culture / L.H. Stallings.
      p. cm.—(Black performance and cultural criticism)
Includes bibliographical references and index.
    ISBN-13: 978-0-8142-1056-7 (cloth : alk. paper)
    ISBN-10: 0-8142-1056-2 (cloth : alk. paper)
    ISBN-13: 978-0-8142-9135-1 (cd-rom)
    ISBN-10: 0-8142-9135-X (cd-rom)
1. American literature—African American authors—History and criticism. 2. American literature—women authors—History and criticism. 3. African American women in literature. 4. Lesbianism in literature. 5. Gender identity in literature. 6. African American women—Race identity. 7. African American women—Intellectual life. 8. African American women—Folklore. I. Title. II. Series
    PS153.N5H68 2007
    810.9'353—dc22
                            2006037239

Cover design by Jennifer Shoffey Forsythe.
Cover illustration by Michel Isola from shutterstock.com.
Text design and typesetting by Jennifer Shoffey Forsythe in Adobe Garamond.
Printed by Thomson-Shore, Inc.

The paper used in this publication meets the minimum requirements of the American National Standard for Information Sciences—Permanence of Paper for Printed Library Materials. ANSI Z39.48–1992.

9 8 7 6 5 4 3 2 1

for
VanessaMattieRaMondaLatashaJasmineOctaviaEthelPat
VictoriaJudyLizPauletteBridgettAngelaGwenFlorence

Contents

Acknowledgments	ix
A Preface on Behalf of Sex Itself (Written by Herself)	xii
Introduction	1
1. The Black Woman and the Trickster Trope of Unnaming	33
2. The Erotics of a Healing Subjectivity: Sexual Desire, the Spirit, and the Divine Nature of Trickster	82
3. "Mutha' Is Half a Word!": Tar Baby Trope and Blue Material in Black Female Comedy	113
4. Badd-Nasty: Tricking the Tropes of the Bad Man/Nigga and Queen B(?)	150
5. *The Black and White* of Queen B(?)'s Play	184
6. Queen B(?)'s Queering of Neo-Soul Desire	221
7. Representin' for the Bitches: Queen B(?) in Hip-Hop Culture	256
Conclusion	
Trickster's Gift: A Language of Sexual Rights through Polymorphous Erotics and Voluptuous Black Women's Sexualities	281
Notes	295
Works Cited	311
Index	329

Acknowledgments

I'd like to thank my mother-father, Vanessa Horton, for sustaining me from wild child to unnamable being that I am. My accomplishments are a mere fraction of the sacrifices and love given so unconditionally from her. I thank my grandmother Mattie Walker for sticking with me long after she departed this world. I am grateful for the love and support of my two sisters, RaMonda and Latasha. As we grew up, "poor, black, and female" in inner-city Durham, we helped each other redefine that subjectivity so that we could survive and succeed where we were meant not to (in this world). I also appreciate the time I get to spend with my nieces and nephews, Jasmine, R.J., Eli, and Octavia. Together, they continue to remind me of the importance of radical Black female subjectivity for Black women and men of the future. I also acknowledge my aunts: Paulette, Liz, Ethel Mae, Pat, Judy, and Victoria. My first examples of radical Black women were you, and each year I realize my good fortune in having been schooled by you.

Thank you, Adrienne Israel at Guilford College, for critically and enthusiastically encouraging me to pursue graduate studies. I give thanks to the Appalachian State University crew (Bruce Dick, Georgia Rhoades, Edelma Huntley, T. J. Arant, and Thomas McLaughlin), who helped lay the foundation for my early development as a scholar-teacher.

The four years that I spent at Michigan State University provided me with fruitful experiences and valuable friendships. Phyllis Burns, Tammy Wahpeconiah, and Dolores Sisco, thank you for all the laughter, as well as your creative intellect, friendship, and lasting love. Without the rigorous guidance of my dissertation committee and readers, Kenneth Harrow, Geneva Smitherman (Dr. G.), Greg Thomas, Theresa Melendez, Scott Michaelsen, Bill Lawson, and Issac Kalumbu, *Mutha'* would not exist. I'd like to thank Kenneth Harrow for providing me with invaluable suggestions and advice that motivated me to challenge the boundaries of critical theory.

I am especially thankful to Dr. G., Greg, and Dr. Gloria Randle for showing me the type of teacher-scholar I could be. A shout-out to Greg for recognizing the value of my trickster implications for female hip-hop when not too many other people did. Big ups to Dr. G. for mentoring country when, and only when, country needed mentoring. I'd also like to thank Trudier Harris, Deborah McDowell, Carole Boyce Davies, Hortense Spillers, and Patricia Williams for doing an atypical seminar class in spring 2000 at MSU. That seminar helped me formulate what questions and concerns I had about Black women's culture, and those concerns form the foundation of this text's purpose.

My first three years at the University of Florida have proven to be delightfully challenging and rewarding. I am grateful for the support of my department chair, John Leavey. I'd like to thank Mark Reid, Kenneth Kidd, Pamela Gilbert, Malini Schueller, and Marsha Bryant for making sure that a sista was always all right. Holla, holla at the young-gifted-and-Black, and their light-light-skinned counterparts, for keeping me sharp on Black literary and cultural theory as I made my revisions to the manuscript. Marlon Moore, Marlo David, Craig Smith, Maryam El-Shall, Angelique Nixon, and Daniel Holder: I know that your work and voices will contribute a great deal to your chosen fields. Thank you, Amy Ongiri and Barbara Mennel, for countless dinners and a stopover spot that helped me balance out work and play. You are wonderful scholars, devoted teachers, and thoughtful friends.

Thank you, Greg, Keith Byerman, Joyce Petis, Valerie Lee, and Kevin Quashie, for reading early drafts of this manuscript. Your input was heard, appreciated, and used to improve. Chapter 2 is a heavily modified version of "From Mules and Turtle and Unicorn Women: The Gender-Folk Revolution and the Legacy of the Obeah" published by Peter Lang Press in *After the Pain: Critical Essays on Gayl Jones,* the only book-length collection of critical essays on Gayl Jones. North Carolina State University published a portion of chapter 3, which was an essay entitled "Re-Reading Ann Allen Shockley through the Queen B's Queering" in *Obsidian III* vol. 4, no.1 (Fall/Winter 2002–2003). I gratefully acknowledge both presses. Thank you Sandy Crooms and Eugene O'Connor, my hard-working and generous editor, for all of your efforts in making this a good book. The research of *Mutha'* was made possible due to institutional support from the University of Florida, and especially the Schomburg Research Institute for Black Culture. The Schomburg Center allowed me time and access to invaluable files for this project and my next.

To William and Kifu, I am eternally grateful for the way you each welcome me into your hearts and life. I thank Kifu for love and support that rejuvenated my personal beliefs and academic theories of radical Black female subjectivities. I am grateful to William—partner for life—for coming into my life, staying in my life, and loving the not-so-nice girl I was and the unwifeable woman I've become. The last eighteen years have been a wonderfully amazing journey. I feel very fortunate to have found two people who contribute to my evolution as a radical Black female subject. Thanks for accepting trickster into your lives, despite the chaos and disorder. Thank you both for loving trickster 'cause trickster shoul' loves you!

A Preface on Behalf of Sex Itself[1] (Written by Herself)

As this is a work dedicated to the tradition and techniques of Black female oral culture, I'd like to begin the way all good folktales begin, by telling a story within a story. . . . Though this book has been a project in process for some time, recent practical experiences from my own classroom have humorously validated its theoretical tasks and arguments time and again. During one spring, I learned from one of my Black female students that one of my advertised courses for the fall semester had been designated the "pussy class." The student, whom I'd previously taught in three classes, told me, "Dr. Horton-Stallings, a few of us registered for your pussy class next semester." That was not the title of my course.

"My what?" I asked. I could feel a slow smile creeping onto my face. Could it be that all my hopes and dreams were realized? Was I the pussy teacher of the pussy class? My student replied, "Yeah, yeah, that's what we're calling it since you got all those books on pussy." My student was exaggerating, but clitoris, vagina, cunt, and pussy were in some of the text titles tentatively listed in the course description and reading list. Still, the purpose of the class was more than a sensationalist and sweeping nod to female genitalia. I envisioned it as a politically charged class on female sexual militancy. Its themes and goals arose from a startling experience I had with a previous class on neo-slave narratives. In that class centered on gender issues and neo-slavery, a different studious Black female student and self-proclaimed "frequent enrollee in African American–anything courses" delivered a presentation on the representation of Black women in rap videos as comparable to European representations of Sara Baartman, the Hottentot Venus. The student delivered a PowerPoint presentation of the well-known pictures exaggerating Baartman's buttocks and vulva, and she completed a feminist reading of the slides and videos. In explicating on the details of other medical photo-diagrams, she stumbled over details in one diagram: "I don't know if that's called the labia or the clitoris. Whatever it's called."

"The clitoris and clitoral hood," I almost shouted. Given the importance of this flesh-art for humanity's very own existence, its influence on many individuals' love and sex lives, as well as the significance of it to my work, I was, to say the least, appalled that she was either embarrassed or did not know what to call the parts of it: and if she didn't know, she more than likely did not know the possibilities and wonders of "whatever it's called." Throughout the semester, Black females in my neo-slave narrative class had voiced concerns about the images of Black women impressed upon them by society and the powerlessness brought on by the images. Yet clearly some of them never took the time to consciously decide how they saw themselves. Even as they could dissect the dress or undress of so-called video vixens, most of them rarely critiqued their own various states of undress in my classroom. In addition to lacking general knowledge about their bodies, their politics seemed to clash with their fashion sense. Because desire is so complicated, there seems to be an impasse between performances of gender, representation, and how to visually and vocally articulate individual sexuality (hetero, homo, virgin, or skank) and its depths as influenced by individual life experiences that even the clothes on one's back cannot overcome. Ironically, the majority of my students had taken women and gender studies classes and African American studies courses, but somehow in the process of learning highly sophisticated theoretical bits on race, gender, class, and sexuality, they did not know what to call it and failed to consider the intricacies of desire and sexual subjectivity beyond concerns of stereotypes. The student's presentation and responses to it had given me the blues, so I took Ida Cox's words, "Wild women don't worry, wild women's don't have the blues" ("Wild Women Don't Have No Blues"), into consideration when I created my classes for the following semester.

Hence, "Radical Female Pleasure, Politics, and Militancy in Women's Popular Culture," affectionately known as the pussy class, was conceived. It was not a health sex education class, but it was a course about the texts used to create women's bodies and the text of women's bodies. It was designed to offer an inquiry into the empowering force of women's sexual desires as depicted in female culture. Black women's popular culture was featured prominently. In addition to interesting texts, I created assignments such as the p-song assignment. This assignment asked female students to create a song about their bodies, and male students could create songs revealing their thoughts on the female body. There were already hundreds of songs written about the subject in American music. Some of them can be found in the Black music tradition, but the students' assignment was to deal specifically with their own genital philosophy rather than write on the general anatomy of woman.

My research on Black oral traditions validated the pedagogical approach of the exercise in several ways. Oral traditions have been used for years as teaching tools in a number of societies and on a variety of subject matters, so why not sexuality or the female body? In creating oral texts, students must grapple with complex elements that simple written assignments allow them to avoid: They have to confront their perceptions about their bodies and the conflict of language in discussing those perceptions, and find a voice that can convey the intersections of the first two. What language will they use to write their bodies? Will that language go with the voice they speak in? Will it convey that body? The key here is that the written text will never expose the potential conflict between the inadequacies of language, social constraints, and the body. The actual speaking or singing aloud the words comes from the body. If the student has no connection to the body, how it looks, or however she experiences it, then the performance, whether spoken, sung, or presented by PowerPoint, will reveal that ignorance either in the language chosen or in the performance. My hopes were that the new class could make its way through a struggle that has been a part of Black studies for some time.

From the very beginning of Black women's early attempts to create theories for African American females and their culture and articulate a female perspective of African American culture as a whole, we have had to overcome a certain fear and find a sense of daring not only to recover some of those earlier ingenuities in early African American female culture, but also to use that daring to support us in creating new theoretical paradigms. In the ever-important and ground-breaking work *The Black Woman*, the great Toni Cade Bambara established a primary mission for her collection when she assessed the state of Black female liberation:

> If we women are to get basic, then surely the first job is to find out what liberation for ourselves means, what work it entails, what benefits it will yield. To do that, we might turn to various fields of studies to extract materials, data necessary to define that term in respect to ourselves. We note, however, all too quickly the lack of relevant material. (7)

Bambara, a writer and activist, understood how the creative forces that drove her also gave birth to critical paradigms that inextricably linked to a formation of herself that could not be defined as yet. Bambara allowed the collection of essays by activists, writers, artists, and musicians to serve as a communal signifier on the Black female liberation movement during the 1970s. Bambara's anthology serves as a vital introduction to the diversities in approaches, styles, and identities of Black females seeking liberation for their social and cultural identities and presences in U.S. society.

Bambara's decision to incorporate poetry, fiction, criticism, and theory acknowledges the necessity for the presence of creativity in critical analysis in order to equip Black females with the tools they need to really discuss themselves. More than thirty years later the same problems persist, and this work is a tribute to Bambara's call in *The Black Woman*. While we may now recognize that extracting materials from various disciplines helps us to do so, we should also be able to assert what is relevant or not relevant to our quest. *Mutha' Is Half a Word: Intersections of Folklore, Vernacular, Myth, and Queerness in Black Female Culture* is my academic effort to attest that Black folklore and oral forms, and mythical figures in Black folklore and vernacular traditions, provide alternative ways for Black women to conceptualize and represent their gender and sexual desires.

Introduction

Mutha' Is Half a Word: Intersections of Folklore, Vernacular, Myth, and Queerness in Black Female Culture is about the uncensoring of Black women who laugh out loud, curse, sit with their legs open, and selfishly act on their desires. It is about tomboys, not-so-nice girls, and unwifeable women. It looks at the constructions of Black female subjectivities cognizant of autonomous sexual desires. How do Black women use culture to explore sexual desire that is spiritual, intellectual, physical, emotional, and fluid so as to avoid splits or binaries that can freeze Black women's radical sexual subjectivities? It is not easy. In the words of both real and fictional people who have theorized on the predicament of Black women's bodies and desires, a master narrative of otherness works in conjunction with a self-imposed politics of sexuality. As Evelyn Hammonds notes, at the end of the twentieth century Black women were still dealing with their otherness and the politics of sexuality in very specific ways:

> Black feminist theorists, historians, literary critics, sociologists, lawyers, and cultural critics have drawn up a specific historical narrative that purportedly describes the factors that have produced and maintained perceptions of Black women's sexuality (including their own). Three themes emerge in this history: first, the construction of the Black female as the embodiment of sex and the attendant invisibility of Black women as the unvoiced . . . second, the resistance of Black women both to negative stereotypes of their sexuality and to the material effects of those stereotypes on their lives and, finally, the evolution of a "culture of dissemblance" and a "politics of silence" by black women on the issue of their sexuality. ("Black [W]holes" 303)

Taking on what W. E. B. Dubois called the "Damnation of Women" during the early twentieth century, Hammonds notices three very particular historical master narratives that engaged Black women's gender and sexuality. Hammonds remarks on how deciphering and challenging the dominant master narrative of otherness has required multiple tactics: resistance to stereotypes, cultural dissemblance, and a politics of silence. Yet the last two tactics evolve as a result of the historical move to resist stereotypes. Since medical and cultural research continue to expose that there are more than two genders and many sexualities, the most glaring cause of concern within acts of resisting stereotypes surfaces when we do not acknowledge the complexities of having numerous genders and sexualities. Someone's invalidated gender may be someone else's stereotype. One person's indefinable sexuality could be another's promiscuous sexuality. As Black cultural studies continue to address gender and sexuality, we must reconsider who gets to say what is and is not a valid form of resistance to the stereotypes, and why.

The culture of dissemblance and a politics of silence have created what June Jordan might call a politics of sexuality that has persistently hindered resistance to stereotypes and the formation of Black women's radical sexual subjectivity. Jordan observes that "the politics of sexuality therefore subsumes all of the different ways in which some of us seek to dictate to others of us what we should do, what we should desire, what we should dream about, and how we should behave ourselves" ("A New Politics of Sexuality" 132). In regards to gender and sexuality then, dissemblance and silence allows a policing of sexuality that is supported through social and political rhetoric of a group of people. In response to this politics of sexuality in African America, Black women could be rescued by their Black men or ideologically stoned with the markers of Jezebel, Sapphire, or Mammy.[1] The choices given appear to be simple: be the stereotype or be the antistereotype dependent upon patriarchy and heterosexuality. Historically, any other options would be seen as causing more harm than good. But what about radical Black female sexual subjectivities? As Velma of Toni Cade Bambara's *The Salteaters* once voiced: "What good did wild do you, since there was always some low-life gruesome gang bang raping lawless careless pesty last straw nasty thing ready to pounce, put your total shit under arrest and crack your back—but couldn't" (278). Throughout her novel, Bambara works with metaphors and symbols of hunting and wilderness to discuss her protagonist's pursuit to be well. At first, oppressive regimes seem overpowering in keeping subverted "the hunt for self" (267), but it is the search, the desire to look at what is not caged (classified and grouped), that allows for continued resistance against that which threatens to crack Black women's backs. Real resistance to negative stereotypes would entail more than simply reversing the binary logic of stereotypes about Black women's sexuality: it would mean destroying systems of gender and sexuality that make the stereotypes possible. Such action would aid in the initial construction of radical

Black female sexual subjectivities.

At times, the twenty-first century echoes the previous century's proposition for Black women. For this reason, and in response to Velma's question, despite the misogynistic, sexist, racist, and homophobic representations of Black female body parts being displayed in (male- and female-oriented, mainstream/Black-stream) magazines, music videos, mainstream movies, and pornography, I may seem a little out of fashion when I say this book offers varied suggestions on how to read wild sexual women in Black literature and popular culture and not the stereotypes of wild women. It is a dissection of wild women that bell hooks momentarily ruminates on in *Black Looks: Race and Representation*: "Wild is the metaphoric expression of that inner will to rebel, to move against the grain, to be out of one's place. It is the expression of radical black female subjectivity" (49). Wildness is radical Black female subjectivity that consciously celebrates autonomy and self-assertion in the invention process of self. The stereotypes of wild women are caricatures of women who appear to rebel, but there is no context for that rebellion.[2] This text is interested in self-authored sexual desire and radical Black female sexual subjectivity that purposely incorporates that desire as the context for rebellion from the beginning, as opposed to its presence as an afterthought. Such moments provide the required foundation for a new politics of sexuality for Black women and their culture.

With the continued infractions on Black female bodies worldwide by medical institutions and media conglomerates, the increase of human trafficking using women of color, the rapid rate of HIV infection among Black women, the domestic physical and mental abuse endured by Black women, the encroaching conservative threat to lesbian-bi-trans women, the increasing number of incarcerated Black women for performing sex work, the forced sterilization of Black women, and the danger of *Roe v Wade* being overturned,[3] I'm not ready to throw out the "nasty" girl, that "bad" girl, and dress her up in her Sunday best, take her to church, and make her sit all prim and proper with her legs tightly crossed and closed like Vanity and Donna Summer on a Sunday morning.[4] I shudder to think what the world would be like without her. I refuse to let male supremacists, white, Black, and other, continue to get rich from their version of Black female sexuality that they lord over me. Meanwhile, open, unabashed, non-heteronormative, and celebrated versions of Black female sexuality personified in the depictions of and efforts by wild women get mistaken for that other, placed in the closet, put out of house and home, go to jail, get beaten, are violated, or are destroyed altogether. I owe it to the legacies of Sojourner Truth, Harriet Tubman, Zora Neale Hurston, Ma Rainey, Gladys Bentley, Storme Delavarie, Bessie Smith, Josephine Baker, Moms Mabley, Lucille Bogan, Toni Cade Bambara, Billie Delia, Sula, and a whole heap of other real and mythical Black women to read wild women outside of the caricatures and stereotypes and in an uncensored fashion that eliminates the risk of replacing them with an antithetical Victorian model of womanhood that emphasizes chaste and virtuous decorum.

As the twenty-first century arrived, scholars of African American women's culture were fortunate enough to reconsider the predicament of Black women's gender and sexuality. In "Black (W)holes and the Geometry of Black Female Sexuality," Evelyn Hammonds continues to write about Black women's sexuality in general, and Black queer female sexuality in particular. In doing so, she notes that recent theories about Black women's gender and sexuality have revolved around issues of invisibility and silence. Whether it is Evelyn Higginbotham's "politics of silence" or Darlene Clark Hine's "culture of dissemblance,"[5] the historically politicized quiet has made it very difficult to fully discuss Black women's sexual desires beyond the presentation of their existence, even as critics have been able to delve into the issues of representation and stereotypes. Hammond's consideration of Black women's sexuality reminds us that there is a great deal more work to be done.

Tricia Rose's *Longing to Tell: Black Women Talk about Sexuality and Intimacy* moves thoughtful discussion on African diasporic gender and sexuality studies into new territory. Early on she divulges the premise for her premier oral history collection on Black women's sexuality: "This book began as an attempt to answer a scholarly question: How has the history of race, class, and gender inequality affected the way black women talk about their sexual lives? It also began as an effort to take on the call made by many black feminists for more reflection on black women's sexuality in modern America" (foreword, ix). With her proclamation for intimate justice, Rose's work successfully answers the call and continues to lead us in the right direction. One of the most promising aspects of *Longing to Tell* is that its author consciously refuses to classify or separate the women's stories about their sexuality in traditional ways that cement heteronormativity as a master narrative of sexuality. There is no separation of the bisexual from the lesbian, no division of the college educated from the working class, and no judgment passed on the sexual experienced and adventurer versus the lesser experienced. Rose's book manages to convey differences of class, age, geography, and blackness in the expressions of sexual desires in ways that clearly show Black women grappling with the notion that there are many genders and sexualities, but too few existing narratives for the multitude of them.

Yet what remains clear is that century after century Black women's discussions about sexuality in critical and creative efforts, as well as real life and fiction, have been marred by the notion of silence, secrecy, and whispers. Some Black women may have been longing to tell, but there were those

Black women who have been telling, and in the telling they have been bawdy, explicit, and downright shameless in their expressions of sexual desires, despite reprimands they may have received. It is those voices that we still have trouble celebrating. As we will see later in this introduction, recent scholarship underlines the values of these women's contributions. Still, Black women continue to wage an internal battle over the damnation of women, fulfilling desires, and expressing individual sexual desire and representations of those desires. Arguably, if it continues to be a one-image-over-another battle, all Black women will lose. We must continue changing the terrain and the foundations of these arguments.

Stereotypes and misrepresentations of Black women occur because of the way we are taught to read differences. According to Audre Lorde's "Age, Race, Class, and Sex: Women Redefining Difference," "we have all been programmed to respond to human difference in one of three ways: ignore it, and if that is not possible, copy it if we think it is dominant, or destroy it if we think it is subordinate. But we have no patterns for relating across our human differences as equals. As a result, those differences have been misnamed and misused in the service of separation and confusion" (115). Lorde's words expose the way dominant society uses difference as a way to oppress and maintain supremacy over subordinated groups, but it also heightens awareness of the way the oppressed counter stereotypes and misrepresentations. Historically, Black women have ignored, copied, or attempted to destroy difference to fit a "normative" model of womanhood, as well as an authentic notion of blackness. And while race, class, and gender are huge differences, the way sexual desire functions within those differences is the subject of this work.

It behooves women to continuously work to redefine difference while avoiding hierarchies of such differences. As if to illuminate the urgency of such work for Black women, Hortense Spillers's wonderfully verbose style of writing becomes dramatically simple when she chooses to discuss sexual desire and Black women in feminist and cultural studies, stating, "The sexual realities of black American women across the spectrum of sexual preference and widened sexual styles tend to be a missing dialectical feature of the entire discussion" ("Interstices" 91). What Hammonds, Rose, and Spillers command with their words is that we realize that the missing dialectical in our reflections of Black women's sexuality is a redefining of difference, as opposed to deviation.

Arguably escaping the damnation of women, deciding when and where we enter,[6] and revising the historical precepts of Black women's sexual desires hinge on one major consideration: how we read difference. Accordingly, Lorde theorizes that "certainly there are very real differences between us of race, age, and sex. But it is not those differences between us that are separating us. It is rather our refusal to recognize those differences, and to examine the distortions which result from our misnaming them and their effects upon human behavior and expectation. . . . We speak not of human difference, but of human deviance" (115–16). The distinction that Lorde makes between difference and deviation is an essential one for Black women articulating and representing their sexual desires. In order to convey desires without incorporating deviance, critical understanding of this distinction must be reached. How does difference become deviance in the way that Lorde has suggested?

Jacques Derrida indicates in *Positions* that "in a traditional philosophical opposition we have not a peaceful coexistence of facing terms but a violent hierarchy. One of the terms dominates the other (axiologically, logically, etc), occupies a commanding position. To deconstruct the opposition is to above all, at a particular moment, to reverse the hierarchy" (56–57). Derrida's assessment of the Western metaphysical categorization process is exactly what Lorde alludes to in her discussion of difference and deviance. The dispersal of widely accepted oppositions such as presence/absence, good/evil, truth/error, man/woman, positive/negative, and so on demonstrate that binary oppositions are a pair of ranked and contrasted terms, each of which depends on the other for meaning. They classify and organize the objects, events, and relations of the world. The most important revelation of Lorde's and Derrida's critiques is that if we accept any binary logic, then that acceptance establishes conceptual order (39–40). As the field of deconstruction has shown, the conceptual order affects every discourse, from race and class to gender and sexuality. Subsequently, one must not only reverse the hierarchy but also avoid making the reversal an established order. Black female cultural producers, in order to create and sustain radical Black female sexual subjectivity, must embrace difference as a foundation without simply reversing the established order that fosters readings of difference as deviance. The stripper, prostitute, video vixen, gold digger, and sexual exhibitionist cannot continue to be the deviant polarity to the working woman, wife, mother, lady, and virgin. We must locate the differences without ranking them and destroy the conceptual order of Western metaphysics, and in turn dismantle Western ideologies of gender and sexuality. To expose nontraditional desires and sexuality in ways that resist deviance entails some hard work that insists upon locating unique models. Doing so may mean the difference between mimicking misrepresentations or claiming and reclaiming wildness.

However, Lorde misspoke when she suggested that we have no way of relating to human differences as equals. She found the means in her own considerations of tricksters. As opposed to continuing to consider the silences or invisibilities, *Mutha' Is Half a Word* proposes the examination of unacknowledged techniques for uncovering the spaces of the vocal and visible where Black female sexuality is not defensive or concerned with the uplifting of the race, but radical and ever aware of its survival and evolution—folklore and vernacular culture. Currently, a scholarly turn to folklore could be seen as a romantic nod to authenticity and essentialism. However, *Mutha' Is Half a Word* argues that folklore and vernacular undo such predictable moves. Some scholars have already expanded on the unyielding ways that folklore and vernacular traditions have been read by critics. Ann DuCille's *The Coupling Convention: Sex, Text, and Tradition in Black Women's Fiction* notes: "However attractive and culturally affirming, the valorization of the vernacular has yielded what I would argue is an inherently exclusionary literary practice that filters a wide range of complex and contradictory impulses and energies into a single modality consisting of the blues and the folk" (69). DuCille is not alone in her discussion of how folklore has been read as a male tradition; *Authentic Blackness: The Folk in the New Negro Renaissance* by J. Martin Favor dissects the phenomenon of making folklore a predeterminate factor in authenticating blackness. His work refuses to explicitly agree with critics like DuCille who regard folk culture as masculine, but he does suggest an impetus of change in how folklore is used: "The form of folk expression is gendered by exclusion, meaning that when we speak of folk culture, we generally speak of *male* folk culture . . . it points toward how we need to examine more closely the way gender is manipulated to arrive at a notion of authenticity" (18). Although Zora Neale Hurston, at the beginning of the twentieth century, and her followers during the Black women's renaissance of the 1970s might have embraced folklore and vernacular to achieve voice in documenting their gendered experiences, this approach has recently been under fire.

Like DuCille and Favor, many other contemporary critics of Black culture seem to believe that uses of folklore and vernacular culture have been exhausted, and that the forms themselves have been read as limited in their use for considerations of a wide spectrum of Black culture based on distinctions of class, gender, and sexuality. Hazel Carby, in "The Politics of Fiction, Anthropology, and the Folk: Zora Neale Hurston," criticizes the way that Hurston's work is rescued from the abyss of forgotten Black women writers. Carby takes issue with what happens as a result of that cultural recovery: essentialized folkisms. For Carby, the fault lies with scholars who have used Black folklore to authenticate one depiction of Black culture communities over others. She also classifies critics' elevation of Hurston's depiction of Black southern life as "not only a discursive displacement of the historical and cultural transformation of migration, but also . . . a creation of a folk who are outside history" (77). Together, these dilemmas of romanticizing folklore and authenticating blackness through folklore and vernacular potentially form the basis of the small but vocal antivernacular criticism in recent

African American critical and cultural theory.[7] They are all very valid points, especially in motivating us to broaden our perceptions of blackness.

If we read Black folklore as merely a means of authenticity, in the way that DuCille, Favor, and Carby have accused critics of doing, then folklore is limited and obsolete as an introspective model into Black culture today. However, if we consider folklore, myth, and vernacular in the way that Robin D. G. Kelley does in *Yo Mama's Disfunktional: Fighting the Cultural Wars in Urban America*, then perhaps we may be ready to open up another line of consideration for the folk:

> Black music, creativity and experimentation in language, that walk, that talk, that style must also be understood as sources of visceral and psychic pleasure. Though they may also reflect and speak to the political and social world of inner city communities, expressive cultures are not simply mirrors of social life of expressions of conflicts, pathos, and anxieties. (41)

Mutha' Is Half a Word relies on orality, folklore, and vernacular to examine Black females' cultural representation of sexual desire because they are sources of visceral and psychic pleasures that can allow for the reading of differences in desires, as opposed to deviating desires. Once we revise the way we read these traditions, we learn that they are not exclusionary. Rose's *Longing to Tell* is so successful at showing differences within sexual desires without making them deviant because it is an oral collection. It does not have to adhere to the model of logocentric thought, and it remains cognizant of visceral and psychic pleasure. Likewise, instead of turning to trickster, folklore, and vernacular to authenticate Black women's culture, *Mutha' Is Half a Word* argues that these cultural forms offer Black women alternative methods to express their sexual desires and expand blackness in the process.

In addition to concerns of difference being capitulated into deviance, Black women also have to ponder issues of inauthenticity, especially when their desires do not align with aims of authentic blackness or the goals of dignified womanhood. What has mired discussions about Black women's sexuality and expressions of sexual desires is the commitment to a particular type of blackness, one that inherently privileges masculinity, heteronormative womanhood, and heterosexuality. G. T. Hull, P. B. Scott, and B. Smith's collection, *All the Women Are White, All the Blacks Are Men: But Some of Us Are Brave*, bravely questions the role of Black women in developing arguments against inequality in social and political representation. With proclamations such as "we struggle together with Black men against racism, while we also struggle with Black men about sexism" (16) and "we reject the stance of lesbian separatism because it is not a viable political analysis or strategy for us" (17), the editors force us to reconceptualize how we define Black political struggles so that they may account for issues of sexism and homophobia. Such work is pivotal in wrestling difference away from deviation so that desire can be freely pursued and expressed. For what happens when the object choice of a Black woman's desire is not Black, is not male, is plural rather than singular, and so on and so forth? bell hooks explains that "when this diversity is ignored, it is easy to see black folks as falling into two categories: nationalist or assimilationist, black-identified or white-identified" (*Yearning* 29). Likewise, in *Appropriating Blackness: Performance and the Politics of Authenticity*, E. Patrick Johnson suggests, "When black Americans have employed the rhetoric of authenticity, the outcome has been a political agenda that has excluded more voices than it has included" (3).[8] In order to resist reading such women as a lesser model of woman or as not Black (enough), we should seek out what bell hooks theorizes as a postmodern blackness[9] to counter such thinking. In the end, differences of sexual desire can undo and threaten the essential and authentic notions of all those other social categories. How much we desire, how little we desire, who or what we desire, the way we express that desire, and the way we choose to fulfill desire inevitably threatens the rationale, logic, and organization of political identities organized by race, class, and gender. Thus, having and comprehending means, metaphors, or myths to represent those desires are vital for maintaining radical Black female sexual subjectivities. Fortunately, finding metaphors and symbols for both desire and difference as discussed within these pages may not have to be an arduous task if critics remain open to rereading Black folklore and vernacular in less exclusionary terms.

Trickster and Trickster-Troping

Trickster, a dynamic model of oral traditions, serves as the best way for exploring radical Black female sexual subjectivity. Although trickster might seem to be a relic of the past because of its ties to myth and folklore, it is very much a metaphor for futuristic possibilities of identity. As we will see, tricksters are difference and desire personified. In arguing trickster as a minor god, Erik Davis's "Tricksters at the Crossroads: West Africa's God of Messages, Sex and Deceit" asserts, "When we think of tricksters, we generally imagine folk characters and culture heroes, not gods. Tricksters either tend to be associated with animal spirits (such as Coyote), or are Promethean figures, archetypal 'humans' who interact with and upset the world of Gods" (37). In addition to his own theory of trickster as a minor god, Davis's description provides some traditional archetypes of tricksters. In referring to African, Native American, and Greek mythological tricksters, Davis shows that in cultures across the world tricksters assume many forms. Davis also delves into the roles tricksters may play in transforming worlds or societies from the margins. Although derivate of many different societies, the figures tend to share similar commonalities across cultures.

"Mapping the Characteristics of Mythic Tricksters" by William Hynes offers a brief assessment of manifest trickster traits that can be used as a typology: the fundamentally ambiguous and anomalous personality of the trickster, deceiver/trick-player, shape-shifter, situation-invertor, messenger/imitator of the gods, and sacred/lewd bricoleur (34–36). These traits explicitly deny dichotomies that might exclude or limit the development of cultural and social impulses and energies. The traits are concepts of fluid and unfixed attributes. Trickster, through its inability to rank differences, takes difference and makes *différance*. Derrida uses this term to halt and show the rankings of speech and writing, but his theory also creates an undecidable, a tool to disrupt the entire system of logocentrism founded on binary oppositions.[10] Each characteristic of trickster enables various acts of creation that could alter time, place, or person. With such traits, trickster allows difference to be read equally and without classifying elements of difference as deviance. Due to these attributes, trickster symbolizes the meeting point for folklore, myth, vernacular, and queerness, and in Black female culture that intersection often forms a discourse of desire figuratively embodied as various types of tricksters and trickster traits in Black women's texts. In many cases, the strategic use of these elements form a repetition and revision of previous tropes as well as the birth of new tricksters and traits that we might note as "trickster-troping."

Trickster has already been defined as a "taboo breaker," "messenger of sex, deceit, and lies," "baad muthafucka," "minor god," and "cultural transformer" by critics.[11] Troping is the figurative or metaphorical speech or conversation. . . . The composition or use of tropes" (*OED Online*). Trickster-troping, as I am defining in this text, will connote several definitions. Trickster-troping means the deployment and recognition of differences through an equilateral order. Trickster-troping defers the privileging of one difference over another. Trickster-troping is acts of undecidability. The composition or deliberate use of taboo breakers, minor gods, cultural transformers, and baad muthafuckas as metaphorical signs of difference and desire signifies trickster-troping. When writers, performers, and artists utilize a creative technique of constructing anomos narratives, characters, settings, or culture through multiple and simultaneous manifest traits of the trickster, that is trickster-troping. It is also any non-heteronormative act of tactically joining orality and sexuality via one or more of the manifest trickster traits to create a folk-based discourse of desire.

Trickster-troping allows Black women to resist being dominant society's "beached whales of the sexual universe, unvoiced, misseen, not doing, awaiting their verb" (Spillers, "Interstices" 74). It enables Black women to continuously strive for radical Black female sexual subjectivities that are just right for them. In summing up trickster, Carl Jung offers insight as to why trickster-troping derived from trickster works so well: "Anyone who belongs to a sphere of culture that seeks the perfect state . . . must feel very queerly indeed when confronted by the figure of the trickster" (*Four Archetypes* 169). The binaries that Black women in the West are confronted with seek to create a utopia by erasing difference or subordinating difference. Trickster-troping captures Black female writers' and performers' deliberate narrative intersection of folklore, vernacular, myth, and queerness within their texts to interrupt social binaries and express sexual desires.

Mutha' Is Half a Word argues that Black folklore, vernacular, and specific figures of oral traditions do not limit discussions of difference in Black culture and society. On the contrary, these forms and figures make it all the more plausible to articulate difference, outside of race, in a less homogeneous manner than that of nonfolk theories. Within this work, I've kept in mind two goals. First, I create a revised and sharp definition of trickster, especially as it involves the experiences of Black females, and then I show the implications of those revisions in various expressive cultural sites. Next, the primary goal of *Mutha' Is a Half a Word* is to use trickster to broaden the direction of Black female criticism from a limited focus on the rhetoric of sex to a discourse of desire[12] that is more invested in a foundational understanding of the broad spectrum of sexuality in African American female culture. As long as Black female criticism continues to rely solely on the rhetoric of sex, which is foundationally based on Western binary metaphysics such as male/female, homosexual/heterosexual, and man/woman, the radical ideologies of desire present in cultural texts by Black women will be misunderstood or lost.

To this end, *Mutha' Is Half a Word* offers close readings of sexual desire in select texts by Black women. These cultural narratives recommend constructions of sexual desire that consider spiritual, corporeal, emotional, mental, and political destinies of radical Black female sexual subjectivity. Desire marks the female slave's acceptance or rejection of gender, as well as her measurement of freedom, in the slave narrative. Desire leads a woman to her gift as a healer in Gayl Jones's *The Healing*. Desire disturbs conformist performances of gender and beauty in the comedy of LaWanda Page and other Black female comediennes. Desire reveals the rejection of racialized performances of sexuality in Ann Allen Shockley's collection of lesbian short fiction, *The Black and White of It*. Desire acts as a radical ideological weapon against sexual fear and paranoia in music by Meshell Ndegeocello and Lil' Kim. Finally, desire gives rise to a language of sexual rights and polymorphous erotics in the poetry of Cheryl Clarke. However, for readers and consumers to appreciate the empowering use of desire by such artists, they must first understand the rhetorical trickery that goes into the presentations of desire. These women use folk machinations to dramatically enter into singing natural desires of their bodies, as opposed to basking in the quiet dignity of their womanhood.[13] Trickster-troping, the intersection of folklore, vernacular, myth, and queerness, becomes one alternative practice that Black female writers and performers exploit to represent and convey their desires without the damaging repercussions and impediments from the rhetoric of sex or the discourse of race.

My choices of cultural producers and narratives are deliberate. Each author or performer examined within this text commits her cultural narrative to cherishing Black folklore and oral hermeneutics. Each work makes its reader question the rationality and logic of representing gender and desire with simple binary models of gender and sexuality by juxtaposing the rhetoric of sex with some individual form of trickster-troping (the creator's self-devised discourse of desire). And all of the works inevitably offer a race-conscious analysis of gender and sexuality. Finally, *Mutha' Is Half a Word* aspires to examine cultural producers who, like the trickster figure, would live up to or could carry the burden of being an "original outsider." Both personally and artistically, Gayl Jones, Cheryl Clarke, the Queens of Comedy (past and present), Ann Allen Shockley, Meshell Ndegeocello, and Lil' Kim seem emblematic of the trickster title. Since their works often blur the line between the profane and the sacred, their efforts and cultural forms remain underexamined in scholarship on Black female culture, but trickster strategies allow readers to understand the complexity of these women's work. A reassessment of how we define and understand trickster serves as the first step to doing so.

Reexamining the Trickster Trope for Gender and Sexuality

Despite the traditional staging of folk culture as male culture, we must retool such thinking when it comes to the trickster figure and its use in Black cultural sites. For "the trickster is neither a god nor a man, neither human nor animal; he is all of them" (Geertz, "Deep Play" 29). If *he*, trickster, could be all of them, then he could also be *she*. The concern that many critics would want addressed is whether or not there are female trickster figures in African American culture and if so what happened to them? *Mutha' Is Half a Word* asserts that there are female and genderless/dual-gendered trickster figures in African American culture, but scholars have not been motivated to locate or use them.

Though many societies perceive of tricksters as genderless, we must remember that trickster represents the cultural and social values of its producers. Hence, more gender-neutral or egalitarian societies would create genderless figures. In contrast, communities based on a history of racial and gender segregation and ranking would produce trickster figures to reflect those dynamics. If the social fabrications of gender hierarchies exist in a society, then more than likely the tricksters and the trickster tales reflect those hierarchies or challenges to such hierarchies. Consequently, in reference to inquiries as to whether a Black female tradition of trickster exists in the culture of Black Americans in the United States, the answer is an unequivocal yes, but locating it means pursuing a postnationalist reading of folklore, myth, and vernacular.

The difficulty in seeing how crucial folklore and trickster figures can be to revealing the layers of blackness in regard to sexuality and gender stems from the adherence to traditional research and tropes about the trickster. In African American culture, scholars utilize folklore and the trope of the trickster as a heroic figure assigned to concerns of race and nation building. The historical use of the trickster trope in Black cultural analysis and its two concerns eventually result, with few exceptions, in folklore and vernacular (especially trickster) traditions being gendered masculine and hyper-heterosexual. Problematic issues of gender and sexuality within cultural research have not been acknowledged, and comprehension of how gender and sexuality influence research methods and analysis of data has rarely been discussed.[14] Most studies on trickster figures in African American culture base their theories on historical Africanisms and evolved models of oral traditions in Black America.

Africanisms become a chief lineage connection for descendants of the African diaspora, and they serve as the primary way to begin authenticating culture for Black people in the New World and a Black nation within the United States. The initiative to find Africanisms in the oral culture of New World Blacks flourished in the work of Lorenzo Dow Turner. In his work *West African Survivals in the Vocabulary of the Gullah*, presented at an MLA meeting in December 1939 and later published as *Africanism in the Gullah Dialect*, Turner conducted extensive studies about Gullah people in South Carolina to ascertain the first of many viable linguistic links between West African and African American language use. Similarly, linguist Beryl Bailey continued this focus by distinguishing her work *Jamaican Creole Syntax* with a broader non-U.S. context. These texts' focus on Africanist linguistic and language presence were only the beginning. Africanisms in Black culture became more important as critics sought to eliminate sociological and scientific work influenced by white supremacy agendas.

The work of anthropologist Melville J. Herskovits, *The Myth of the Negro Past*, completes an important task concerning this dilemma. Herskovits's study disputes early American thought that Black people in the United States had no past (or culture), an argument used to assert that U.S. citizens need not afford the primitives (African Americans) emancipation or the same political rights as their white counterparts. Herskovits's work was supported with research conducted by the previously mentioned linguists and W.E.B. Du Bois. Herskovits provides evidence for the developing field of Black studies, which would later help activists and critics theorize that the "Negro" (one who has no culture or past) is a Western construct meant to replace the African (who has a history and culture that predate Western society). According to Herskovits, the myth is based on five false ideological foundations, the last three of which are relevant for this work's assessment:

3. Since the Negroes were brought from all parts of the African continent, spoke diverse languages, represented greatly differing bodies of custom, and as a matter of policy, were distributed in the New World so as to lose tribal identity, no least common denominator of understanding or behavior could have possibly been worked out by them;
4. Even granting enough Negroes of a given tribe had the opportunity to live together, and that they had the will and ability to continue their customary modes of behavior, the cultures of Africa were so savage and relatively so low in the scale of human civilization that the apparent superiority of European customs as observed in the behavior of their masters, would have caused and actually did cause them to give up such aboriginal traditions as they may otherwise have desired to preserve;
5. The Negro is a man without a past. (1–3)

Herskovits then goes on to present research that contradicts and belies each of the criteria of Black people in the New World. However, he also forewarns that using research to find Africanisms is merely a start to any work dedicated to eliminating these myths of an absent past (33). Herskovits's work ensures that Western civilization will be held accountable for its initiatives to erase an African past, and he explores the beginning of Black culture's modernity by examining Africanisms in secular life, religious life, language, and the arts of Black people. As Albert J. Raboteau's "African American Religion in America" proclaimed of Herskovits's validation of Black culture, it "turned out to be a powerful heuristic for both scholars and political activists. Some black nationalists defended racial separatism by appealing to cultural differences based on the retention and/or recovery of African culture" (65–82).

Years later Sterling Stuckey's *Slave Culture: Nationalist Theory and the Foundations of Black America* uses the ring-shout (a communal and spiritual dance ceremony) to make explicit what Herskovits implies—descendants of slaves came from a rich cultural background that survived a forced trip from Africa and evolved in the United States. Stuckey does an excellent job of proving what elements from the ring-shout contribute significantly to Africans' culture in the New World. Stuckey insists that the ring-shout was "a principal means by which physical and spiritual, emotional and rational, needs were fulfilled. This quality of African religion, its uniting of seeming opposites, was perhaps the principal reason it was considered savage by whites" (24). Even as whites might have viewed the ring-shout as primitive, Stuckey proves that Black people in the United States revised and adapted the ring-shout's uniting of seeming opposites in various facets of African American life to help them survive slavery and apartheid in the United States.

Stuckey sees the ring-shout as a circle of culture that unites African people from various tribes in the New World, despite distinct tribal origins, the horrors of enslavement, and the process of acculturation. In doing so, he connects folklore and vernacular culture to an agenda of nationhood so as to evolve Herskovits's theories. As Stuckey explains, armed with language, spiritual traditions, and cultural artifacts, slave culture served as the foundation for a growing Black population seeking to be a nation within a nation. The ring-shout is only one cultural practice that allowed and sustained African concepts about capricious corporeality. Incorporating similar theories about unified opposites, the trickster figure endures as a remaining influence on African American traditions and culture in the United States. Like those early Africanisms, tricksters and trickster traditions also helped scholars establish a base of cultural nationalism. Consequently, the aims of cultural nationalism lead to unintentional and intentional gendering of the trickster figure as male in academic research in both African and African American scholarly communities. This is not meant to conflate the two traditions, but several texts on African oral traditions have been widely utilized in African American folklore and trickster research.

In *The Trickster in West Africa: A Study of Mythic Irony and Sacred Delight*, Robert W. Pelton records and archives the tales and antics of trickster figures from various West African nations: Anansi, Legba, Esu, and Ogo-Yurugu. Pelton concludes that "Legba, Esu, and Ogo-Yurugu similarly open up the pattern of trickster-transformer-culture-hero . . . this circularity of the trickster pattern points to its own deepest meaning: the unveiling of the imaginative process that is able to marry disorder and transformation and social order, foolishness and wisdom, history and timelessness" (227). According to Pelton, trickster becomes many things at once and in doing so deconstructs accepted logics of social order. Such theories have proven useful, and it is easy to agree with Pelton's theory of the trickster as it relates to social transformation; however, hero is the most problematic and widely used ideology offered in studies on the trickster. The classifying of trickster as hero assumes that trickster exists to perform the act of rescuing someone or something in need. However, one of trickster's primary agendas is to resist the act of rescuing so that individuals or societies at large may learn from the chaos. In addition, hero speciously imposes masculine attributes into studies that examine trickster in the pattern of trickster-transformer-culture-hero.

Appositionally, Legba and Esu have both been deemed genderless figures. A brief description of the Yorùbá trickster Esu from Adoye Ogundipe's "Esu Elegbara the Yoruba God of Chance and Uncertainty" makes clear that, as a trickster figure, Esu "certainly is not restricted to human distinctions of gender or sex" (119). In *Esu Bara Laroye: A Comparative Study*, critics J. E. and D. M. dos Santos qualify Ogundipe's statement: "He inherits the nature of all ancestors . . . male ancestors, the Egun Irunmale, as well as those of the female, the Iyam-mi Aje" (91). Language becomes a common barrier in representing trickster. For even as dos Santos attempts to write about the non-Western figure, English pronoun usage betrays the implicit cultural values of trickster's gender possibilities.

Beyond language usage, early criticism imposed Western European principles onto studies of tricksters. First, tricksters such as Legba and Esu are often referred to as devils within their own West African cultural context, and to label them as heroic changes the cultural context. More specifically, if researchers of Black folk traditions were to address issues of gender and sexuality by simply relying on existing research for figures such as Esu or Legba, their studies would be haunted by the overwhelming attention critics pay to Esu's penis. In trickster studies, it becomes apparent that critics fetishize Esu's penis: "His masculinity is depicted as visually and graphically *overwhelming*, his expressive femininity renders his *enormous sexuality* ambiguous, contrary, and genderless" (Ogundipe 172–73; italics added). To reflect the true nature of trickster, a more revolutionary statement might play with language and identity: Her massive phallus is depicted as visually and graphically overwhelming.

Alas, academe has not been so adventurous. Esu's erect phallus symbolically represents the figure's characteristic trait of hypersexuality, but critics have made it a symbol exclusively for hypermasculinity and heterosexuality. Even as critics give lip service to Esu/Legba as being both male and female, it appears very difficult for any of us to not notice the elephant in the room, or for this matter the huge phallus, in order to begin talking about deconstructing notions of gender. The fetishization of the erect penis has as much to do with masculinity as it does with heterosexuality. In numerous tales of these two West African figures, listeners or readers learn of their ability to take on different species and forms. The figures' trickeration in this regard often mean that the tricksters discombobulate the usual heterosexual readings trickster research yields. From Greek mythology to West African mythology, tricksters moodily shift from autoeroticism to bisexuality to homosexuality to bestiality to necrophilia and so on. Focus on the physicality of the phallus acts as a tool for the straight mind of Western discourse to eliminate the complications that might arise in a discussion of the polygender and polysexuality of trickster. Such cultural impositions happen too often.

One study of the trickster Anansi (who transforms to Aunt Nancy in Black diasporic trickster tales), R. S. Rattray's *The Ashanti*, reveals the Ashanti elders' response to Rattray's surprising discovery concerning the importance of women in the culture, state, and family of Ashanti affairs: "I have asked the old men and women why I did not know all this. . . . The answer is always the same: 'The white man never asked us this . . . we supposed the European considered women of no account, we know that you do not recognize them as we have'" (84). Rattray's cultural ignorance points out how the privileging of patriarchy in studies of the African oral tradition pervades literature and research on the trickster figure. These contradictions about gender in research on trickster figures become evident in contrasting the work of researchers. Ironically, Herskovits's and Stuckey's work noted the existence of differences based on tribal origins and eventual locations of slaves and their ancestors. Their acknowledgment of these distinguishing features suggests the importance of acknowledging other social variations that exist or develop in Black oral culture.

Nevertheless, the scholastic inconsistencies regarding gender and sexuality in folklore and trickster studies persist. If the study of the African trickster figure has been made masculine in research on African oral traditions, it has been made equally masculine in African American culture since a great deal of research on Black oral traditions and the trickster figure relies on studies of African oral traditions. In a comment that acts as a follow-up to the analysis of Pelton's use of hero to define trickster, Nathan Huggins makes a provocative comment regarding masculinity in African American folklore: "It is easier to imagine men as roustabouts, vagabonds, bums, and heroes, and harder to draw sympathetic females whose existence is their bodies and instincts . . . women, whose freedom has natural limitations—they have babies—are essentially conservative" (*Harlem Renaissance* 188). Huggins explicitly expresses the problem of the hero and the masculine gendering of Black folklore. Though we should disagree that bodies and instincts represent the traits of figures in folklore, regardless of gender, Huggins's comments actualize how embedded assumptions of gender have hindered the actual possibilities of folklore and vernacular traditions. The birthing of a child and the caring-for of that child are heroic acts, but Huggins's reading of gender denies that fact. As we will see in chapter 1, the "natural limitations" (childbearing) of freedom presented in Huggins's vision of Black women's folklore is a figment of some male and female critics' imaginations, and it is their ideals, rather than folklore itself, that imperils the development of nonconservative radical Black female sexual subjectivity in Black women's culture. Despite the work of Pelton, Levine, and others, trickster should not be seen as similar to heroes because to do so may assign a gender value system not originally intended for the figure. Huggins's comments may be dismissed due to his lack of knowledge in folklore studies; other critics cannot be dismissed as easily.

While African American literary and cultural studies remain aware of the theoretical gender and sexual implications of the figure, the fields do not make full use of such knowledge. To date, the most notable works dedicated to the study of trickster figures in the African American community comes from Henry L. Gates and John W. Roberts. Gates's *The Signifying Monkey* metaphorically utilizes trickster to establish a Black literary theory model. Gates's work is a notable deconstruction project influenced by race and nation: "Whatever is black about Black American literature is to be found in this identifiable black signifyin(g) difference" (20). Gates samples vernacular scholarship from the likes of Claudia Mitchell-Kernan, Geneva Smitherman, and Roger Abrahams to define his theory of signifyin(g) as "a black trope of tropes, the figure of black rhetorical figures" (51). The importance of his theory is that rhetoric supplants semantics (signifier/ signified),[15] and Gates applies the trickster figure as a cultural corroboration of his notion of signifyin(g) as a distinct Black aesthetic. Trickster traditions found in vernacular culture function as focal points for Black theories about formal language use, define the role of the figurative, and qualify traditions of indeterminacy and interpretation in African American texts (21–22).

However, what cannot be ascertained from the text is how to locate difference within the distinction of blackness. Notably, while investigating the tricksters of West Africa for his own study, Gates broaches the subject of gender with one statement: "Metaphysically and hermeneutically, at least, Fon and Yoruba discourse is truly genderless, offering feminist literary critics a unique opportunity to examine a field of texts, a discursive universe, that escaped the trap of sexism inherent in Western discourse" (30). In the end, Gates dismisses taking on the issue by suggesting that feminist literary critics take advantage of the unique opportunity. Oddly enough, Gates examines texts by women writers to explicate on how the act of signifyin(g) disrupts the conceptual order or logocentrism of speech and writing, but he does not contextualize his trickster-dependent theory, as affected by gender or sexuality, in the production of the Black women's texts that he reads.

Conversely, Roberts's pioneering and still relevant study *From Trickster to*

Bad Man: The Black Folk Hero in Slavery and Freedom reflexively depicts concerns of gender (masculinity) even as it may not have been written to do so. Although Roberts's study does situate itself as thematically about folk heroic traditions, he expands on theories of African American trickster traditions as reflective of, and connected to, an evolving Black consciousness of survival and resistance episodically examined in Lawrence Levine's *Black Culture and Black Consciousness*. Like those of Levine and Gates, Roberts's study was monumental. From the very beginning of the text, Roberts fixates his study on the hero:

> We often use the term "hero" as if it denoted a universally recognized character type, and the concept of "heroism" as if it referred to a generally accepted behavioral category. In reality, figures (both real and mythic) and actions dubbed heroic in one context by one group or people may be viewed as ordinary or even criminal in another context by another group. (1)

Roberts perceptively questions the Western definitions of hero and heroic. He admits that these terms are subjectively based on specific cultural contexts and social beliefs. What is heroic in Black culture may not be seen heroic in white culture. This seems rather obvious today, but at the time Roberts raises a point that challenges the notion of universal values. Since Roberts is concerned only with race, his argument prepares the way for him to establish the trickster tradition and figure as heroic in Black America.

Despite Roberts's thesis that we examine African American cultural values for their definition of heroic and hero, rather than Eurocentric definitions, Roberts plants the Western model of hero precisely in the middle of Black culture when he accepts the premise of trickster as a hero tied to cultural nationalism:

> A hero is the product of a creative process and exists as a symbol of our differential identity.... In this regard, heroic creation is very much like culture-building—the means by which a group creates and maintains an image of itself.... In many ways, this approach to folk heroic literature reveals the intimate relationship that folklorists envision between folklore creation and culture-building and reflects the assumption, implicit in folkloristics, that folklore should support culture-building. (4)

Roberts rightly asks that we consider the hero as a product of an individual community's goals and agenda. In the case of Black America in Roberts's work, one major goal of culture building means nation building. Yet heroes are inherently connected to patriarchal nationalism. For Africans in America, culture building cannot be separated from issues of nation and race. Roberts admits the implicit connection. Roberts, like Pelton before him, considers his claims in comparison to Western notions of the hero. The first passage indicates that different racialized or non-Western communities may find heroes in different places, but he limits his point to the social blocks of national boundaries and race. Therefore, if hero creation is very much like culture building, it has to be male culture, called Negro or Black culture, but one that is always gendered masculine or hypermasculine.

Roberts specifically maintains his connection to masculinity by exploring masculine-equated functions and aesthetics in animal tales such as Br'er Rabbit, African oral tales, and the slave narrative of Frederick Douglass (19). The final and most potent display of masculinity occurs as Roberts explores how the human trickster morphs into the Bad Man-as-outlaw-hero (174).[16] The works of Roger Abrahams, Harold Courlander, Joel Chandler, and other male scholars of Black folklore support the remainder of Roberts's text.[17] The quandary with Roberts's examination, as well as those previously mentioned, is that they fail to mention whether their research is expressly concerned with Black male culture. They also assume that the human trickster tradition becomes a male tradition. While Roberts and Gates cannot be expected to cover the whole of Black culture in single texts, we must now recognize these omissions and move the tradition forward lest it continue to be categorized as inherently male and exclusionary. This project embraces Roberts's assessment of folklore as culture building, but it broadens that use so that it is not monolithic to the point of exclusion.

This is not to suggest that critics such as Gates and Roberts have made feminine a tradition that is masculine, but to insist that not all of the folk tradition's ties to the trickster have masculine schemas. If one buys into conventional phallocentric theories of folklore and vernacular, these general assumptions can diminish the work of critics who study oral traditions in African American women's culture. In a response to Kimberly Benston's appraisal of the oral in "Performing Blackness," Cheryl A. Wall falls victim to these ideologies: "Women were, of course, historically denied participation in many of these traditions; for instance, speechifying, whether in the pulpit or on the block, has mainly been a male prerogative" (188). Wall is right to be concerned, but the pulpit and the block are not the only forms of oral performance, and women did and do engage in oral forms that may take place in the kitchen, beauty salon, front porch, or elsewhere other than the block. Many critics have simply chosen to privilege those other forms. In addition to examining the way we research trickster, folklore, and vernacular traditions to reflect the gender and sexual values of Black women, we must also participate in aggressive and jarring shifts in Black women's cultural studies.

A Necessary Rhetorical Shift in Cultural Studies

For decades, Black critics have debated about if, how, and when Black women's sexual desires might be represented or discussed. Solutions have been limited by the regulations of the rhetoric of sex (biological), the manifestos of womanhood (social), and the monosimplistic voice of nationhood (political). This work aims to offer a rhetorical shift. Major works, written by Black women and men, in Black women's cultural studies made tremendous strides in the 1980s and 1990s in contemplations of feminism and race. Calvin Hernton's *The Sexual Mountain and Black Women Writers* and Michael Awkward's *Negotiating Difference: Race, Gender, and the Politics of Positionality* primarily address gender as opposed to sexual desire. Patricia Hill Collins's *Black Feminist Thought: Knowledge, Consciousness, and the Politics of Empowerment* contextualizes gender and feminism in ways specific to Black females that draw from contemporary debates and models and the historical legacy. And while many other texts by Black female critics were published, two major texts by Barbara Christian and Hazel Carby forged new ground on race, gender, and cultural production and also touched briefly upon desire in the context of racial and sexual violence in Black women's lives.

The main purpose of Barbara Christian's *Black Woman Novelists* is to recover and reread texts written by Black female writers. Christian's work addresses how stereotypes of Black women (Mammy and licentious Black woman) and ideologies of womanhood informed Black women's early literary tradition. Of womanhood, Christian outlined the implicit contradictions Black female writers faced when they accepted the social discourse of gender as a way to counter stereotypes: "Beyond the question of its relationship to truth, the image itself contained contradictions. A lady was expected to be a wife, a mother, and a manager; yet she was expected to be delicate, ornamental, virginal, and timid" (8). Christian observes that society deemed female slaves as incapable of possessing any of those traits. She concludes that Black women novelists used the medium of literature to counter negative stereotypes and representations by aligning their subjectivity with the cult of womanhood.

Expanding Christian's study, Hazel Carby's *Reconstructing Womanhood: The Emergence of the Afro-American Woman Novelist* investigates the novel tradition of Black female writers. Like Christian's study, Carby's work becomes, first, an examination of stereotypes about Black women, and second, a monument dedicated to representing the utmost moral character of Black females. Carby's view on the cult of womanhood and the female slave refers to the slave's status as laborer, breeder, and sexual concubine: "Slave woman, as victim, became defined in terms of a physical exploitation resulting from the lack of assets of white womanhood: no masculine protector or home and family, the locus of the flowering of white womanhood" (35). Carby declares that an ideology of womanhood provides the Black woman novelist with a way to counter misrepresentations formed from her historical experience of sexual exploitation. Carby's arguments work to fashion a moral culture of true Black womanhood because the "ideology of true womanhood attempted to bring coherence and order to the contradictory material circumstances of the lives of women" (24). Sexuality, then, becomes a site of oppression, not liberation.[18]

Both Christian and Carby are right to identify the horrors of female bondage because the abuse of the Black female body makes it impossible to figure Black female subjectivity into a discussion of womanhood. Prior to these initial queries there were no substantial discussions about the function race plays in cultural representations concerned with virtues and gender, but the work to locate a self-defined ontology of sexuality for Black females that exists outside roles of slave, wife, and mother is just beginning. Since technology has influenced the rhetoric of sex (biological intents to procreate can be manipulated), should not critical inquiries reflect such changes? As Hammonds claims, "we know more about the elision of sexuality by black women than we do about the possible expression of sexual desires" (309). By continuously engaging the discourse of womanhood and the rhetoric of sex, which by their very nature seek to prohibit any discussion of independent and autonomous female sexual desire, critical inquiries of Black female culture have been incomplete. Carby's text comes close to broaching the importance of this issue: "The sexual ideology of the period thus confirmed the differing material circumstances of these two groups of women and resolved the contradiction between the two reproductive positions by balancing opposing definitions of womanhood and motherhood, each dependent on each other for its existence" (25). Carby's statement provides a wonderful foundation from which to move forward.

First, we must ascertain the sexual ideology of our current period and reassess the material circumstances of Black women. In "Mama's Baby, Papa's Maybe: An American Grammar Book," Hortense Spillers details the historical and material experiences of Black women and their bodies: "First of all, their New-World, diasporic plight marked a theft of body—a willful and violent (and unimaginable from this distance) severing of the captive body from its motive will, its active desire. Under these conditions, we lose at least gender difference in the outcome, and the female body and the male body become a territory of cultural and political maneuver, not at all gender-related, gender specific" (259). As captive bodies during chattel slavery New World Blacks, like tricksters, remain genderless. Yet what happens when bodies are no longer captive in chattel slavery differs for Black men and women. What do we make of Black female bodies' motive wills and active desires upon their emancipation? As this text will explore in greater detail in the next chapter, some Black women, those past and present invested in radical Black female sexual subjectivity, choose to work from the knowledge of their bodies as a territory of cultural and political maneuvering rather than accept false gender ideologies of whatever time period they exist in. *Mutha' Is Half a Word* argues that this is their way of ascertaining the sexual ideology and reassessing the material circumstances of their era.

The second way to effectively balance the rhetoric of sex with discourses of desire entails resisting thinking of female corporeality solely in terms of sexless or asexual reproductive positions. When Spillers deconstructs New World mothering for Black women, she formulates that "we might guess that the 'reproduction of mothering' in this historic instance carries few of the benefits of patriarchilized female gender, which, from one point of view, is the only gender there is" ("Mama's Baby" 268). Yet if we complicate the belief that there was only one female gender, that of patriarchilized female gender, then the discursive practices of speaking of many genders and then many desires become wholly possible. Such a move offers one way to resolve the age-old contradiction between womanhood and motherhood that still influences Black women's critical and practical lives. In Western societies, "womanhood" and "motherhood" depend on each other because they are part of the same gendered construction that seeks to reinforce a white patriarchal system. As long as we continue to accept these terms, the manifestations of alternative Black female genders and desires will always seem to either deviate or mimic and aspire to be within the two patriarchal positions, as well as motivate Black women to ignore more liberating possibilities.[19]

Thanks to lesbian writers such as Barbara Smith and Audre Lorde, Black feminist scholarship now works to establish a platform to engage issues of gender, race, sexuality, and desire in new and exciting ways. With its queer reading of Toni Morrison's *Sula*, Barbara Smith's "Towards a Black Feminist Criticism" creates a minor shift from a strict adherence to gender oppression, and, as we will see in the next chapter, Audre Lorde's poetry, fiction, and critical essays also changed the terrain by using African mythology to discuss same-sex desire. The work of these Black lesbian writers forced others to reconsider the role of sexual desire in their own works. Always one for dissecting the intersectionality of race, class, and gender, Patricia Hill Collins recently included sexuality in her work on Black women, *Black Sexual Politics: African Americans, Gender and the New Racism*.

In addition to Tricia Rose's work on oral histories and Black women's sexuality, in recent years other intellectuals have relied on folklore, vernacular, and oral traditions to examine gender and desire in Black women's culture. Critics such as Trudier Harris prove that Black folklore and desire is important to the writings by Black female writers.[20] Notably, the introduction from Harris's *Saints, Sinners, and Saviors: Strong Black Women in African American Literature* questions the model of asexuality in texts featuring strong Black women as protagonists. In search of other methods to illuminate Black females, editors of the collection *Female Subjects in Black and White: Race, Psychoanalysis, and Feminism* discuss "whether the academy acknowledged only methodologies that fell within the Western intellectual tradition" to discuss Black female subjectivity (3). Angela Davis's *Blues Legacies and Black Feminisms* examines domesticity and sexuality in the music of female blues and jazz artists. Like Carby before her,[21] Davis's work covers heterosexual and homosexual desire in cultural forms of blues and jazz. More recently, Gwendolyn D. Pough's exceptional book *Check It While I Wreck It: Black Womanhood, Hip-hop Culture, and the Public Sphere* looks at the way Black women deploy the rhetoric of wreck in hip-hop as an exploration of gender and sexuality in their recent and varied cultural manifestations. Valerie Lee delves into the differences of Western science and folk medicine in one chapter from her *Granny Midwives & Black Women Writers: Double-Dutched Readings*. Lee's narrative positions folk traditions as relevant material to base her theory of Black female literary tradition, but it also explains the benefits of folk traditions over Western science, specifically the use of folk medicine as an alternative to Western medicine in examinations of Black female bodies and reproductive health care.

Finally, in *Moorings and Metaphors: Figures of Culture and Gender in Black Women's Literature,* Karla F. C. Holloway explores the manner in which folklore and myth act as lenses to critique discourses of gender and sexuality in West African and African American women's culture. In an approach that pays homage to the folk belief in ancestors, Holloway argues a symbolic connection between the goddess and ancestral presence: "I believe that far from being a coincidental selection of metaphor, the ancestral presence in contemporary African American women's writing reconstructs an imaginative, cultural (re)memberance of a dimension of West African spirituality, and that the spiritual subjective figuration is fixed into the structures of the text's language" (2). As Holloway demonstrates, African American women's appreciation of West African spirituality consistently manages to include issues of sexuality (the body) into its spiritual manifestations.

All of these texts validate this work's thesis concerning the use of trickster as a figurative model to create discourses of desire for the representation of Black women's genders and sexual desires. Holloway's book engages her metaphor to indicate how "there is a textual place where language and voice are reconstructed by black women writers as categories of cultural and gendered essence" (11). *Mutha' Is Half a Word* shifts in a more contested direction to assert that there is not a single gendered essence, but a shared experience of liminality stemming from the inability of Western discourses on race, gender, and sexuality to discern fully the subjectivity of New World Black females. This project seeks out the uncomfortable spaces between constructions of gender and sexuality. Such an endeavor does not preclude taking into account the historical experiences of Black females, but it also does not rely on artificial and finite categories of gender and sexuality. Folklore, vernacular, and myth have a way of interrupting dominant master narratives that can be illuminating.

A brief deliberation on the phrase embedded in this text's title affords further insight as to why trickster might apply as a metaphorical sign of difference and desire in Black female culture. It is obvious by now that, despite its title, this book is not about mothering or motherhood.[22] The phrase "mutha' is half a word" is excerpted from comedienne and actress LaWanda Page's 1970 comedy album, *Mutha' Is Half a Word*. When Page spoke the elegiac words, she did so to signify on that old guttural street slang "muthafucka" and her own trickster nature. Trickster is sacred and profane. Muthafucka is a sacredly profane word, and one that, according to sociolinguists and the OED, has its origins in Black America. The use of the term is usually discussed in reference to Black men's culture. However, Page made it poetic, the great actress S. Epetha Merkerson proclaimed it as her favorite cuss word, and most importantly poet Carolyn Rodgers wrote a poem, "The Last M.F.," that depicts the way the word can discombobulate people and their discourses of nation, gender, sexuality, race, and class. If trickster had a favorite word, this might be it since it is used with some frequency in animal and human trickster tales. Sexual vernacular, when used strategically by Black women, has literally been a disruption of master narratives on Black womanhood and motherhood.

Language should always be a key consideration in any discussion of Black women's cultures, bodies, and desires. Capable of expressing linguistic parameters of function and structure, as well as denoting corporeal expressions of thought, language's connection to the body cannot be disentangled from conversations about subjectivity, identity, and forms of culture. Analysis of the importance of mother tongues in the social, economic, and sexual colonization and decolonization of people of color proves this fact. Muthafucka blurs the line that separates the sacred and the profane, and its usage in African America does the same with the binary of good and bad, since its meaning can have either positive or negative connotations. In correlation to the usage and meanings of the term and Page's phrase, this text's title seeks to consistently remind readers of the sometimes censored, politically incorrect, taboo, and non-heteronormative desires of Black women everywhere.

Page's signifyin(g) phrase signifies on notions of silence and all the revered expectations of motherhood as they conflict with the hushed implications of female desire signified with the slang term "fucka." Though the phrase has never denoted one who has sex with a mother,[23] the implications of the phrase do imply removing the mother from a sacred and domestic space and placing the figure into a public realm where the purpose of sexuality is something other than reproduction and false intimacy. If the two words "mutha" and "fucka" are ever placed together (explicitly or in censored code), then the unmentionable and private is exposed. Page's "mutha' is half a word" dismisses the culture of dissemblance, the politics of silence, and the politics of sexuality historically incorporated into studies on Black women's sexual desire. Embedded within Black vernacular is an understanding that desire has the tendency to trample established boundaries and codes of morals, gender, race, and sexuality.

In discussing the purpose of British sexual vernacular "getting a bit of the other," bell hooks explains how vernacular might be transgressive: "Contemporary working-class British slang playfully converges the discourse of desire, sexuality, and the other . . . as a way to speak about sexual encounter" (*Black Looks* 22). What is most useful in hooks' analysis for this text is what she says about "fucking" and otherness: "Fucking is the Other. Displacing the notion of Otherness from race, ethnicity, skin-color, the body emerges as a site of contestation where sexuality is the metaphoric Other that threatens to take over, consume, transform via the experience of pleasure" (22). That's right, pleasure, the other benefit of sexuality that hooks and other Black women cultural producers have insisted that we not forget. If we extend hooks's theory, we can de-essentialize blackness, explode binary models of gender and sexuality, and remain aware of class differences, but to do so we must insist upon an analysis of pleasure in the representation of sexuality and the discourses of sexuality. For every one's pleasure will not feel or arise from a fountain of universalisms. *Mutha' Is Half a Word* argues that oral traditions have been allowing producers of Black female culture to dismiss the rhetoric of sex and constructs of gender for centuries.

Yet, to date, a number of critics continue to engage the tradition of Black female culture in ways that center on motherhood and womanhood with little regard for the function of sexual desire in each category, perhaps out of legitimate concerns over sexual stereotyping, exoticness, and primitiveness.[24] However, folklore and vernacular comprise a wealth of Black female culture that considers the sexual self as separate from the philosophical designs of partiarchical gender. These traditions are not solely wrapped up in the reproductive concerns of the body (sex–biology), and the social network of womanhood (gender–the social) serves as a secondary issue. *Mutha' Is Half a Word* takes on the subject of these alternatives by returning to the very core or individuality and difference within a community—as Spillers calls it, the body's motive will and active desire—and then explains how these oral mechanisms of desire shape Black female communities.

Trickster-Troping, a Culturally Relevant Discourse of Desire

For Black women who produce cultural texts invested in depicting sexual encounters and representations of their desire materialized, trickster converges the discourse of desire, gender, and the other as a way to speak about sexual encounter. While trickster may seem like a relic of the past, Jung noted its influence on past, present, and future when he claimed, "In many cultures his figure seems like an old river-bed in which the water still flows. One can see this best of all from the fact that the trickster motif does not crop up only in its mythical form but appears just as naïvely and authentically in the unsuspecting modern man" (*Four Archetypes* 167). Or modern woman. Trickster plays a key role in postmodern blackness because it recognizes differences without ranking them, but also because it signifies desire. Desire is overwhelming, and it can elicit change in various facets of life. Intrinsically, desire opposes values of deviant and normative values. Jacques Lacan's concept of desire suggests it as the *difference* or gap separating need from demand: "Desire is produced in the beyond of the demand. . . . But desire is also hollowed within the demand, in that, as an unconstitutional demand of presence and absence, demand evokes the want-to-be" (*Ecrits* 265).

To read Black female culture through a discourse of desire, as well as the rhetoric of sex, would allow us to examine individual and cultural representations of what is wanted and yearned for without regard for societal restraints or policing. As Samuel Delany explains, "Power is what distinguishes the psychic discourse of desire from the social rhetoric of sex . . . desire, to the extent that it is a material and social discourse, commands power enough to found and destroy cities, to reform the very shape of the city itself ("Rhetoric of Sex" 20). For this reason, the progression away from Western traditions of gender and sexual desire focuses this work toward consideration of the trickster figure. Since *Mutha'* seeks to destroy those models with unacknowledged alternative models of gender and sexuality, desire is the revolutionary tool to do so.

Delany's clarification of desire sounds remarkably similar to the purpose of trickster in Black communities. John Roberts found that "Africans created and re-created tales of the animal trickster to serve as a model of behavior" and to counter "conditions of destructive material shortages and control of a socio-political system they did not accept as legitimate" (34). Trickster and desire are both designed to handle material and social elements of a community. Some might even say trickster is desire.[25] If desire "is a movement, a trajectory that asymptomatically approaches it object but never attains it" (Grosz 188)[26] and it "is concerned only with its own processes, pleasures, and internal logic, a logic of the signifier" (65), then trickster acts as a trope of desire. In reference to desire's logic of the signifier, "while such a logic can support social laws and values, it is also able to subvert or betray them, based as it is on expelled, socially inappropriate, repressed wishes" (65). Trickster and desire create and destroy systems but not without replacing those with temporary ones that can also be changed and adapted based on needs of the communities. Since trickster symbolizes undecideability, it follows the path of desire: "An element necessarily lacking, unsatisfied, impossible, misconstrued, an element that is called desire" (Lacan, *The Fundamental Concepts of Psychoanalysis*, 154). For nonacademics, desire simply exists and springs forth without rationality or boundaries. This is why an analysis of Black women's popular culture is a vital part of this text. If part of the work of radical Black female subjects entails crossing boundaries of public and private space to share their awareness of radical Black female sexual subjectivity with others, then there have to be comprehensible ways to transfer these notions of desire in less abstract ways than previously discussed. Such issues are not only the problem of Black women. In Judith Butler's essay "Desire," the author asserts, "It seems that language is bound up with desire in such a way that no exposition of desire can escape becoming 'implicated' in that which it seeks to clarify. This means that language is less than 'clarifying' when it comes to desire" (369). Consequently, there is already a gap when it comes to language and desire in general, but the gap increases once we turn to the detrimental historical assault on Black people's languages and bodies by white supremacy across the globe. Thus representations of Black female sexuality must intuit the conflicts that stem from language and experiences of desire and overcome them. When Black women cultural producers engage in trickster-troping, they do equalize difference and lessen the fissure between desire and language.

After all, Sarah E. Chinn argues that "sexual desire and sensation of sexual contact seem part of that subterranean world, outside of our abilities to express ourselves" (181). Trickster rules the subterranean world Chinn speaks of, and since it is the gap that makes some Black women hesitate in their presentation of radical Black female sexual subjectivity, we must turn to it for expressing sexual desire and sensation. And though Elizabeth Grosz is correct when she devises that "the most intense moments of pleasure and force of their materiality cannot be reduced to terms that capture their force and intensity" (65), the trope of the trickster can signify that force and intensity once it is placed in the appropriate perspective. Further, if we return to bell hooks consideration of sexual acts or encounters, trickster-troping simplifies the complexities of desire with action.

But this is not the only meaning. Butler observes of desire's historical precedents, "Desire has been thought of in many ways: in terms of its origins in the body or in a more expansive set of passions; in terms of its *ends,* those that are considered more sensuous, those considered more spiritual, and an ambiguous range in between" ("Desire" 369). In the following chapters, we will see how Black female cultural producers rely on trickster's trait of sacred/lewd bricoleur to cover the many ways that desire has been understood. Cultural narratives embedded with a discourse of desire, based on trickster, enable a social discourse that could adapt and change as material conditions of Black women's communities change. Tricksters are the very embodiment of difference and allow us to move beyond a system of biological-based binaries. As perfect models of indeterminacy, they mirror desire as "lack and repetition" (Samuel Delany 19), but because they are communally conceived in different societies across the globe they enable us to locate culturally specific references for the representation of such desire. In the end, trickster-troping often results in a shift of desire from the margins of a text to its very center so that readers can value and reevaluate varied genders or fluid sexuality in cultural products.

In addition to creating a greater rhetorical shift from gender to desire in Black women's cultural criticism, trickster-troping hopes to document class influence on the representation of Black women's desire in culture. Currently, cultural studies on Black women, Black queer studies, and Black feminism seem wholly invested in bourgeois models of Black culture and Black cultural production in those designated fields. In doing so, critics have excluded philosophies on desire presented in culture produced by lower-class masses. Such a narrow scope is another major reason that trickster serves as the figurative model for this study. John Roberts concludes that because Africans endured a loss of control over other aspects of their lives, they "placed a high value on native intelligence as a way of dealing with situations that disadvantage the individual" (28). Since trickster is the discourse of the disadvantaged lower echelons of a social community, and Black women are ranked at the lower echelon of Black political and social communities, the use of trickster as a trope for gender and sexuality in Black culture automatically challenges bourgeois notions of gender and sexuality by placing value on Black women's genius.

Despite trickster's outside status, *Narrative Chance: Postmodern Discourse on Native American Indian Literatures* by Gerald Vizenor submits that "the trickster is a communal sign of a comic narrative; the comic holotrope (the whole figuration) is a consonance in tribal discourse . . . [whereas] the instrumental language of the social sciences are tragic or hypotragic modes that withhold communal discourse" (9). Vizenor's criterion of trickster demonstrates why trickster might be an effective alternative configuration for Black female desire. Viewed as an absence of whiteness, man-ness and woman-ness, Black female subjectivity, identity, and desire will always appear tragic in Western social scientific language. However, in the world of folklore, myth, and vernacular, tragic interpretations become one of many ways to view Black females and their culture.

The proliferation of tricksters in Black oral traditions poses an alternative space in regards to gender and sexuality, the folklore sphere versus the scientific sphere. The existence of the trickster serves as a community's subconscious belief in the myriad possibilities in regards to gender, sexuality, and desire. In the same way that man and woman are the personification of Western constructs of gender, trickster is the personification of varied genders and many desires. The former may be more corporeal and institutionally supported, but the latter is no less real or true than its physical form. Vizenor's critique on the language of social sciences addresses the way poststructuralist thought and the logic of binaries have narrowed the infinite possibilities of vernacular subjects and culture.

In *Writing Tricksters: Mythic Gambols in Ethnic American Literature*, Jeanne R. Smith explores the importance of tricksters in her assessment of ethnic American literature. Smith declares, "Perhaps trickster's biggest contribution to the postmodern is the notion that identity can be multiplicitous and the deconstruction of a falsely unitary language" (3). Trickster's ability to evolve and move beyond the confines of language proves that it is the greatest trope of difference within difference. The following chapters explore how Black women use trickster (troping) to move desire away from the tragic language of social sciences.

Mutha' Is Half a Word does not purport to create a Black feminist reading of trickster or a Black womanist tradition of trickster. The aims of the work do not include representing the wide continuum of Black female folklore experiences in the way that Roberts's *From Trickster to Bad Man* does. The goals of *Mutha'* are less dedicated to authentication and linear connections of the tradition found in Gates's text. The objective of this study is to reveal vital ways of reading folk and oral traditions into queer, race, and gender theory, and then assert these readings as one of the most productive ways to engage Black female culture that thematically addresses sexual desire. It exposes how trickster-troping allows Black women to reclaim and represent their rights to desire and be desired without fear of reprisal from the problematic codes of normativity and Western morality.

In chapters 1 and 2, this work defines and explicates on the trickster trope of unnaming, a method which supplants the rhetoric of sex in presentations of Black female identity and culture. Chapter 1 provides a revision of the trickster in African American culture. It also surveys important trickster tropes in Black female culture, from slavery to the present, that produced alternative models of trickster to serve the needs of Black female communities. From there, *Mutha' Is Half a Word* delves into more specific monikers of trickster as a sign of desire. Chapter 2 includes a reading of Gayl Jones's *The Healing* to demonstrate how writers build on the trickster tropes established in their particular cultural site. In the case of Jones, I show that she returns to literary models established by Zora Neale Hurston and Audre Lorde to explore the spiritual and ambiguous nature of sexual desire.

The last four chapters move away from a rigid focus on extended written narratives and become more concerned with the way trickster-troping shapes ideologies of gender and sexuality in Black female popular culture. Chapter 3 investigates the intersection of visual and oral performances of the trickster tradition through a queer lens. It symbolically incorporates Tar Baby tales and criticism of Tar Baby folklore to argue that Black comediennes utilize orality to interrupt a socially influenced drag performance aimed at conforming to the illusion of gender so that they can represent their real subjectivity and desires.

Chapter 4 covers racialized sexuality, folklore, and two central trickster figures, the Bad Man/Nigga and the Queen B(?), to disturb the production of heterosexuality in Black folklore studies. It offers a theory that Black male and female communities create these figures to counter racialized sexuality, and in the process create a folk philosophy of sexuality where queerness and blackness can occupy the same space with little or no conflict. The Queen B(?) figure will take center stage and remain pivotal for the rest of the chapters. Having established the relevance of the Queen B(?) as a trickster figure, chapter 5 examines the significance of the Queen B(?) figure as a way to comprehend the presentation of Black lesbian desire in Ann Allen Shockley's controversial collection of short stories, *The Black and White of It*.

Chapters 6 and 7 explore the depiction of a more radical Queen B(?) figure that exists outside the realm of literary production. Critics have rarely examined the divine sexuality and sexual violence contained in some of the more adult trickster tales. In documenting the Queen B(?) figure in Black women's music, the text uncovers how the trait of sexual militancy within trickster figures has gone unnoticed in any previous analysis of trickster culture. Meshell Ndegeocello and Lil' Kim serve as my primary models. The study concludes with an assertion that if we accept trickster-troping as a discourse of desire, then students and scholars will be better equipped to comprehend and appreciate future texts produced by and about the wide range of Black queer peoples and cultures like Cheryl Clarke and Red Jordan Arobateau. *Mutha' Is Half a Word* reminds readers that Black women's desires allow them to exist and represent themselves outside of prescribed social bodies of nationalist thought, racial discourse, and limited gender constructs.

1

The Black Woman and the Trickster Trope of Unnaming

The ordering of black female bodies and the attempt to silence their voices and make absent their desires happens through one specific means: language. While delineating on the position and subjectivity of Black women in the United States, Toni Morrison explains how historical discourses have failed to grasp Black women's subjectivities:

> True the black woman did the housework, the drudgery; true, she reared the children, often alone, but she did all of that while occupying a place on the job market, a place her mate could not get or which his pride would not let him accept. And she had nothing to fall back on; not maleness, not whiteness, not ladyhood, not anything. And out of the profound desolation of her reality she may have well invented herself. ("What the Black Woman Thinks" 63)

Despite the resourcefulness of Black women to invent themselves, when confronted with material realities and the absence of an acknowledged discursive model, outsider interference to the process of self-invention remains a problem. In Zora Neale Hurston's *Their Eyes Were Watching God*, Hurston uses protagonist Janey to explore the contradictions of language in the construction of self. After Janey is questioned as to whether she knows her own self, she provides a response that reveals a great deal: "Dey all uster call me Alphabet 'cause so many people had done named me" (9). Both Morrison and Hurston address the multiplicity of being Black and female, and the failure of those classifications with the lived experiences in discussing Black women.

Janey's situation reflects the condition of many Black females who have erroneously been named by someone other than themselves. If Janey is known as Alphabet, and the alphabet is comprised of twenty-six letters, it is no wonder that Janey does not know herself. Depending on the purpose and rules of any given language, Janey could represent one specific letter of the alphabet at any given time, the entire alphabet at one time, or select letters from the alphabet meant to form words at any time. For without an understanding of the grammar of self, meaning can be imposed on her body using someone else's grammar book.[1] If she does not know herself, then she cannot sustain her own process of self-creation and culture building. However, Black female culture relies on trickster-troping to circumvent the dislocation of self that erroneous naming may cause. The tricketer trope mechanism of unnaming is the key to empowering liminality that can interrupt the logic of Western gender. In the end, this trickster-troping then allows them to defer gender so that Black females can continue stating freely their desires.

The central consideration of this chapter argues that for centuries Black female cultural producers in the United States have been promoting an act of gender unnaming, a process of unranking and challenging gender through a manipulation of language to elide the troubles and violations of language in the West. It further expounds that trickster-troping offers numerous and various means of carrying out the act of unnaming to counter the institutionalized rejection of difference as propagated by the false assumption that the biological (physical factors such as ovaries, uterus, and eggs) is more real than the social factors of gender, race, and sexuality. In *Bodies that Matter*, gender-anarchist Judith Butler argues that the biological, like the social, has no real meaning until humans forcefully provide elements with such meaning: "In this sense, then, 'sex' not only functions as a norm, but is part of a regulatory practice that produces the bodies it governs, that is, what regulatory force is made clear as a kind of productive power, the power to produce—demarcate, circulate, differentiate—the bodies it controls" (1–3). Likewise, Spillers's "Mama's Baby, Papa's Maybe" discusses the queer inventions that go into representations of Black bodies. Spillers particularizes the historical gendering and degendering of Black females and male bodies. Rather than examining Western medicine and scientific racism, Spillers examines how the institution of slavery creates sociocultural mechanisms that make gender. In one of her chief points, Spillers determines the master's systematic privilege of naming as crucial to the *pornotroping* of African American bodies: "The captivating party does not only 'earn' the right to dispose of the captive body as it sees fit, but gains, consequently, the right to name and 'name' it. . . . the opening lines of this essay . . . demonstrate the powers of distortion that the dominant community seizes as its unlawful prerogative" (263). The governing society's control, its "ownership" of the captive body, grants it the tools for gendering and degendering practices withheld from the captive bodies. Together, Butler and Spillers expose the collusion of the social and the biological as mere fictitious accounts by oppressive communities seeking to maintain reigns of supremacy.

Trickster-troping discloses the nonexistent gap between the social and biological by suggesting desire as the form that interrupts the subjective fictions of skin color, ovaries, uterus, and so on. Thus desire becomes a primary tool in self-invention and the reading of difference. Like the Black female cultural producers to be discussed at length in this text, difference and meaning are at the heart of Black women's culture. The earlier statements made by Morrison and Hurston make obvious that self-creation and a process of naming (but, more radically, unnaming) are key factors for reading difference, as well as determining meaning for Black female subjectivity and representation of desires. Desire and folklore are connected in a complex matrix that works to counter stereotypes and obsolete approaches to attend to such misrepresentations, but desire and folklore are also necessary for the self-creation and unnaming that occurs before relevant cultural representations can take form. By exploring select slave narratives and neo-slave narratives, this chapter explains that the experience of the Black female slave and her slave narrative genre establish the precedent for negotiations between the rhetoric of sex and the discourse of desire in Black female culture, as well as the need for the metaphorical use of tricksterism and trickster by Black female writers, artists, and performers to articulate that desire without making them deviant through a hierarchy.

If Black females hoped to accomplish these goals in their culture, they would need to find a way to displace what Butler calls the logic of intelligible genders: "Intelligible genders are those which in some sense institute and maintain relations of coherence and continuity among sex, gender, sexual practice, and desire" (*Gender Trouble* 23). Fortunately, the historical experiences of Black females show their very subjectivity as one that defied the logic of intelligible genders. It is also what makes them different from other women. Angela Davis's *Women, Race, and Class* documents the experience of nonhierarchical values of biological sex in African American communities historically formed during the institution of slavery. She completes a reexamination of the history of Black women in slavery and explores the multidimensional role of Black women within the family and slave community as a whole. Her analysis argues against the works of Daniel Moynihan, E. Franklin Frazier, Herbert Gutman, and Eugene Genovese in order to move beyond much of the negative rhetoric about the Black family as a destructive matrilocal biological structure.[2]

Davis notes, "The economic arrangements of slavery contradicted the hierarchical sexual roles incorporated in the new ideology. Male-female relations within the slave community could not, therefore, conform to the dominant ideological pattern" (12). Whereas the work of the other controversial critics suggests that the structure destroys the Black family and contributes to the social and economic problems of Black communities, Davis sees the resulting community as a deconstructive development that potentially dismisses the conventional rhetoric of sex and gender:

> The salient theme emerging from domestic life in the slave quarters is one of sexual equality. The labor that the slaves performed for their sake and not for the aggrandizement of their masters was carried out on terms of equality. Within the terms of their family and community life, therefore, black people managed to accomplish a magnificent feat. They transformed that negative equality which emanated from the equal oppression they suffered as slaves into a positive equality: the egalitarianism characterizing their social relations. (18)

Davis shows that the Black family structure potentially possesses the qualities of gender fluidity and equality that was not common for white U.S. society in the eighteenth and nineteenth centuries. Nevertheless, the egalitarian dynamics of Black females and males are consistently displaced by biological and social explanations of men and women as freedom is sought. Prevailing society connects the Western rhetoric of sex with the discourse of race to simplify the complicated subjective positions and experiences of Black females. Black female artists counter this through a complex understanding of gender. They understand that

> [g]ender is a complexity whose totality is permanently deferred, never fully what it is at any given juncture in time. An open coalition, then, will affirm identities that are alternately instituted and relinquished according to the purposes at hand; it will be an open assemblage that permits of multiple convergences and divergences without obedience to a normative telos of definitional closure. (Butler, *Gender Trouble* 23)

In addition to Butler's explanation of gender, this text acknowledges that the deferment of gender occurs in culturally specific ways that are influenced by factors such as race and class. In order to create and sustain radical Black female sexual subjectivity, Black female artists promote unnaming to interrupt the intelligible logic of gender, and they continue to defer with trickster-troping.

Although Morrison confirms that the Black female invented herself, Janey from Hurston's *Their Eyes Were Watching God* reveals that Black women may have little to do with naming themselves. Self-invention and naming are major reasons that expression of Black female desire remains so complex. Davis's, Carby's, and Morrison's descriptions of the historical experiences of Black females parallel the typology of trickster as a fundamentally ambiguous and anomalous being, and it also references the Black female as an imitator of gods since she does create herself. Be she trickster or Black female, Jacques Derrida acknowledges that names cannot define or fix the being of God in language (*Margins of Philosophy* 27). Therein lies the problem: fixing Black females' historical subjectivity in language and attempting to name unnameable beings.

Slave traders pilfered the act of naming away from generations of Black people. Though much has been covered with respect to how important naming is in the African diaspora, the basis for that knowledge inevitably assumes that upon emancipation former slaves and their descendants took back the act of naming by renaming themselves. However, with the enslaving, renaming, and assimilation of Africans into the New World one must wonder if simply renaming was enough to sustain a process of self-invention. Further, analysis of these acts of naming and renaming are based solely upon racial discourse with no assessment of gender and sexuality within scrutiny of naming and unnaming. Historical experiences and current issues about representations of Black women suggest something all together different. Naming, of course, remains important, but it is the revision of the act by Black women that demonstrates a willingness to carve out radical Black female sexual subjectivity. In terms of broader social categories and implications, the "Black woman" represents an invented character by cultures not of her own making. As the Combahee River Collective implies, the term unsuccessfully attempts to join the narratives of woman (white) with that of Black (man).

The process of naming Black females as "Black women" disturbs the self-invention of the subjects and results in a confining and violent confrontation between the two separate subjects—Black woman and Black female. Though these two subjects/bodies, like race and sex, are social and biological constructs whose meaning is enforced and determined by powerful oppressors, such theoretical meanderings doesn't make the fissure or conflicts stemming from them any less real. Since, as Butler notes, the body has no meaning until we assign it, I will continue to use Black woman and Black female interchangeably to discuss what really is a subjectivity and body whose meaning is determined by its active will and desire. However, because that meaning is subjugated by other forces, Black women must find a way to deny oppressive regimes.[3] Fortunately, deceptions by slaves attempt to return acts of naming and meaning to the individual. In the case of Black women, one can literally unname herself by acknowledging or claiming, "I'm not what you say I am," or one can pursue a more metaphorical and symbolic path to unnaming—trickster-troping. Throughout the remainder of this chapter, we will see how Black women literally unname and trickster-trope to unname. Such trickster-troping, which may never look the same and may occur through several vehicles, allows Black females to defer gender for their own needs and desires.

Unnaming is not necessarily a new term, but it is a revised one. The topos of (un)naming seems to be a prevalent tool in African American culture. After emancipation, one way in which slaves expressed their freedom was to change their given slave names to names of their own selection. In discussing his theory on the topos of (un)naming as it concerns Ralph Ellison's *Invisible Man*, Kimberly Benston avers that "the ambiguities he (the invisible man) learns to confront in 'being' at once a subjective absence and total self-presence (invisible/man) arise from the comedy of his vain desire to achieve an empowering name" ("I yam what I am" 159). Benston's theory of (un)naming, through its parenthetical coding, really implies unnaming to rename, an act many Black people condoned. For example, Olaudah Equiano's, Malcolm X's, and Amiri Baraka's decisions to (un)name themselves by replacing their slave names with an X or an African/Afrocentric name have been deemed a defiant act against racial oppression. Since the surnames of many Blacks can be traced back to the owners of their ancestors' captive bodies, the renaming of one's last name became a symbol of ownership and self-determination for African Americans. This (un)naming is a personal process on the reflection of self. Yet there has also been a larger process on naming that we should consider in our reflections of race, gender, and sexuality. I am speaking now of unnaming. Unnaming is an act of liminality that seeks to disrupt limited discursive models. This text's theory of "unnaming," devoid of any parenthetical coding, hinges on a subject's willful, infinite, multiple, and continuous process of defying classification/naming.

Unnaming engages the larger identity crisis of an oppressed group of people subordinated because of social differences such as race, gender, and sexual orientation. It also showcases the ideological and institutional apparatuses for resolving said identity crisis. When Sterling Stuckey charts the process of naming for Black people in the New World, he dissects the factors of identity and ideology in what he calls the naming controversy: "If in Freudian terms even simple distortions of name, conscious and unconscious (slips of the tongue), constitute acts of aggression, then the act of language—and only partial names at that—must be regarded as a serious act of aggression, as a reflection of a subordinate state" (198). As Stuckey briefly discusses the personal naming and (un)naming (or renaming) of Douglass, Garnett, Truth, and others, he also dissects the unnaming of Blacks as a group of people. Charting the shifting political climates that call for the use of African, Colored, Negro, Black, African American, or Afro-American in reference to

African descendants in the United States, Stuckey exposes that the naming of Blacks in the New World, as a group, is really a liminal process of unnaming to fit specific social and political situations and climates of various time periods in history.[4] A change in name would certainly mean a different rhetorical strategy was being engaged in agendas of liberation and equality for Black communities. Arguably, this process of unnaming operates in the way I am proposing. Today, the various ways in which Black people refer to themselves and each other varies with meaning derived from markers of class, gender, geographical location, politics, and so on.

Since Stuckey charts the name controversy as it is relevant to race, we can now examine this name controversy in respect to gender. If, as Stuckey, Turner, and Bailey show, a great many of Africans enslaved were stolen from western areas of the Congo-Angola, Nigeria, Dahomey, Togo, the Gold Coast, and Sierra Leone, then we must consider Oyèrónkẹ́ Oyěwùmí's argument that discloses how the invention of "woman" begins in the West and through imperialism makes its way into societies whose rendering of gender is more multifaceted:

> The usual gloss of Yoruba categories *obinrin* and *okunrin* as "female/woman" and "male/man," respectively, is a mistranslation (of Western influenced thought) . . . these categories are neither binarily opposed nor hierarchical. The word *obinrin* does not derive etymologically from okunrin, as "wo-man" does from "man." *Rin* the common suffix . . . suggests a common humanity; the prefixes obi and okun specify which variety of anatomy. Eniyan is the non-gender specific word for humans. (33)

In her important investigation of three simple words, Oyěwùmí illustrates that in precolonial Yorùbá societies, physical bodies were not necessarily social bodies.[5] If Blacks endured a traumatic experience because of forced changes in personal name and in their renaming from African to Negro, then the mistranslations or distortions of gender naming was a similar act of aggression. Although there is no historical record of Black men and women undergoing a names controversy about gender in the way that they did in terms of race, there has been the simple distortion of names with regard to gender that Black women have been unconsciously engaging for years.

Spillers has already shown how this happens with the captive bodies of those Blacks held in chattel slavery and the descendants thereof:

> Even though the captive flesh/body has been "liberated," and no one need pretend that even the quotation marks do not matter, dominant symbolic activity, the ruling episteme that releases the dynamics of naming and

> valuation, remains grounded in the originating metaphors of captivity and mutilation so that it is as if neither time nor history, nor histography and its topics, shows movement, as the human subject is "murdered" over and over again. ("Mama's Baby" 261)

So while naming and renaming have been very important in the cultural history of African Americans' racial liberation, the threat of linguistic murder to Black racialized and sexualized bodies had to be attended to through another means—unnaming. The unnaming of gender may not be specific to Black women. Black gay studies and masculinity studies could glean out the specific ways in which unnaming occurs for particular Black male cultures. Indeed, later chapters of this work disclose such knowledge in folklore. However, the focus of this study remains the underengaged phenomenon of trickster-troping in Black female culture that seeks to articulate various sexual desires. Further, because Black women, captive and liberated, do not benefit from the naming and raking of gender in the way that Black men have,[6] they turn to unnaming as is being defined within these pages.

Malcolm X's, Amira Baraka's, and Ellison's invisible man's (un)naming is about a shared commonality aside from race—their masculine status. Conceptually and traditionally, it seems easier to discuss (un)naming on a personal level as it concerns race, but it might also be relevant to discuss it in terms of gender. Despite the discussion of the invisible man as a subjective absence; there exists a privilege in being a total self-presence that derives from being a human being, but most notably in the ranking of male over female in Western societies. The invisible man must (un)name to rename so that he might access the power and privilege that comes with the social standing of manhood. It is about accessing power, as opposed to true self-invention. As Benston notes, it is a rather vain desire, and Black females cannot benefit from the act in the same way.

On the other hand, if Toni Cade Bambara's, Assata Shakur's, or Ntozake Shanghe's name changes were defiant acts against "gender" oppression in addition to racial oppression, then they are more reflective of a type of tricksterism because they stem from the plurality outlined by Morrison and Hurston rather than the absence highlighted by Benston and Ellison. The name changes suggest self-creation and not power plays. If Spillers is correct, and I argue she is, when she claims that "the loss of the indigenous name/land provides a metaphor of displacement for other human and cultural features and relations, including the displacement of genitalia, the female's and male's desire that engenders future"("Mama's Baby" 268), then unnaming takes center stage. I suggest that, as opposed to mimicking or attempting to align themselves with dominant models, some Black women—and some Black men—understood the benefits that could come from this displacement and in turn created a process of unnaming for Black women to self-author the narrative of self in ways that allow it to be revised and reread over time.

"How She Came By Her Name" by Toni Cade Bambara demonstrates how one Black woman believes that the process of naming should not result in permanent stations. In detailing the change of her name from Toni Cade to Toni Cade Bambara, Bambara explains that she cannot choose only one name because she is a different person at different times with different people. She also suggests that her choice to unname arises from a feeling that her birth name no longer reflects her current self. Bambara's experience dictates the definition of unnaming (no parenthesis) in this text. Her unnaming reflects that there is no true self but many selves. Unnaming is based on liminality and fluctuation in subjectivity and identity. In this sense, unnaming in this text differs from Benston's (un)naming. Unnaming mimics trickster's shape-shifting abilities. The freedom afforded to a subject engaged in unnaming stems from the way the liminal procedure allows a subject to shift when the political terrain changes.

Black females have been committed to the process of unnaming themselves for years. For the process of unnaming in Black females' lives is as much about gender as it is about race, and for that reason their Black cultural experience of unnaming does not seek renaming, but instead a continuous process of unnaming. Though the theoretical concept of (un)naming/unnaming does not evolve until the later part of the twentieth century, the actions of selected historical figures and their experiences reveal a dynamic process of eluding definitions and boundaries for their subjectivity, specifically for African American females. These actions, based in orality, folklore, and vernacular culture, can now be shown as an initial precursor or early attempt by Black females to unname themselves as slaves and as "Black women."

For example, when Hurston had Nanny proclaim that "de nigger woman is de mule uh de world so fur as Ah can see" (*Their Eyes* 14), she utilized a timeless strategy of using folk tales and animus parallelism to interrupt the intelligible logic of gender and unname the Black woman through trickster-troping. In African American female culture, unnaming traditionally has been extracted from trickster's trait of indeterminacy. Before reading slave narratives, close readings of various trickster tails that analyze the presence of gender conflicts may foster a greater sense of why and how Hurston, and writers before her, came to rely on lessons from folklore and trickster tales to begin their tradition of trickster-troping that would counter the discourse of race and the rhetoric of sex's false naming.

Pedagogy of the Oppressed—Trickster Tales

As Davis previously documented, on the plantation there is no separation of the sexes that would foster an initial separate oral tradition. Patricia Hill Collins's *Black Feminist Thought* also notes that "Black women's centrality in Black family networks should not be confused with matriarchal or female dominated female units . . . Rather, African Americans' relationship to the slave political economy made it unlikely that either patriarchal or matriarchal domination could take root" (52). Both Collins's and Davis's comments should then be connected to Sylvia Wynter's thesis in "Novel and History, Plot and Plantation" to comprehend how these facts contribute to folk revolutions. Wynter explains that slaves created a separate social and cultural landscape: "Around the growing of the yam, of food for survival, he created on the plot a folk culture—the basis of a social order—in three hundred years. This culture recreated traditional values—use values. This folk culture became a source of cultural guerilla resistance to the plantation system" (99–100). Wynter's claim that folk culture possesses its own social order echoes Davis's theory of egalitarianism in slave culture. Consequently, the egalitarian mode of social organization and the use of folk culture as resistance did not cease to exist once slaves were freed. All ex-slaves needed to be concerned with was survival: if they would live, how they would eat, stay with family, or leave. African American females continued to work in agriculture to help support their families. As the narrative of Sara Brooks recalls, "We never was lazy cause we used to really work. We used to work like mens. Oh, fight sometime, but worked on" (39). Material conditions took precedence over social repression. Some early animal trickster tales reflected these nonhierarchical values.

In one trickster tale, "The Fox and the Goose," the original configuration of trickster as genderless is restored through a retelling of how Fox tries to trick Goose into being his/her next meal:

> Fox said, "You ain't afraid of me, is you? Haven't you heard of the meeting up at the hall the other night? . . . Why, they passed a law that no animal must hirt any other animal. Come down and le me tell you about it. The hawk musn't catch the chicken, and the dog musn't chase the rabbit, and the lion musn't hurt the lamb." (Hughes and Bontemps 12)

As Fox works to coax and convince Goose to come out of the tree, a dog barks and causes Fox to assume a hiding position. As the dog's bark grows louder, Fox sneaks off and this encourages Goose to ask, "Fox, you ain't scared of the Dog, is you? Didn't all the animals pass a law at the meeting not to bother each other" (12). Goose wisely notices Fox's trickery and the game of wits ends in a stalemate. Goose does not get eaten and Fox escapes the dog. No clear victorious or heroic figure exists, but both characters survive. Though Fox seems very clever in its imagined suggestion of the passing of a new law, Goose's keen intelligence to assess Fox's action at the barking of the dog indicates the figure's own wiliness. As with some African oral epics and myths, the lack of gendering of animals in this particular tale suggests the original ambiguity of tricksterism.

The pedagogy of the tale also remarks on the notion of difference. Fox attempts to use the notion of a universal and harmonious animal kingdom to fool Goose. As a monolithic nation, under the supposed new law, they must not hurt each other. Goose is not the same species as Fox and is therefore an outsider who can be consumed, but Fox can't eat or oppress until Goose has released notions of difference. As Audre Lorde argues, "Institutionalized rejection of difference is an absolute necessity in a profit economy which needs outsiders as surplus people" ("Age, Race, Class" 115). "The Fox and the Goose" provides a powerful analogy of how to avoid the pitfalls of monolithic rhetoric of race, nation, gender, and sexuality.

Black Culture and Black Consciousness formulates that trickster tales told during the institution of slavery function as tools to teach about Black experiences in the New World. The tales, "because of their overwhelmingly paradigmatic character . . . were, of all the narrative of social protest or psychological release, among the easiest to relate both within and especially outside the group" (Levine 102). It comes as no surprise, then, that the trickster figure endures as a pedagogical apparatus for the Black community during slavery. Animal trickster tales reflect a community's material conditions and social repression. African American slaves had to consider both in their daily lives, and depressed material conditions were the result of social repression. Many times these conditions led slaves to translate or relate trickster tales to their own lives.

Since African American culture lacked the spiritual world of its African mother, where hierarchies were conveyed via deities/trickster-gods, divinities, and humans, the most pivotal way to represent those dichotomies in early African American culture was via gender constructs of the empire during slavery. When stories highlight the ranking of gender in African American folklore it is not necessarily an indication of accepted beliefs in the social construct of gender or the biological rhetoric of sex, as much as it is a strategy to show ranking in a New World way. Traditionally, "the primary trickster figures of animal tales were weak, relatively powerless creatures" who depended on wit and guile, and their counterparts were physically bigger and relied on brute strength (Levine 103). Hare/rabbit, tortoise/turtle, spider, lion, tiger, hyena, and elephant may have been enough to represent battles about material conditions, but this work proposes that the doubling of weak versus strong conveyed by traditional characters and gender markers of "sis" or br'er" are an attempt to handle the more complicated issues of social repression facing Africans in the New World:

> "Ole Sis Goose, I'se got yer now, you'se been er-sailin' on der lake er long time, en I'se got yer now. I'se gwine to break yer neck and pick yer bones."
> "Hole on der, Brer Fox, hold on, I'se got jes' as much right to swim in der lake as you has ter lie in der weeds. Hits des as much my lake as hit is yours, an we is gwine to take dis matter to der cotehouse and see if you has any right to break my neck and pick my bones."
> And so dey went to cote, and when dey got dere, de sheriff, he wus er fox, en de judge, he was er fox, and der toruneys, dey wus fox, en all de jurymen, dey was foxes, too. En dey tried ole Sis Goose, en dey victed her and dey scuted heer, and dey picked her bones. Now my chilluns, listen to me, when all de folks in de cotehouse is foxes, and you is des' er common goose, der ain't gwine to much justice for you pore cullud folks. (Hughes and Bontemps 13)

In "Ole Sis Goose," the woes of the African American community and the U.S. legal system provide a folkloric rendering of how race affects the outcome of justice. Gender status seems to be employed in this animal tale as a way to parallel the superior levels of creativity, ingenuity, and cleverness with those of a given society's measurements of superiority. In the case of the United States, the ranking of male over female, as well as white over black, is one way to show rank. However, creating oral stories that explicitly evoke the unfair and oppressive realities of slaves through race might have resulted in harsh punishment if white oppressors overheard. Gender became the most viable alternative.

Examination of more tales validates the need for deeper explication of gender and sexuality in folklore. The marker of "sis" in the animal tale suggests gender as the safest way to express the injustices of the world. The superficial lesson to be learned is that justice refers to just-us (white) declared citizens of society. Not every animal judging the case is Sis Goose's kind. The foxes clearly represent white people and their presence in U.S. courts, while Sis Goose represents the Black race. More subversively, the tale exemplifies how folktales counter any dominant social ideals. As slaves, Blacks are deemed property and the language of ownership that would enable Sis Goose (Blacks) to swim in the lake remains unavailable to her. As Sis Goose learns, only those making the laws can expect to reap the benefits of the privilege they might afford individuals.

In research on animal trickster tales, the presentation of gender relations is rarely broached. Yet in the Sis Goose tale, gender emphasizes the overall theme of inequality. Race doesn't become a primary factor in the tale until the end. From the very beginning, Br'er Fox's attempted trickery of Sis Goose is positioned as a masculine/feminine dynamic. If gender were of no account, the qualifier of "sis"—dialect for sister—would be unnecessary. Br'er Fox stands as the stronger and more cunning figure in comparison to the more docile and weak goose. Fox possesses characteristics attributable to masculine qualities, while Goose possesses representative traits of femininity.

The proliferation of such tales make obvious that these pedagogical legends use the rhetoric of sex to teach Black people not only how to negotiate the oppressive racial realities of Blacks to whites in the New World, but also how to negotiate the oppressive/repressive status of gender and sexuality in the community and culture of Blacks in the United States. Yet the latter function is dismissed for a focus on race. As Levine demonstrates, critics encounter few problems demonstrating the tales' connection to issues of race and stature. However, connecting the tales to other conflicts in Black life remains to be done.

Over time, the tradition of animal trickster tales changes to reflect both a concern with material conditions and social repression, especially as it concerns women. In another tale, "Brer Rabbit and Sis Cow," the issues of gender relations in the Black community are more clear-cut. In this particular tale, Br'er Rabbit tricks Sis Cow for his own means:

> Br'er Rabbit see Sis Cow an' she have a bag plumb full of milk, an' it's a hot day an' he ain't had nothin' to drink for a long time. He know 'tain't no use askin' her fur milk 'cause las' year she done 'fused him onct. . . . he say: "Sis Cow would you do me the favor to hit this persimmon tree with yore head an' shake a few of dem persimmons." . . . Sis Cow . . . hits the tree, but no persimmons come down. . . . So den Sis Cow git mad . . . an' hit dat tree so hard dat her horns go right into the wood so fur she can't pull 'em out. (Hughes and Bontemps 4)

Once Sis Cow becomes stuck in the tree, Br'er Rabbit brings his family to the tree and they proceed to milk and feast on the milk of Sis Cow.

Br'er Rabbit's trickery triumphs again. If he had not used it, his family may never have received the milk it needed. The lesson to be learned from this tale suggests that wits win out over brawn every time. However, tales such as Sis Cow and Sis Goose demonstrate a pattern that consistently places animal figures assigned a less powerful status into the gendered position of the Western construction of woman, as well as being the tricked rather than the trickster. Such tales make it difficult to believe these animal trickster tales hold any of the original genderless qualities of the African trickster figures, or that they could represent various positions in Black subjectivity. However, since trickster tales are about material circumstances and material conditions change over time, so do the tales. It should not be seen as coincidental that these elements begin to change in the same period as talk of emancipation and women's voting rights begins.

With the goals of freedom in mind for nineteenth-century Blacks, the trickster tradition evolved from animal trickster tales to human trickster tales about a Black male named John who has a hard-work philosophy and superior physical endurance that wins out over machine technology.[7] During the transition of trickster tales, the tradition becomes split along the plots and themes of gender. The tradition of John is merely one trickster in the human trickster cycle. Annie Christmas is another.

Annie Christmas, Female Trickster Figure Countering the Tradition of John

In *Tricksters Make This World*, Lewis Hyde argues that "all the standard tricksters are male" (335). The first question, then, is whose standards guide the research and focus? As discussed in the introduction, if the reading and use of trickster is a recouping of nation, heroism, or masculinity, then the standard would be male. If the community or group that produces trickster is hierarchically arranged along gender divisions, where masculinity is privileged, then the standard will be male. Yet what happens when none of the aforementioned is a consideration. What happens when women's culture uses and reads trickster as the genderless or multigendered being that it has been referenced as being? Hyde extends his argument by suggesting three perfectly (il)logical reasons for trickster traditions being male no matter what: "First, tricksters belong to patriarchal mythologies, one in which the prime actors are male. Second, there may be a problem with the standard itself; there may be female tricksters who simply have been ignored. Finally, it may be that the trickster stories articulate some distinction between men and women, so that even in a matriarchal setting this figure would be male" (335). Since trickster, based on years of research in various disciplines, is by its very existence and definition an anomaly that should never be referred to in the same breath as standard anything, we must challenge Hyde's assumption that all tricksters are male. There are matriarchal mythologies where the trickster is female, there is an obvious problem with the standard, and as Hyde's own words offer, female tricksters have been deliberately ignored just because of their being female.

While the figures themselves may not be Western, the concept of trickster is a Western term and concept that delimits the original possibilities of trickster. In accordance with this belief, William Hynes suggests that more characteristics, in addition to the six manifest trickster traits, might be found: "More characteristics could be chosen, but these six serve as a modest map, heuristic guide . . . thus, these initial six characteristics invite and anticipate not only the intricacies of the careers of particular tricksters, but emendations" ("Mapping the Characteristics of Mythic Tricksters" 33). In that sense, the figures we classify as tricksters should not be appropriated or changed, but the definition of trickster should be tinkered with at some point through the values of the specific communities and time periods that it remains a part of. Tales of one folk figure reveal how Black women continued evolving trickster strategies in animal tales and slave narratives in their daily lives.

Beyond animal trickster tales, we find one underread human trickster tale, "Annie Christmas," wreaking havoc on the laws of intelligible gender in Black oral traditions in the early twentieth century. Black diaspora oral and folk traditions are filled with stories of trickster-gods/goddesses and animal and human tricksters. Aside from all the tales of Tar Babies, Signifying Monkeys, Br'er Rabbits, John Henrys, and Stackolees, we should also examine the few tales on Annie Christmas in Black females' folk and vernacular culture. In the folktales of Annie Christmas, we find the beginning of indeterminacy and the implied complications of gender and sexuality for African Americans and this text's revision of the trickster figure in Black culture. Annie Christmas, a Black U.S folk figure, is one of the first figures to provide a revision of the masculine trope of the human trickster in Black U.S. culture:

> Oldtimers say that the Negro longshoremen and all life on the riverfront are not what they used to be. Its gone soft now, say they. In other days men were really men, yet the toughest of them all was a woman. Her name was Annie Christmas. She was six feet, eight inches tall and she weighed more than two hundred and fifty pounds. She wore a neat mustache and had a voice as loud and as deep as a foghorn on the river. (Hughes and Bontemps 13)

Annie Christmas has been described as the female version of John Henry, the superhuman hero of Black folklore. Yet such a reading of the story, like that of John Henry, would mean accepting the traditional reading of gender and heroic figures. On the other hand, trickster-troping uncovers the real potential of the tale. The story of Annie Christmas reminds us that issues of gender and sexuality are very much a part of Black vernacular culture. The lore of Annie Christmas remains a part of levee life or riverboat/dockside culture of America. Often described as a life dictated by the river, levee culture expresses "the life of a community within a community,—a society of wanderers who have haunts but not homes, and who are connected with the static society surrounding them by common bond of State and municipal law" (Hughes and Bontemps 211). Hence, levee habitats facilitate trickster's liminal or transitory life.

In states dependent on docks and ports for economic subsistence, African Americans once again made up a great deal of the labor force. Referred to as roustabouts, their "pariah existence and wholly sensual enjoyments" provide this author with plenty of trickster material (Hughes and Bontemps 213). These figures epitomize trickster's ability to be both marginal and central to the community's culture. Although historians show roustabout life as a male culture, folklore presents alternative narratives. One cannot partake of the rowdy, rambunctious tales of sailing adventures, booze, violence, and women without encountering the tales of Annie Christmas.

Annie Christmas highlights the trickster-like existence of Black females and their culture. The description of Annie takes the contradictions of Black female subjectivity to their greatest heights by exaggerating the socially conceived physical attributes usually ascribed to either men *or* women and embeds them in one being. Annie, previously undefined as a trickster, reflects Hynes's six original characteristics of trickster. In addition to the tale itself serving as a signifier of the importance of gender and sexuality in women's folklore, the recording of the tale exposes the influence of gender and sexuality in the research and study of folklore.

There are two very distinct versions of the Annie Christmas story.[8] The first version, as quoted above, is extracted from Langston Hughes and Arna Bontemps's compilation *The Book of Negro Folklore*. As we will see, the variations of the story are attributable to the gender of those collecting or telling the stories. The version found in the Hughes and Bontemps collection contains vivid descriptions of Annie Christmas as a drinking woman: "Annie could outdrink any man in the south. She would put down a barrel of beer and chase it with ten quarts of whiskey, without stopping" (13).

In this version, the bio-logic[9] of Annie's gender runs contradictory to the bio-logic of woman. That Annie's strength and gendered fluidity seems more male than female comes from the realization that Annie chases beer with whiskey, where typically it would be the reverse—with mortals using beer to chase the stronger and harder liquor of whiskey. Drinking establishes Annie as something not quite man or woman. The focus on drinking hard liquor typically is assigned as a masculine pastime.

Nevertheless, when the story implies that Annie is more masculine than feminine, the ideologies of gender are once again interrupted: "Whenever she got ready to have a baby, she drank a quart of whiskey and lay down somewhere. Annie had twelve black sons, each seven feet tall, all born at the same time. She had plenty other babies, too, but these were her favorites" (Hughes and Bontemps 14). The tale reveals Annie as a biologically fertile female. Yet Annie's ability to consume large quantities of alcohol and birth twelve sons at the same time undermines Western bio-logic that positions females as physically and emotionally weak. The tale of Annie Christmas certainly serves as evidence to discredit Nathan Huggins's comments about the natural limitations of freedom creating conservative women in folklore.

Another version of Annie Christmas, recorded in *Herstories*, a collection of folktales compiled by female folklorist Virginia Hamilton, delivers an almost identical version of the story of Annie Christmas, but with some noticeable changes:

> Annie Christmas was coal black and tree tall. She stood seven feet barefoot, and she weighed two-hundred and ninety-nine pounds . . . the strongest [woman] that ever lived. . . . She was a keelboat operator. . . . She had a mustache too. She could make fists hard, and she would fight boatmen by the dozen and beat them down everytime. . . . They say her baby boys were born one right after the other for twelve days. (84)

In this version, Annie gives birth to boys one after the other, and there is no mention of her drinking like a man. The variety in versions of the tale is attributable to the ideologies of gender and the purpose of the collection.

In the Hughes and Bontemps collection, we have a version recorded by two men, collected for a general collection of folklore. In that version, the exaggerations of masculine qualities seem to be reemphasized. The Hamilton version, told by a woman and collected by a woman for inclusion into a collection of Black folklore for girls, focuses less on the masculine attributes. Perhaps Hamilton's version, while still imbuing Annie with great strength with which to beat many men, does not refer to Annie's drinking habits because it buys into ideologies of drinking as an activity or vice that should not be promoted. It is, after all, a collection of tales meant for young girls. The Hughes and Bontemps version includes the drinking to defeminize the character for believability of her status as riverboat captain. The possibilities for the inclusion/exclusion of certain factors in this particular context suggest how a tale with a limitless subject figure can be shaped by social creeds. However, the tale and figure itself consistently refute the influence of dominant beliefs that there are only two genders.

In both versions, Annie possesses both masculine and feminine traits, and she has the hypersexuality of trickster, as evidenced by her twelve children. Incidentally, the description of Annie with facial hair disrupts the discreet order of gender. Facial hair has been touted as a masculine trait, but women also experience facial hair growth. Annie's moustache, height, and weight subvert constructed ideas of gender and biological feminine aesthetics. Conceivably, she is male *and* female. In addition, her very existence works to change the community in which she lives. In one adventure, shape-shifting, a manifest trickster trait, prevails: "I'll tell you about the time Annie decided to dress up like a fine lady. She shaved that mustache real close so it wasn't there. She piled her raven hair up and stuck peacock feathers in it" (*Herstories* 85).

The shaving of Annie's moustache represents an acknowledgment that femininity is a performance written by the discreet order of gender identities. Annie's bionatural state is to have a moustache, and her decision to shave gives her an unnatural but now normalized physical appearance as a "woman." The relegation of biology into familiar gendered categories is motivated by normative readings that are invested in dominant social gender constructs. Ironically, as many of Annie's girlfriends are prettying themselves for boat rides with male suitors, Annie sets to sail by herself in her keelboat. Annie Christmas's story makes it hard to believe that the trickster figure has contributed to a purely masculine line of folk descendants. The figure consciously moves back and forth between Western constructs of gender, but Annie never really adheres to the logic of such discourse. The endings of the separate tales emphasize the possible disruptions.

The endings of the Annie Christmas stories present another primary inconsistency in the two versions of the tale. Both tales end with Annie committing suicide because she fell in love with a riverboat captain who did not want her. However, the reactions and subsequent finality changes from tale to tale and depends on who is telling or retelling and collecting the story. In the Hughes and Bontemps version, Annie commits suicide directly after the rejection: "Finally Annie met a man who could lick her and then she fell in love for the first time in her life. But the man didn't want her, so Annie bedeckered herself in all her finery and her famous necklace and committed suicide" (223). In this version, Annie simply gives up and dies, while the captain seems to go on living.

The presentation of this Annie Christmas tale subsequently makes the captain a victor or a more powerful agent in the life of this Black female. Where she was once the toughest of all (men), her attempt to capture a man's love weakens her. The Hughes and Bontemps version of the tale clearly indicates an unhappy ending for Black females who do not adhere to model ideologies of womanhood. It suggests that women can be different, but those women should be prepared to face the consequences of that difference—man's rejection of them and their love. Further, it implies that while Annie had her independence and freedom, she could not be completely happy unless she had a man in her life. As someone who unashamedly possesses both "masculine" and "feminine" qualities simultaneously, Annie exists liminally because she moves back and forth between the social constructs of male and female. In this version, suicide appears to be the only way for Annie to alleviate her anomalous physical fluctuations.

However, in the Hamilton version, Annie does not accept society's norms and decide to kill herself right away. After the captain rejects Annie, we learn:

> Well, that hurt Annie, to be put off like that. She was in love and then out of love in about a minute flat. "I hope some big trouble gets you," she told the captain. "You'd better watch out this night. Your crew too. For all that's bad is right with you!" With that Annie Christmas got on her own boat and tore out of there. (*Herstories* 86)

Hamilton's version positions Annie as the more active and powerful agent. After the rejection by the captain, Annie is not silent. She speaks before she commits suicide and briefly places herself back into a position of power. Although she still commits suicide, she does not seem to falter at the established norms. In fact, Annie rejects those standards by altering the course of the captain's life with her curse. Her actions change the outcome of the story; the captain and his crew die, "but he haunts the big devil river. You can hear him cursing the weather, the sky" (86).

In addition to the captain's death and his angry haunting of the river in New Orleans, Annie's unhappy predicament in death changes. Ironically, tellers of the story forewarn: "Now you can believe this last, or not. But this what the black folks say" (88). The need to address the believability about the rest of Annie's tale concretely conveys the importance of who is telling the story, as well as who is listening. It also seeks to prepare the listener for a more provocative ending: "Annie Christmas is still on the big river . . . sitting on her own wood grave, singing a river tune to the thundering sky" (88). The ending of Hamilton's version enunciates the differing perception of suicide in the two tales. The captain dies and curses everything in his afterlife, while Annie, almost gloating, sings triumphantly on the river. Hamilton's ending remarks about the gendering of this Black female. It figuratively unnames Annie Christmas as a Black woman. Unmistakably, this Annie is not the weakened, dejected, and dead female of the Hughes and Bontemps version, but something much more.

Annie's actions mirror Br'er Rabbit, Signifying Monkey, and the tradition of John. She signifies, she tricks, and she possesses a superhuman quality that ensures her survival in lore. As a spirit, she is now free to embrace her trait of indeterminacy in a way she could not have as a human. Characteristics and elements of magical realism and hoodoo revamp Annie's image and transform the figure into a trickster-god(dess) for the masses. She lives as the strong, indeterminable self that she originally was. Her spirit state suggests the full reality of what was at one time her corporeal experience. She could only maintain this state in an alternate world, and that is what Black folklore suggests for Black people and Black culture—to find other discourses that sustain liminal subjectivity rather than accept false or static options. The complexity of Annie Christmas shows the complication of gender and desire in African American communities. As mythical as human tricksters like John and Annie may have been, human trickster tales were frequently based on some real-life person. Nowhere is this more obvious then in the individual accounts of former slaves who took to presenting their stories in extended written narratives.

Pregeneric Myths of Slave Narratives

Just as folklore becomes evidence in proving that Blacks have a culture in which they can stake their claim in nationalism, so too does the slave narrative. In both their experiences as slaves and as authors of slave narratives, ex-slaves relied as much on tricksterism learned from Black folklore and myths as they did on the Western tradition of writing and discourses of religion and enlightenment. However, it is the slave narrative based on the experiences of males that shapes many discussions about Black culture so that it parallels and benefits the aims of nation building in folklore. In *From behind the Veil: A Study of Afro-American Narrative*, Robert Stepto reminds us that African American culture, like all cultures, has "canonical stories" or "pregeneric myths, shared stories or myths that not only exist prior to literary forms, but eventually shape the forms that comprise a given culture's literary canon" (ix). According to Stepto, the slave narrative shows that freedom and literacy are the pregeneric myths for African American literature. Subsequently, few have questioned this universality of pregeneric myths.

Stepto's designated pregeneric myths seem to deny the hierarchies that existed in institutions of slavery (field slave/house slave, man/woman, and darkie/mulatto). He totalizes the slave experience, and if the slave experience were universal then we would not have the development of the Black female slave narrative. What are pregeneric myths of the female slave narrative, and how do they shape the tradition of African American women's literature? These questions have not been fully answered. Clearly, we have analyzed the importance of gender and sex in contexts dealing with history, themes, and the representation of the Black woman, but there has not been a moment of recognition of these pregeneric myths, if they exist.

Stepto's argument later influences the work of Henry L. Gates, who bases his theoretical *The Signifying Monkey* on Stepto's opinion. Later, in *Loose Canons: Notes on the Culture Wars*, Gates corroborates Stepto's earlier opinions:

> After Descartes, reason was privileged, or valorized, among other human characteristics. Writing, especially after the printing press became so widespread, was taken to be the visible sign of reason. Blacks were "reasonable," and hence "men," if and only if—they demonstrated mastery of the "arts and sciences," the eighteenth century's formula for writing. (54)

By asserting that literacy was the way for slaves to prove their humanity, Gates validates Stepto's pregeneric myths. He relies on a number of male slave narratives to confirm his major argument—the trope of the talking book. Gates is not alone in this theory of writing one's self into being (*Signifying Monkey* 33–37, 48–49).[10]

Ronald T. Judy's *(Dis)forming the American Canon: African Slave Narratives and the Vernacular* moves beyond these established assumptions about the vernacular and literacy in African American literary tradition. In reference to both the slave narrative and Black folk and oral traditions, theories of being suggests exactly what Judy claims in his work: "[T]he mute African body is overwritten by the Negro, and the Negro that emerges in the ink flow . . . is that which has overwritten itself and so become the representation of the very body it sits on" (89). Judy challenges the previous statement made by Gates, which proposes that the slave writes himself into being through the narrative and that before the moment of inscription there was no valid being. With his dismissal of theories of slaves writing themselves into being in ways that Western man can understand, Judy attempts to revise the canons of American and African American literature to find a place for African-Arabic slave narratives through a theory of indeterminacy. Judy makes solid claims that a Black narrative tradition exists before Africans in the New World construct it. Rather than relying on traditional slave narrative from the West written in English, Judy refers to Ben Ali's *Diary*, written in Arabic, as "an augmentation of Afro-American canon formation" (22). Judy's critique of Ben Ali's African-Arabic slave narrative and its sense of indeterminacy highlight how issues of authenticity and essentialism have narrowed conceptions of Black experiences and culture.

Interestingly enough, Judy's work could have offered interesting insights about the issue of gender in the African American literary tradition, but, as indicated by Wahneema Lubiano, Judy chose not to focus on those insights:

> Being is a set of terms—a male new set of terms; "making a man" is "being" on male grounds, for neither Kant nor Douglass's humanness makes "female" humanness possible. And if Ben Ali's manuscript's indeterminancy has feminist implications, then their articulation in Judy's work is sotto voce indeed. Judy not only doesn't comment on the masculinist language and imaginings of the texts or the discourse of reason, he doesn't make an argument for why gender does not have to be addressed, and I mean gender not only in terms of what is left out—because apparently it did not occur to Judy to take up gender as something to consider even if only to dismiss its importance (xxii).[11]

Lubiano masterfully details how recent attempts to rethink blackness still eliminate gender and sexuality from those considerations. These revisions share one commonality. Be it through the articulation of pregeneric myths or metaphors of authentication, the narrative tradition of African Americans is problematically assessed through an ontology of deformity and deficiency. The Negro lacks culture, lacks tradition, lacks history, and therefore lacks identity. So focused on the idea of proving what the Negro lacks and the Negro's attempts to "be," we never ask what/who we mean when we say "Negro." Incidentally, as Lubiano alluded to earlier, the concept of "being" and being Negro is primarily conceived as masculine,[12] and as such, critics reach for the most widely perceived masculine forms of the oral and vernacular to continue incorporating Africanism with nationalist agendas. Such representations of blackness mask the distinctions and differences we currently find ourselves trying to account for in the identity of Blacks. Uncovering unnaming and trickster-troping in the female slave narrative moves scholarship beyond conceiving of Black narrative tradition and identity as an ontology of lack, but suggests that identity can emerge through a simultaneous presentation of multiple and fluctuating processes that don't have to be fixed or limited.

The African American female tradition evolves from a foundation of nonhierarchical roles of gender, an understanding of occupying space that is deemed masculine, feminine, and other. Black females who were once slaves do not attempt to write themselves into being, because they already know they exist. Instead, their works seek to translate their liminal subjectivity to societies or cultures obsessed with finite categories of race, class, gender, and sexuality, while denying dominant society's classification and naming of their subjectivity. Essentially, Stepto's concerns over pregeneric myths (freedom and literacy) help to reveal the counternarrative in Black female slave narratives. Freedom acts as a major factor in most slave narratives, but literacy fails to be a significant factor not only because it was a male privilege and priority, but also because literacy, in the sense that Stepto imagines it (writing in English), connects to Western discourses that mistranslate or misrepresent Black female subjectivity. Slave narratives about female protagonists do incorporate the pregeneric myth of freedom. However, unlike the male slave narrative, that freedom does not hinge on the acquirement of literacy. For female slaves, freedom depends on the disruption of racial and gender categories. In the end, their historical methods of trickster-troping stems from their quests to resist being either Negro or woman. The desire to resist "being" shapes Black women's goals of freedom and developing culture.

Signifyin(g) Sojourner Truth and the Historical Figuration of Mythology

For all their profuse appreciation and support of learning to read and write, critics' privileging of writing as most important in Black literary tradition must take a back seat when we examine the rhetorical strategies used by most authors of slave narratives.[13] Strategies of trickery learned from folklore traditions, specifically trickster tales, become just as important as literacy. Learning how to write is one thing, understanding how to manipulate that skill to write a pass for freedom is quite another. Even the most skilled writer and follower of Rousseauean ideals of democracy, Frederick Douglass, needed a little Br'er Rabbit to help him (un)name himself and work the antislavery lecture circuit. In the case of Black female slaves, trickster tales provide as many worthy models for their material conditions as Br'er Rabbit did for their male counterparts. While the historical experience of the Black female calls for the act for unnaming, her strategies of unnaming arise from her oral culture and, in this case, animal and human trickster tales. The intersection of rhetorical strategies of animal trickster tales with that of concerns of liberation for Black men and white women erupts in the oral rendering of one female slave's life into the written narrations of slave tradition, *Narrative of Sojourner Truth*.

Truth's narrative functions very much along the same narrative strategies of folk tradition, with the one exception that it is veritable fact. Still, the forces of divine myths make their way into Truth's autobiography. When Truth discusses her post-emancipation move to unname herself as Isabella, she states, "An' so I went to the Lord an' asked him to give me a new name. And the Lord gave me Sojourner, because I was to travel up an' down the land, showin' the people their sins, and bein' a sign unto them.... Afterward I told the Lord I wanted another name [other than Sojourner], cause everybody else had two names ... the Lord gave me Truth, because I was to declare the truth to the people" (*Narrative of Sojourner Truth* 126–27). Truth's rhetorical involvement with truth and signs exhibits intellectual strategies that are trickster-like in nature. Ironically, like a true trickster, the two names the Lord bestows upon her non-hierarchically oppose each other. "Truth" connotes absolutism. While Sojourner Truth claims that her first name represents her function as a sign. Notably, "for any one sign there may be several interpretations."[14] Truth engages in a personal (un)naming (renaming herself) to counter the personal subjugation forced on her by the institution of slavery, but in assigning herself opposing names that cancel out the meaning of each other, she also unconsciously unnames to counter the discursive binaries of Western discourse. This unnaming metaphorically challenges the binaries that comprise ideologies of gender, race, and sexuality. Truth's unnaming revelation documents the way Black women used and continue to use myth and metaphor to invent themselves as subjects and express their desires.

Like the tales of Br'er Rabbit told to Joel Chandler Harris by Uncle Remus, Truth's life story is told to two white women suffrage activists, Olive Gilbert and Frances Gage. Truth's narrative tends to lack the authority and strength of voice of other narratives, such as Douglass's, but that doesn't make the logic of her most famous speech any less valid. Though her story is narrated by Gilbert and Gage, the logic and ideals clearly derive from the point of view of a female slave raised in a world filled with folklore. From Gage's account, Truth's famous speech at the 1851 Women's Rights Convention in Akron, Ohio, confronts social ideologies of womanhood and the bio-logic of gender:

> "Dat man ober dar say women needs to be helped into carriages and lifted into carriages, or ober mud puddles, or gives me any best place," And raising herself to her full height and her voice to a pitch like rolling thunder, she asked, "and ar'n't I a woman? Look at me! Look at my arm!" And she bared her right arm to the shoulder, showing her tremendous muscular power. "I have plowed, and planted, and gathered into barns, and no man could head me—and ar'n't I a woman?" (Gage 133)

Truth's rhetorical strategy mirrors that of Br'er Rabbit and Sis Goose in animal trickster tales. She positions herself as the lower and weaker foil, but she uses wit and guile to move herself into a position of power or control. She draws attention to the inconsistencies within the social and biological discourses on gender.

The speech also resonates with the elements associated with the human trickster tale:

> Looking back upon the past, the slaves and their descendants painted a picture not of a cowed and timorous black mass but of a people who, how-

ever circumscribed by misfortune and oppressions, were never without their means of resistance and never lacked the inner resources to oppose the master class. (Levine 389)

Truth's narrative allows her to emphasize her inner resources of strength. Levine explains that the creation of human trickster tales was meant to foster a sense of resistance. Human trickster tales empower African Americans to move from a subjectivity of powerless victim. In the same way that ex-slaves mythologized their ancestors in slavery, Truth makes herself a trickster against her opposing master classes of white men, white women, and Black men. Like the tradition of John Henry, "Ain't I a Woman?" epitomizes the basic qualities of the human trickster tale.

Rather than assuming a position of victimhood dictated by ideals concerning gender, virtues, and biology, Truth opts for a trickster discourse. Unnaming is a performative tactic of the vernacular similar to José Muñoz's disidentification. In *Disidentification: Queers of Color and the Politics of Performance*, Muñoz examines cultural performances by queers of color that "must negotiate between a fixed identity disposition and the socially encoded roles that are available for such subjects" (6). However, where Muñoz's work speaks of performances that refashion mainstream and heteronormative ideololgies as a form of resistance, unnaming is a form of resistance to counter and destroy dominant types and models with myths from the subjects' culture.[15] Unnaming, in the way that Truth does it, is a process of redefining difference as postulated by Audre Lorde where we can use "human difference as a springboard for creative change within our lives" ("Age, Race, Class, and Sex" 116). The effectiveness of Truth's speech relies on how she understands difference. She brilliantly conceptualizes difference as something that is not deviant. Trickster acts as a subtext to her approach.

As a performer of African American communal discourse, she becomes Gerald Vizenor's definition of the comic (ironic) holotrope in racial and gender inequities. Biologically, Truth places herself in the arena of females, but socially she explodes the ideologies of "woman" with her position as slave labor. She possesses feminine attributes of female reproduction, but she remains physically capable of manual labor. Her historical line, delivered in her vernacular tongue, signifies on her oppressors in the same way that Monkey signifies on the lion in the well-known African American trickster tale "The Signifying Monkey":

> For up jumped the monkey in the tree one day and laughed
> "I guess I'll start some shit . . ."
>   . . . King of the jungle, ain't you a bitch,

you look like someone with a seven year itch . . .
"Whup! Motherfucker, don't you roar. (B. Jackson 164–65)

The trickster figure is brash and unapologetic but aware of Lion's possible reaction. Truth's rhetorical demeanor and trademark line, "ain't I a woman," replicates the repetitious taunting nature of the animal trickster and its plot device of pitting weaker (oppressed) against the stronger animal (oppressor). She dares those with more power to challenge her with each refrain by making use of their own rhetoric of sex and womanhood. Truth's signifyin(g) exposes the secret intersection between the rhetoric of sex and the discourse of race. The use of her folk tongue serves as a way to unname herself, as opposed to renaming herself woman. As Claudia Mitchell-Kernan assessed early on:

> The Black concept of signifying incorporates essentially a folk notion that dictionary entries for words are not always sufficient for interpreting meaning or messages, or that meaning goes beyond such interpretations. Complimentary remarks may be delivered in a left-handed fashion. A particular utterance may be an insult in one context and not another. What pretends to be informative may be persuasive. The hearer is constrained to attend all potential meaning carrying symbolic systems in speech events—the total universe of discourse. (314)

In order for Truth's signifying to be successfully understood, her audience has to appreciate and comprehend the cultural foundation that she is mining. Though Truth and the white women she addresses are biologically female, all parties must understand the social discourses denied and available to Truth. The discourse of womanhood is denied to her, but her folk universe gives her trickster's signifyin(g). Though the logic of Truth's speech attempts to disrupt the biological determinism that creates the hierarchical ranking of sexes, it is undermined by the intrusion of white females and their suffrage objectives.

Gage and Gilbert could not attend to, and perhaps did not care to, all the meanings of Truth's signifyin(g) "ain't I a woman." She uses the term "woman" in the same way that the monkey uses motherfucker. Her signifyin(g) undoes the intelligible logic of gender because it is a "boast by indirect verbal or gestural means" (Abrahams, *Deep Down in the Jungle* 264) to suggest that no nineteenth-century language exists to adequately define her subjectivity. Truth's "Ain't I A Woman" speech is a trickster narrative, and trickster-scholar Anne Doueihi convincingly argues that trickster narratives are "about the difference between, and the undecideability of, discourse and story, referential and rhetorical values, signifier and signified, a conventional mind and one that is open to the sacred" (200). Signifyin(g) acts as Truth's method of trickster-troping. She replaces the rhetoric of womanhood with her own culturally specific discourse of desire to be something more than woman, to unname herself as Black woman. The only problem, then, is that audiences (past and present) ignore the reality of Truth's "trash-talking," a folk machination. This is after all, a person who is a walking contradiction since she defines herself as a sign and the truth.

As always, it is the transmission from oral to written that begins the problematic use of Truth and the historical figuration of "the Black woman." Besides Truth's question of womanhood, we see something else taking precedent in the narrative—Truth's body. Before Truth bares her unwomanly arms to reveal muscles usually accorded to men, Gage focuses incessantly on Truth's height. As Truth performs, her narrative relates that she is slouching at first, but then she raises herself to her full height. Gage previously discloses that "the leaders of the movement trembled on seeing a tall, gaunt, black woman" (*Narrative of Sojourner Truth* 133), and that "Old Sojourner, quiet and reticent as the 'Libyan Statue' sat . . . her chin resting upon her broad, hard palm" (134). Gage reveals that Truth's body commands as much attention as her words.

If the point of Truth's speech is truly to underscore her subjectivity as woman and connection to sisterhood, then surely we can realize the mockery in her words "ain't I a woman" in front of the apparently scared-as-hell white "liberal" masses. If white female leaders and social activists saw Truth as Gage does, then what is it they saw, anyway? An unexplainable other! Gage's attempt to destroy ideologies of womanhood by writing Truth's narrative appears admirable, but she does so at the cost of Black female subjectivity. Gage, while disclosing Truth's life, manages to construct early feminist thought and build its very foundation through an othering of the Black female body.

As the text progresses, Gage's comments become more centered on Truth's physical presence being antithetical for "woman." "There were *few women* in those days that dared to 'speak in meeting' . . . every eye was fixed on this *almost Amazon form*, which stood nearly six feet high" (*Narrative of Sojourner Truth* 135; emphasis added). After Truth made her speech, Gage recalls, "I have never in my life seen anything like the *magical influence* that subdued the mobbish spirit" (*Narrative of Sojourner Truth* 136; emphasis added). Rather than reading Truth's difference and using it as a springboard for change, Gage makes Truth deviant and other. Throughout Gage's narrative, Truth becomes object and othered. The text is as much about Truth's words as it is her body. Even after delivering the powerful words that have made her a preeminent figure in history, Truth's othered body would still be an issue with the white masses of her time. At the request of a man, Truth had to bare her breasts to prove that she was a female, which is not necessarily woman, as seen in the narration of Truth's speech.

Clearly, from Gage's rendering of Truth's narrative, the white male was not the only one having trouble grasping the figure of Sojourner Truth. Gage manages to connect Truth to every negative image of Blacks from magical/mystical Negro to all-body-no-intellect stereotypes. Truth's body elicits fear and trembling, and Gage takes great measures to place Truth outside the sphere of "normal" body aesthetics. Further, instead of describing Truth's persuasion of the mob as something of great intellectual superiority, Gage manages to reduce Truth's genius to magical influence. Gage's narrative of Truth's life sets up a parameter for judging Black female feminist thought that continues in the work of current feminist criticism. This parameter asserts that feminist criticism should covertly use the historical position of the Black female as its intended goal and theory, but never acknowledge it as the basis of its own white feminist hope. White feminists like Gage can extract the benefits of Truth-like subjectivity, but they might also exceed her subject status as a result of their skin-white privilege. Consequently, this suggests why Black females need to unname themselves in their own lives with discourse distinct from the rhetoric of sex.

Critics such as Denise Riley and Constance Penley inaccurately see Truth's proclamation as a desire for the construction of womanhood to fit her, but they should also be able to recognize that Truth's words acknowledge woman as a frame that could never replace her actual being.[16] As this text has shown, Truth did not need a new language, white suffragists and feminists needed a handbook on signifyin(g). In one chapter of *The Changing Same*, Deborah McDowell uncovers the truth and colors feminist theory in her assessment of the value of Truth. McDowell suggests that "Truth and the knowledge of that name help to construct concerns about Black feminist thinking within the general parameters of feminist discourse," but she also argues that Truth "as a metonymn for 'black woman' is useful in this context both to a singular idea of academic feminism in general, and in particular, to ongoing controversies within that discourse over the often uneasy relations between theory and politics" (158). Other Black female critics support McDowell's claim, and they prove that the "Black woman" also serves as a metaphor, myth, or historical figuration of myth for white feminist thought.

Karla F. C. Holloway's *Moorings and Metaphors* reveals vital information to expose how myth of the historical figurations of Black women might come to be as a result of Truth's statement. Holloway explains, "Mythologies are not discrete units of structure as much as they are features of a surviving sense of how language enables the survival and transference of memory" (94). Truth's statement survives centuries within the machine discourse of feminist theory, and as a result we are able to gather insights from her memory of grappling with her subjectivity as a slave, a female, and an African in America. However, as McDowell and Holloway point out, upon reading these words we must always remember that language, that of white female activists, enables the initial survival, transference, and distortion of Truth's memory.

Truth's original trickster-troping of signifyin(g) is displaced in the women's suffrage machine. Holloway continues: "Because memory is critical to mythologies, then the privilege that memory traditionally represents over myth—that of representation (accuracy) over figuration (metaphor)—is dissolved within the disappearance of the chasm between memory (history) and myth (figuration). What remains are historical figurations of mythologies" (94). Truth's all-powerful statement serves as a representation (accurate) of her flexible and indefinable subjectivity that then becomes the figuration (metaphor) for an early white feminist movement.

Truth's words do not create this figuration since she does not exercise authorial control over the publication of her speech. The suffrage movement uses Truth to initiate a cataclysmic call for women's voting rights that does not apply to her. In reality, she functions as a theory to dispute biological reasoning of why women shouldn't be allowed to vote because they are physically and emotionally weak and unable to bear children and conduct politics. She becomes a mascot for a (white) women's rights movement. The radical trickster-troping and unnaming are displaced, and the memory of Truth's understanding of her subjectivity is dissolved in the chasm between memory (history) and myth (figuration), along with any desires that she may have.

As McDowell and Holloway explain it, Sojourner Truth becomes the theory in feminist theory. What remains with us are historical figurations of Black females still trying to fit into the gendered discourse of womanhood and historical figurations of mythologies—Black Woman, Venus Hottentot, Mammy, Sapphire—the emasculating matriarch, Jezebel—the sexually licentious Black woman, the diva, and the Strong Black Woman. When tied to feminist thought, the discussion of Black female subjectivity fails to move into the realm of creating distinct goals and discourses for her subjectivity. Truth's narrative reveals the material conditions and social repressions that Black women will experience in the New World. Her mistranslation by white culture, like the human tales of John Henry and Old Massa or Uncle Remus and Br'er Rabbit, exposes the biological, moral, and social discursives that Black females will have to manipulate with folk cunning and wit. As a human trickster of the past, Truth's example heeds that we accept Anne

Doueihi's conclusion of trickster: "The joke is on us if we do not realize that the trickster gives us an insight into the way language is used to construct an ultimately incomplete kind of reality" (200). Truth's strategic use of the vernacular was a way to note the deficiency of gender.

Sojourner Truth should remind critics that in order to fully comprehend and describe Black female subjectivity in any written narrative, we must begin with trickster-troped readings of gender. Like the ontology of Negro for the African, Woman cannot serve as a substitute of the formerly enslaved Black female. Woman can't become the representation for the African female in the New World. When Truth uttered her famous words, she was speaking from a learned dynamic of folk traditions. Truth's words become all the more powerful when we remember that Black women and men are working with incomplete kinds of reality.

"Mr. Johnson": The Allegorical Strap-On of Early African American Literature

Truth was not the only ex-slave to emulate the trickster tradition in rhetorical strategies of written narratives. After reading William Wells Brown's *Clotel*, how could one ignore the queer trickster implications of his novel? But ignore it we have. Ann DuCille's "Where in the World Is William Wells Brown? Thomas Jefferson, Sally Hemings, and the DNA of African-American Literary History" argues that *Clotel* "remains a book in need of both reading and re-readings, an originary, enabling text in want of analysis and deep theorizing—perhaps in want even of a tradition" (451). Trickster-troping is that tradition. Sara Blair's "Feeling, Evidence, and the Work of Literary History: Response to DuCille" offers the most convincing case of how and why we should reread Brown's *Clotel*:

> [T]his work . . . unabashedly conjoins autobiographical narrative, travelogue, political oratory, medical discourse, sentimental lyric, popular song, biography, advertising and book reviews, folklore and urban legend, and proslavery and abolition pamphlets, to say nothing of the intricacies and intimacies of melodrama, vernacular speech, the picaresque, the gothic, and allegory. (463–64)

Clotel's reliance on many narrative forms and modalities to reveal that authors of slave narratives and fiction were just as keenly aware of the rhetoric of gender as they were of race in their aspirations for liberation and equality.

Although *Clotel* is written by a man, the novel helps establish a tradition and early protocol of Black female protagonists who triumph over adversity. *Clotel* is a fictional story that features a female slave trickster, Clotel, reportedly based on Sally Hemmings. Brown employs the trickster trait of shape-shifting to advance his fictional world: "As shape-shifter, the trickster can alter his shape or bodily appearance in order to facilitate deception. Not even the boundaries of species or sexuality are safe, for they can be dissolved by the trickster's disguises" (Hynes, "Mapping the Characteristics of Mythic Tricksters" 36). Clotel, the namesake and female protagonist of the novel, escapes slavery through these very measures. She passes as a white man with Brown as her slave.

What is significant about Brown's novel is the way the text and characters navigate the true cult of womanhood. Brown's fiction accomplishes what other narratives written by men seldom did. It explores the ramifications of gender on freedom. As a male fiction writer, some would say a satirist, Brown is less inclined to adhere to the ordinances of propriety so vital to early Black women's autobiographical strategies concerned with womanhood. *Clotel* documents the potential for the vernacular to disrupt socially established boundaries of gender. For Black female culture, Brown's novel acts as a notable admission by Black males that gender entails trickster strategies of deception and performance.

While Brown's protagonist is based on the Sally Hemmings controversy, he also turns to other stories about Black women to create his heroic protagonist Clotel. Brown specifically appropriates details from a unique slave narrative *Running a Thousand Miles for Freedom; or, the Escape of William and Ellen Craft from Slavery*. In this narrative, two slaves successfully elude capture when the wife, Ellen Craft, passes as a disabled white man with her husband pretending to be her slave. Though the story is about the escape of husband and wife William and Ellen Craft, the husband's voice dominates the narrative:

> Knowing that slaveholders have the privilege of taking their slaves to any part of the country they think proper, it occurred to me that, as my wife was nearly white, I might get her to disguise herself as an invalid gentleman, and assume to be my master, while I could attend as his slave, and that in this manner we might effect our escape. After I thought of the plan, I suggested i to my wife, but at first she shrank from the idea. (32)

The radical agency that could be achieved for the Black female slave is displaced by the lack of consciousness on Ellen's part, as well as her voice, in the subsequent carrying out of the ruse and the telling of the escape on the antislavery circuit.[17] With the exception of being credited with the idea to feign disability to hide their illiteracy as slaves,[18] Ellen's boldness and cleverness becomes subsumed under her husband's calm demeanor and calculating plan.

Brown's Clotel, however, imagines the full possibility of Ellen Craft's actions as he cleverly emphasizes the instability of the rhetoric of sex as it relates to slaves, and specifically to Black female slaves. For Clotel mimics and opposes Ellen. She is literate where Ellen is illiterate, she is fearless where Ellen is fearful, and she carries out and performs the ruse from every aspect: thinking it up, creating the look, and carrying it out. Most importantly, while Clotel does have a male companion, she does not have to adhere to a husband and all that entails. Omniscient narration ensures the independence and voice of the female protagonist. For example, after Clotel's former master, Mr. French, cuts her hair very short before selling her to a "kinder" owner, Clotel's new confidant (Brown) says of her hair: "Yes, . . . you look a good deal like a man with your short hair" (213). Brown records Clotel's thoughts and responses: "'Oh, . . . I have often been told that I would make a better looking man than a woman . . . If I had the money I would bid farewell to this place.' In a moment more she feared that she had said too much, and smilingly remarked, 'I am always talking nonsense.'" (213). Brown establishes that Clotel's appearance lends itself to slipping through anatomical destinies, and that should she ever choose she could easily switch her illusionary gender. And in being aware of her words to Brown, Clotel comes across craftier than one of the women she is based upon, Ellen Craft.

Later, as Clotel devises her escape strategy this ability of gender passing becomes a major plot development that was foreshadowed in her earlier remarks to Brown. In addition to dispelling myths about the permanence of gender, Brown also deconstructs racial identity. However, unlike other passing novels, it is not racial passing alone that dictates the novel's progression. In trying to help Clotel come up with a suitable escape plan, Brown offers: "There Miss Clotel, you said if you had the means you would leave this place; there is money enough to take you to England where you will be free. You are much fairer than the white women of the South, and can easily pass for white" (214). Clotel's fair skin makes it possible for her to pass as a white woman, but an exchange with Brown divulges that racial passing is not enough to achieve true freedom.

Clotel replies, "I will take the money only on one condition . . . and that is, that I effect your escape as well as my own. . . . I will assume the disguise of a gentleman and you that of a servant" (214). Even as Brown previously says that Clotel, with short hair, looks very much like a man, he deftly uses a vernacular strategy to complement the visual illusion and compel characters and readers alike to continue to see Clotel as a male during their escape. Like

Truth, he has at his disposal two traditions, one written and one oral. Time and again, persons interested in Black female experiences return to their folk heritage to counter the rhetoric of sex.

In taking on the ruse, we learn that the masculine dressed Clotel travels "under the assumed name of 'Mr. Johnson'" (214) to facilitate her disguise. There are two possible explanations for the use of "Mr. Johnson," but both help signify the same meaning. Brown simply returns to the narrative of William and Ellen Craft. In the Crafts' narrative, the name is given to Ellen:

> The captain of the steamer, a good-looking jovial fellow, seeing that the gentleman appeared to know my master, and perhaps not wishing to lose us as passengers, said in an off-hand sailor-like manner, "I will register the gentleman's name, and take the responsibility upon myself." He asked my master's name. He said, "William Johnson." The names were put down, I think, "Mr. Johnson and slave." The captain said, "It's all right now, Mr. Johnson." He thanked him kindly, and the young officer begged my master to go with him, and have something to drink and a cigar; but as he had not acquired these accomplishments, he excused himself, and we went on board and came off to Wilmington, North Carolina. (56)

Brown could have simply reincorporated the Craft's experience along with those details into his narrative. Yet that explanation ignores the wiliness of most slave narratives and the nature of Brown's use of satire and irony. As fugitive slaves, the Crafts would not reveal the name they used in their escape because such references might have led to their recapture. Instead of choosing Smith, Washington, Doe, or any other vague and general surnames, they chose one that implicitly aligns with Ellen's gender passing. Johnson becomes an allegorical hint at a masculine feature Ellen does not possess, a phallus. Both the Crafts and Brown employ the vernacular as an aid in their ruse. The place in which the naming incident occurs is in a levee culture. The Crafts are boarding a ship in Wilmington, North Carolina. The captain of the ship is said to provide the naming that connotes male genitals in levee vernacular. Beginning in the nineteenth century, sailors used "Johnson" to serve as a common surname, used in low slang to describe the penis (*OED Online*). It is not coincidence that the captain supposedly names the fugitives. Given that the Crafts were clever enough to pull off such an elaborate ruse, it follows that such intelligence would also make its way into the narrative. Taking up a name that connotes gonadal masculinity serves as much a vital part of the ruse as the cutting of hair, the fake arm injury, and the glasses Ellen wears. Further, most literal and rhetorical trickery in slave narratives arises from concerns of audience. The very way in which William Craft's narration consistently apologizes for his wife's overstepping the boundaries of gender suggests that placing the responsibility of naming on the captain is a way to placate audience and maintain the artfulness of Ellen's gender passing.[19]

However, if the Crafts were not responsible for the namesake of Ellen's persona, the influence on their gender passing is recognized by others. What solidifies "Mr. Johnson" as an allegorical strap-on is Brown's act to recoup the name within his own text. If we accept previous critics' claim that the genius of Brown stems from the satirical and ironic nature of his writing, then a repetition of fact into fiction grossly underreads the use of "Mr. Johnson" in Brown's *Clotel*. Before becoming a writer, Brown was a former shipmate familiar with slang of river life, like the Crafts' steamboat captain. In his novel, he emphasizes and draws attention to the name Mr. Johnson through the use of quotation marks. These markers are both a nod to the Crafts' story and a play on the vernacular. Clotel's visual presence allows her to pass as a white man, and her vernacular unnaming provides her with the anatomical piece missing from her act. Brown's vernacular use of slang acts as an allegorical strap-on to assist Clotel's attempt to achieve freedom. In this case, the allegorical strap-on is more about the transgression of gender through performance rather than fulfilling sexual desires.

Using the manifest trickster trait of shape-shifting, Brown's trickster trope joins orality and sexuality together to express Clotel's desire for freedom. She will perform race and gender in any way that will gain her freedom, even if it means encroaching on the boundaries of virtue and sex. "Mr. Johnson," a verbal appendage that can be removed and used again at Clotel's whim, connects more to the liminality of unnaming due to her biological status as anatomically female, but temporarily male. While initially it might seem as if Brown is privileging the penis, we can look to the text to dismiss such an argument. As previously seen, Brown exhibits a deep appreciation for the way that Clotel can shift her identity, a fluidity that stems from being a Black female, nonwoman subject.

Brown's authorial decision to have Clotel risk her escape in order to free her male companion also says volumes about how folklore and vernacular provide truly revolutionary tactics in dismissing gender. His narrative technique to advance the plot and theme of freedom depends on the tradition of shape-shifting, or some aspect of it, found in animal trickster tales of birds, rabbits, and turtles and vernacular slang.[20] Since their freedom depends on Clotel's ability to pass as a white man, Brown and Clotel have to let go of all the falsehoods and privileges that might come with accepting a fixed gender identity. Complete freedom for Black males and females requires that they let go, even if momentarily, of Western canons of gender and accept the logic of trickster. Truth and Brown used the school of trickster to take on the rhetoric of sex and cult of womanhood, but Harriet Jacobs attends to the discourse of desire.

Fooling Master (Narratives)

In one African American folk song, the slave's trickery is boldly acknowledged: "I fooled Old Master seven years./Fooled the overseer three./Hand me down my banjo./And I'll tickle your bel-lee" (Botkin, *Lay My Burden Down* 9). As the song progresses, it states without apology that trickery, a part of the past and present, will also be a part of the future: "Fool my master seven years. Going to fool him seven more" (9). The slave narrative, autobiographical and abolitionist propagandist in nature, adopted the slave's philosophy of fooling master (narratives) of the United States, which positioned Black people as property and inhuman. Black female culture readily accepted this role of fooling master, fooling master's discourse, and fooling master narratives of gender by borrowing from its tradition of folklore. While Truth, the Crafts, and Brown offered presentations of literal unnaming and trickster-troping to unname gender, Jacobs engages in trickster-troping to defer gender and unname sexuality for her era.

Typically the subject of tricksterism in Harriet Jacobs's *Incidents in the Life of a Slave Girl* focuses on Jacobs as deceiver and trick player because she escapes from her master by hiding in his garret.[21] However, this text examines Jacobs's rhetorical strategy of deploying the manifest trickster traits of deceiver and trick player to interrupt the social constraints of gender. Jacobs establishes her trickster-troping by slyly positioning non-heteronormative socialization as essential to real Black female freedom. The boldness of her act is often disguised by her manipulation of the discourse of womanhood, melodramatic references to virtue, unrequited love, Christian ethics, and an undermining of her own intelligence. When Jacobs deceives and plays tricks, the reasoning behind her actions very often stems from her willingness to submit that she, as a female slave, has desires, both emotional and sexual. Jacobs's narrative admits that sexual desires cannot be separated from the desire to be free. To act on sexual desire inherently becomes the multifarious articulation of freedom as something more than physically breaking the bonds of chattel slavery. To be truly free means pursuing the object of one's desire, especially if that object is self.

Because the slave narrative was the first extended written narrative of African American literary tradition written in English, questions about its authenticity, reader reception, and purpose arose. To ensure the success of the narratives and the antislavery movement, the slaves' narratives became rife with rhetorical tricks. William L. Andrews's *To Tell a Story: African American Autobiography* shows that "white America was willing to suspend disbelief and assume the sincerity of an autobiographer it identified as a political peer and a racial equal. However, the knowledge that they (the writers) could not predicate their lives on this racial credulity and trust forced Black autobiographers to invent devices and strategies that would endow their stories with the appearance of authenticity . . . the very reception of the narrative as truth depended on the degree to which the artfulness could hide his art" (224). Writers of these slave narratives and autobiographies employed rhetorical tools that would both authenticate the facts of their bondage and covertly establish their selfhood and identity to an America that did not want to see them as equals. Authorial control exposes the controversy surrounding the facts of slave narratives and beliefs about who wrote them.[22] In those machinations of authenticating, placating, persuading, and converting lay distinguishing narrative strategies of an African American literary tradition.

While authenticating documents such as the parenthetical "written by herself" or letters from white editors or abolitionists attested to the truthfulness of the narrative, other techniques were used to persuade readers to see the evils of slavery. Writers from Oladuah Equiano and Frederick Douglass to Mary Prince and Harriet Jacobs cleverly manipulated American ideals of democracy and Christian morals in their texts. They used the Bible and the U.S. Declaration of Independence to make a connection with their readers (Andrews 76).

Christianity serves as one mode of discourse in which Jacobs attempts to critically evaluate the institution of slavery. According to Jacobs, her subjectivity and spirituality is shaped by her mother's belief in Christianity. She refers to the conflicts of Christianity and slavery without explicitly passing judgment. When her first mistress dies, the conflicts of spirituality and subjectivity become clear:

> After a brief period of suspense, the will of my mistress was read, and we learned that she had bequeathed me to her sister's daughter, a child of five years old. So vanished our hopes. My mistress had taught me the precepts of God's Word: "Thou shalt love thy neighbor as thyself." "Whatsoever ye would that me should do unto you, do ye so unto them." But I was her slave, and I suppose she did not recognize me as neighbor. (344)

As Andrews claimed, Jacobs manipulates the Bible for her strategic purposes. She manages to use biblical logic to criticize whites who believe that they are practitioners of Christian morals and ethics. Repeatedly, Jacobs describes herself as a good Christian waiting for her prayers to be answered, for promises to be upheld, and for the word of owners to be made good by the will of God. So as not to alienate her readers, Jacobs portrays herself as a good and faithful servant who never formally admonishes whites for the institution of slavery. Yet she continues to prove that even in the face of death, the conflicts between subjectivity and spirituality go unresolved and are ignored by those in the business of human bondage.

Due to the artfulness of most slave narratives, we may never know for sure if the authors' descriptions of such things served as their honest beliefs in the dominant culture's religion, if they were simply rhetorical strategies to convince their white readers of their likeness to them, or a little of both. The fact that they needed to be concerned about such issues indicates a problem that does not get solved by writing one's life story. The issue of authorial control divulges the conflict as to how one writes him- or herself into being in the dominant discourse while still being true to that self. Jacobs consistently uses Christianity as a narrative device to convince her readers of antislavery arguments based on morality. Yet to convince them of her humanity and remain true to her developing individual selfhood, she must embrace the cult of womanhood while unnaming herself as a Black woman. In doing so, Jacobs's cleverly hidden philosophy on desire risks being just as misinterpreted as Truth's signifyin(g).

The Black female slave narrator's task was more complicated than that of her male counterpart, and as a result she produced clear moments of trickster-troping. Unlike the male slave narrative that articulates freedom in terms of humanity, but more specifically in terms of manhood, the female slave writer's argument for freedom essentially was asking for something beyond what the women's suffrage wanted for white women and the antislavery movement wanted for Black men. Due to their precarious and anomalous status, Black female slaves articulated an autonomy that had yet to exist or be discussed. In addition, their complete freedom might be seen as impeding the freedom of Black men and white women. Though it may not seem as daring as Ellen Craft passing as a white man, Jacobs's means of expressing and obtaining freedom and self-determination also happens through masking and disguise.

In addition to morality, the themes of feminine virtues and sentimental or romantic love differentiate the female slave narrative from the male narrative. The most proficient way of distinguishing between the two is to explore the virtues of woman and how they do or do not apply to Black female slaves. Jacobs's early focus on Christianity in the narrative establishes a credible claim that Jacobs represents the essential characteristics for a virtuous female. If slave women have virtue, then they are worthy of being saved from immoral men who attack or rape slave women. This is not to suggest that Jacobs accepts or does not accept the cult of womanhood. Because she remains so aware of her audience, she recognizes how vital a strategy the cult of womanhood and its ideologies become in persuading readers. In a recounting of one specific experience that concerns literacy, sexuality, and self-determination for Black women, Jacobs exposes an important pregeneric myth of the slave woman's narrative, sexual freedom:[23]

> One day he caught me teaching myself to write. He frowned, as if he was not well pleased; but I suppose he came to the conclusion that such an accomplishment might help to advance his favorite scheme. Before long, notes were often slipped into my hand . . . I would return them saying, "I can't read them, sir." "Can't you?" he replied; "then I must read them to you." (365)

Notably, Jacobs does not resort to trickery to learn to read and write, but she does narrate how she resorts to trickery to maintain control of her bodily rights. She relies on the belief in the illiteracy of slaves to thwart her master's sexual exploitation. She constantly faces the threat of rape and other sexual violence by her white master, Dr. Flint, and his wife, Mrs. Flint.

At this point in the narrative, Jacobs has already established the threat of sexual rape from her master. She makes it quite obvious that, as a good Christian female, she not only has to worry about the threat of rape, but she must also fear her mistress's perception of these sexual transgressions. Both the mistress and the master identify their female slave as without morals and humanity. Jacobs's previous focus on Christianity in her life establishes a record of morals that the readers can see. When Dr. Flint questions her ability to read, the "quest" to read is denied and rejected so that she can ignore the sexual advances of her master. Trickery in reference to literacy in the male narrative attributed to Eshu's trickery as divine translator and linguist is denied in the female slave narrative.[24] Trickery becomes less of a linguistic referent and more cognizant of gender referents in the female slave narrative.

After conclusively showing how the Flints make unwanted, and sometimes violent, sexual advances toward her, Jacobs moves from discussing the rape of the female slave to positing that the slave has a will to love. In a sentimental gesture, Jacobs asks her readers, "Why does the slave ever love? Why allow the tendrils of the heart to twine around objects which at any moment may be wrenched away by the hand of violence?" (369). Throughout the narrative, Jacobs moves from the virtues and elements of womanhood to notions of romantic love. Jacobs uses the language of sentimental love as a device to emphasize how slavery deprives her of the most basic human freedom—the attempt to love and be loved by one of her own choosing. Dr. Flint denies her every right accorded free persons, be it love or physical freedom. Due to the threat of sexual violence, both racial and sexual repression constitutes the way the Black female defines freedom for herself. With this comprehension of freedom, Jacobs comes to believe that to repress her own desire would be as harmful to her humanity as Dr. Flint's sexual violence upon her body.

When Jacobs "falls in love" with a free man of color, her mistress and master object to the courtship. Their objection stems from the rules of property: An inanimate object as property can't love. In their eyes, granting Jacobs a marriage ceremony would be akin to calling her human. Once Jacobs asks for permission to marry, Dr. Flint explains, "Well, I'll soon convince you whether I am your master, or the nigger fellow you honor so highly" (371). Dr. Flint's statement submits marriage as another institution established to preserve the status of white males. He assumes that the institution of slavery takes precedence over the marriage institution for Blacks in the New World. Jacobs also understands that slaves and free Blacks' attempt to practice or adhere to the sacraments of marriage seems oxymoronic:

> Again and again I revolved in my mind how all this would end. There was no hope that the doctor would consent to sell me on any terms. . . . My lover was an intelligent and religious man. Even if he could have obtained permission to marry me while I was a slave, the marriage would give him no power to protect me from my master . . . then, if we had children, I knew they "must follow the condition of the mother." (371)

In revealing the desire to love, Jacobs can create another bond with readers of the narrative who believe in marriage as the ultimate fulfillment of true love. For Jacobs to pursue a focus on sentimental love versus the idea of marriage as an institution for the exploitation of women would specifically appeal to white women influenced by a Victorian women's culture that believed wholeheartedly in a redefinition of the concept of marriage as less of a financial and property-based institution. In addition, Jacobs's assessment of the institutions of marriage and slavery begins the unnaming of her already degendered self.

The earlier devices of romantic love serve only as precursors to the ideologies of (white) womanhood that Jacobs exploits for her purposes in this narrative. Consequently, in discussing her own subjectivity with the ideal attainment of "woman," Jacobs's narrative can't help but document the inconsistency between the two and the failure of Western dominant discourses to translate her:

> But, O, ye happy women, whose purity has been sheltered from childhood, who have been free to choose the objects of your affection, whose homes are protected by law, do not judge the poor desolate slave girl too severely. . . .

> I wanted to keep myself pure; and under the most adverse circumstances, I tried hard to preserve my self-respect; but I was struggling alone in the powerful grasp of the demon of slavery. (384)

Jacobs caters to her readers by implicitly asking them not to judge her, and she makes the reader aware that she has broken a cardinal moral rule—premarital sex.

Yet she explicitly explores how her legal status as property sets her on an altogether different path of morality. As she formulates it, she isn't evil personified. The institution of slavery is the monster responsible for whatever beast she becomes. By constantly spotlighting her inclination and pursuit for love, chasteness, purity, innocence, and "self-respect," Jacob proves all the more the humanity of the slave "woman." Still, in the midst of her catering to womanhood, is the struggle for Black female subjectivity, and the inconsistencies of Jacobs's narrative are where the author moves beyond her Northern, white, middle-class readership to assert her own subjectivity.

Jacobs's trickery and manipulation of her own words make ambiguous her actual belief in the ideologies of white womanhood, virtues, and morals. Can readers believe any of the narrator's words when her logic about virtue, marriage, and romantic love do not match her actions? Jacobs's pursuit of marriage with a free Black man and her verbal rejection of and opposition to her master's desires seem geared toward foreshadowing her prolific discourse on sexual rights. Jacobs's sexual rights, or her sexual desire, lead to the taboo interracial relationship Jacobs will have with a white male suitor at the age of fifteen. If Jacobs were merely content to argue her virtues and the wrongs of slavery, then editing out this particular relationship would not have hurt. Since, at the time, there is nothing more non-heteronormative than this relationship, Jacobs potentially risks undoing her previous alignment with the cult of womanhood. However, it is instead a trickster-troping maneuver that seeks to unname the woman she constructs herself to be. It also follows that the unnaming of gender defers gender long enough for her to also unname her sexuality away from otherness or chasteness. As a slave, she is genderless and thus logics of desire and object choice do not apply. As Spillers claimed earlier, she becomes a pansexual subject. As a pansexual subject, Jacobs illuminates the importance of choice, perceptively the freedom to pursue any object choice, as key to considerations of sexuality.

Though she proclaims to strive hard to maintain her virginity, it becomes very clear that she views her sexual desires as a way to exert independence during her time of bondage. In discussing her relationship with her new "lover," Jacobs speaks forcefully of free will and choice:

> I knew the impassable gulf between us; but to be an object of interest to a man who is not married, and who is not her master, is agreeable to the pride and feelings of a slave, if her miserable situation has left her any pride or sentiment. It seems less degrading to give one's self, than to submit to compulsion. There is something akin to freedom in having a lover who has no control over you, except that which he gains by kindness and attachment. A master may treat you as he pleases, and you dare not speak. (385)

This statement is revolutionary not only for a Black female slave, but for any female in the 1800s, when women were still considered property. What school of womanhood is Jacobs from that would compel her to believe that such free will and desire are inalienable rights? Her words bridge the gap between sentimental literary narratives and free-love ideology of the time. This provocative combination would appeal to women readers in ways that biblical allusions might not. Though somewhat akin to the betrothment of white women in marriage, Jacobs's status as a female slave has decidedly altered her concept of the freedom females should have. If this text is examined as strictly a written narrative, then the retelling of this particular incident in Jacobs's slave autobiography appears perplexing. How does the slave, Jacobs, perceive that she has any choice or control over which white man may pursue interest in her? Does she, in fact, enjoy free will with this particular white male, or is this simply another narrative device to persuade her readers to the rightness of her argument? No clear answer abounds.

Yet viewing her narrative in terms of an oral tradition comprised of trickster tales, other readings are possible. Authorial control becomes even more complicated when we return to her desire to marry a free Black man. Both marriage and slavery project themselves as institutions dedicated to the maintenance of white patriarchal supremacy systems. Jacobs's participation in either institution seems susceptibly linked to Jacobs's strategy of appeasing her white female readers and white male abolitionists through moral guises. As is evident from her attempt to marry and her "choice" to take a lover, she quite possibly did not see marriage as anything more than two people of color sharing love and equal status as free Blacks, and her interracial relationship as a mutual agreement to culminate mutual attractions. Jacobs possesses two ideals of her gender status: the one she knows white America believes in, and the one she has received through her status as a Black slave in the New World.

Consequently, in referring to her earlier argument about choosing whom to love, Jacobs understands the complexity of the argument she formulates. To avoid frightening her readers, she explains, "There may be sophistry in all this; but the condition of the slave confuses all principles of morality, and, in fact renders the practice of them impossible" (385). That simple phrase and Jacobs's actions in regards to both the Black man and white man in her life returns us to elements of animal and human trickster tales. As almost every folklorist from Roger Abrahams to Lawrence Levine has asserted, "Africans enslaved in America freely and repeatedly testified to the fact that they envisioned the physical control of the slave masters over them as placing them in a situation where the demands of physical survival took precedence over the morality of behavior in the peculiar social environment of slavery" (Roberts 34). In conciliating her readers with apologies and humility, Jacobs returns to the model of trickster to construct her argument and persuade her readers. This strategy allows Jacobs to define herself as woman, to persuade white female abolitionist of the evils of slavery, and then unname herself over and over again.

In order to be free, Jacobs reveals that she must maintain that same model of thought taught through human trickster tales. Like Truth's book, Jacobs's narrative manipulates the discourses available by signifyin(g) on those models. In *Talking Black*, Roger Abrahams observes that signifyin(g) can be used "in recurrent black-white encounters as masking behavior" (33). The slave narrative, with its Black author and its majority white audience, and through its function as an abolitionist tool, exemplifies an author's use of both masking and indirection in such black-white encounters. As a fugitive Black female slave, Jacobs must simultaneously dismantle the rhetoric of race and gender in as subtle a way as possible. Hence, Jacobs is quick to use dominant society's misrepresentations and stereotypes to obtain her heart's desire. With every action, she asserts that she suffers from the slave's amoral disposition to hide her disturbance of the rhetoric of sex. The radical way that Jacobs envisions man and woman stems from her status as a slave. Jacobs has insights about the status of women that she should not have.

However, instead of forcibly suggesting equality of the sexes, Jacobs excuses herself from the criterion of woman: "Still, in looking back, calmly, on the events of my life, I feel the slave woman ought not to be judged by the same standard as others" (386). She reduces her multifaceted view of male/female relationships to confusion because she is well aware that her ideals conflict with Christian morals and societal discourses on the treatment of women. In the process, she casts doubt as to whether she really believes in such ideas.

In concluding her narrative, Jacobs supports all of her trickery to elude the rhetoric of sex and exposes how the concepts of woman and gender impede her quest for freedom in one last subtle way: "Reader, my story ends with freedom; not in the usual way, with marriage. I and my children are now free. We are as free from the power of the slave holders as are the white people of the north; and though that, according to my ideas, is not saying a great deal" (513). There are many implications in this brief passage that closes out Jacobs's trickster-troping. She does, after all, basically imply that just because she is married, it doesn't mean that she is free. Her comparison of her story ending with freedom through marriage to the experience of Northern whites is purposeful. During Jacobs's time, history has shown that Northern territories were at the political and economic mercy of Southern states that controlled much of the capital that contributed to the early economic growth of the United States. White Northerners had to promote the elimination of slavery for its own peace of mind and vision of the United States. As the Civil War and the Emancipation Proclamation proved, Jacobs's assessment of how free Northern whites really were from the power of slaveholders was accurate. Her rhetorical comparison alerts savvy readers that just because she ends her story with marriage doesn't mean that freedom has been obtained. With her afterthought about white Northerners, Jacobs closes her text with the Black act of signifyin(g) and rejects all the prioritizing toward cults of domestic womanhood that she has used promotionally throughout her text.[25] Jacobs notes that her race and gender, at this time, in no way allow her to enjoy privileges (limited as they were) that free Black males might receive.

Further, she is not afforded the rights of womanhood because of her race. Jacobs says as much as she can about her liminal state of freedom. At the end of Jacobs's narrative, the authenticator of her narrative, Amy Post, divulges that Jacobs expressed disgust at someone paying the monetary price for her freedom. Jacobs claims that the purchase robs her of any victory. Her reaction fully expresses the failure of language to express her subjectivity beyond that of Negro woman. The payment for her body enables society to define her as first a slave, and then to name her as Negro or Black woman in freedom. However, Jacobs's trickster-troping allowed her to desire, and briefly express desire, as a part of freedom. Her example would propel twentieth-century Black females to do the same through other trickster traits.

Audre Lorde and the Rebirth of Trickster-Gods: Fabrication of the Erotic

Jacobs's revelations about her interracial relationship allow her to risk presenting a discourse of desire for heterosexual Black females that Zora Neale Hurston would take up in the 1930s, but a deliberate discourse of homosexual desire would not be found until the later part of the twentieth century. The egalitarian dynamics of Black females and males is displaced by biological explanations of men and women, but the tales of Annie Christmas foreshadow a pivotal combination of human trickster figures and divine trickster figures that one writer would employ in a more succinct way to recover those dynamics and speak of same-sex desire. No study on the use of trickster figures in African American female culture would be complete without assessing the work of Audre Lorde, who, in her own way, worked to redefine the trickster tradition in Black culture: "Recreating in words the women who helped give me sustenance. . . . Mawu-Lisa, thunder, sky, sun, the great mother of us all, and Afrekete, her youngest daughter, the mischievous linguist, trickster, best beloved, who we all must become" (*Zami* 255). With the publication of *Zami*, Lorde posits that cultural or familial myths allow Black women to participate in performances of unnaming. Lorde critically engages trickster in ways that the previously mentioned writers and critics failed to do. And while she too rarely avoids the characteristic of employing trickster as a tool of cultural nationalism and nation building,[26] she does reveal how uses of the figure could recognize differences and avoid the pitfalls of Western imperialism. Like the African American male tradition of trickster tropes, Black female tradition has vacillated between utilizing animal and human trickster tales and briefly delved into elements of the divine not usually associated with African American trickster figures. Lorde completely commits to the idea of a divine-human trickster.

She provides significant insight into the functions of gender and trickster figures as they relate to the construction of voice and identity by questioning the representation of woman:

> My mother was a very powerful woman. This was so in a time when that word-combination of woman and powerful was almost unexpressable in the white American common tongue, except or unless it was accompanied by some aberrant explaining adjective like blind, or hunchback, or crazy, or Black. . . . Therefore when I was growing up, powerful women equaled something else quite different from *ordinary* women, from simply "woman." It certainly did not, on the other hand equal "man." What then? What was the third designation? (*Zami* 15; emphasis added)

The implications of Lorde's novel title make readers aware of the naming/unnaming process for Black females. Finding a new spelling of her name may have been the beginning, but it was not the end. As the passage suggests, Lorde's predicament was one wrought with the inadequacy of language and terminologies as it concerns Black female subjectivity. For someone seeking to make sense of gender and sexuality as it concerns Black females, there were few options. In addition to the state of folkloric research, Black feminist criticism on gender and sexuality was too new or too conservative. By creatively theorizing about a third designation for gender and later tying that designation to the trickster figure, Lorde creates her own theoretical apparatus—the Zamian model. Instead of turning to a strictly African American tradition of animals and humans, perhaps reflective of her experience as a Black immigrant, Lorde chooses to revise the African trickster figure through a focus on the divine.

The words of Lorde that opened this section imply why this figure was chosen and not another. Before Lorde evoked the figures of Afrekete and Mawu-Lisa, Melville and Frances Herskovits describe the mother, Mawu-Lisa, in *Dahomean Narrative* Mawu-Lisa, as Herskovits notes, "[i]s the creator . . . one person but has two faces. The first is that of a woman. . . . The other side is that of a man. . . . Since Mawu is both man and woman, she became pregnant" (125). Herskovits's general description of Mawu-Lisa lends itself to a debate about Mawu-Lisa as a figurative model for constructing revised readings of gender and sexuality. Herskovits describes Mawu-Lisa as bigendered, rather than genderless. In addition, he hyphenates the name of the being so as to separate the figure into two beings for the purposes of making it more intelligible to Western readers. Even as language attempts to confine the transgression of social boundaries represented by the divinity, the myth of the figure resists.

In another account of Mawu-Lisa pertinent to the issue of gender, sexuality, and language, *Dahomean Narrative* records Mawu as the Fa, "the author of man and destiny" (203), who at one point gives each of her seven children their own language different from her own and each other's. For her youngest, Legba, Mawu grants the trickster-god the capabilities of understanding all of the languages (126). Gates has already taken this example to its full literal extent with regard to writing and difference in *The Signifying Monkey*. Yet if we incorporate the symbolic meaning of the myth, Fa is the Fon's discourse on identity and subjectivity. How telling is it, then, that each child has its own individual language, that Mawu could think up seven distinct languages, or that Legba could translate each and every language. The system of subjectivity resists binary or monolithic formations of identity and subjectivity. With the existence of multiple languages or discourses, it would be impossible to become static, fixed, limited, and pornotroped by one discursive model's oppressive representations. Unnaming would be deemed obsolete. Unfortunately, Black people in the United States are not the Fon, but Lorde posits that such systems may be possible if we want them to be.[27]

The compelling revelation that within one being two unranked binary oppositions exist provides a welcome distinction from the violently opposed binaries provided by Western orders. We know the binaries are unranked from the detail of Mawu's self-fertilization. The figure exists as both the man who impregnates and the woman who is impregnated, and this is possible because neither face dominates. How does one know where male begins and female ends? That cannot be determined, and it does not have to be. Lorde saw that within Dahomean creation myth lay vital strategic devices for self-creation and autonomy in subjectivity pertinent to Black female cultural products and society. She'd found difference without deviation. Lorde's third designation for gender parallels Herskovits's detail of Mawu as a self-reproducing being. Because Lorde comprehends the myth of Mawu-Lisa, she can also develop the underlying philosophies of the myth to counter traditional discourse about the trickster, gender, and sexuality.

Calling upon Dahomean culture, Lorde uses Afrekete and Mawu-Lisa to theoretically attempt to find a space and discourse for Black lesbians' mutable subjectivity:

> Being women together was not enough. We were different. Being gay-girls together was not enough. We were different. Being black together was not enough. We were different. Being black women together was not enough. We were different. Being black dykes together was not enough. We were different. (*Zami* 245)

Lorde articulates the necessity for a model that might be close enough to represent the layers of Black lesbian subjectivity and desires. Just as concepts of unranked binaries impact Dahomean culture and language, so too can the use of myths and figures that represent fluidity in gender as figurative models reveal a philosophy of nonhierarchy in African American texts. Mawu-Lisa emblematically signifies the concept of gender undecideability or gender disruption.

In *Margins of Philosophy*, Jacques Derrida explains this potential of undecidability in Western culture with his concept of *différance:*

> There is no essence of différance; it is that which could only never be appropriated in the as such of its name or its appearing, but also that which threatens the authority of the as such in general, of the presence of the thing itself in its essence. That there is not a proper essence of différance at this point, implies that there is neither a Being nor truth of the play of writing such as it engages difference. . . . There is no name for it—a proposition to be read in this platitude. This unnameable is not an ineffable Being which no name could approach: God, for example. (27)

The changeable appearance and subjectivity of Annie Christmas and the indeterminacy of Mawu-Lisa as a goddess/trickster figure all represent the gender equivalent of *différance*—a goddess, but most importantly a subject being both male and female that exists as a play of gender to engage the distinctions without ranking them since there exists no one master truth about gender and sexuality. According to this paradigm, the figures resist the definition and naming that might fix their subjectivities so as to continue their mutability.

More applicable to this discussion than Derrida's theory of *différance* is a strategy derived from a specific (pre-)poststructuralist theoretical logic of gender in Black communities. Toni Cade Bambara's "On the Issues of Roles" assesses the dismissal of gender as a revolutionary tactic that must be completed for true Black liberation:

> In the last few years I have frequently been asked to speak on the topic of the Black woman's role in the Revolution. . . . I'm not altogether sure we agree on the term "revolution" or I wouldn't be having so much difficulty with the phrase "woman's role." I have always, I think, opposed the stereotypic definitions of "masculine" and "feminine," not only because I thought it was a lot of merchandising non-sense, but rather because I always found the either/or implicit in those definitions antithetical to . . . what revolution of self is all about—the whole person. (101)

Establishing a praxis for her theory, Bambara contextualizes the importance of destroying gender assumption in Black communities.

She later adds, "Perhaps we need let go of all notions of manhood and femininity and concentrate on Blackhood" (103). Bambara remains aware of the genetic differences between male and female, but she wishes to assassinate the social dictatorship that enforces limited practices of gender and desire. Once all notions of manhood and womanhood are released, what do we call ourselves? As Lorde theorizes, we become trickster-gods like Mawu or Afrekete, ineffable beings that no names can approach. Once the categories of gender are dismissed, sexual desire no longer has to properly align with any particular sex. By being unnamable, we can sustain control over the deferment of gender, explore individual sexual desires, and become equipped with a mother tongue to discuss our subjectivity.

Lorde's novel connects the subjectivity of trickster figures to alternate considerations of gender and sexuality in African American culture and cultural theory to facilitate unnaming, but this method also keeps in mind the author's task of desire and expressing desire. Like W.E.B. DuBois's *The Souls of Black Folk* in African American culture, Lorde could rarely resist the ethereal in her trickster applications of difference, desire, and gender in configurations for Black women folk. Inevitably, Lorde's use of trickster in her fiction derived from her theory of desire as defined in her nonfiction. In her gyneocentric essay "Uses of the Erotic," Lorde explores her concept of the erotic as one that embraces spiritual and physical factors of desire: "There are many kinds of power, used and unused, acknowledged or otherwise. The erotic is a resource within each of us that lies in a deeply female and spiritual plane, firmly rooted in the power of our unexpressed or unrecognized feeling" (53). As we have already seen, trickster has often been deemed a community's unrecognized or unexpressed feelings, as well as a manifestation of divinity. Within the uses of the erotic we can see the trickster and her actions.

Lorde further attends to how the erotic functions: "The erotic is a measure between the beginnings of our sense of self and the chaos of our strongest feelings. It is an internal sense of satisfaction to which, once we have experienced it, we know we can aspire. For having experienced the fullness of this depth of feeling and recognizing its power, in honor and self-respect we can require no less of ourselves" (54). Lorde envisions desire that aids in transformation, desire that simultaneously roots and uproots one's sense of self, desire that creates rather than destroys from its tensions and differences, and desire that transforms from the inside out. What she depicts as the erotic is trickster. In addition to understanding these values of trickster traditions, Lorde also corroborates with the trickster tradition in her fiction and poetry because of how orality can disrupt the rhetoric of gender and sexuality.

Ineffable sensations and beings that occur because of desire can rarely be configured through concrete and surface mechanisms such as writing alone. Visual representations are surface mechanisms that carry with them the weight of being concrete and real because they can be universally seen with the eye. Visualization is privileged over orality in the West. The exorbitant amount of scholarship spent on dissecting desire includes the ranking of the visual in concerns of difference (Lacan's mirror, Du Bois's veil, the gaze, etc.).[28] However, throughout her career, Lorde made us aware of other hypothesis of desire that did not rely on the visual, the erotic. In "Uses of the Erotic," she theorizes concepts of desire and love that interrupt the importance of visualization in Western expressions of desire. She claims, "The erotic has often been misnamed by men and used against women. It has been made into the confused, the trivial, the psychotic, the plasticized sensation . . . confusing it with its opposite, the pornographic" (54). Lorde hones in on the way visual mechanisms tends to make static images and freeze objects. The visual makes subjects into objects: Orality and aurality maintain subjects in process. She demands a vital reconsideration of love, desire, and sexuality in ways that seek to resist the pornotroping of female bodies. Thus she chooses trickster for the way it displaces the domination of visual over oral in matters of desire.

Published in 1982, *Zami*'s use of Mawu-Lisa and Afrekete is significant in that it comes five years before the most significant studies of the trickster and its relation to African American texts, namely, Roberts's *From Trickster to*

Badman and Gates's *The Signifying Monkey*. Lorde stakes a claim to redefining trickster, specifically in terms of gender and sexuality. Initially, Fon and Yorùbá discourse directs Audre Lorde's conceptualization of Afrekete in her life and work. Lorde's Zamian model is as much reflective of Dahomean culture as it is of U.S. Black female culture. If we have learned any lesson at all from Lorde's affection for Mawu-Lisa, it is the lesson Mawu-Lisa's story offers to her tricksters in terms of language. Unnaming through trickster-troping is the starting point.

Annie Christmas's trickster flirtation with gender-bending takes us to the next logical step in Black female trickster traditions, that of Black female desire. As Lorde notes, desire is more complicated than gender: "I have always wanted to be both man and woman . . . to enter a woman the way any man can, and to be entered . . . to be hot and hard and soft all at the same time" (*Zami* 7). Lorde's choice toward the divine nature of trickster acknowledges the limitations of the animal and human trickster tale in that those figures might never be able to represent the ethereal depths of desire. The divinity of trickster can. In addition, she was haunted by the same nationalistic aims as previous scholars of trickster tradition, with the exception that her nationalistic aims belonged to the developing Black queer nation. Ideologically, the divine trickster as represented by Mawu-Lisa and Afrekete could not be anatomically or sexually pigeonholed in the way animal and human trickster figures had been.

In the end, in the remainder of *Mutha' Is Half a Word* I hope to continue Lorde's ingenuity while avoiding the conflicts of appropriation. The remaining chapters provide a glimpse into the way African American female communities adapted and continue to adapt the Black diasporic trickster tradition to their own material and sociopolitical needs. As we will see in remaining chapters, this may mean redefining blackness to incorporate concerns of class and gender, or unfreezing racial and sexual identity to coalesce objects of desire that fundamentally disturb the boundaries of rhetoric on race and sexuality, or accepting the logic of the illogical.

The Erotics of a Healing Subjectivity
Sexual Desire, the Spirit, and the Divine Nature of Trickster

With *Zami*, Audre Lorde explores how cultural or familial myths could keep women from looking away from the importance of the erotic in their lives. Lorde imagines that women could welcome the erotic into their lives by participating in performances of unnaming. Her use of the trickster suggests that Black women use nonvisual resources of expressing desires to keep visual means from corrupting or making deviant those desires. This chapter demonstrates how Gayl Jones's *The Healing* embraces the Zamian model to explore the ramifications of desire in Black women's lives. Jones performs trickster-troping by having her characters displace dominant models of gender and sexuality with their own familial cultural myths, by returning to trickster as communal discourse and exploring the divine nature of trickster sexuality. However, whereas Lorde's text testifies to the need for Black women to invent selves, she only alludes to the possibilities that could occur after trickster has left her imprint, the felt power of the erotic.[1] But, as bell hooks has assessed, the actual process of self-creation is not the end of self-invention:

> Opposition is not enough. In that vacant space after one has resisted there is still the necessity to become—to make oneself anew. While contemporary writing by black women has brought into sharp focus the idea that black females must "invent" selves, the question remains what kind of self?—usually remains unanswered. (*Black Looks* 51)

As if in response to hooks's statement, Jones goes one step further to provide an example of what kind of self might remain. Further, Jones's novel about a traveling faith healer explores touch and orality as the most feasible means of expressing desire for Black women.

As seen in the previous chapters, Black females' invention of self can take on many ruses and forms, and the possible configurations for trickster-troping are endless. Signifyin(g), passing, deception, and deities are simply the beginning. In accord with a proclamation made by Carl Jung, healers, like shamans and medicine men, derive from the psychic experience or parapsychological nature that is trickster:

> Since all mythical figures correspond to inner psychic experiences and originally sprang from them, it is not surprising to find certain phenomena in the field of parapsychology which remind us of the trickster.... Since he has on occasion described himself as a soul in hell, the motif of subjective suffering would seem not to be lacking either. His universality is co-extensive, so to speak, with that of shamanism, to which, as we know, the whole phenomenology of spiritualism belongs. There is something of the trickster in the character of the shaman and medicine-man, for he, too, often plays malicious jokes on people, only to fall victim in his turn to the vengeance of those whom he has injured. For this reason, his profession sometimes puts him in peril of his life. (*Four Archetypes* 160)

Jones's *The Healing* creates a representation of trickster's psychic or parapsychological nature. By making her protagonist a healer, Jones can engage the motif of subjective suffering and attend to the benefits of pleasure in Black women's lives. She also reincorporates trickster's quest for pleasure and its spiritual destiny into her formulation as to how significant sexual desire is in making radical Black female subjectivities. *The Healing* serves as the most recent textual embodiment to recall the importance of conjure, hoodoo, and animal trickster tales for creating a discourse of desire for Black females. In *The Healing*, unnaming, through divine acts such as healing, allows the protagonist, Harlan Eagleton, to reject the construction of woman and traditional gender ideologies concerning Black females. Jones uses the phenomenon of faith healing to unname her Black female protagonist.

Harlan's rejection of traditional womanhood comes from the ethics instilled in her by her family, most notably her mother and grandmother. These ethics are presented in unique and phantasmal familial myths:

> I was a turtle before I became a human being, said my grandmother. She was taking a new order of beauty products out of the boxes and restocking the shelves ... Then I saw this handsomest young man and took a liking to him,

she said as she put the superior beauty products on the shelves. Do you want to know how far I followed him? She chuckled. I followed him until I turned into a human being. Is that far enough for you? (133)

With her characterization of Grandmother Eagleton as striving to become human, Jones situates her reader with a predicament that Black slaves also faced, establishing their humanity. In the case of Grandmother Eagleton, like the female slave narrators, the Black female question is about humanity and womanhood. Jones establishes the pregeneric myth of her novel as one most concerned with self-invention in the midst of other influential discourses. Because they are having this conversation as they are stacking beauty products, Jones implies that it is the ideals of womanhood and beauty regimens and standards that negate that self-invention. She also submits that the desires and needs of men, such as Grandmother Eagleton's husband, may also be a factor. Jones posits that we consider Grandmother Eagleton's predicament: How far will you go to become human, or, more specifically, woman? She then juxtaposes it with her own question: How far will you go to become yourself? Will you engage in a process of self-invention if the result is not a unified self that aligns with limited concepts of woman, blackness, and sexuality? Will you, Black women, unname yourself? As we will see, familial (cultural) myths of trickster keep Jones's protagonist true to her sense of self and enable her to deploy the uses of the erotic in her life in ways that are literally healing.

Grandmother Eagleton's crediting the man she loves with the change in her mutable subjectivity from turtle to human echoes Annie Christmas's feminizing of herself to attract the riverboat captain. Sadly, Grandmother Eagleton does not enjoy the reinvention of self in the way Annie Christmas does. Grandmother Eagleton does not have the last laugh herself. The man she perceives as being responsible for her change from a Turtle Woman to a real woman leaves her. It seems neither could ever fit the mold of womanhood because of their multifarious subject position. As Carole Boyce Davies concedes of Black females in *Black Women, Writing and Identity*, "it is the convergence of multiple places and cultures that renegotiates their identities . . . once Black women's experience is accounted for, assumptions about identity, community and theory have to be reconsidered" (3). Davies understands the liminal subjectivity of Black women and chooses to use the term and tool of "migratory subject" primarily because her text is concerned with the impact of nationalisms and nationalist borders in her deconstruction of Black females and Black feminist thought. However, for factors not as definitive as land and nationalist boundaries, Gayl Jones interrupts and dismantles the rhetoric of gender with Black folklore and trickster traditions in a manner similar to Zora Neale Hurston's *Mules and Men* and Audre Lorde's *Zami*. She then proceeds to unname the Black woman so that we can consider various desires, classes, and cultures that renegotiate identities. As she accounts for these experiences, her text reconsiders identity, community, and theory on Black females.

Jones creates her particular trickster-troping through a joining of two trickster traditions, animal and trickster-gods. Her narrative mixture of mythical turtle trickster tales combined with a story about a faith healer allows her to accomplish this achievement. The turtle serves as a metaphor for Black female subjectivity, and healing acts a symbolic discourse of desire for Black female subjects. Together, these two folk heuristics imply that joining the secular and the sacred enables Black females to resist the psychological and physical damage to sexual desire that might occur due to the erroneous naming—the historical othering of her body and internalized racism.

In *The Healing*, readers are introduced to Harlan T. Eagleton, a black female jack-of-all-trades who becomes a faith healer. Yet from the very beginning of the novel's immediate meditation on a tin of "Spirit of Scandinavian Sardines, floating in mustard sauce" (3), the reader comes to understand how Jones has taken the traditional healing protagonist (the conjurer woman from Charles Chestnutt and Eulalia, the hoodoo priestess from Hurston), and made it into a character touched by her own voice and ideologies. The novel discards historical figures of Black females in favor of a more suitable archetype of Black female subjectivity, that of trickster. As a healer, the most dominant trickster trait Harlan exhibits is that of messenger and imitator of the gods. As William Hynes prescribes: "Often of uncertain or impure birth, the trickster can be both a messenger and imitator of the gods. Admixing both divine and human traits . . . (s)he may bring something across this line from the gods to humans—be it a message, punishment, an essential cultural power, or even life itself" ("Mapping the Characteristics of Mythic Tricksters" 40). As this chapter reveals, the origin of Harlan's healing powers remains uncertain in the eyes of the novel's characters. And though Harlan exhibits other trickster traits, this particular trickster trait acts as an essential cultural power and life. It reminds readers of the divine nature of trickster.

In the canon of African American women's literature, *The Healing* is not the first contemporary novel to make use of conjurers, healers, and magical realism. On the contrary, Toni Cade Bambara's Minnie Ransom and Velma in *The Salteaters*, Paule Marshall's Rosalie Parvay and Avery Johnson in *Praisesong for the Widow*, and Gloria Naylor's Sapphire in *Mama Day* are characters who have all been touched by or bestowed with healing gifts in various ways. As some critics have argued, there are some common variables in the traditional healing protagonists.[2] As Athena Vrettos explains in "Curative Domains:

Women, Healing and History in Black Women's Narratives," the purpose of conjure tradition in Black female narratives serves a purpose: "Through representations of healing, Black women writers seek the inspiration and authority to heal, locating in language a new curative domain" (456). Vrettos further states that Black women writers "envision the fragmentation and alienation of Afro-American culture from traditions of its past as a disease that can be healed, and healed specifically by Black women" (471). While Jones, like each of the aforementioned novelists, does explore healers and healing in a similar and traditional way—to document and examine the psychological ills of African American women—*The Healing* modernizes the concepts of healing in Black women's fiction in several ways.

Through her characterization of Harlan, Jones revises the healer character type: where Minnie was an outcast in Bambara's *The Salteaters*, Harlan's ordinariness and ability to shift her stations in life and community are emphasized time and again; where Minnie and Sapphire may have been asexual or nonsexual, Harlan comes to know her healing gift because of her sexual transgressions; and where laying on of the hands usually focuses on the healer laying hands on a body other than her own, Harlan's first experience of laying on of the hands puts her in contact with her own body. These divergences from previous healing protagonists exist in Jones's text for a reason—to move the subjectivity of Black females away from traditional discourses of gender to a discourse of desire.

Negative images and representations about Black women have long endured. Positive images of Black females and historical moments of survival and triumph have been distorted or eclipsed. The attempt to locate suitable discourses for Black female subjectivity has been the subject of critics who examine the issues of healing and the psychological ills of Black women. In "This Disease Called Strength," Harris is concerned with the prevalent type character of the Strong Black Woman in literary texts by Black women. Harris's text adamantly claims that the repetitive manufacturing of the Strong Black Woman type exemplifies a psychological disease/illness, "a disease called strength" (110). Overall, Harris proves that strength is a disease of Black female characters in many texts. However, Jones's novel moves beyond these previous notions of strength in Black female characters. The novel reveals that the ideology of the Strong Black Woman is another failed attempt to create a discourse for Black female subjectivity.

Jones often mocks the ascribed elements of womanhood (femininity, weakness, and physical beauty) through a concerted examination about the ideas of beauty held by her Black female characters. Harlan Eagleton is a former beautician, as was her grandmother. *The Healing* cleverly takes on the dialogue of beauty and the bio-logic of gender to explore existing hierarchies of gendered subjectivity for Black females through Turtle Woman tales and Unicorn Woman stories. Grandmother Eagleton implies that through the love of her husband, she achieved humanity, specifically womanhood. Harlan recalls her grandmother's tale: "She say that he could see the genuine woman behind that fake turtle shell" (135). When Harlan's grandmother—a retailer of beauty products—discusses with Harlan her status as a once-upon-a-time Turtle Woman, not yet human, we must metaphorically ascertain that the discourse on gender is so faulty that Black females cannot use the rhetoric of sex to see themselves as women.

Coincidentally, Harlan's grandmother sees herself as a woman primarily because someone else sees her as such. This introduction to the Turtle Woman demonstrates that womanhood, specifically notions of Black womanhood, are illogically defined by persons who are not Black females. The grandmother's story reveals that there is a secondary reading of gender occurring in the text. By characterizing Harlan and her grandmother as beauticians, Jones could simply address the internalization of racist values and an inferiority complex over beauty in Black female culture. Beauticians, after all, are master illusionists in the art of gender performance. However, there is a disruption of gender in the text that stems from Grandmother Eagleton's real subjectivity and her counter-reality as a Turtle Woman subject. In returning to the figurative metaphor of trickster-god(dess), we must now explore how the internalization of the logic of intelligible gender had, and still has, quite a bit to do with Black females' battle to see themselves. The ability of dominant discourse and criticism to distort its subjects has truly lent credence to Audre Lorde's suggestion that "the master's tool will not dismantle the master's house" ("The Master's Tools" 112).

While there are a number of ways that Jones could have taken up the question of Black female subjectivity, she chooses to refer to the Black diaspora's cultural appreciation of healing because of the way it can also suggest the importance of language in diagnosing and curing illness. In *Planet Medicine*, Richard Grossinger offers a connection between the practice of healing and language: "We assume we know disease by the feel of internal organs of our body but that is not true ... it must first be brought to the surface, as concepts, as language as one's self, and, finally, as language with the society and its doctors" (16). In *The Healing*, Jones utilizes a complex structure of orality and myth in ways that reflect Grossinger's views. She merges and intertwines the health and well-being of African American women with the use of language. As with Lorde's creative and critical work, Jones's text explores her own mythologies for female culture. She examines how mainstream misrepresentations and distortions can sometimes become mythic influences in the lives of Black females. Jones also explores how self-made or communal mythic influences exist to aid

Black females in the struggle to conquer and destroy the former. Jones replaces mythic models such as the "Black woman" or the "Strong Black Woman" with her own trickster models of the Turtle Woman and the Unicorn Woman to create a discourse for Harlan T. Eagleton. In order to recognize these models, we must first realize that an unnaming is taking place.

On the surface, naming appears to play a minor role in the theme and goals of the novel. For example, in discussing her long-lost grandfather, James B. Eagleton, Harlan reveals that the B. stands for Booker (T. Washington). Grandfather Eagleton's middle name goes to the political type of man that he may have been since we never really see him, only hear of him through Grandmother Eagleton's Turtle Woman story. James Booker Eagleton, like his namesake, seems to understand the need for racial empowerment in the way he vocally admires and raises Grandmother Eagleton's esteem by saying he could see the real woman in her. However, much like Booker T. Washington's economic empowerment ideologies, his own methods of Black female empowerment are flawed because they accept the classification of gender. The Eagleton family utilizes a trend of bestowing upon themselves the names of influential African Americans. Harlan's own middle initial, T., stands for Truth.

Upon closer examination, Harlan's full name symbolizes the question of Black female subjectivity and a lack of language for that subjectivity:

> So my name's Harlan Eagleton. Harlan T. Eagleton, but I do not tell anyone what the T. stands for, because I don't think it's a name that anyone should be given. Well, I'll tell you. It's Harlan Truth Eagleton, named for Sojourner Truth, not Truth itself. (252)

Harlan's desire to softly reject her middle name is significant because embedded in that desire lays the marker that highlights the necessity to unname the Black woman. Jones tropes on the meaning of Harlan's name. As indicated in chapter 1, Sojourner Truth's name was about truth itself. First, Harlan's rejection of her middle name implies that there is no such thing as an absolute Truth (as posited in Enlightenment ideology and aesthetics) but a multiplicity of truths. Harlan's rejection of her middle name is an acceptance of the divinity that she will become. Harlan knows the importance of multiplicity in discussing herself.

In *Black Women, Identity, and Cultural Theory*, Kevin Quashie documents the importance of liminality that can be achieved through Harlan's rejection of her middle name. Though different in scope and purpose, in a discussion of liminality of girlfriend selfhood, Quashie proposes a liminality of otherness for Black women that is "a surrender that embraces what it is to be other, a practice of tension between two essential principles: 'I am (a) me' and 'I am someone's an/other.' This recognition . . . is an invocation of spirituality, an awareness of the fluctuating dimensions of identity" (78). The original Sojourner Truth's unnaming was about accepting liminal subjectivity. Harlan's unnaming is certainly about assuming this practice of embracing the tensions of what it means to be her "me" and someone's an/other. In a move that accepts her liminality of otherness, Harlan unnames herself and begins her journey toward invoking the spiritual nature of desire that will mark her as healer. Harlan cannot allow herself to be defined or fixed as one absolute. By rejecting the notion of an absolute truth, Harlan makes it possible to accept many truths about her own subjectivity as a Black female, rather than a detrimental monologic discourse of truth about woman.

Harlan's full name semantically embodies trickster-god. As with divine beings, Harlan's name hints at her status as an unknown being. She is not called God, but her very name itself creates a space of the unknown and temporal for its being. Harlan might traditionally be seen as a male name; Jane, a woman's name; Truth, an ambiguous name (male or female); and Eagleton, her family name. Hence, Harlan might very well be made to acknowledge "I am that I am," that phrase we attribute to that which we cannot name. She does not fit an either/or dichotomy, but she does occupy a liminal discursive space of multiplicity and polyphonic discourse. "This liminal . . . subjectivity exposes and complicates the binaries that constitute a socially accepted notion of reality, especially of how bodies are imagined, marked, and controlled" (Quashie 79).

Harlan seems apprehensive about the name because of its sacred place in time and history, but she also appears to understand the logic and discursive baggage that comes with that name. If there is no absolute truth, then Harlan, like the Sojourner Truth after whom she was named, must ask herself that all important question: Is she a woman? Harlan must decide how to interpret this question and whether to reject or embrace its answer in the shaping of her identity. Does she accept the discourse that comes with the question, or does she, unlike her grandmother, move beyond the one absolute truth? Harlan goes further because she allows herself to be unnamed. Her first small step in doing so becomes visible in her desire to reject her middle name. Harlan's rejection of her middle name is hardly enough to maintain the state of liminality that will position her to be more than a woman—a Black female with an empowering gift to heal. Harlan needs to find other alternatives and tools for unnaming herself, and she finds them in the communal elements of healing, primarily in witnessing, testimony, and touch. Jones makes this possible by creating a true trickster narrative based on communal discourse.

Trickster Narrative

With *The Healing*, Jones revises the blues aesthetics from her previous work, and she demonstrates how these revised blues mediums must be employed to discuss healing. Healing symbolizes a gift from the divine, a commitment to appreciate and understand the wonders of the flesh and spirit, and constant rebirth—a return to life rather than death. *The Healing* uses a divergent structure based on liminality and an oral narrative structure and discourse defined by desire that differs from Jones's blues aesthetic narratology used in her previous novels. In *The Healing*, plot and characters rely on a mythic understanding of faith healing produced by oral traditions and grounded in what cannot be named or defined—divinity. Simply writing about these acts is not enough for Jones. In discussing her own work, Toni Cade Bambara once deliberated over why plain English would never be enough, stating that English "has been stripped of the kinds of structures and the kinds of vocabularies that allow people to plug into other kinds of intelligences, [at a time when] certain types of language 'mysteries'—for lack of a better word—were suppressed" ("Searching for a Mother Tongue" 48). For Jones, too, English lacks the depth to discuss the pain and trauma of slavery and racism. Jones must be able to translate divination so that the readers can grasp its power, and orality is the preferred method. In *Liberating Voices*, Jones says of the potentiality of the oral tradition: "Oral tradition . . . provides techniques and suggests new structures for the writer" (12). Because healing is essentially based on divination, Jones creates a narratology based on divination—the language/discourse of that which is unknown (higher power) to discuss what is unknown, the subjectivity of Black females. "The engagement of liminality is, as a practice, synonymous with finding god in oneself, a self-divinity that is a key aesthetic principle in the African Diaspora" (Quashie 83). Trickster is a divine linguist and minor god. Thus, Jones creates a trickster narrative to convey this huge undertaking of finding the trickster-god in oneself and using it to express desires.

As Jones says, "Oral forms can likewise be examined and studied for their dramatic structure, conflict patterns, actions, verbal play and interplay, points of views, characterization, transitions, tone and vigor, visual and auditory imagery, conceptions of time and value" (*Liberating Voices* 13). Jones uses all of the above elements found in animal trickster tales in African and African American tradition to supplement her own human trickster tale. The major indicators of this divination narrative strategy are liminality, soulful raps or flowing usage of words, and indirection through disjointed testimonies, interruption of a rap session, communality, and the presence of omnipresent myth(s). As a rhetorical mode, it may in some way seem akin to the Black rhetorical mode of signifyin(g). However, the characteristics and elements of signifying (indirection, cajoling, punning, playing on words, and introduction of the semantically logically unexpected) almost always operate from a knowable referent.[3] Since divination heralds itself as the writing of the divine,[4] its referent is always unknown. Creating a narrative structure and discourse based on an unknown referent leaves subjectivity in a liminal state and allows characters to avoid misrepresentation and static symbolism. Gerald Vizenor assessed, "The trickster narrative situates the participant audience, the listeners and readers, in agnostic imagination: there in cosmic discourse, the trickster is being and nothingness and liberation; a loose seam in consciousness; that wild space over and between sounds, words, sentences, and narratives" (7). However, Jones does not allow her trickster narrative to be dictated by clever mechanical strategies of omniscient writing because she needs her text to reflect agnostic imagination. As Quashie notes of liminality, "Liminal subjectivity is not exactly an achieved state; instead, it is a series of uncoverings" (78). Omniscient narration would aesthetically fix her characters into an achieved state. Jones uses her liminal narrative, specifically the disjointed testimonies of secondary and minor characters, to create a communal discourse that reveals the series of unconvering Harlan as a liminal subject. Jones unnames the protagonist.

Witnessing as Trickster's Communal Discourse to Unname

Jones's narrative technique acts as a testament to the need for multiple truths in healing the discursive ills that can occur for subjects or subjectivities without a discourse. The deeply developed recursive structure (repeated and circular rather than linear) of the novel may initially make it difficult to recognize how Jones is taking up the maladies of Black women. However, the communality that can be achieved from these oral acts demonstrates that the author is focused on communal healing rather than individual healing. Jones emphasizes this belief in her previous novels but makes notable changes to it in *The Healing*.[5] Harlan often gives up narrative control to those who witness for her because in ritual and spiritual spheres testimony acts as learning and teaching tools. Subsequently, because the witnessing and telling of an incident are never the same, rebirth and life are always possible through community exchanges of oral traditions. The continuous rebirth leads to unnaming.

Unnaming in African American females' texts, as Jones demonstrates with *The Healing*, must be about remaining unnamed and sustaining a state of liminality. Harlan's second phase of unnaming—the ability to maintain liminality and unnamability—comes through Harlan's first witness, Nicholas. The purpose of witnessing is revealed in the correlation between Harlan's sidekick's name and Nicodemus:

> And N'Orleans that ain't my true name, that just his sometimes name for me.
> Then he whispers, He's free.
> Who's free? Nicholas?
> They freed Nicodemus.
> Who's Nicodemus? Nicodemus? Oh, yeah, yeah. Nicodemus.
> That's good. (35)

Again, there are moments when the reader may be unsure of who is actually speaking, but in this brief passage Harlan's witness and former bodyguard becomes associated with Nicodemus. The name suggests a number of possibilities for understanding the character but most importantly for understanding myth and ideas of healing. Nicholas could represent Nicodemus—the righteous Monk of Mt. Athos; Nicodemus—the Runaway Slave; Nicodemus—the Jewish King; John 3:11's Nicodemus (What must I do to be saved?); or the nineteenth-century Negro exodusters from Kentucky who settled on land in Kansas.[6] All of the images share a common link to the notion of rebirth, new life, separation from mainstream society; and they have a connection to healers and function as witnesses or legacies to an important moment in a race/nation's history or birth.

In *The Healing*, Nicholas becomes all of these representations in some way. He serves as the most significant witness to Harlan's work. Harlan explains, "I thought about hiring me another 'witness' but that would be duplicitous and Nicholas the true one witnessed the first healing, and that ain't the same as a hired witness" (10). Later Harlan expands on the role of the witness: "All I know is Nicholas usedta tell the tale with more fanfare, more flourish, more confabulatoriness. And when he tells about that healing; it don't sound like no confabulatory tale. Least the way he usedta tell the tale of that healing. Now he tends to be kinda dry" (11). Nicholas serves as a witness to Harlan's work. As the first person to see Harlan go through her rites of passage into healing, Nicholas lives up to the legend of the monk, runaway slave, Jew, and exoduster by giving up his own life to witness for Harlan. His task is to help make evidence of healing for those in pain. In this novel, witnessing and testifying replace absolute truths and long-held stereotypes.

In many African and African diasporic cultures, witnessing of healing acts as an important part of the process. E. E. Evans Pritchard's "The Morphology and Function of Magic: A Comparative Study of Trobriand and Zande

Rituals and Spells" found in Zande healing spaces that "the corporation of medicine-men possess powerful magic known only to the members of the corporation. That their magic is genuine is proved by legends which show how in the past great medicine-men performed remarkable feats through its medium" (11). Healing is a performative art that depends on more than the actual act itself. Healing depends on the witnessing of the act. It can only work if the healer and those who are coming to be healed believe in the existence of such a thing. What good is the gift if no one is there to recognize the act, to call it, or give it a language for its very existence? As the first witness to Harlan's gift, Nicholas becomes a messenger, an outsider, and unintentional leader directing the sick to the healing woman.

Karla F. C. Holloway's *Moorings and Metaphors* provides evidence to suggest that Nicholas's repeated testimony and witnessing construct a myth meant to displace misrepresentations of Harlan as Black woman:

> Myth vitalizes language, giving it a presence outside of the interpretive mode and forcing its significance to a level where the community's shared meanings are the basis of its understanding and interactions with both the spiritual and physical worlds; it is both of them. In its ways of recursive signification, it is the perfect vehicle for signification. (25)

By constantly retelling the first healing, the story becomes mythical. Nicholas's tale influences the doctrine of faith, and consequently, the lives of all that come to be healed. Nicholas's selfless act makes it possible for those coming to be healed to have faith in Harlan's gift, and it also provides Harlan with the faith that she needs to believe in herself and sustain her abilities. Harlan temporarily becomes the healing woman. Each and every time Nicholas testifies he helps to sustain the process of unnaming Harlan by helping to develop a space that permits her to temporarily misplace or replace the Black woman with the healing woman, but she never has to choose one over the other.

In another prehealing testimony, Nicholas revises his dry tone and narration as he speaks of Harlan's first healing, and in the process he creates a space for Harlan's changing subjectivity:

> I thought she were some witch at first, says Nicholas. Even she didn't know.... Maybe that's who she is. The healing woman healed herself first....Well I'm here to testify that she healed herself first. I'm here to testify that she healed herself first. I'm here to testify that this healing woman healed herself first. And now she trying to heal everybody that want to be healed. (*The Healing* 33)

Nicholas's testimony returns us to Holloway's theory of historical figurations of mythologies, where the chasm of representation (accuracy) over figuration (metaphor) disappears (94). Nicholas's witnessing relies on his own accurate memory, but the telling of the memory introduces a figure that was not a part of the original memory. When the healing occurs, only Nicholas and Harlan are present. With his statement about a witch and uncertainty about who Harlan was, Nicholas's testimony welcomes a stranger into his memory, the healer.

Quashie's examination of an other self constructed by Black women explains the importance of this other that Nicholas constructs: "The trope of the stranger is almost by definition a metaphor for liminality—the stranger is a spirit self, a self that exists as an idea, a force, an energy, as a tenuous and tenacious" (82). Nicholas repeats four times that Harlan heals herself first. His repetition establishes a distinction between Harlan and Harlan the healer. He makes a distinction between the ordinary and the divine. Nicholas aka Nicodemus is witness to the construction of a space and language for Black females' subjectivities beyond Harlan. In addition, the liminality Harlan obtains could potentially enable liminality for the community in need. In *Healing Narratives* Gay Wilentz makes a statement about Bambara's *The Salteaters* that parallels the significant logic behind Harlan's own self-healing process in Jones's novel: "This novel . . . takes individual healing beyond personal well-being, so that healing also becomes a responsibility for those who have gone through the cure" (35). Nicholas's insistence assures the sick that Harlan's commitment to healing is real and true because she accepted the responsibility to heal herself and is now taking responsibility to heal others. It also ensures that those who are healed might find a way to heal through their own divine forces.

Again, Holloway reminds us that "myths are not discrete units of structure as much as they are features of how a sense of language enables the survival and transference of memory" (94). Nicholas's repetitive testimony helps to create a myth that reveals Harlan and the myths that she carries with her as verbal power to use alongside her gift of healing. Nicholas's testimony on the illusive definability of Harlan's subjectivity provides a preliminary state of being for Harlan. Testimony and witnessing initially launch a process of unnaming for Harlan by providing myths to counter the historical figuration of mythology at the center of the text—the Black woman. As an international healer, Harlan's other witnesses also assist the practice of unnaming as evidenced in discussions of Harlan by the gossipers, Martha, Zulina, and Josephine. They say that "Dottoressa is what they calls her there in that Milan. . . . Curandera's what they call her in Brazil" (13). Because the act of healing is different every time, Harlan is different each time. As seen in her unnaming across the world, her experiences and subjectivity as a healer can be influenced by culture, geography, sex, and class. She is never the same at any one point, and her unnaming reflects that she is not a static subject. The testimony of Nicholas and other witnesses removes Harlan from the static subject position of Black woman, and it places her into a liminal space where reevaluation of the discourse of gender and sexuality and Harlan's subjectivity as a Black woman can begin. If Harlan wishes to avoid the mistake of her grandmother by letting others name her, then she should not accept or become the historical figurations of mythology created by her witnesses.

As exhibited with Sojourner Truth, such figurations can be costly if the individual becomes defined as the figuration itself. Nicholas recognizes the uncertainty of Harlan's identity and subject position. He questions whether she is a witch or something else. Even Harlan does not know, or she does not know what to call herself. Harlan does not need to be unnamed as the Black woman only to be named again as some "other." She must not fall into the trap of accommodating traditional discourse. Testimony and witnessing build myths, but it is the remaining historical figurations that Harlan must learn to navigate to achieve an empowering position. The historical figurations are no good to Harlan if they become a fixed identity. Only in the transitory existence of these remaining historical figurations can Harlan begin the important progression of unnaming through her familial myths. The turtle is the key.

Turtles, Divination, and Healing

More than a predilection for animism, Turtle Woman stories evoke various trickster myths about turtles and tortoises. As Harlan tells us of her grandmother's unnaming in Brazil while on tour with the carnival: "One of them Brazilians named her Jaboti instead of Turtle Woman. . . . Jaboti . . . was a turtle trickster in Brazilian folklore" (203). As both land and amphibious animals, turtles demonstrate a trait of adaptability. They symbolically represent the connection between heaven and earth. In addition, the turtle/tortoise shell links it to adaptability, immortality, and enduring strength and resistance. For these reasons, turtle is seen as a likely representation of healing, and many cultures associate the animal with shamanism (*African Mythology* 245).

For Jones, the turtle functions as the best way to carry her metaphorical narratology whose purpose is to explore faith healing as the representation of desire in Black female culture. She uses the Turtle Woman story as the beginning of her critique of womanhood. She constantly makes the reader aware of how and who defines womanhood and for what reasons. In a discussion with her grandmother, Harlan learns how these discourses work in the lives of Turtle women:

> ... and that them other men just thought of her as freakish, as one of them freakish women, whether or not they believed in the reality of that turtle's shell. She say that he [Grandfather Eagleton] could see the genuine woman behind that fake turtle shell. She say he say that she more a genuine woman than any woman he know, a category he say ain't just limited to colored women, which some mens do. You know how some mens do. They'll compare you to other colored women, but not to womanhood itself, and refers every other man's woman to they own. (135)

Harlan's divulging of her grandmother's tales about her carnival experience as a Turtle Woman is essential to disrupting ideologies of womanhood and gender. The focus on freakish womanhood and carnivalesque atmosphere reminds readers of how Black female subjectitvities become freakish in dominant discourses of Western gender and sexuality. Jones employs turtle to overturn the rhetoric of sex.

Turtles, tortoises, and terrapins have long been figures of tricksterism in African American folklore and literature. Levine explains that the turtle and terrapin occupy trickster spaces in African American folklore: "In the popular tales featuring a race between a slow animal and a swifter opponent the former triumphs not through persistence, as does his counterpart in Aesopian fable of the Tortoise and the Hare, but by outwitting and capitalizing on his weakness and shortsightedness. Terrapin defeats Deer by placing relatives along the route with Terrapin himself stationed by the finish line" (115). Levine's reading explores the trickster as strictly humanly deceptive. As I indicated before in the analysis of Annie Christmas, the divine elements of the trickster figure are displaced. This traditional reading of turtles/tortoises/terrapins reveals little as to why Jones utilizes the Turtle Woman figure in her myth of healing. However, as Grandmother Eagleton alluded earlier, there is a surprising parallel between Jones's Turtle Woman and the tortoise as trickster in African diasporic folktales.

Herskovits's *Dahomean Narrative* describes elements about the tortoise in African oral stories that become essential in fully understanding the importance of the Turtle Woman in *The Healing* and a connection to trickster and divination:

> All the animals and birds go at sunrise to the fields to eat. Tortoise whose skin is like stone, also goes out. There was a bird called Awele. When he saw Tortoise, he called together all the birds. None of them had ever seen an ani-

mal like that, an animal with skin like stone. Awele said to the other birds, "... and today a stone comes to eat with us." ... Since Tortoise walks slowly, the birds flew down to see what was inside this thing Awele said was a stone. But they saw nothing for the Tortoise stopped still. (191)

The tale continues that all the animals are perplexed by the stone that came to eat with them. They take their concerns to Mawu and ask the divine why a stone should eat with them. Eventually, Mawu reveals tortoise as an animal and tells the other animals, "Tortoise is the diviner for birds and animals" (Herskovits 192). Tortoise's shell distinguishes it from the other animals, but it also enables tortoise to be a trickster.

In another story, Tortoise is told, "You will always be a diviner because you have suffered much" (Herskovits 193). The connection between trickster and the divine is embodied in the tortoise. In many of these tales, the tortoise is also a genderless trickster who is diviner. The significance of subjectivity, identity, and indefineability cannot be overlooked in these Dahomean tortoise tales. Tortoise is an outcast amongst other animals and unlike anything they have ever known or seen. Tortoise's distinct subjectivity means that the figure will suffer much, but it will be divine. The elements of trickery with divinity in the turtle/tortoise are the basis for Jones's trickster-troping mechanism.

Through the Turtle Woman myth, Jones makes a case that the representation of the shell, the shell being an allegory for the "Black woman," hides and distorts the actual being that exists. Only through the trickster-god(dess)'s divine intervention—a disruption of the discourse on intelligible gender—can a discourse be provided for Black female subjectivity in the novel. Harlan's grandfather does not view Grandmother Eagleton as freakish. The grandfather sees Harlan's grandmother as a human female, but because he defines womanhood for her grandmother, the change is never really a true self-transformation. Throughout the text, readers must recognize that Grandmother Eagleton, like Sojourner Truth, moves between troubling constructs of womanhood, from Turtle Woman to human woman, and she never really dismisses any of the false ideologies. Harlan's name significantly draws us back to the subjectivity of Black female and how to translate it. In a scene in which Harlan has asked her mother if she ever believed in the grandmother's turtle stories, Harlan's mother replies, "Yeah, I suppose I did. I suppose when I was a little girl I did ... I even imagined that I was a turtle woman transforming myself to free myself from the tyranny of others" (277). Harlan's mother may not have had the means to go back to the process of unnaming that the turtle stories represent, but as a healer, Harlan has the means to accomplish such a feat.

Harlan's goal, then, is to believe the confabulatory tales of her grandmother and see their usefulness in her own life. Understanding that ideologies of womanhood are problematic for Black females because historical discourses of gender remain unavailable to them, Jones continues to create her own discourse of gender for Black females through the oral story of the Unicorn Woman:

> A lot of people when they would see that sign advertising the Unicorn woman, they'd think she was a white woman, you know, cause all the unicorns in the storybooks is white, cause that's supposed to be a sign of purity, you know, and even the colored people that come to see the Unicorn woman, theys's as surprised as the white people that she ain't a white Unicorn woman, cause even colored people think that white's a sign of purity, and she is a genuine Unicorn woman, but a colored one.... I heard someone say that even if she's a real Unicorn woman, she still a fake one, just by virtue of being colored. (136)

Harlan's grandmother repeatedly relays these tales to her as a child, and in their repetitive and recursive orality they become myths for Harlan to process. The Unicorn Woman is bound by the same ideologies of the Turtle Woman. Never the "true" woman, no mater how unreal gender may be, colored unicorns and colored women lack the authenticating element—whiteness. People assign hierarchies based on racial and gender discourses that attempt to define individual subjectivity. Carnival goers view the Unicorn Woman as an inferior and fake version of a unicorn simply by virtue of her color.

If readers juxtapose the myth of the Turtle Woman with the Unicorn Woman, they can envision the choices of womanhood left to Harlan. These myths document that each woman of color lacks a language for her subjectivity and is inclined to choose an inappropriate language so that she might be useful to society or a part of a community. Western culture's failure to accommodate their differences, and their own internalized misnaming of themselves, means that these females find themselves working in a carnivalesque-type environment such as the circus. That venue attempts to exploit their outcast status. They have been relegated to the margins, and the margins are a space for the exotic and monstrous footnotes of society.

In the case of Harlan's grandmother, someone else conceives that there is a failure of language to articulate her subjectivity and attempts to name her. Although Harlan's grandmother asserts her humanity and womanhood, it is a false one because the discourse does not apply to her. Eventually, someone else renames Grandmother Eagleton woman. Still failing to perceive the course she must go, Harlan's grandmother ascertains that she might have remained a Turtle Woman had it not been for her husband. She reaches womanhood because someone else saw her as a woman. She never finds an empowering space for her subjectivity, and she no longer has the man who gave her an identity.

In asking the critical questions, Harlan draws from her grandmother a wealth of wisdom that a young Harlan cannot yet begin to comprehend, and that the grandmother has yet to admit in her own life. In expanding further on the Unicorn Woman, Grandmother Harlan states:

> [B]ut it takes a true mythical woman to be the ideal of true womanhood, colored or ain't. Why even the proprietor of the first carnival she was at became obsessed with her, until he found him a woman that he thought the more ideal of womanhood than herself. Then he sold the Unicorn woman to another carnival, cause he didn't want them two competing ideals of womanhood. (138)

It might seem as if Jones is endorsing the use of mythical womanhood as a way of empowerment for Black women; however, the mention of competing ideals of womanhood is important because it reveals, once again, that womanhood is not the business of woman but that of men. Men created the ideologies and buy and sell these representations of women at will, but never for one moment can there be competing ideals because that would cancel out profits from exploitation of the women. Jones does not wish to replace mythical womanhood with another; she simply wishes to corrupt the discourse of gender with myth.

Comparing Grandmother Eagleton's story with Audre Lorde's "Black Unicorn" provides a way to observe that Jones's novel metaphorically suggests that folk dialogics be used by Black females to rebel against the Western rhetoric of sex that has been used to shape or define them: "The black unicorn is restless. /The black unicorn is unrelenting. /The black unicorn is not free" (*The Black Unicorn* 3). The unicorn as a metaphor for the Black woman implies that Black females will not be free, until, as Lorde has asserted through strategic hermeneutics in her other works, they can find new spellings of their name by which she meant new discursive models for their historical subject and experiences. AnaLouise Keating's *Women Reading, Women Writing* explores Lorde's "use of imagination, language, and mythic conversion principles to invent new individual and collective gendered and ethnic identities" (146). As Keating points out, in Lorde's collection of poems *Black Unicorn*, the poet uses her work to expressly take on what she had always acknowledged as the lack of language to convey the experiences and subjectivity of Black females. The title poem, "Black Unicorn," makes significant comments on the subjectivity of Black females: "The black unicorn is greedy. / The black unicorn is impatient. / The black unicorn was mistaken / for a shadow / or symbol / and taken . . ." (3).

In this poem, as with the entire collection, Lorde is concerned with Black females being construed as signifiers without meaning, like Sojourner Truth and Grandmother Eagleton. It is no longer the entire being itself that we understand and know but the distinct characteristics divorced from the being itself, and this is the sad historical experience that comes with accepting the term "Black woman" in society. The uniqueness of the black unicorn's presence becomes a shadow without light and a symbol without a context, but it also possesses the ability to be a floating signifier if it is not made "other" in the text. The only way to find a way to keep this floating signifier from being othered is to find a discourse to speak about the black unicorn—the Black female. Symbolically, Lorde's conception of the black unicorn, as a symbol and shadow, mirrors the way in which Jones uses the Black Unicorn Woman in her novel. It is not that Jones draws from Lorde's specific concept of the black unicorn for her text, but Jones's work in many ways demonstrates an appreciation and perhaps a worthy response to "The Black Unicorn." Like the black unicorn, Harlan must find a way to avoid the false recognitions and mistranslations of her subjectivity. The words of her grandmother offer a direction.

In *The Healing*, Grandmother Eagleton ruminates over womanhood with Harlan by remembering and repeating a conversation with a man she'd met after transforming from a Turtle Woman to a human woman. The man exclaims to her grandmother, "The man to woman you. Who'd have the nerve to woman you. Who'd have the nerve to woman a woman like you?" (253). By making "woman" a verb, Jones can use the unidentified man's simple statement to reveal the inadequacies of biological meanings of sex and the social rhetoric of gender to convey Black female subjectivity. It becomes clear that women, especially women of color, can become true women with the help of a strong and courageous man. As man remains the primary signifier, woman can only receive meaning from man. The statement reveals finite definitions of gender and that, yes, men define womanhood, and men impose womanhood onto women. For women of color, the imposition often results in Black females being unable to define themselves by their own ontological, epistemological, and phenomenological visions.

Grandmother Eagleton's misconceptions about her subjectivity do not have to be passed onto future generations due in large part to an intentional discourse based on tricksterism, liminality, and divination. Harlan acknowledges:

> When I grew older, I didn't believe the Turtle Woman stories, not the magical ones. Not the tales of how when she was a turtle she'd had to play all kinds of tricks to keep from getting caught by humans . . . I believed the one about

the carnival, and even the tales of the confabulatory Unicorn Woman, but not that one. Not the tale of metamorphosis, of how when human beings chased her, like every turtle, she ran so slowly that in order to avoid getting caught she had to transform. (164)

The point of those stories is clear. The turtle must play tricks to remain free from the prison of human hands. However, Harlan's doubts stem from her belief in social systems and beliefs that devalue magic and folktales. They are they same systems and beliefs that devalue Black female bodies. Coupled with Grandmother Eagleton's story of transforming from a Turtle Woman to a human, the magical turtle tales told by Harlan's mother and grandmother create a canon of trickster tales about shape-shifting necessary for Black women. Harlan's statement reveals that she once believed that such stories were real and significant. Her goal, then, is find a way to believe in the magical turtle stories in order to avoid the mistakes and misrecognition of her grandmother before her, and she soon does. The turtle stories are a destiny that she must accept. Initially, Harlan does not recognize the significance of these transformation tales as somewhat representative of what she must achieve in order to heal herself and others, but she will.

Even before Harlan acquires her healing gift, we can see that she is different because she defies societal notions of womanhood. As Harlan recounts the details leading up to her divorce from her husband, Norvelle, she remembers how uncomfortable she felt during a conversation with Norvelle's sister:

> I hope you's a nice girl. I hope you's a nicer girl than you looks like you is. It depends on what you mean by a nice girl, I said. I hope you's a nicer girl than you looks like you is what I mean. Cause you don't look like you's a wifeable woman at all to me. (169)

Again, Jones forgoes the use of quotation marks to help continue the stream-of-consciousness narrative. These references to nice girls, wifeable women, and men that can woman a woman irrefutably deny that standard conceptions of gender contain any plausible moments of which to confess sexual desire that has little to do with motherhood or marriage. Throughout Harlan's life, she constantly confronts the denial of herself in such discourses, and this struggle leads her to finally accept the magical stories of unicorn women and myths of turtles that transform to keep from being caught.

Harlan's failed marriage to the medical anthropologist Norvelle brings her face to face with the necessary non-Western discourses of gender, healing, and change that intertwine to influence her life as a "Black woman." Harlan asserts, "Even when I went to Africa with Norvelle and heard African transformation tales which sounded very much like that one [the turtle story], I still didn't believe it or I thought it was just folklore" (164). Harlan's disbelief doesn't dispel the influence of the turtle and unicorn stories on her evolution as a healer. They compel her to seek out similar apparatuses for her own transformation. After all, she does leave Norvelle in Africa after some serious soul searching.

Despite her irritation with Norvelle's work on the Masai medicine woman, the experience enables Harlan to choose a myth that will allow her to evolve her own subjectivity:

> It was only that Masai medicine woman who disoriented me because he wanted to stay with her, because he wanted to keep following her from Korogwe to Morogoro. . . . And I guess I envied her independent life, traveling about, curing folks. I guess the only way she could express her wanderlust even though the Masai are traditionally nomadic people was by being a medicine woman. (228)

Harlan's decision to leave Norvelle in Africa and pursue her own self concerns the Masai medicine woman as much as it does the Unicorn Woman she heard so much about as a child. Harlan's grandmother states, "There's plenty of mens crazy about her, like I said, crazy in love or infatuation and even follow her from carnival to carnival, her being a mythical-type ideal woman, but she ain't follow none of them. . . . if it's possible for a woman to follow her ownself, it's her. Free and independent" (139). Norvelle's academic pursuit and study of the Masai medicine woman sounds very much like those men who came to see the Unicorn Woman. Harlan's decision to leave Norvelle acts as a critical experiment to see if she can, like the Masai woman and the Unicorn Woman, follow herself.

Uses of the Erotic: Or, The Healing

Since Harlan learns her lessons of gender and sexuality from stories about turtle and unicorn women, as opposed to Mary and Madaglene or Eve and Lillith, she uses her life to follow herself. In doing so, she participates in the uses of the erotic: "When I speak of the erotic, then, I speak of it as an assertion of the lifeforce of women; of that creative energy empowered, the knowledge and use of which we are now reclaiming in our language, our history, our dancing, our loving, our work, our lives" (Lorde, "Uses of the Erotic" 55). Both Harlan's familial myths and the examination of her envy of the Masai woman unravel the possibilities of her own life. The Maisai woman allows her to reclaim a life-force that leads her to a subjectivity away from normative models of womanhood.

In the process of following herself, Harlan becomes manager to a rock star, Joan the Savage Bitch, and continues to be faced with the importance of her decision to leave her husband to his own dreams and to follow her self. In a discussion about women, Abio, one of Joan's friends, claims not to be a "feminista," and tells Harlan, "I only think a woman should be true to who she believes herself to be. Or who she wants herself to be. I don't know what I mean, or whether I'm true myself, to any of that. I don't think there are many of us who are true to our possibilities" (238). Again, Lorde's uses of the erotic impel us to accept our inner longings and desires into our lives without fear or shame. Throughout the text, such statements work to address Harlan's courage to accept her subjectivity as a Black female, and then as a healer. Harlan acquires the gift of healing, precisely because she began healing herself a long time ago by trying to be true to her possibilities. She could not have come to such a critical consciousness without the stories of turtle and unicorn women that were a part of her childhood.

The healer is born, but not realized. Harlan's ability to not fear her desires teaches her the key to healing. For when Lorde assesses that "the fear of our desires keeps them suspect and indiscriminately powerful, for to suppress any truth is to give it strength beyond endurance" ("Uses of the Erotic" 57–58), she is speaking about oppressive forces that silence women. Yet, her words might also reflect how fear and self-doubt can, when improperly treated, become a disease that invades and ravages the body. Harlan's familial myths allow her to address the psychological aspects of her body, but to avoid creating another conceptual order that privileges mind and spirit over body, Harlan must acknowledge and recognize the pleasures of the body. Once she no longer fears those joys, the process of self-invention can continue.

It takes a different type of magic to make Harlan be true to all of her possibilities—"The erotic—the sensual—those physical, emotional, and psychic expressions of what is deepest and strongest and richest within each of us" (Lorde, "Uses of the Erotic" 56). Harlan heals herself after being stabbed by Joan Savage. Harlan was sexually involved with Joan's ex, James. Joan, still in love with James, stabs Harlan because of the sexual relationship. Here, Jones makes it clear that sexual desires are as much a part of turtle trickster tales as divinity. The distinction of Harlan's sexual appetite is foreshadowed when Harlan tells Joan that Norvelle could not be sleeping with the Masai medicine woman because the Masai "got a tradition that the healing women are celibate or something. I think that their tradition" (159). While it may be the Masai's tradition, Jones toys with the notion of Harlan as a celibate or asexual healer. Early in the novel, gossipmongers Martha, Zulina, and

Josephine discuss Harlan before they witness her healing. Harlan's sex life becomes the topic for one of their many conversations: "Some say she was loose-virtued before she become celibate" (16). Harlan's celibacy during her period as a healer is mere rumor and conjecture since it is never confirmed. However, the conversation continues when they compare Harlan to saints: "Naw, there is female saints that also begin as sinners" (16). The blurry division between the sacred and profane or the sacred and secular are highlighted in reference to Harlan time and again: "A healer ain't necessarily no saint, is it, Martha. You can be healer and don't mean you a saint" (19). Jones refuses to let her character slip into categories of good versus evil or flesh over spirit. The trickster can be spirit and flesh. It can desire and love.

In the end, Joan stabs Harlan not simply because she's still in love with James, but because she recognizes that Harlan is more than a fling. In explaining her failed relationship with James to Harlan, Joan claims that she never minded his affairs, but that maybe "if it was more than a fling, more than infatuation," she would be hurt (104). After initially catching Harlan and James in yoga-like sexual positions (67), Joan seems unconcerned and nonchalant. However, as Harlan's story continues to unfold we see Joan's doubts. Before playing for one concert audience Joan asks the crowd, "Have you read the Kama Sutra?" and later she poses the same question to Harlan (152, 153). She even goes so far as to brush off her interest in both Harlan and the Kama Sutra, "I mean when I caught him with you that was nothing to catch him with you. . . . And you're still chewing on that old chestnut. I mean you're a girl scout you're a schoolgirl compared to what's in that book, the Kama Sutra, I mean. You're still in grammar school, girl-friend" (159). But Harlan is not in grammar school. As a matter of fact, she seems to approach her sexuality in a way that most wifeable women and nice girls would not. Long before Harlan becomes distinct because of her healing gifts, she possesses a self-intuitive knowledge about herself that allows her to be sexually free in ways that the keepers of womanhood would frown down on.

Throughout the novel, Harlan's commitment to being a "woman" or honoring the ideology of a woman is made an issue. Harlan forgoes the domestic destiny of traditional womanhood for her true self. She divorces her husband because she does not wish to be the dutiful wife and follow him across the African continent. She engages in extramarital sex with single and married men while sporting her wedding ring (51). Indeed, after she refuses to be a traveler with her husband, she becomes a woman traveling the United States alone to promote musicians. The fact that Harlan is stabbed because of her sexual desires suggests that the way she wants to live her life and the way the world perceives that she, as a woman, should live it are at odds with each other. Joan, a woman concerned with the rhetoric of womanhood (79), represents the reckoning of the world with Harlan's problematic subjectivity and individual desires. Joan's motives for stabbing Harlan are revealed in her conversation about Norvelle and the medicine woman. Joan asks of Harlan, "Aren't you at least jealous that he's met a woman who's sensual, spiritualized sensuality, or sensualized spirituality, not the vulgar sensuality of the West" (161). Joan's words remind us of trickster's importance of connecting the sacred (spirit) and secular (flesh) in sexuality. This is James's ideal woman, a being Joan could never be. So the inquiries about the Kama Sutra are revealed to be Joan's doubts and inklings that perhaps Harlan is a female who is that very being. The Kama Sutra, a work dedicated to connecting the sexual and the spiritual, returns us to the nature of the turtle, or in this case, turtle women. While Joan knows that Harlan was indeed spiritualized sensuality or sensualized spirituality, Harlan does not know. The knife wound reveals her trickster-like nature.

After Harlan heals the stab wound, Harlan recalls Joan's disbelief: "'I thought you were a real person,' she says. 'But you're not even a human woman, you're not even a real human woman,' and Harlan says in response, acknowledging, 'This is the truth of it. The knife fell out. I put my hand to the wound and it healed'" (280). Harlan's act of healing, as does the turtle, represents desire and divination. In "Cultural Transmission and Female Diviners in Gullah Slave Society," Margaret Washington explains that "divination was the process of unmasking private drives, sin and vices, which interfere with the flow of society. On the plantation the diviner might also serve as medicinal healer, midwife, or prophetess. Spiritual mothers directed and guided seekers through their symbolic travels into the wilderness or world of the dead" (5). Like the colored unicorn and the black unicorn competing against whiteness, competing models of womanhoods interfere with the flow of Black female evolution and culture.

Because Harlan's first healing is on herself, it remains a significant indicator of her role in healing Black females. Once Harlan's self-healing is placed in the context of lessons gleaned from Turtle and Unicorn Woman stories, the lesson learned from Harlan's trickster stories then are meant as an aid for curing the affliction of Black female disembodiment and dysfunction caused by the social rhetoric of gender and race. Joan's words are a way for the author to return to her critique of womanhood and the historical figuration of myth—the Black woman. After Harlan heals herself, she remains unaware of and unprepared for the act of healing in her life. It is only through the continued use of her gift that she will come to know her true self and full possibilities.

In many Western myths, female desire can be corruptive, destructive, and damaging, but Jones presents it as an empowering force that can transform those who wield it and the world around them. Harlan's boldness in searching for her self, through her independence and sexuality, allows her to locate Lorde's conception of the erotic: "For the erotic is not a question only of what we do; it is a question of how acutely and fully we can feel in the doing. Once we know the extent to which we are capable of feeling that sense of satisfaction and completion, we can then observe which of our various life endeavors bring us closest to that fullness" ("Uses of the Erotic" 55). Harlan discovers one use of the erotic. Harlan's ability to heal through touch showcases her surrender to how acutely and fully she feels in pleasing/pleasuring herself. She observes through acts of pleasure, a life endeavor that brings her closest to that fullness, her gift for healing. Jones does not end Harlan's life with tragedy, regret, or death; rather, she resolves to prolong her life with healing and hope. Her decision suggests that the gift of healing that Harlan acquires helps her find a place for her subjectivity. In the performative arena of healing, Harlan can generate a space in which she can invent language for that which the world cannot deal with, her autonomous sexuality.

The presentation of Harlan as a sexual person moves beyond traditional ideals of healers as asexual persons. Since her first healing act happens because of her sexual relationships, we can be sure that Jones wishes to distinguish Harlan from other literary healers. Since Harlan heals through touch, as opposed to herbs, potions, or spells, her sexual desires have as much to do with her healing as her Turtle Woman upbringing. As a healer, what is secular becomes sacred. Sexual desire serves as the equivalent of spiritual energy, and spiritual energy is sexual desire. Jones makes Harlan sacred without making her inhuman. In Jones's text, the act of healing is a symbol for divination and the manifestation of sexual desire that reflects trickster's origins in Africa and Black America.

Touch

When Harlan says, "I don't just heal physical ailments, I heal ailments of the spirit" (24), readers should understand that the foundational roots of Harlan's healing derives from African beliefs that promote a healthy balance between the spirit and flesh. From the testimony of one witness, we learn that

> [d]octors couldn't do nothing or didn't want to. I would go from doctor to doctor and none of them could heal me, or didn't want to . . . then she looked at me and know my trouble. She said the trouble would end, and touched me, and it did. That's what I mean by she heal by healing. . . . Sometimes she speaks a word and it's done. Other time she got to lay on hands. She don't

prescribe none of them herbs and roots and potions, though. She ain't that sorta healing woman. (16)

The witness's testimony places Harlan in the realm of diviners, medicine men, shamans, and conjurers. In many Western narratives, conjurers or healers are depicted as men. However, Alfâ Ibrâhîm Sow contends of African tradition that the woman acts as a "prime mover and vital element essential to the good functioning and continuation of social institutions. The source and seat of fertility and prosperity, she is also the guarantor of custom. She preserves the traditional methods of healing" (63, n.2). In the case of Harlan, she not only preserves but also adapts those traditions for new ills and diseases. Touch of the trickster ensures that cultural transformations can occur.

Of the traditional conjure, Leonora Herron and Alice M. Bacon assert in "Conjure and Conjure Doctors" that "the conjure doctor's business was of two kinds: to conjure, or 'trick' a person, and to cure persons already 'conjured'" (360). Embedded within early research and writings on conjure by whites and Blacks is a compelling vernacular linked to tricksterism. Harlan is the new prototype in African American tradition. Harlan's act of healing may seem far removed from these configurations of conjuration, but Jones reveals Harlan's faith healing as divine trickery. As the witness notes, Harlan does not employ any of the "tricks" of the conjurer with regards to roots or herbs. However, she does possess other powers that align with conjure lore: "Powers of all kinds are attributed to these doctors. The healing art in various degrees is their gift, and the so-called 'diseases' which they possess exclusive power to cure, as one informant puts it, these: tricks, spells, and poison" (361). Many Western narratives on conjuring mistakenly perceive that these spells, tricks, or poison will be physical or mythical and mystical. Yet the representation of conjurers in African American literary tradition has always dissected the impact of slavery and segregation on the physical and psychological health of Black people and implied divine touch as a way to heal. In addition, conjure representations reconnect the figure back to African traditions in which

> [t]he African tradition led slaves to recognize multiple and non-contradictory levels of causality. Spiritual and temporal worlds interpenetrated one another, as did present, past, and future. By manipulating these realms simultaneously as they saw fit, slaves recognized the fundamental connectedness of physical, social, and emotional aspects of affliction, while the dominant culture then, as now, failed to see the connections. (Goldsmith 88)

Harlan's gift for healing reiterates the need to understand and work with multiple realms of humanity.

Since Harlan is not a conjurer or a hoodoo priestess, we must hone in on what she type of healer she is in the context of the novel. The previous testimony on Harlan's healing method makes note of the tradition of laying on of the hands. To "lay on hands" places Harlan's faith healing in an African diasporic tradition that coincides with the text as trickster's communal narrative. In "A Laying on of Hands," Joanne V. Gabbin defines "laying on of hands":

> The term signifies the ancient practice of using hands in a symbolic act of blessing, healing, and ordination. By its very act, it appears to bestow some gift.... Thus it is associated with the healing powers of Christ as he lays hands on sufferers and they are cured. Others see the practice as central to the concept that the African concept that the spirit and body are one. Thus sensuality is essential to the process of healing and rebirth. (247)

The witness's testimony of Harlan's healing affirms the importance of communal healing: touch, sound, and physical exchanges are emphasized over herbs, roots, and potions. It also reflects what Joan saw in Harlan before she became the healing woman. Joan saw sensual spirituality. Sensualized spirituality, or a laying on of hands, is how Harlan heals. Had she never had the courage to explore her desires for fear of not measuring up to the ideologies of true womanhood, she might never have realized her gift for healing.

In Jones's previous novels, witnessing and testifying may have been enough to alter the path to healing. However, the inclusion of "laying on of hands" suggests that more needs to be done, for in the process of laying on of hands, we see power through a discourse of desire. If, as Delany mentions, that desire commands the matrix of power, then both the healer and the sick must submit to desire to heal and be healed. They must all participate in a simultaneous possession and submission of the body. It is a sacred-sexual act that hinges on touch. Gabbin's analysis refers back to the concepts of unranked binary opposition in African metaphysics. The spirit and body coexist in one space, and they need not be split, separate, or ranked as they are in Western Christian religious discourse. In addition to Harlan's sexual desires with James, Harlan learns the power of touch from other sources as well.

Harlan inherits this knowledge about the power of touch from her grandmother, in the same way she inherits myths of turtle and unicorn women. Turtles are the perfect metaphor for this notion of untouchable and touch in Black female culture. They are at once hard and soft, and strong and fragile. Yet there is possibly another way that Harlan learns the value of touch. As a beautician, the grandmother is economically engaged in the business of visually perfecting beauty. However, beauticians and beauty shops are people and places of healing too. The material value of the beautician has often outweighed the spiritual and sensual value. Yet the beautician engages in touch in the most intimate ways. The parting of hair, the massaging of the scalp, the nourishing of the scalp with oils and lotions, and the washing of the hair are all acts that mimic the closeness encountered in the most torrid representations of foreplay. The twisting, curling, dredding, picking, plaiting, braiding, brushing, and combing represent an erotic orgiastic experience of touch culminating in an amazing hairdo. The sheer physical proximity that one might endure in the process of doing and getting her hair done places women in an exchange of intimate bodies and energies that likely provides pleasure to the beautician and her client. Such exchange could be represented as a form of healing due to the psychological impact of the visual improvement or the physical effects of the process. Grandmother Eagleton's profession as a beautician provides Harlan with knowledge of how important touch is to the physical body, emotional makeup, and psychic and spiritual makeup of humans. Such lessons benefit a future healer.

In Jones's novel, it is impossible to imagine that a healer who could heal the ailments of the body would not know the wonders and pleasure of it for herself. How could Harlan heal without knowing how to touch, and without comprehending how touch affects the human body? Through her creation of Harlan, Jones reveals how ridiculous the notion of an asexual healer should be. Her work does more than speculate on the ideologies and institutions of sexuality, it creates a space in which the act of sex, the fulfillment of desire through the body, and ongoing moments of touch cannot be ignored in representations of desire. Harlan cannot become a healer if she represses her sexual desire, the very thing that grants her psychic knowledge about the intimate workings of the body. The acts of healing based on touch explain what the spiritual fulfilling of sexual desire can feel like and how it can benefit people. The way the body experiences pain and pleasure is key to Jones's creation of Harlan Eagelton as a healer.

In a discussion of S/M, Sarah Chinn argues that "S/M pornography comes the closest to capturing what sex feels like, since it . . . heavily depends on sensation and sublimity of sensory extremes. Writing about S/M means paying minute, exquisite attention to the maelstrom of experiences that play along the surfaces of the body but are so often invisible" (182). Though I am not interested in reading Jones's novel with an S/M subtext,[7] I cannot ignore the implications of Chinn's statement as it illuminates the importance of touch to a healer. In theory, a laying on of the hands, as done by Harlan, depends on the sensation and sublimity of sensory extremes. Because Harlan claims to be able to heal physical and spiritual ailments, her actions are as much about pain as they are pleasure. Elaine Scarry discusses pain as a psychic event, and psychic events are the dealings of trickster: "The events happening within the interior of another person's body may seem to have the remote character of some deep subterranean fact, belonging to an invisible geography that, however portentous, has no reality because it has not yet manifested itself on the visible surface of the earth" (3). As both Chinn and Scarry explain, pain and pleasure are psychic experiences within the body. Surely the healer must pay minute, exquisite attention to the subterranean experiences to successfully heal. Touch is the most logical way to do so. Harlan must access the point of pain in the sick body, but she must also access points of pleasure in her own body to make better the ill.

These tensions of pleasure and pain are the erotic, the chaos of our greatest feelings. The emphasis on touch in *The Healing* reminds us to maintain such uses of the erotic as power. Lorde warns us of what might happen without this recognition and exchange of how we touch each other:

> When we look away from the importance of the erotic in the development and sustenance of our power, or when we look away from ourselves as we satisfy our erotic needs in concert with others, we use each other as objects of satisfaction rather than share our joy in the satisfying, rather than make connection with our similarities and our differences. To refuse to be conscious of what we are feeling at any time, however uncomfortable that might seem, is to deny a large part of the experience, and to allow ourselves to be reduced to the pornographic, the abused, and the absurd. ("Uses of the Erotic" 59)

As a technique of healing, laying on of hands encourages the mutual sharing and exchange of each other's similarities and differences. Touch becomes the link that keeps both parties conscious of feelings, despite uncomfortableness.

Further, Jones suggests that healing is not a solitary process, but is instead a communal course of action that impacts those coming to be healed and the healer herself. Gabbin's definition of healing through laying on of the hands, confirms that Jones opts to implant in her protagonist and story an African concept of body and spirit as a way to dispel imagery of the healer as otherworldly or unnatural. Jones's concept of faith healings, as indicated earlier, differs from those of other African American female writers in that Harlan is not the exiled freak. Because this is the story about a trickster, difference is conveyed through the uses of the erotic. Remember, according to Lorde, the erotic functions in many communal ways: "The first is in providing the power which comes from sharing deeply any pursuit with another person. The sharing of joy, whether physical, emotional, psychic, or intellectual, forms a bridge between the sharers which can be the basis for understanding much of what is not shared between them, and lessens the threat of their difference"

("Uses of the Erotic" 56). A laying on of the hands allows the community to remain linked during what might traditionally be conceived as supernatural acts. Therefore, the healer cannot be othered and outcast, and the healed can physically embrace what they may not know or understand. Difference can be acknowledged without making deviance. Hence, body and spirit can be one in the construction of Harlan T. Eagleton. The divine elements of Harlan overcome the limitations of the bio-logic of her body, and the testimonies of witnesses provide a liminal space for her subjectivity.

Because Harlan lived her life in a way in which she could explore and be a participant to the wonders of her body and others, through uninhibited and unrestrained sexuality, the healing power becomes a manifestation of that sexual energy. Further, it also reconnects to trickster being able to occupy many spaces at once—to be male and female, or sexual and spiritual at the same time. Harlan can perform a laying on of the hands on her own body to heal herself because she accepted her flesh with her spirit long ago. She accepts her subjectivity despite not having a discourse for it, and this acceptance is a powerful act that enables her to transcend her corporeal form. When Harlan places her hands over the stab wound, she prolongs her life through healing. Harlan admits as much: "And when you discover that you can heal yourself, that you can simply put your hand to a wound and it heals, you soon discover that you can heal others. From a horse suffering from a fractured phalange, and then a Turtle Woman" (281). Furthermore, the gift of healing does not come from external forces but from her inner being. Harlan has carried her gift of healing with her the whole time; she simply had not recognized it in herself. Her end goal is to continue healing herself as she did that first time. In order to continue healing others, she must face her own fears, despair, pain, and disbelief about herself.

Years after she has healed herself, Harlan recognizes that the earlier words spoken by Joan Savage were incorrect, a failure of language to convey what she is:

> I didn't even ask for the spirit gift, I begin softly. I weren't even prepared for the spirit gift. But it came, it came.... A lot of y'all looking at me and just seeing an ordinary woman, and asking y'allself how come a ordinary woman like me to be given the gift of the spirit, how come a ordinary woman like me to be given a spirit gift? But that the point of them spirit gifts, the point of them spirit gifts, is that I am just a ordinary woman. I am just a ordinary woman, that is the point of the healing. (34)

Because she uses the resource of the erotic, Harlan lessens the threat of difference between herself and her clients. As with Lorde's use of "zami" to discuss ordinary women and difference, Jones refuses to make Harlan a deviant but does not downplay her difference. Harlan is not freakish, inhuman, or otherwordly. She is ordinary *and* divine. Instead of making those two elements opposing factors, Harlan forms a coalition between the ordinary and divine. She allows herself to surrender to the margins and in-betweeness of herself. This way of discerning her desire "yields a liminal identity, a subjectivity that is material and corporeal but which also transcends the limits imposed by corporeality, visual culture, and colonization—a selfhood that challenges the normative constructions of 'self'" (Quashie 78). Harlan's succumbing to the desires of the flesh makes her as real as Joan Savage, but her divinity gives her the language to express that reality. She admits the truth of it to herself and those coming to be healed. Healing is simply a space whereby she can exist and know herself.

In the end, Jones adeptly disrupts the construction of gender in Western discourse, specifically the construction of the "woman" as the primary cause of psychological illness in the lives of Black women. Jones utilizes the oral myths of the Turtle Woman and the Unicorn Woman to explore how Black women can depict their gender and sexual desires by locating their subjectivity through mythical discourse and metaphors. Harlan decides to exist liminally between the historical figuration and her own self. She will not let the myths (or stereotypes) define or restrict her. She will use them at her leisure to remain free from the prevailing discussions of gender. This liminal state keeps Harlan from being static and choosing to embrace one subjectivity over another. She does not have to choose to be society's definition of woman and human or the myth's definition; she can navigate between the various worlds.

Gayl Jones has always understood the need for locating new ways of knowing and that's the point of them healing gifts, the extraordinary comes from the ordinary that can find its own language. In assigning Harlan a transformative identity, the novel provides a methodology that makes it possible for Harlan and other Black female subjects to move away from essentialist and totalizing telos that might determine Black female subjectivity. Finally, Harlan can be like the turtle she claimed not to believe in. She can live up to her own possibilities, be whatever she wants, and all the while defy and elude those who seek to catch and name her. Such sentiments reclaim a major strategy of the trickster.

"Mutha' Is Half a Word!"
Tar Baby Trope and Blue Material in Black Female Comedy

All of this talk of gender and sexual desire in Black women's culture, serious as it may be, does not always have to be so heavy and metaphoric. The very real complexities of Black women's subjectivities and locating figurations to translate them can also be presented in a less serious light. At least that's what one trickster said some time ago: "I love myself when I am laughing.... And then again when I am looking mean and impressive" (Hurston, *I Love Myself* i). Impressive has already been broached, mean will come later, but the importance of laughter and humor in destroying restrictive gender and sexual traditions is the subject of this chapter. Even after locating that mother tongue, the vernacular organ that makes speech possible, we may need additional means to help us construct and love our own subjectivity and resist damaging representations to the self. Performance of comedy, with its play between public and private spaces, becomes one such means in which Black females' self-invention and desire can flourish.

In this chapter, the performance of vernacular and gender will be scrutinized to reveal another route of trickster-troping in Black women's culture, campy spaces and drag performances. In a move akin to Marlon Ross's examination of queer resources in the nationalist invective,[1] I'd like to discuss the camp aesthetics of Black female stand-up comedy and its importance in Black women's performativity of their sexual desires. Consequently, in a return to nineteenth-century Black writers' clever use of vernacular slang, and Annie Christmas's performance of femininity, this chapter presents an argument that some Black stand-up comediennes engage in trickster-troping through elements of cross-dressing vernacular performances and drag to explore other venues for unnaming their false gender status, promote expressions of desire, and evolve radical Black female subjectivity. No longer inhibited by concerns over propriety, Black females' comedic performances of "blue stuff" or "blue material" (raunchy and oftentimes sexually explicit subject matter) continue a Black female trickster tradition dedicated to creating oral cultures, divergent language practices, and initiatives to change definitions and boundaries of gender and sexuality in society.

The existence of vernacular and its possible uses are already transgressive, but as LaWanda Page forecasts with her prophetic reminder that "mutha' is half a word," witty performance of vernacular can be more transgressive. In returning now to the title of this book and chapter, Page's Black taboo lingua franca phrase previews the raw and raunchy subject matter of Page's recordings. As previous analysis in this text's introduction showed, Page's signifyin(g) performance of the vernacular, "muthafucka," relies on the messiness of desire to discredit and disprove the so-called truths of womanhood, motherhood, feminism, and gender roles. Historian Darlene Clark Hine has suggested that by practicing secrecy and "achieving a self-imposed invisibility . . . ordinary Black women accrue the psychic space and harness the resources needed to hold their own" (915). Yet the bold disturbance of gender by Page's "mutha' is half a word" offers another space attuned to the difference of women based on certain class connotations. "Mutha' is half a word" is both censored and uncensored because of the way it omits the "vulgarity" while at the same time mocking self-imposed silence and invisibilities. Page does not speak the entire word, but she pointedly refuses to remain quiet about the sex act implied with the word. Since performance is a public action that denies the domestic privatized destiny of "woman," it incorporates considerations of class. The function of the female field slave or the post-emancipated Black female who cannot choose or afford to work solely in the house/domestic sphere is a public one. Therefore, a more empowering discourse for women not included in the occult of womanhood would be visible and not silent. Page's phrase and this chapter continue to explore how some Black women opt for, and rightly so, a cultural practice less based in silence and invisibility. While vernacular is encoded with cultural codings of desire, performance of vernacular and desire potentially circumvents performance of gender. Even if it is not defined as so, the provocative nature of the phrase, "muthafucka" derives from the fact that it vocally connects sexual desires to the female systematically positioned as mother. Coincidentally, Page seemed remarkably aware of how much more she could transgress the boundaries of her slated roles (wife or mother) as a woman if she spoke in her class-based vernacular tongue, which does not have to adhere to the cult of womanhood. The phrase allows her to separate herself from the rhetoric of sex and social contract of gender so as to express her individual desires. Like a three-piece suit and top hat for Gladys Bentley, or a sequined evening gown and wig for RuPaul, vernacular becomes Page's drag. Ironically, Black stand-up comedy is not a traditionally female space or cultural form. Yet this chapter proposes that it is an unacknowledged queer space that African American women have been manipulating for their very own drag performances meant to annihilate heteronormative prescriptions of gender and sexuality.

For years now, performances of Black men in drag have garnered more attention than that of African American women in drag. Without the work of critics like Judith Halberstam or filmmakers like Michelle Parkerson, we might assume that Black women in drag were a thing of the past. Further, recent work on Black women in drag focuses on the drag ball/hall spaces and performances of masculinity. During an interview with *ColorLines* magazine, Judah Dorrington, the musical director for DKSG (Drag Kings, Sluts & Goddesses, a Boston-based theatre production run by lesbian/bi women of color), explains how drag can be empowering for Black women in such spaces: "For many African-American performers, DKSG is an unique opportunity. To sing in church, I'm expected to put on a dress. With DKSG, I was able to wear a suit and tie and croon. I even learned how to apply a beard. It has become more than a theater company; it has really affected the community by bringing GLBT women of color together to explore ideas from our own lives" (Katz 3). But outside of balls, clubs, and theater halls, are we to assume that drag performances cease to exist for Black women? We shouldn't. Black women have been in drag performing masculine, feminine, and indefinable and untranslatable genders for more than a century in spaces that White America has not deemed queer. Stand-up comedy is one unacknowledged field.

If we reconsider the historical position of the Black woman as both a break in the rhetoric of Black as male and woman as white, then Black females exist in a liminal space. In discussions formed more by the social than the biological, they might be considered genderless, multigendered, or transgendered. Kate Bornstein, in her book *Gender Outlaw*, notes the benefits of humor in the gender wars when she writes, "It's frightening to be genderless. What makes it easier is a sense of humor, and that's where camp comes in. . . . It's a sense of humor developed in response to oppression based on a unique gender identity, and a minority sexual orientation" (135). Although for some Black people it may not seem politically astute to place Black females in such a queer sphere, the reality of Black females' experiences, past and present, suggests that they do have unique gender identities and minority sexual orientations. As I am arguing, blue material in Black women's stand-up comedy develops in response to systematic oppression based on their racialized gendered identity and minority sexual orientation as asexual and hypersexual representational others. Consequently, camp elements can often punctuate the performances by these Black female comics.

Black female stand-up comedy has historically, purposely and coincidentally, deferred gender and opened up the possibilities for sexuality and expressions of sexual desires through its own visual and verbal performances. Though an examination of performances by LaWanda Page, Jackie Moms Mabley, Laura Hayes, and Adele Givens, this chapter reveals queer dynamics that allow comic performers to teach other women how to avoid the abyss of universal womanhood, dominating spaces of masculinities, and an absolute nothing of blacklessness. It argues that these female comics exist as perfect modern-day tricksters because they offer a visual drag parody of gender and sexuality, which they then subvert with their oral vernacular presentation. Black comediennes employ techniques such as Arthur Spears's "uncensored mode" and the trickster trait of sacred/lewd bricoleur in their blue material to serve as verbal cross-dressing techniques to defer their drag performance as woman. Once the verbal performance happens, they can translate their sexual desires without fear of mistranslation from prevailing discourses of gender and sexuality.

In her appreciation of trickster, Jeanne R. Smith revels in how "trickster challenges culture from both within and without, strengthening and renewing it with outrageous laughter" (3). Desire and the sex act itself provide humanity with many funny moments and myths, but in the representation of Black female experiences and desires there have been few moments of laughter. Hortense Spillers captures the predicament when she writes:

> Let's face it. I am a marked woman, but not everybody knows my name. "Peaches" and "Brown Sugar," "Sapphire" and "Earth Mother," "Aunty," "Granny," God's "Holy Fool," a "Miss Ebony First," or "Black Woman at the Podium": I describe a locus of confound identities, a meeting ground of investments. . . . My country needs me, and if I were not here, I would have to be invented. ("Mama's Baby" 257)

If we continue to commit to the rhetoric of sex alone, then certainly Spillers's words will forever haunt Black females and their cultural production. The violent physical, emotional, and visual abuses of Black women's bodies and sexualities are regarded as staid matters that have been taken up time and again, but what of the beauty, ordinary, foolishness, and the downright obvious missing focal point of pleasure derived from the act of sex? Do Black women not need or seek it for themselves, or attempt to represent it in their lives? Though Black women's sexual desires can be divine and transformative, they can also be bawdy and funny. Black women's blue material is an important consideration because it reminds us of pleasure in the sex act, and because it provides us with pleasure. It challenges us to see what is possible after the historical pain delivered onto Black women's bodies.

Yet if we never move beyond bourgeois forms of culture such as the novel, then it will be difficult to comprehend how lower-class folk communities and their tricksters laugh at social inventions not of their own making before transforming them at will. Discussions of literary tricksterism tend to focus on characters being trickster-like or narrative strategies as resembling patterns of trickster, but similar readings are possible in other cultural forms. The dotted lines of myth can more readily be connected on the written page. When we move away from the written text, connecting the dots becomes a more rigorous undertaking. We must pay attention to more than plot and theme of trickster. We must also return to the greatest elements contributing to trickster's ability to be critic and creator—performance and masquerade. These arenas allow trickster to serve as Gerald Vizenor's comic holotrope and representative of communal discourse. Clowns and jesters have traditionally been labeled as comic tricksters. In modern times comedians have also been assigned the classification of trickster. Yet William Hynes insists that while "there are various real-life, twentieth-century tricksters, more often than not the tenor of their character tends not to be as rich, multivocal, or polychronic as that of mythic tricksters" ("Inconclusive Conclusions" 204). Black female comics who perform stand-up challenge Hynes's theory on the death of trickster.

In order to recognize the humor of any comic, the public audience must be privy to the personal and private identity and subjectivity of the performer as well as the hermeneutics the comic may be using. The audience must feel some sameness or connection to the comic performer. As seen in the previous two chapters, mainstream society's propensity to make incomprehensible Black female subjectivity hinders such a possibility, and the scholarship on Black female comedy that might help remedy this is virtually nonexistent. With the exception of Mel Watkins's *On the Real* and Elsie A. Williams's *The Humor of Jackie Moms Mabley*, Black female comedic tradition continues to be undervalued, understudied, and misunderstood by mainstream critics and Black popular culture studies.[2]

Yet, the innovative use of blue material by Black female comediennes to disturb their own complicit visual performances of gender offers a needed critique on both the social construction of the Black woman and the representation of Black female desire that should be valued and underscored as innovative. Their trickster-troping makes these real-life tricksters every bit as rich, multivocal, and polychronic as their mythic ancestors. Before completing close readings of these comediennes, a brief examination of the common goals of comedy for African American women and camp for white gay culture would benefit any readings.

When Black drag queen RuPaul Charles teamed up with comedienne LaWanda Page for his music singles and videos "Supermodel" and "Back to My Roots," the connection between folklore and vernacular culture with queer culture was confirmed before the entire country. RuPaul's male subjectivity seems not as important as the way his reading of Black female culture allows him to bend gender constraints. For his performance as a drag queen is only possible because he recognizes the queer spaces within Black female culture, moments that this text intends to explore more queerly so that we might see the constructivist nature of woman making. African American women's stand-up tradition and Black drag culture share common aims and techniques to help accomplish the dismantling of binary systems of sex. RuPaul, Page, and the Queens of Comedy are all performative tricksters who challenge the illusion of gender and form distinct discourses of desire. Although chapter 2 briefly touched on the elements of physical beauty that configures models of normative womanhood in literature, attention to the criteria of physicality in other forms of Black culture should also be examined. In her pioneering study of drag artists, *Mother Camp*, Esther Newton offers three elements that are always present in camp: incongruity, theatricality, and humor (109). Notably, these are all traits and tropes of all tricksters. Each element exists in Black female stand-up tradition. As we will see, the interaction between Black female stand-up comedy and camp arise from the aforementioned elements.

However, camp inevitably is attributable to white gay male culture in the early twentieth century in that it seeks to unseat the models of masculine and feminine through purposeful drag performances. Of drag queens, Newton claims that "the clever drag queen possesses skills that are widely distributed and prized in the gay world: verbal facility and wit, a sense of 'camp' (homosexual humor and taste), and the ability to do both 'glamorous' and comic drag" (3). On the other hand, Susan Sontag's "Notes on 'Camp'" establishes very early on that camp is indefinable, and as such camp is not necessarily sheltered in the confines of homosexual culture (63). Still, she does note, "Camp is a certain mode of aestheticism. It is one way of seeing the world as an aesthetic phenomenon. That way, the way of camp, is not in terms of beauty, but in terms of the degree of artifice, of stylization" (54). Camp, then, seems somewhat influenced by non-Western traditions of orality. It is a less pigmented version of signifyin(g). It uses the visual and oral side by side without ranking one over the other. In Black female stand-up comedy tradition, the aesthetic phenomenon, the degree of artifice, and stylization stem from oral traditions. Sociolinguists have already exposed the priority of oral stylization in Black talk.

Both Black women and gay men have historically been oppressed within the United States, and they have produced cultures from this particular position. Each group forced Western societies to reconsider their axiological categorization of gender and sexuality. The methods for culturally assessing and thwarting oppressive regimes and representations coincide or intersect based on models of how governing communities read or imagine the subordinated groups. Both are read through a rigid fabrication of white masculinity. In reference to Black women's language practices, sociolinguist Marcyliena H. Morgan concedes that the social and scientific pattern has been to approach Black women's language practices, and in the end their cultural items, from concerns of normativity based on white masculinity: "African American women's issues are hypermarginalized and are considered typical neither of all women's issues (because the women who face them are not black) nor of black issues (because the blacks who face them are not women). It is not surprising, then, that all linguists—whether they include, marginalize, or fetishize black women—always at some level, take a position" ("No Woman No Cry" 28). Whatever position linguists take doesn't matter since "language is a social act," and the study and research of it "constitutes social and cultural production that is influenced by issues" of power (26). Therefore, if dominant society could comprehend the magnanimous historically fluid subjectivity of the Black female, then that knowledge would inevitably result in the dismantling of categories of gender and sexuality that would make less powerful those social communities in power. Since this is not in the interest of the oppressor, governing society attempts to regulate the economical and social successes of racial minorities through language policies that privilege standard English.

Fortunately, Black female comedy's application of vernacular resists these stipulations of society. Lawrence Levine speculates that Black people use laughter as a hermeneutical tool in battling their oppressive social position during slavery, in the Jim Crow era, and during our present era of Neo-colonialism. In *Honey, Hush,* Daryl C. Dance compiles a welcomed and serious collection on the rich tradition of Black female oral tradition and community of laughter. Dance describes the humor in Black female communities as healing:

> We (African American women) have had our share of tragedy and pain, and often even in the midst of that pain, we have found the relieving balm of humor. Humor hasn't been for us so much the cute, the whimsical, and the delightfully funny. Humor for us has been a means of surviving as we struggled. (xxii)

Dance includes humorous statements from notable Black female figures, folk sayings and traditions, jokes, mimeographs, poetry, and short fiction by and about Black female communities dating back to the 1900s. However, with the exception of a few excerpts from Jackie Moms Mabley's comedy routines, Whoopi Goldberg's Fontaine, and Butterbeans and Susie, there are few inclusions of Black female comedy/stand-up performance. The omissions signify that the means of resistance against oppressive dominant discourse may be influenced by concerns for respectability. In words that run parallel to sentiments of camp in gay culture, *Honey, Hush* evokes a closeted culture. Dance's collection showcases an internal conflict of humor, class, and gender that influences the revolutionary potential of African American female communities when she observes:

> African American women's humor has been an *in-house* affair. . . . [The] reason for the concealment of African American women's humor is that it was not considered ladylike to tell jokes or even to laugh too loud publicly. . . . One wonders if this could possibly have anything to do with the popularity of an almost formulaic responses to jokes, witty remarks, signifying comments—"Honey, hush!" It really isn't a suggestion that the person stop talking, but rather a friendly encouragement . . . or a suggestion that one is telling truths that are prohibited. (xxiii)

Dance's comments expose the reality that some Black women chose to separate their humor into spheres of public and private to be mindful of attributes that would qualify them as part of the occult of true womanhood. Blue performance, like camp, develops in secret. Dance's collection rests on the foundation that humor by African American females can be liberating even without the inclusion of blue material. Yet Dance's assumption appears to correlate to the tenuous position of African American females in the majority of African American communities.

Black feminist critics such as Barbara Christian, Hazel Carby, Angela Davis, and Patricia Collins have outlined the conflicts and tensions that enunciate the historical experiences of Black females in the New World. Therefore, as Dance points out, "honey, hush" becomes the tricksters' signifyin(g) to indicate the way Black females cloak their culture of comedy and laughter from the outside world that seeks to control and contain their presence. Though Dance attests that "honey, hush" is not prohibitive signifying, Dance later acknowledges key observations in her research on Black female humor: "No obscene language or sexual innuendos entered these conversations, perhaps because even when they let their hair down in the privacy of their own home they were ever aware of their images as college educated descendants" (xxiv). Dance's comments reveal why she may have omitted stand-up comedy in her collection, and they acknowledge class distinctions. Once the need to censor self-expression persists, Black females' initial representations of desire pause. Radical Black female subjectivity freezes. Such censoring, as opposed to signifyin(g), prohibits the unnaming of gender position that would lead to an uncensored pronunciation of sexual desires.

Dance's descriptive focus on the females as descendants of college-educated families implies a certain economic status not enjoyed by all Black females. The introduction unintentionally informs its reader how Black middle-class females remain mindful of colluding with or representing any of the stereotypes that project Black females as loud, rambunctious, licentious, or unfeminine, even as they create humor meant to resist those images. In this case, Black female humor always runs the risk of censoring itself or deliberately masking its language practices for the sake of propriety. If this masking was not tactically used to connect Black female subjectivity to false ideologies of womanhood, then it could be seen as empowering. Despite Dance's inclusion of humor with sexual themes, she, like her respondents, shares concerns over propriety that run counter to trickster traditions because trickster "myths of several nations include comic figures, even stories of sexual improprieties, although they are usually suppressed as formal religious traditions are developed" (Doty and Hynes 58). In the case of Black females, formal religious traditions and the rhetoric of sex unsuccessfully attempt to suppress Black female sexual desire. Dance's commentary proves how model womanhood and middle-class economic prosperity hinge on ideals of respectability.

On the other hand, lower-class communities must upset the status quo to prosper. Blue material in Black female stand-up comedy is really a lower-class phenomenon in that the public performance of taboo subjects shows no concern with issues of respectability. Whereas the middle class has more to lose in making public its private matters, the folk class has more to gain in that their voice might finally be heard and impel change to their social status. Black female stand-up comics' language practices draw from the historical well of comedy and tricksterism to exert control over their so-called anatomical destinies. Tricksterism offers a fundamental understanding of the foundations for Black female comedy. Although the folk tales may be long forgotten, the hermeneutics from them thrive in contemporary Black female culture. In the context of Black female stand-up comedy, the elements of a camp culture, argumentatively shaped by race, exists in African American folklore and vernacular culture. Its earliest beginnings can be gleaned from the trickster tales involving Tar Baby and Br'er Rabbit as they offer symbolic models of signiyin(g) or camp aesthetics that recent comic performers emulate.

Getting Down and Dirty with the Tar Baby Drag

Tar Baby tales illustrate the folk's more radical solution to problems of language, race, gender, and desire. Because "Tar Baby" is a tale that "warns against accepting illusion for reality" (J. Roberts 42), it stands as a satirical tale about drag performances. In addition, since "Tar Baby" also implies that "one should not forget one's cultural roots" (42), it contains valuable lessons relevant for Black female subjectivity, corporeality, and desire. In human-animal versions of the tale, a white master creates Tar Baby to get the better of Br'er Rabbit. In animal-only versions of the tale, Br'er Fox or a community of animals replaces the white master and attempts to exact revenge on Br'er Rabbit for his past trickery. In both versions, Tar Baby symbolizes an illusion constructed by those subjects in power to undermine the less powerful beings' attempt to move beyond oppressive circumstances:

> One day atter Br'er Rabbit fool 'im wid dat calamus root, Br'er Fox went ter wuk en got 'im some tar, en mix it wid some turkentime, en fix up a contrapshun w'at he call a Tar Baby, en he tuck dish yer Tar-Baby en he sot 'er in de big road, en den he lay off in de bushes fer to see what de news wuz gwine ter be. En he didn't hatter wait long, nudder, kaze bimeby here come Br'er Rabbit pacin' down de road—lippity-clippity, clippity lippity—dez ez sassy ez a jay-bird. Br'er Fox, he lay low. Br'er Rabbit come prancin' 'long twel he spy de Tar-Baby, en den he fotch up on his behime legs like he wuz 'stonished. De Tar Baby, she sot dar, she did, en Br'er Fox, he lay low. (Harris, *Uncle Remus* 17)

Supposedly recorded in the slave's (Uncle Remus's) speech pattern, Tar Baby's tale emerges. In this tale, the trickery of Br'er Fox works, to an extent, when Br'er Rabbit attempts to talk to Tar Baby. Tar Baby does not respond.

When Tar Baby does not speak to Br'er Rabbit, he loses his wits. As Br'er Rabbit arrogantly tries to physically bully an unresponsive Tar Baby into speaking, he becomes stuck in the tar. Br'er Rabbit's arrogance leads him to become displaced in the illusion of the Tar Baby. He frees himself from Br'er Fox's trap by delivering a performance of humility and helplessness: "'I don't care what you do with me, Br'er Fox,' says he, 'Just so you don't fling me in that briar patch. Roast me, Br'er Fox,' says he, 'But don't fling me in that briar patch'" (Lester, *Uncle Remus* 14). Br'er Rabbit uses his wits to convince Br'er Fox that the briar patch would be the worst punishment, when it is really his home and saving grace. He triumphs and gets the last laugh at the expense of Br'er Fox. Traditionally, the story has been read as an allegorical tale about power in race relations on the slave plantation. It suggests that Blacks must remember their roots if they are to survive in the New World.

Yet to comprehend the tale's meaning to the representation of Black females' sexual desires, it should also be read as a metaphorical tale about power in gender and race relations. In the tale Tar Baby is gendered female, while Br'er Fox and Br'er Rabbit are gendered male. Theoretically, if we remember that the "Black woman" is as much of a false construct as the Negro, then Tar Baby serves as a symbolic reference to false configurations created by a more powerful subject meant to trick the disenfranchised. The story forewarns African Americans to see beyond illusion, a strategy necessary for Black females overcoming the debilitating limitations of the rhetoric of sex. Further, Br'er Rabbit's tale underlines the aesthetic deployment of verbal camp, signifyin(g), and dragging: "To camp is a mode of seduction—one which employs flamboyant mannerism susceptible of a double interpretation; gestures full of duplicity" (Sontag 56). Br'er Rabbit greatly exaggerates his fear of the briar patch. He uses indirection, a element of signifyin(g), to save himself. His flamboyancy at indirection comes across in the detail that he would prefer the fiery fires of roasting to the dense bushes of the briar patch. His verbosity seduces. Likewise, the degree to which the Tar Baby ruse fools Br'er Rabbit offers a type of campiness in the tale. For "all camp objects, and persons, contain a large element of artifice. . . . camp sees everything in quotation marks. It's not a lamp, but a 'lamp.' . . . To perceive camp in objects is to understand Being-as-Playing-a-Role" (55). Notions of being and role-playing, artifice and illusion, remain at the heart of the Tar Baby tales.

In addition, in less Western models of the Tar Baby tales, gender becomes all the more a prevalent factor. In another interpretation of "Tar Baby," one which returns Tar Baby tales to West African mythology of the Tar Lady, Toni Morrison once said of her modification to Tar Baby: "Tar Baby is also a name, like 'nigger,' that white people call black children, black girls, as I recall. . . . At one time, a tar pit was a holy place, at least an important place, because tar was used to build things. . . . For me, the tar baby came to mean the black woman who can hold things together. The story was a point of departure to history and prophecy. That's what I mean by dusting off the myth, looking closely at it to see what it might conceal" (LeClair 102*).* Morrison's statement and her revision of the Tar Baby in her literary work *Tar Baby* position Tar Baby as an active being, less constructed by other individuals or beings but still caught in between roles and representations and one's own self.

In either case (if we position Black females as Br'er Rabbit, or as a revisionist Tar Baby who is active rather than passive), the tales' important demonstrations of the tensions and interplay of orality versus visual are crucial to African American female culture. The plot and lesson of the tale hinge on visual trickery and the use of oral wit and guile to overcome the visual tricks.

Though the story has only been applied to literary texts, Tar Baby tales serve as a significant component to see how truly trickster-like Black female stand-up comics might be. The visual drag of Black women reflects Br'er Rabbit's performance of humbleness and subordination to greater society symbolized by Tar Baby and the creator of Tar Baby. However, oral wit, conveyed in blue material, allows Black females to land in their own cultural briar patch so that they might better express themselves.

Drag culture encompasses many elements for various groups. Women who perform as men are drag kings, and men who perform as women are drag queens (Newton, *Mother Camp* 3). However, drag also has broader implications. In one of the greatest versions of "If You Don't Know Me by Now," Patti LaBelle makes a speech in the middle of her live cover performance: "So you fasten your clothes, you check your speech, and you check out your drag and everything else, your face and you find out that you're still in trouble." In appropriating "drag" from gay culture, LaBelle attributes drag to makeup, wigs, and whatever else, aside from anatomy that goes into making women "woman." She suggests drag is something that all women, straight or gay, perform at some point. Years later, queer theory formally articulated how drag utilizes and manipulates many physical attributes and masking techniques to create a unified picture of "woman." In *Gender Trouble,* Judith Butler writes that the performance of drag is an art form of parody that plays "upon the distinction between the anatomy of the performer and the gender that is being performed" (175).

Like many other women, Black women invest heavily in drag techniques to create a unified picture of "woman" and femininity. For Black females, white supremacy foundations of feminine beauty make their performance as subversive as the male who would perform woman. The financial success of Madame C. J. Walker, gained from her empire of hair-straightening products, and the profits enjoyed by cosmetic companies peddling makeup and skin-lightening products to Black women, demonstrate how racially influenced categories of femininity are, as well as how willing Black females are to submit to those versions of femininity. Some women oppose complete submission to these versions of femininity so that they can avoid a restriction of their sexual desires that may not align with prescriptions and object choices for those versions. Various drag performances, specifically the "glamorous" and comical, possess the tendency to blur the Western coherence of desire with prescribed social roles of gender. Despite some of the best work done on Black vernacular traditions, little has been done to investigate the strong queer dynamics operating within the performative space of the comedy stage. I'm not asserting that anyone from Moms Mabley to Sommore "Diva of Comedy" is a lesbian. Black comedy has sporadically been a prime haven for homophobia and misogyny, but there have been obvious instances of Black comedic tradition revealing its queer space. Black female comics remain aware of and embrace camp's attention to glamour and comic performances of woman. In occupying a trickster-like subjectivity and the performative arena of the stage, Black female comics have engaged those queer spaces through an unintended nod to drag culture.

Black comedy has been fearless in its critical appreciation of how race influences its drag illusions. In African American culture one need only recall the chitlin' circuit act of Freddie and E., an entire act that consisted of two men impersonating women; or Flip Wilson's Geraldine character and persona; or the implied queer associations from Whoopi Goldberg's one-woman show *Fontaine . . . Why Am I Straight?* to observe how the homophobic takes a backseat to boundary-breaking performances established by tricksters such as Eshu, Annie Christmas, and Afrekete. Gender ambiguity and androgyny have survived and thrived in Black lower-class culture of blue material in Black comedy, just as intentional exaggeration of gender and sexuality remains. Blue-Black comedy and queer aesthetics derive from one and the same Tar Baby trickster root: the goal of remaining aware of false social illusions and remembrance of cultural roots as an empowering way to manipulate the dominant society for one's own need. Since camp is "the triumph of epicene style (the convertibility of 'man' and 'woman' . . .)" (Sontag 56), Black female stand-up comedy and gay drag culture share similar aims. RuPaul and LaWanda Page proved that individually and cooperatively.

In RuPaul's autobiography, *Lettin' It All Hang Out,* he admits that as a child he was uncomfortable with his masculine side, but he also admits how subjective gender can be. As RuPaul extols the benefits of drag, he discloses how gender stability can be as temporal as a full moon:

> Just as I have explored different female looks—black hooker, gender fuck, and supermodel—now I am exploring different drag male looks—J. Crew, preppy, sexy homeboy, and executive realness. Just as when I am in drag, I feel totally at ease with my feminine side, now for the first time in my life, I feel totally at ease with my masculine side. (xi)

RuPaul astutely explains the metalevels of performance involved in the act of gender. Individualist considerations take priority over universal discourses about when or how people, especially people of color, should accept or reject fixed identities of gender. In the successive years of 1992 and 1993, music lovers across the video-viewing world were treated to two RuPaul videos featuring LaWanda Page. Page, the bluest of all female comics and a regular on the Black sitcom hit *Sanford and Son*, portrayed a maternal figure in RuPaul's "Supermodel" and "Back to My Roots" tracks and videos. Here, it is necessary to move beyond RuPaul's drag performance and delve into the way Page represents queerness. Page's liminal position as a Black woman posits her as queer; it is this queerness that RuPaul recognizes, uses to access his own queerness and perform it in empowering ways that might not be possible otherwise. Further, RuPaul's admission, through his incorporation of Page, allows Page to also perform and embrace her queerness as a trickster in a form other than comedy.

"Supermodel" is a catwalking ode to the production of gender by models and drag queens around the world, and "Back to My Roots" considers Black hair, culture, and heritage. The inclusion of Page in the vocal and visual aspects of these products conveys how revolutionary comic performances can be in regards to the representation of Black female desire. It is RuPaul's turn to Black female culture that showcases the influence of Black women's trickster-troping in the lives of Black men and women. In "Supermodel," Page recounts, in her inimitable oral delivery, the inspiring story of Supermodel's (RuPaul's persona) rise from the projects of Detroit to the runways of Paris. The decision of these two artists to collaborate with each other emphasizes the negotiations that producers of Black culture make and understand concerning gender and queerness.

Of why he desired Page for his work, RuPaul proclaims, "I always loved her—her voice and delivery. I had a wish list for the album and LaWanda Page was at the top."[3] RuPaul's statement attends to another aspect of successful drag, voice and delivery. As we saw with *Clotel*, successful drag performance completes its visual fantasy with complementing oral and aural work. As seen in Page's well-known lines "watch it sucka" and "mutha' is half a word," Page's voice and delivery receives its aesthetic appeal from Black folklore tradition and vernacular culture. Black female stand-up comics pit visual and verbal against each other to articulate their sexual desires away from the social handicap of gender logic.

Superficially, the Page and RuPaul pairing may have seemed innovatively odd because of the age gap and the different arenas of performance. RuPaul enjoys success as a drag queen that exceeds previous queens, and LaWanda Page, at her career peak, performed as one of the most shockingly funny comediennes. RuPaul acknowledges the opposing appreciation and love he had as a little boy for Page, as well as Diana Ross and other Black performance divas. Ross and Page exemplify the opposing factions of femininity in Black America. Where Ross had long hair, light skin, and keen facial features associated with white women, Page had short, coarse hair or a wig, dark skin, and broader facial features. In a sense, RuPaul's drag performance allows him to be within Ross's same range, but his affinity for Page also underlines the need for culturally specific versions of the feminine and supports the belief that people find beauty in the woman or performer who doesn't perform gender in the way that he does. RuPaul's appreciation of Page's style and vice versa points to the shared commonality—disturbing any socially prescribed notions of gender. While RuPaul's technique would typically be grouped under camp delineated by white gay culture, Page's technique of unnaming and expressing sexual desires was acquired from her early days as a performer on the chitlin' circuit.

Perhaps it was the no-holds-barred environment of the chitlin' circuit, but Black comedy performances have surely been queer longer than they have been homophobic. The chitlin' circuit reconfigures elements associated with camp to include issues of race. Though the chitlin' circuit and its sister avenues, traveling tent shows and the TOBA (Theater Owners Booking Association), did not explicitly perform for sexually queer audiences, they did address the needs of Black people consistently ascribed to the realms of non-heteronormativity. The chitlin' circuit, a direct descendant of the traveling tent shows of Black vaudeville and burlesque in the early 1900s, epitomizes Black camp (Watkins 372). These nightclubs and hall venues existed on the margins of communities alienated for their racial and class differences. As Mel Watkins notes of the clubs on the circuit, "You usually needed a ghetto guide to find them" (373).

The birth of Black stand-up can be linked to the TOBA and the chitlin'circuit (380). In these performance arenas, incongruity, performance, and humor flourished. Black female stand-up comedy that unnames gender and articulates its sexual desires reverts to the modes of camping found in the chitlin' circuit or the traveling tent shows. Symbolically and performatively, the chitlin' circuit could be said to do exactly as camp does for white gay culture: "Camp is a practice of suturing different lives, of reanimating, through repetition with a difference, a lost country or moment that is relished and loved. Although not innately politically valenced, it is a strategy that can do positive identity—and community—affirming work" (Muñoz 128). Akin to the practice of camp's function to suture and reanimate through repetitions with a difference, the chitlin' circuit, and its namesake chitterlings, represent the gathering of purportedly unusable remains of dominant society's taste and values and seasoning them with a distinct flavor so that they become a nourishing staple in one's lives. Black female stand-up comedy exploits the unusable remains of womanhood and the projected excessiveness of their Black bodies to produce intellectual feasts and entertaining critiques of gender, race, sexuality, and class for marginalized audiences. Would that we could create phrases such as "chitlinfyin(g) drag" (a combination of chiltin', signifyin(g), and dragging in the margins of the margins) and "chitlinality" (positionality as opposed to identity that considers the performative intersections of class, gender, race, and sexuality and the unusable remains of those discourses) to denote this soul food intersectional exploration of race and class into camp. Auspiciously, the examples of Black female stand-up comedy provide more fruitful analysis than name games.

LaWanda Page's early career demonstrates that the continued existence of the circuit had a lot more to do with it as an operating space of freedom for Black lower-class mass expression, as opposed to the noble, but bourgeoisie agenda of Broadway or mainstream touring. In Cleveland, Ohio, at the age of fifteen, Page actively pursued a professional dancing career. She later relocated to St. Louis, where she worked as a waitress at Ned Love's Tavern. Dedicated to her dancing aspirations, she soon began stripping. Since performers on the chitlin' circuit could avoid the censorship that came with mainstream bookings and TOBA, burlesque traditions flourished. Page was known for stripping in nightclubs predominantly affiliated with the chitlin' circuit. The environment that she performed in permitted her to construct a type of drag performance of otherness. Page's eventual incorporation of fire-swallowing into her striptease earned her the title "The Bronze Goddess of Fire."[4] During the act, Page would fearlessly light cigarettes with her fingertips, swallow the fire, and torch her body with the burning fire sticks. Page's act reveals an audience and a subculture interested in queer engagement with the body. Moving beyond a binary theory of gender (male and female), Page's performance as "The Bronze Goddess of Fire" acts as another possible gender performances, the other.

Newton has already explained that drag queens explore the performance of femininity, but other critics of camp and drag offer ways to reread Page that now seem invaluable. In "Mackdaddy, Superfly, Rapper: Gender, Race, and Masculinity in the Drag King Scene," Judith Halberstam investigates the way race shapes drag king culture for African American women: "I define the drag king as a performer who pinpoints and exploits the (often obscured) theatricality of masculinity. The drag king can be male or female; she can be transgendered" (104). By turning to race, Halberstam documents the production of drag culture in spaces that are not inherently white and gay. Her work locates camp culture in women's communities of color. Hence, based on the early and now broader implications of drag, Black women, like Page, have several options they may exercise in their drag performances: masculinity, femininity, trans, and othered. In the case of Page, she pinpoints and exploits the theatricality of otherness.

Before Page made a career of making people laugh, she attended to her prescribed role as an othered woman. Page, like RuPaul who follows her, manipulated the Black body for audiences who remained limited by their own societal boundaries of race, class, gender, and sexuality. Likewise, RuPaul's blonde-haired, blue-eyed Supermodel persona is as much a humorous exaggeration of white femininity as Page's exaggeration of Black othered femininity. The pairing of RuPaul and Page explores the shared space of sexual and gender drama. They both exploit Page's chitlinfyin(g) drag beginnings and her performance as the homely and unfeminine Aunt Esther on *Sanford and Son* to solidify RuPaul's contemporary violation of gender and sexuality. Given that Page met Redd Foxx, the star of *Sanford and Son*, when they toured on the chitlin' circuit, it seems quite possible that Page's comic genius and the Bronze Goddess othering of herself resulted in her being cast in the ideal antiwoman role of Aunt Esther. In a number of *Sanford and Son* episodes, Black females' deferring of gender is highlighted. Page's flawless performance as the character of Aunt Esther symbolically connects to Tar Baby tales. Like Tar Baby's unresponsiveness to Br'er Rabbit, Page's Aunt Esther refuses to perform gender in the way the signifyin(g) Fred Sanford wishes. She unnames herself through vernacular ploys in the same way she employs the visual to other herself as a stripper.

In numerous episodes of *Sanford and Son*, Fred refers to Esther as "the creature from the black lagoon," and those comments negate Esther's "less feminine" (dark, not white or light) looks in comparison to Fred's divinely feminine Donna or Elizabeth. In a sense, Page's dark skin color positions her as the Tar Baby to Fred's Br'er Rabbit. The two participate in the dozens, and Fred's funniest lines often refer to Esther as a failure in feminine beauty. In addition, the Aunt Esther character moves between silent Tar Baby (actively signifyin[g] through certain looks to Fred) and Morrison's revisionist strong Black woman Tar Baby (comically throwing up her fists to pummel Fred or vocally proclaiming, "Watch it sucka"). These are the vernacular mechanisms that RuPaul finds so appealing. On *Sanford and Son*, the two tricksters duke it out time and again, with Fred, like Br'er Rabbit, being the victor. However, years later, all that Esther stands for appears vindicated by the appearance of Page in RuPaul's work.

What happens when the blackest of the black, Aunt Esther, gets matched with Supermodel—the most glamorously feminine in the whitest Western ways—supplies ample cultural criticism about gender and desire. As the maternal figure in both videos, Page serves as a representation of antiwoman through her voice and appearance, but the subversion occurs when viewers realize it is the anti-woman who gives the world the ultrafeminine Supermodel. Page's comedic presence allows RuPaul, even as he engages in the theater of gender, to ironically mock it in a way that calls attention to the way that race influences that exhibition.

Of drag performance Butler asserts: "But we are actually in the presence of three contingent dimensions of significant corporeality: anatomical sex, gender identity, and gender performance" (*Gender Trouble* 175). Butler's assessment remains markedly powerful except when we take into consideration issues of class and race; except when we are dealing anatomically with third sex/intersex/hermaphrodites; except when we take into consideration those corporeal moments of not only the performer but the audience as well; and except when drag, a mainly visual artform, intersects with vernacular culture. Fortunately, Halberstam rectifies the absence of race and vernacular culture within such discussions.[5] For example, in her study of race and masculinity in the drag king scene, Halberstam returns to male impersonation by Black blues women of the early twentieth century to serve as historical evidence of a tradition of male impersonation in African America. When she states that "the image of the blues woman in drag singing to another woman also guards against what Ann DuCille has called the 'feminization of the blues,' which she describes as the mass production 'of the black female as sexual subject'" ("Mackdaddy" 114), the symbiotic relationship between drag and verbal cross-dressing remains clear. In the case of blues women, who more readily dispersed sexual themes within their music, visual drag lessens the risk of Black female performers being seen solely as sexual subjects. In a way that Judith Butler had failed to do but Halberstam does, Page's decision to participate in RuPaul's music and videos offers an assessment of race and drag. In the case of Black female stand-up comedy, the orality of Black vernacular culture, signified by Page's presence, interrupts the privileging of the visual epitomized by RuPaul's exaggerated performance of Western white woman. This play between orality and the visual creates formulations of Black females as radical sexual subjects who can control and manipulate their markers of agency without becoming sexual objects.

In order for gender to be subverted, it must be exaggerated, imitated, repudiated, and rejected. During her portrayal as Aunt Esther, Page refuted and rejected gender roles. She fetishistically and comically unnamed herself. As a stripper, Page exaggerated her role of woman, not simply through a bold sexual performative display of her body, but in an othering of that already alien Black body, one in which she projects herself as spewing fire from her body. Just as RuPaul's performance as woman has the potential to be othered if he does not tuck (the technique of making less visible the penis), Page's fire stunt submits her as monstrous other. Page's decision to pursue stand-up comedy and later participate in RuPaul's videos hints at her own understanding of how visual tactics undermine attempts at radical Black female subjectivity, but blue material in Black female comedy empowers her by serving as a disruption of the visuality of drag performance.

Drag and Vernacular Cross-Dressing

In Debra J. Robinson's now dated documentary *I Be Done Been Was Is*, viewers are treated to one of the few female interpretations of Black female comedy. Rather than assume a fictional or less critical film genre, Robinson allows the documentary to speak on the role of gender and sexuality in Black female stand-up comedy. The title of the film communicates the numerous subject positions Black females occupy, and it uses Ebonics' invariant "be" to signal its answer to discussing that liminal subjectivity outside of the language of wider communication. It is a brief, clever comment on the failure of European languages and Western metaphysics. The title foreshadows Robinson's documentary of Black female comedy as a trickster narrative or a narrative about trickster. The documentary contains clips and interviews of four, at the time, up-and-coming comics: Marsha Warfield, Rhonda Hansome, June Galvin-Lewis, and Alice Arthur. Warfield, a regular on the 1980s sitcom *Night Court*, was the most successful and recognizable to mainstream audiences. Because it was a low-budget, independently made documentary, *I Be Done Been* lacks the glitz and glamour of the most recent film on Black female comics, Walter Latham's *Queens of Comedy*. Although *I Be Done Been Was Is* and *Queens of Comedy* differ in presentation and purpose, both films verify that blue material in Black female comedy allows comics to interrupt their drag so that they may better present their sexual desires without worrying over matters of decorum. *Queens of Comedy* may have made more money, but *I Be Done Been* historicizes Black female comedic tradition in a way that deepens *Queens of Comedy*'s value beyond that of entertainment.

Robinson readily conceived of a project that should historically contextualize itself in the world of Black cinema and comedy. Robinson shoots the film in various locations. She cinematically moves from the dark and barely lit venues of comedy and night clubs to interaction between comics and camera and director in various uncontrolled environments. The camera and the director always hold as its subject the Black female comic speaking or performing. In the nightclubs, we barely see or hear the audience. Our sole focus stands on stage, a nondomestic space.

The film opens with short clips of each female's routine. Warfield, Arthur, and Hansome are in makeup, while Galvin-Lewis performs *sans* makeup. After the last clip of performances, the film's title streams across the screen. As it streams, audiences are aurally treated to Moms Mabley's well-known Klan routine about her performance in a southern nightclub. Robinson establishes the context in which we should view *I Be Done Been*. The film addresses Black female comedy as the liberatory practice from racial and gender oppression:

Visual illusions coupled with biting comic voices serve as the strategy to freedom.

By beginning with Moms Mabley, if only in a snippet, Robinson implies the mechanisms of drag utilized by early Black female stand-up comics. As Watkins notes, during her performances Moms Mabley appeared in "oversized clodhoppers, tattered gingham dresses, and odd-ball hats, and affecting the persona of a sage, down-to-earth, older woman" (390). Moms's character or personae isn't the Bronze Goddess act of Page, but it clearly serves as the basis of Page's Aunt Esther character. Both implicity perform another gender. The beginning of the documentary offers evidence for this text's consideration of unnaming and drag. In the past, Black women comics took up comic drag to serve as their method of unnaming through performance. For Robinson, these purposeful visual transformations of oddball hats and clodhoppers connect to the issue of gender. As the filmmaker records the answers to questions such as "Why are you a comic?" or "How'd you get into the business?" the answers seem no different than the response might be for a male comic: "Because I'm funny . . . because humor is wonderful . . . because I thought I could." Despite such generic answers, Robinson lets her film provide more detailed retorts. In a beautiful montage on the history of Black female comics, the camera pans on photographs, posters, and pictures of previous female performers while audio commentary narrates and explains the subjects before the camera. Moving away from the universal assumptions of her two opening questions, Robinson reveals that Black female comedy didn't necessarily begin as a separate and open field.

Black female entertainers served as either chorus girls or waitresses in early twentieth-century show business. In an epigrammatic assessment of minstrel and vaudeville shows, Robinson completes a roll call of Black female comedic performers, some known, but most unknown: Princess Pee Wee—a singing comedian in Barnum and Bailey, Ladle Thompson of the Ziegfeld Follies, Ada Overton, Landi Williams, Anita Bush, and Mae Barn. In a moment of historical analysis that compels us again to understand the queerness of Black performance of comedy, Robinson remarks on the prominence of male/female comedy teams in vaudeville and the chitlin' circuits. Clearly, the teaming of Butterbeans and Susie and Vivian Harris and Pigmeat Markham provide an early peek at blue material that knew nothing of the boundaries of gender etiquette and sexual decency.[6]

Robinson's emphasis on the outrageousness of these performances transitions the documentary into a very valid examination about the public comedy performance on stage and the public performance of woman, and each one's role in the interruption of gender binaries and hushing of desire. In words that explore this text's theory of blue-Black performance as queer, an oral cross-dressing to counter their drag performance of woman, Robinson asks, "What if Ada Overton hadn't been beautiful, couldn't sing, act, or cake walk, would being funny have been enough?" And she later explains, "Even Pearl Bailey . . . had to play down her looks and to settle for the ordinary chatting, wise cracking lady." In recalling Sontag's criteria of camp as performing comic or glamorous drag, it seems clear that Black women on stage had to move back and forth between the two options. Robinson's comments show that there is no such thing as a universal comedic stage presence working for Black female comics, even if they don't admit it. In order to succeed, Black female performers had to manipulate oral and visual elements to both defer gender and refer to their sexual desires.

Early Black female comics had to intuit what audiences wanted from them and subversively give it in a way that seemed nonthreatening. Well versed in the role of trickster as an outsider who changes the community as it engages communal discourses, Black female comics realized that in order to be successful on the circuit or stage, Black female performances had to play within and exceed the boundaries of gender performance at a schizophrenic pace. Even as Robinson notes that "today's Black female comediennes approach the industry through a direct route of comedy," it seems very obvious that in 1984, those comics being studied still had to worry about the politics of gender and the art of drag:

> Comediennes have no groupies. You know (to the director), men are intimidated. It seems from the time you walk on the stage . . . you know, you've done something women don't do . . . so you've automatically taken yourself out of the realm of desirable women. (Marsha Warfield)

Makeup, jewelry, certain hairstyles, and clothing help place the Black females on stage closer to the desirable realm of woman. However, as Warfield argues, the stage presence of these female comics seems to somehow defer the performance of woman because it is an undomesticated space. Rather than simply submitting to a logic of universal womanhood, some Black comediennes revel in their dislocation as desirable woman and emphasize it though sexually explicit routines. While audiences may remove these women from the realm of desirable womanhood, their response or reaction to the women on stage doesn't alter the fact that the performers have desires of their own that might be hushed to partake in the privileges of womanhood. Consequently, once these comediennes are projected as undesirable, a liminal space is opened up in which they can express their own desires without the inclination of censorship that might occur when one is attempting to maintain an image of desirability for dominant audiences or communities. Like the blues singers who represented liminal figures who explored sexual potential (Halberstam,

"Mackdaddy" 114), the stage and the vernacular degender the Black female comedienne, and these Black comediennes become exemplary figures of sexual agency who can do and say what other women simply dream about doing.

If these women really are performing gender, doing drag, then how can they showcase that fact so that it does not seem as if they are imitating woman or buying into the fabrication of gender? Blue-material lengthens the subversion of gender and sexuality that begins with drag. In one scene, Warfield observes of her comedy, "All of my material is XXX rated . . . but my material never seems vulgar . . . or offensive." In response to negative reactions to her blue material, she counters such rhetoric and emphasizes that she works "nightclubs where people are drinking and smoking." Warfield sharpens the camp sensibilities of Black female stand-up. Blue material is for a specific audience who shares the sensibilities of the comic performing. The liminality of Black women's subjectivity allows them to operate in spaces that do not align with representations of "woman." Blue material continues to defiantly interrupt the visual performance of woman. Blue material becomes both the greatest defense to drag performance as woman and the greatest example of drag's subversive potential.

Later in the film, Hansome compares her use of blue material to Black male comics doing blue material: "Even though it was not true about Richard Pryor, Redd Foxx, or about Eddie Murphy, the one thing that was stressed to me by the showcase club was that if you do blue material you won't be accepted . . . I don't like that." Despite the freedom the stage allows in terms of performance, that stage is still owned by persons who may wish to adhere to prevailing discursive models. Warfield and Hansome's comments demonstrate why Black female stand-up relies on the tensions of drag performance and the politics of vernacular and trickster culture to unname and desire. In mainstream environments, the showcases, the pontification of desire cannot occur without an unnaming process that defers gender. As opposed to alienating the audience, which leads to a loss of profits, Black females must consciously play with/up representations that audiences are comfortable with before they can ensue the contravention of language and moral values.

As indicated by Page and Mabley's routines, they must offer either excessive otherness or gender neutrality. Since the comediennes of the film are performing during the 1980s, clownish and buffoonish appearances are substituted for the androgynous aesthetics of funk and punk. For Warfield that means the wearing of pants, a natural afro, and a a less-than-soft demeanor coupled with a polished and made-up face. She conveys soft butch. Hansome wears her hair dyed and spiked, and flamboyantly colored wardrobe and bright makeup complete her image. Both comics' stage presence releases each comic from the confines of womanhood in a nonthreatening manner. Their attention to drag gets them on the stage, while their use of blue material, the vernacular, allows them to deconstruct their own performances of "woman" and "othered." Like signifyin(g), the successful practice of blue material depends on similar shared cultural values between audience and performer. Without this understanding, "honey, hush" might become a permanent marker of Black female culture. Nowhere is this more evident than in the production of Latham's *Queens of Comedy*.

The Black stand-up comics in *Queens of Comedy* choose to draw in their audience with drag acts that highlight the appearance of glamour, while still deploying the verbal cross-dressing of blue material. Though *Queens of Comedy* is originally intended for entertainment purposes mainly, it offers an education on the material lives of its performers. The film's narrative technique reiterates and strengthens the main theme and nature of the females' comic performances—for gender to be altered through a process of unnaming and Black females to express desire. The filming of *Queens* occurs in a semicontrolled setting. The special was shot at the Orpheus in Memphis, Tennessee, and televised on the cable network Showtime. The audiences, both the live participants in the film and the cable-paying spectators, are at the heart of *Queens of Comedy*. Where Robinson's *I Be Done Been* wishes to reveal as much as possible about the role of gender in comedy performance, *Queens* attempts to represent female desire and meet the voyeuristic demands of their audiences. Audiences who are set on having their need for sexual satire and gender performance satisfied can use the stage or television to separate them from whatever unexpected social criticism the comedy acts may produce.

The stage consists of an Egyptian-themed set with pyramids and hieroglyphics meant to correspond to African royalty, but these attempts to authenticate the Blackness of the women, as well as their connection to legitimate lines of royalty that exalt Black femininity where it has typically been denigrated, are dismissed by the clever way camp shapes their acts. *Queens*'s opening scene shows four women: Adele Givens, Laura Hayes, Sommore, and Monique driving to their concert destination. As the film opens, we hear Givens say, "I'm such a fuckin lady." The women pose for photographs. With the exception of Sommore, everyone is casually dressed and *sans* makeup. The director and producer team of Steve Purcell and Walter Latham make a point of dispersing segments about Black female corporeality throughout the filmed performances of these women. The juxtaposition of the comedy routines with the random but deliberately themed clips expose how much of a drag competition blue-Black comedy can be.

Once the routines in the film are under way, the camera focuses on the first comic, Laura Hayes. She enters the stage wearing a flowing and flattering pants ensemble. Her long, colored hair and nails are extravagantly done.

This comic clearly exists in the realm of desirable woman. Everything from her hair, clothes, and nails project the soft and delicate nature of "woman." After Hayes finishes one segment of her routine, the film interjects a clip of the four females having their hair and makeup done before the show. Again, the ordinary and barefaced women are a far cry from the polished queens we see on stage, and they good-naturedly joke about the differences. However, the clips are jarring not because the women look so horrible without makeup, but because it aesthetically does not seem to connect with Hayes's routine before or directly after the clip in the stage delivery of her comic monologue. Yet Hayes's closing and her introduction of the next comedienne cue astute home viewers to comprehend the thematic connection between the beauty salon clips and the concert scenes, for there is an underwhelming connection to the performance of gender and the representation of desire.

Latham's cinematic narrative zooms in on the tensions of the vernacular performance in opposition to visual performance. In the absence of the filmmaker's narrative context that Latham constructs in the editing and filming of the show, the live audience must turn toward those frictions alone. Hayes relies on trickster skills of exaggeration and mimicry to ensure that the audience acknowledges the role race plays in the representation of gender and female desire. In a segment on how Black females move from ladies to bitches when one of their own is harmed, Hayes begins pantomiming a boxer getting ready to fight a man who has abused her sister. The climax of the routine comes when, in preparation for the fight, she begins removing her drag—rings, earrings, and finally the long flowing, colorful wig that adorned her head are thrown to the floor. The audience erupts in laughter because the soft, feminine lady has been replaced by a "thugged-out bitch." In this case, Hayes's Tar Baby disguise is gone, and she now becomes Br'er Rabbit in the briar patch. Because she remembers her mutable subjectivity as a Black woman and her class roots, she can protect her own by any means necessary.

Hayes's routine works because she was able to emphasize the decorum and motives of performing woman, motives that seek to adhere to audience perceptions. Makhail Bakhtin's exploration of masks affords a way to explain how Hayes's comic timing serves as indicator of herself as a trickster, as opposed to just another woman: "[T]hese masks take on extraordinary significance. They grant the right *not* to understand, the right to confuse, to tease, to hyperbolize life; the right to parody others while talking, the right to not be taken literally, not 'to be oneself'" (Bakhtin 163). To be sure, I am not conflating dragging and masking. What is most useful about Bakhtin's statement as it relates to Hayes's performance comes in how it draws our attention to the campiness of Hayes's routine: "Camp in this context clearly refers to a somewhat ironic gender practice within which gender traits are exaggerated for theatrical and often comic effect" (Sontag 58). In drag, Hayes can accomplish all of the assignments that Bakhtin outlines because Hayes's comedy mirrors the previously mentioned camp mechanisms of Br'er Rabbit in the Tar Baby stories. When she undresses before the audience, she signifies woman as a performance and not as being. A female who accepts the parameters of gender would not be as willing to unveil the smoke and mirrors that go into the illusion of femininity. All of the items that Hayes removes threaten to undermine Black female subjectivity and replace it with a performance of white femininity. However, her willingness to comically showcase the visual reveals Black females' defiance to mirroring white womanhood. Whereas maintaining drag composure, the artifice, is essential for drag kings and queens, for the Black stand-up comic to expose the flaws of gender performance, she has to publicly dismantle the drag artifice. Keeping it on is not as subversive as publicly removing it. Again, the division between the public and private serves as a means to an end.

In addition, Hayes's routine draws on camp's glorification of character and the unity and the force of the person (Sontag 58). In the beginning of Hayes's act she glorifies woman as a character. Hayes walks in ways that emphasize her feminine appeal. Her hips sway, she speaks in demure, flirtatious tones with her audience, and she giggles like a girl. Yet she also engages us in another character, the thugged-out bitch. The way she walks and talks changes. Hayes's performance of this character becomes as much a performance of dragging as her depiction of a lady. Hayes plays with stereotypes of Black women, essentialized woman, and issues of authentic Blackness. In each instance, Hayes's work demonstrates a distinctive drag performance. Take, for example, Halberstam's discussion of Gladys Bentley and Storme DeLaverie as Black women doing male impersonation. In her assessment of the two entertainers, she locates what separates male impersonation from drag kinging: "The ability of the drag king to make a show out of male impersonation. The theatricality, or lack thereof, in the drag king performance depends, for example, on whether the performer is attempting to reproduce dominant or minority masculinity, whether she relies totally on impersonation, or whether her own masculinity flavors the act" ("Mackdaddy" 115). Although Hayes is not interested in drag kinging or male impersonating, she relies on drag's theatricality for her act. She makes a show of both female impersonation and bitch impersonation. As I will argue in another chapter, perhaps bitch becomes a separate marker of gender in and of itself, making desire more polysexual for some Black women.

Notably, after this particular scene, Hayes introduces Adele Givens via Givens's signature line: "She's such a fuckin' lady." Givens, upon entering the stage, asks the audience, "Do I look like a fuckin' lady or what?" As seen in the close of Hayes's performance and in Givens's line, the question that these women and the comic film pose is: What does it mean to look like a lady? Givens returns to a verbal cross-dressing, as opposed to Hayes's visual unveiling. Because Givens revises her signature line in a way that draws attention to her physical appearance, we consistently see the importance of appearances and performances in this particular film concert. Visually, these Black females, with the assistance of wigs, extensions, and makeup, can temporarily emulate the model of woman (white) just as RuPaul could, but it is their blatant disregard (Hayes's throwing off her wig or Givens's "fuckin' lady") toward the mainstream idea of concealing how much of a performance gender is that destabilizes the construct.

In her essay "Stripping, Starving, and the Politics of Ambiguous Pleasure," Katherine Frank suggests of gender that "more 'legitimate' performances carry privilege. . . .Working-class women and Black women, then, cannot play with gender as freely as white middle-class women" (196). In addition, RuPaul also notes that "you're born naked, and the rest is drag" (iii). Many females dress in drag to perform woman. As exemplified by Hayes's routine, "others" simply have to work harder at it. Drag displays depend on visual chimera *and* vocal or verbal disguise. Black female comedy epitomizes the idea that what you say and how you say it is just as pivotal as how you look. Blue material serves as a strategy that allows Black females to resist the commodification and sexual exploitation so regularly imposed on the Black female body. Given the examples from LaWanda Page and *I Be Done Been*, it is important to remember that subversion of gender must occur differently for Black females than for white females. It must be an aural or oral subversion as well as a visual one because any corporeal reference makes more monstrous what is already perceived to be so.

Letting Go of Gender to Vocalize Sexual Desire

Instead of adhering to ideals of womanhood, Black female comediennes' performances often reflect the dissident practices of trickster in their performative language customs. Tricksterism becomes a way to change society. Taken from the vernacular and folk culture of Black America, as a way to avoid bourgeois assumptions about gender, the most dominant trickster trait found in the humor of Black females is that of sacred/lewd bricoleur. This is where the crossing of boundaries and violation of taboos can become a major factor in language practices of Black female humor. William Hynes believes that one of the major characteristics of the trickster figure is that of sacred/lewd bricoleur:

> The bricoleur is a tinker or fix it person, noted for his ingenuity in transforming anything at hand in order to form a creative solution. Because the established definition or usage categories previously attached to tools or materials are suspended/transcended for the bricoleur, these items can be put to whatever inventive purpose is necessary. . . . The trickster manifests a distinctive transformative ability: . . . can find the lewd in the sacred and the sacred in the lewd, and new life from both . . . seems impelled to violate all taboos, especially those which are sexual, gastronomic, or scatological. ("Mapping the Characteristics of Mythic Tricksters" 42)

Though some people might be hesitant to find the lewd in the sacred and vice versa, doing so enables a sense of freedom from restrictive and oppressive societal boundaries. To disrupt the constructed axiologically opposed binaries of Western aesthetics reveals how deeply detrimental flawed ideologies based on simple either/or and wrong/right dynamics can be. In this way, if a female comic wishes to dismiss the problematic constructions of gender and sexuality, she has to do so through language. She must become the sacred/lewd bricoleur.

As the sacred/lewd bricoleur, the Black female stand-up comic configures blue material so that it becomes a verbal cross-dressing to counter her performance as woman. Because language can be an accessory to an outfit, a prop, or an effect in a performance, the disturbance of the rules and regulations of language etiquette, situated by race, class, gender, or nation, can also reveal the triumph of Sontag's epicene style. As we saw with *Clotel*, language figures into the convertibility of man and woman. Stand-up comedy provides the best way for Black female comics to become sacred and lewd bricoleur. The tensions between public humor and private matters help exaggerate the taboo-ness of blue material in Black female comedy. The presence of blue material in African American female comedy prevails throughout several generations. Many critics would argue that Jackie Moms Mabley was one of the most successful to complete the task of sacred/lewd bricoleur. However, this work continues its focus on LaWanda Page's antiwoman model. In Page's canon of comedy, *Mutha' Is Half a Word, Watch it Sucker!* and *Pipe Laying Dan*, she consistently discusses moral hypocrisy and female desire. Page's expression of her sexual desires surely served as another possible reason for RuPaul's admiration of Page. Though both figures engage in drag performances, Page seemed better able to express her sexual desires through Black vernacular culture. As a part of commercial drag, RuPaul represents, as José Muñoz notes, a "sanitized and desexualized queer subject for mass consumption" (99). However, Page opposes RuPaul's desexualized queer subject. Page's knack for remaining uncensored and sexual stems from her ingenious use of

Black vernacular styles.

Since Page possesses gender liminality she can revert to the most artful form of expressing desire and critiquing gender, the sacred/lewd bricoleur. On *Watch It Sucka!*, Page leaves behind the visual trickery of the Bronze Goddess to elevate herself as a sacred/lewd bricoleur in vernacular art during her routine entitled "Whores in Church":

> Yeah, honey . . . the whores in such bad shape. One whore said to the other whore, she said "Honey, it ain't no money on these streets no mo. Hell I'mma join the church." So the other whore, she didn't really believe she was gone join the church you know, so she say, "Well bitch if you gone join the church I'm going that Sunday to see you join." So that Sunday, the damn bitch join the church honey. So the preacher came down out of the pulpit and he says, "We know you a whore." He say "But I want you to tell your determination!" The bitch got up and she say, "Well brothers, sisters, members, and friends." She says, "I wanna speak my determination." Yes honey, she talked to em' a while baby. She say, "You know I'mma whore out on the streets." This other whore, her friend, she sittin' in the back listenin'. She say, "And the money got bad out there, but the money didn't mean nothing to me. One night I was laying in the arms of a sailor, the next night I was laying in the arms of a soldier." She say, "But tonight, I'm laying in the arms of Je-esus!" And the other whore she jumped out of her seat and said, "That's right bitch, fuck 'em all!"

Robert Pelton suggests that tricksters unite "'high' and 'low' in a language of sacred ribaldry" ("West African Tricksters" 130). A number of Page's recordings concern subject matters on religion and sexuality that typically contain philosophies that undervalue female desire. Page's "Whores in Church" is an act filled with profanity, sexually explicit references, and a critical assessment of Christian devised representations of women—sacred ribaldry. Her voice never falters or hesitates over intertwining the sacred, secular, and so-called lewd. This play between sacred and lewd is exactly what formulates Page's blue material as verbal dragging.

In drag, binary and fixed assumptions about gender are highlighted and dismissed. Sade Huron, self-proclaimed "lesbian drag queen with a dick," estimates what the process of drag does for her in a way that coincides with the way sacred/lewd performances work in blue material:

> So I stood up and sang a few Shirley Bassey songs—that's how it all started. . . . I remember feeling like a drag queen. It was the way I wanted to express myself. I wasn't dressing up trying to be Shirley Bassey, rather I was dressing

up as a caricature of a woman. An ultra-feminine woman—something that I've never felt, even though I feel 100% woman. It's that kind of over-the-topness; more of a woman than a woman could ever be. It was very exciting taking on that persona of a drag queen. (Atherton 228)

Huron's performance complicates ideologies of gender and sexuality. That she defines herself as a lesbian drag queen observes lesbian as a type of third gender, and as a third gender the way she places her performance of femininity in the realm of queen rather than drag king further corrupts the intelligible logic of gender and sexuality. In many ways this is how the transformative sacred/lewd bricoleur trait works within LaWanda Page's blue material. In its use of profanity and its juxtaposition of sacred representations with lewdness, Page's routine makes a caricature of the binary models of heteronormative womanhood and non-heteronormative womanhood. Her repeated use of "bitch" and "whore" in the already tabooed themes of whores in church delivers an over the topness of other womaness, and the final use of "fuck" with regards to Jesus then makes the other women all the more othered. Additionally, Page, who recounts the story, becomes more non-heteronormative than the sex workers in church and her trickster-troping of desire is complete. Central to this verbal cross-dressing is the analytical understanding of "woman" that Page brings to her act.

Epitomized through the Virgin Mary's Immaculate Conception, mothers and virginal women are viewed as sacred entities. The prostitutes represent society's idea of lewd people. The irony Page reveals, through her mixing of the sacred and lewd, is that prostitutes perceived as morally bankrupt and unredeemable people are as conscious of morality and redemption as the next person on the pew. Like other parishioners coming to be saved, the prostitutes come to the church when they have nowhere else to go. Page's introduction of the prostitutes into this sacred institution mocks the hypocrisy that may be present in Black church venues. Though all persons seeking redemption should be welcomed into the church, quite often those who have sinned are the subjects of many negative criticisms. The reverend's public outing of the prostitute's lifestyle in front of the congregation leaves him and the congregation open to whatever may come from the prostitutes' testimony.

Page reworks the Black testimonial call-and-response tradition that usually occurs in both church (sacred) and club (lewd or secular) spaces. She uses it to uncover repressed sexuality. Unlike the signifyin(g) honey hush, Page's humor is street humor and trickster in nature. Its comedy derives from breaking taboos. Taboos can't be broken if one veils the criticism or the transgression. The stage allows her to take sexuality out of the bedroom. The sacred and spiritual testimony of the first prostitute is remade and reenvisioned by the witnessing and subsequent "lewd" response of the second prostitute. The idea of Jesus Christ fornicating with a prostitute clearly draws from a controversial theory of Christ—the savior and Magdelena—the prostitute.[7] Page's routine suggests that the depiction of an asexual Jesus and Mary may have a lot to do with man's repression of sexuality.

Beyond religion, Page's act suggests that money, or lack thereof, influences issues of morality. The second prostitute's initial doubts about the first prostitute's commitment to being saved refer to trickster's task of overcoming pitiful material circumstances. Consequently, Page's use of profanity to describe the women's actions hints at the duplicitous nature of her tale on human morals. The testimony ritual used by Page equalizes the first prostitute's repentance of her sexual behavior with the second prostitute's ecstatic and admiring response of the first prostitute's testimony. Where some people will hear redemption, others will hear sexual mastery. However, since they take place in a sacred space, they are both valuable testimonies. Page's point is made. The use value of female sexuality is subjective and individual, and it deserves visible and vocal social institutions and discourses that reflect that. She uses the stage and her performance to do so.

Though Page's jokes violate a number of taboos for some people, they reveal a lesson about practicing forgiveness and compassion being extended to all. Page's routine divulges how, as a trickster, she "both exposes and transforms that dirty bottom" and "invites humans to contemplate what they will become and to hope for what they already are—a world large in its intricacy, spiritual in its crude bodiliness" (Pelton, "West African Tricksters" 135). Page's monologue reveals that Black females have to be particularly adept at finding the sacred and the lewd, and use it to destroy problematic social configurations that would make deviant individuals' sexual desires. If they were not able to critique, as Page convincingly does, established boundaries, borders, and definitions in their own version of a mother tongue, then they could not sustain an empowering radical subjectivity. Camp reviewer Pamela Robertson's discussion of lesbian camp exposes how Page's function as sacred/lewd bricoleur connects once again to drag sensibilities:

> Camp as a structural activity has an affinity with feminist discussions of gender construction, performance, and enactment; and that, as such, we can examine a form of camp as a feminist practice. In taking on camp for women, I reclaim a form of female aestheticism, related to female masquerade, that articulates and subverts the image- and culture-making process of which women have traditionally been given access. (57)

In this routine, Page does not risk othering herself in the way her chitlin' circuit act does. She uses the uncensored mode to subvert the typical image-

and culture-making process that woman has access to. This discursive trickster practice of finding the sacred in the lewd and vice versa serves as a language strategy to criticize and take society to task for its oppressive and limiting system of binary divisions. Laced with profanity and sexually explicit subject matter, Page's blue comedy material offers an initial transformative query into Western fabrications of gender and desire.

Aside from Page's exercise in sacred irony, Trudier Harris once classified a classic Moms Mabley's routine as a "refusal to believe that human beings should compartmentalize their sexuality to the early years of their lives" ("Moms Mabley" 768); Mabley also utilized the language practice of the sacred and the lewd in her performance. Playing on the ideas of wisdom and old age, Mabley contends:

> "I never will forget my granny," Moms quipped; "You know who hipped me, my great grandmother. . . . This is the truth! She lived to be 118 years old. . . . One day she sittin on the porch and I said, 'Granny, how old does a, does a woman get before she don't want no more boyfriends?' She was around 106 then. She said, 'I don't know, honey, you'll have to ask somebody older than me.'" ("Grandma" routine)

Mabley knows that women are traditionally taught that they shouldn't openly discuss sexuality, and such wisdom also lessens the importance of sexuality in identity formation of those in advanced age. However, in this particular bit, the wisdom pertains explicitly to sexual desire, and sexuality remains a factor for Mabley's elderly granny. It does not become less of an issue for females: they simply become wiser about discourses surrounding it.

Mabley's strategy of preparing the audience or making them feel comfortable with discussing sexuality and aging becomes possible through the language strategy of the sacred/lewd bricoleur and her own appearance. She explodes established ideals to make her point. Her stage name elicits a maternal connection, and her nonthreatening, comical appearance desexualizes her. She is not overtly feminine or glamorous. Often dressed to look like a domestic worker or bag lady, she appears asexual. The visual desexualization does not prohibit expression of sexual desire, it merely unnames Mabley as woman. It allows for a bold show of sexuality through its deferring of gender. Whenever audiences might assume they are being provided with less taboo subjects, such as family or the sacredness of a grandmother, Mabley refers back to less comfortable discussions of sexuality and age. She never allows the audience to separate sexuality from gender, age, or race. Her strategy makes it impossible for anyone to establish fixed boundaries or "norms," and because it takes place in the arena of comedy people can accept what they otherwise might not.

The sacred/lewd trope of the familial is a verbal edifice of drag performance in African American female stand-up comedy. Adele Givens, one of the most recent comediennes to leave a lasting impression for Black females in the twenty-first century, provides a tribute to her grandmother that mirrors the earlier Mabley tribute to her great-grandmother and the continuation of the trope. Givens was the first female to perform on the male-dominated Russell Simmons's *Def Comedy Jam*, an after-midnight weekly comedy show on HBO in the mid-1990s. Though proclaimed by other, elder comedians as "a black minstrel show,"[8] *Def Comedy Jam* enjoyed years of critical and commercial success. While Moms Mabley and LaWanda Page turned to chitlinality at certain times in their career, Givens, from her initial start on *Def Comedy Jam*, resorts to Page's attention to excessive otherness. Much later she turns to the *Queens*' affinity for glamour drag to clear a space for herself. In her most notable *Def Comedy Jam* routines, Givens plays up the sexual theatricality of Black women with full lips. Givens incorporates the physical distinctions of some Black women's features versus that of white women, saying, "I know by now that ya'll then noticed that I got some big-ass lips. Yeah, I know they some big muthafuckas. Hey, I know they some big muthafuckas. Yeah, all my lips are big" *(Def Comedy Jam* 1992). Though it is not as exotic as the incorporation of fire into a striptease, Givens's attention to her wide-painted facial lips accomplishes what it needs to.

First and foremost, the statement acknowledges, through its explicit reference to her facial lips and her implicit reference to her vaginal lips, representations of Black women as sexually excessive, and rather than defend herself against such statements she pinpoints the theatricality of her performance as other on a stage dominated by Black male comics. This rhetorical wink to sexual representation mimics camp strategies. Kate Davy's "Fe/Male Impersonation" offers some clues as to how the subversive wink works in gay culture: "But instead of realizing the promise and threat of its subversive potential for imagining and inscribing an 'elsewhere' for alternative social and sexual realities, the wink of Camp (re)assures its audiences of the ultimate harmlessness of play" (142).

In opposition to camp, Black female stand-up comedy winks, but it also enforces the threat of subversive potential with its own cultural signifyin(g) that insists upon playing with purpose. In one joke about her lips, a tic-tac, and a whale, Givens plays up the threat of her sexuality swallowing men whole. Givens's attention to and then dismissal of sexual representations of Black women enables her to subvert gender, express sexual desires, and get paid. Givens's success on *Def Comedy Jam* is one of the reasons that she is showcased in the concert and touring show *The Queens of Comedy*. Like Hayes before her, Givens chooses an outfit that adheres to mainstream aesthetics of feminine wear. Though she does not wear a dress or skirt, Givens dons a sheer-flowing duster outfit with open-toed heels to accentuate her femininity. This Queen of Comedy knows the tightrope of Black female representation that she walks. Caught in between hypersexual other and asexual Mammy, Givens adjusts her performance to the times. Givens's visual performance of a ladylike woman is interrupted when a male audience member yells at her to do her notorious tic-tac routine.[9] Givens refuses and tells the audience:

> No, cuz I'm on my grandma. I need to tribute to her. I love my grandma. In fact, she's the reason I'm still standing here doing comedy. Cuz you know I had got discouraged. I said I wasn't gone do it. Cuz I had did a show and gave it my all . . . and I gave a great show one night and a lady came up to me and said, "Adele, we loved you, you was funny as shit," she said. "But you have a filthy mouth" . . . When somebody tell you how you should talk, that's a muthafucka that want to control you. . . . My grandmother talked to me and she said, "Look bitch you don't quit unless you want to quit. The next time somebody tell you you got a filthy mouth, you let 'em know: It ain't what come out of your mouth that makes it filthy, it's what you put in there. And you tell them you wash all the dicks you suck, here." (*Queens of Comedy*)

In the past, Givens's comic routines have focused on her sexual prowess, but she refuses to become a sexual object at the whim of her male audience members. At her discretion she can pontificate on sexual excessiveness or ignore it all together. Her choice to do so, or not do so, is what moves her into radical Black female sexual subjectivity. The stage and her theatrical performance of woman enable her to maintain control over her self-representation.

Beyond her refusal to follow the audiences' prescribed notions of her comedy, the story she relates about her grandmother teems with solid examinations of language, audience, and gender. Be it the dozens or some form of signifying, her verbal performance rescues her time and again from models of womanhood that dominant masculine society wishes her to perform at its request. While Sade Huron subverts her drag queen act with a false phallus, Givens depends on blue material to subvert her drag. Another drag artist, Valerie Mason-John, offers some insight into how the performance of gender affects her female audiences: "Women enjoy me but they're scared. I act out some of their secret fantasies; I do break boundaries. When I was performing at the Fridge, Venus Rising, one night, I wore a top hat and tails, Victorian bloomers and a strap-on dildo. Women really did enjoy it" (216). Parallel to Huron and Mason-John, when Givens becomes the sacred/lewd bricoleur by performing blue material, she frightens and breaks boundaries. That she emphasizes a glamour version of the feminine while doing so explains how her female audience could laugh at her hilarious antics and then later reprimand her. She acts out their fantasies to boldly exclaim their desires to the world while appearing as feminine as her audience. Her blue material and her appearance devour the division between the heteronormative and non-heteronormative, and she queers herself and her desires in the process. This manifestation of queerness unnames and self-represents her desires so that even as she embellishes her femininity, her exoticness, or her otherness, her verbosity will not allow anyone to reduce her to the performance of "woman" or othered object.

Initially, Givens's refusal to do the tic-tac routine assumes to take a turn to the serious and sentimental, and though she does tribute to her grandmother to express her love and appreciation for her grandmother, she never allows her comedy to forget its foundations in sacred/lewd maneuvering so as to represent bold, Black female desire. Like Mabley, she understands that sexuality remains a topic for the ageless that should be explored without regard for language or decorum. If wise elderly women can talk about sexually explicit subject matter, then society's preoccupation with what women should talk about and how they should talk about it is an issue that needs to be investigated. Givens's confession about almost quitting comedy because someone didn't like the language she used is the second issue that needs to be discussed in reference to African American female comics doing blue material. As demonstrated by Moms Mabley, LaWanda Page, and now Adele Givens, the use of profanity becomes a marker of blue material that very much exposes the conflicts of language and ideologies of womanhood. Like the sacred/lewd hermeneutics, profanity in the comedy of Black female stand-up comics occurs for a reason. In order to deconstruct binary oppositions of gender, race, sexuality, and class, blue material has to be laced or articulated via a mix of normative discourse and the uncensored mode.

According to Arthur Spears, uncensored mode recognizes that "individuals operate effectively within different evaluative language norm contexts—which is true of language users world wide" (227) Most importantly, Spears notes that "[t]he labeling of expressions as profane varies socially, regionally, and temporally. If profanity is considered with regard to its essence, we are really talking about what is considered, by some people on some occasions, as unacceptable speech, which covers not only expressions, but also topics, tropes, and aspects of grammar" (227). Convincingly, Spears draws our attention to how language reflects relations of power and dominance. Consequently, when Black female comics perform comedy, blue or otherwise, they might be viewed as profane regardless of what they say or the subject matter they discuss because they are not typically in dominant positions of power. It all depends on the audience interpreting the material. Black female audiences, then, might react differently to blue material based not only on gender, but on class status as well.[10]

On *Def Comedy Jam*, Givens's routine often began with her trademark line, "I'm such a fuckin' lady," and perhaps it was the very cleverness of this phrase that held the door open for other Black female comediennes to perform on the male-dominated show and be successful: "Hey! What's Upppp!!! Do I look like a fuckin' lady or what? Ladies in the house tonight! I like bein' a fuckin' lady, especially in the 90s. We get to say what the fuck we want to. Don't we girls?" Givens's signature line immediately makes the audience aware of the false ideologies of womanhood that stipulate that she should not be partaking in this particular comic venue.

However, by devising her speech with the uncensored mode, Givens can signify[11] all over the constructions of gender and sexual ideologies that do not apply to her. In *Black Talk*, Geneva Smitherman notes that "fuck" in the language community of African America is "used in reference to various non-sexual events to show emphasis or indicate disapproval . . . used to dismiss something or someone as irrelevant or unimportant; in the sense of 'forget that'" (139). In a sense, each time Givens speaks the phrase, she is saying, "Forget that assigned gender subjectivity, I'm creating this new one for myself." In the same way that queer critics have theorized butch lesbian as a possible third gender, "fuckin' lady" could be read as a separate gender category. As it did with Craft's and Brown's use of "Mr. Johnson," the vernacular becomes an artifice in the drag performance. In its uncensored mode, it propels further the transgressive properties of drag.

In the struggle against conventions, the drag apparatus takes on special significance and allows trickster to rip apart visual masks and "betray to the public a personal life, down to its most private and prurient little secrets" (Bakhtin 163). As "fuck" appears as an adjective before the noun "lady," it becomes clear that Givens wants to dismiss Western, bourgeois societal notions of what's feminine or ladylike as irrelevant. Only then can the audience move beyond partaking in those ideologies and on to more relevant discussions of Black female subjectivity—voicing one's desires: "Cause you know in the old days they couldn't say the shit they wanted to say. . . . They had to fake orgasms and shit. Today we can tell men. I wanna come motherfucker" (*Def Comedy Jam All Stars* 2001). LaWanda Page and Moms Mabley demonstrated that Black females before Givens's time have been very vocal about discussing issues of sexuality, roles of women, and the like in front of audiences. She continues that tradition with a revision from comic or chitlin' drag to glamour drag.

Since the uncensored mode subverts the visual of drag, Givens can fulfill a trickster task of demonstrating the metalevels of experience. This trickster goal seeks to "destabilize absolute perspectives and essentializing definitions" (Smith, *Writing Tricksters* 143). Once she has done that, Givens can then move into her routine of bringing to light her experiences and sexual desires as a Black female subject moving from a Victorian-modeled past to the present:

> That's right I learned to appreciate that pap smear. Talkin 'bout once a year. Bull-sshit I'll see you tomorrow motherfucker. Ten inches—of iron, hard, safe shit. When he finish, I smoke a fuckin' cigarette. . . . And some women like foreplay you know, if you creative enough you can get foreplay with that fuckin' pap smears. Oh yeah all you got to do is say some shit like "Ah doc, can I get a breast exam before the pap smear. There may be a knot in this muthafucka (rubbing breast) why don't you check it out." I know I know, I know what you saying, "She's so fuckin' feminine and lady like. She's such a fuckin' lady." *(Def Comedy Jam* 1992)

Noticeably, before changing subjects in her act, Givens consistently goes back to her mark phrase—"fuckin' lady." When she struts across the stage or touches her breasts, she further removes herself from the realm of desirable woman and virtuous lady (white), but that is the point. She reminds the audience that she knows that boundaries are being trespassed. Consequently, she seeks to remake the definitions of gender and sexuality defining Black females.

Esther Iverem's review of *Queens of Comedy* understands that the subject matter and strategies of Black female comedy are dictated by trickster subjectivity and historical experiences of Black females too often ignored and repudiated by mainstream society:

> There is a particular sista thang. It's hard to describe other than we know it when we hear it. . . . At its best, it's speaking truth to power. On its coarser level, it's speaking truth about our raw humanity, which usually involves beatdowns, jail, sex, physical imperfection and the comedy of oppression. How else can we laugh HARD at someone being called an illiterate mother-f*$#&*? It is the coarser sista thang, the salacious tradition of Moms Mabley and Millie Jackson that fuel the often hilarious "Queens of Comedy" special.

Irverem's ability to understand the language practices and traditions of Black females' blue material in comedy alters her perception and enjoyment of the concert film. Unlike the previous criticism by male critics,[12] she delves into aesthetics of the show that are particular to Black females.

When African American female communities can throw off the shackles of language that seek to control and fix them in limited positions, they can move beyond oppressive situations. The performative ability to manipulate visual illusions, use the uncensored mode and the sacred/lewd trickster trait provides a systematic folk rejection of present canons of gender and sexuality. Symbolic lessons of Tar Baby and Br'er Rabbit exist in the comedy of African American female communities. Blue material acts as a cultural root meant to continuously evolve the communities, rather than demean them. These mechanisms provide African American females with trickster-troping measures to construe representations of their sexual desires and gendered identity in ways that are less traditional, and less limited, than mainstream feminist discourse practices.

Badd-Nasty

Tricking the Tropes of the Bad Man/Nigga and Queen B(?)

What is bad, carnal, nasty, freaky, tawdry, and taboo remains subjective, but the intangible tensions of anyone's "love bizarre" also stem from the variant possibilities of choice available for the object of one's desire. Preceding chapters revealed how trickster-troping permits Black women to use non-heteronormative means to express their heterosexual desires in opposition to white femininity, but those divisions only briefly assessed how trickster-troping might occur if Black females' desires were not heterosexual or supported by communal discourses of race and class. The work of exploring trickster-troping for the expression of queer desires begins in this chapter with the words of queer theorist Eve Sedgwick:

> It is a rather amazing fact that, of the very many dimensions along which the genital activity of one person can be differentiated from that of another (dimensions that include preference for certain acts, certain zones or sensations, certain physical types, a certain frequency, certain symbolic investments, certain relations of age or power, a certain species, a certain number of participants, etc. etc. etc.), precisely one, the gender of the object choice, emerged from the turn of the century, and has remained, as *the* dimension denoted by the now ubiquitous category of "sexual orientation." (*Epistemology of the Closet* 8)

Sedgwick offers an imperative analysis of gender as the advantaged object choice of desire that establishes the logic of sexual orientation. Though Sedgwick may be correct about how Western science has theorized gender of the object choice as the foremost marker of sexual orientation, Black female culture has been singing a different song about object choices all together, in less Eurocentric validated spaces. Whether it's Nina Simone's "See-line Woman" or Adina Howard's "Freak Like Me," gender has not always been represented as the object choice of desire in Black females' culture. These are the queer facts.

While we have recently accepted and began to theorize about the homosexuality of a Bruce Nugent, James Baldwin, Audre Lorde, or Samuel Delany in the writing and activism of African American culture, what critical and theoretical analysis can we offer for the Black bisexual, transsexual, transvestite artist and her/his work in the twenty-first century? As we will see in this chapter, human trickster tales in African American culture had already initiated this discussion, which Black formal analytical discourse had not been ready to broach with any real complexity until recently. Black folklore offers a realm of expression for queerness that is loving and monogamous; queerness that is masochistic and sadomasochistic; queerness that is transgendered and transsexual; queerness that is pornography and sex toys; queerness that is orgiastic and polymorphous; queerness that may be incestuous; queerness that is not reactionary, conservative, or defensive about itself because it is Black. Because "Black" is still trying to belong and find a place in the norm, rather than being abnormal, these folkloric machinations may be controversial in that they potentially threaten political objectives of Black nationalism. Yet trickster figures and their vernacular tendencies offer artists a way of explicating on the argument that object choice(s) for sexual desire need not be universal or coherent to gender or racial identities/identity politics.

As we've already seen throughout the first part of this work, dominant culture has offered a consistent characterization of Black female characters as outside the norm, while their own historical experiences tend to disrupt the logic of gender anyway. In the remaining chapters we will see how object choice(s) of Black women's sexual desire can lead to some Black women, in the register of the Black nation and the cult of womanhood, being labeled as wild women, nasty girls, freaks, jezebels, bad girls, and a host of other stereotypes when those object choices contradict with the political aims of the nation. Sedgwick, as well as other critics,[1] began criticizing the early nature of sexual identity politics to dismantle the very binaries that created inequalities based on sexual orientation. Because object choice is such a major factor in one's sexual orientation, any forms of culture that depart from normalized object choices adherent to gender logic (man & woman, woman & man), as well as race, class, and national boundaries, deserve to be examined for their radical rhetoric and representations of sexual desire.

The remainder of this book insists that Black females' cultural tendency to explore sexual desires outside of traditional heterosexual tropes of womanhood occurs through Black outlaw culture and illegal bodies presented in Black folklore and figures. The use of illegal Black bodies and outlaw culture in Black folk and oral aesthetics and figures forms a queer collective consciousness. In the works of Black female cultural producers, this queer collective consciousness is personified in the trope of a Queen B(?) figure. The Queen (B?) is this text's encompassing revision of three cultural folk and urban figures in Black women's communities: Queen Bee, Queen Bitch, and Queen Bulldagger. As this chapter argues, the Queen (B?) figure allows Back women to represent their non-heteronormative sexual desires so as to resist the negation of normality construed by mainstream ideologies and policies. Black female cultural producers embrace folklore's acceptance of shifting object choice to express sexual desires in an unlimited but coherent manner.

This chapter begins with an essential examination of why outlaw tricksters are necessary as a parallel discursive model to analytical formulations of sexuality and sexual representation. I then examine African American folklore stories about two trickster figures, the Bad Man/Nigga and Queen B(?), to understand, through a continued evaluation of manifest trickster traits, how we can comprehend variant sexualities in African American texts that are typically read as mono and heterosexual representations. Black female culture devises a theoretical framework for the trickery of a Queen B(?) figure, as opposed to the dominance of Queen Bee in Black female folklore. The Bad Man/Nigga and the Queen B(?) possess the wily guile of Br'er Rabbit, the brash outspokenness of the Signifying Monkey, and outsider subjectivities parallel to that of Annie Christmas.

However, as illegal pariahs of specific communities, the Bad Man/Nigga and Queen B(?) characters draw their appeal from breaking and crossing boundaries. Traditionally, the boundary crossing is represented as breaking the law, but this work delves into the figures' breaking and crossing of established sexual boundaries of heteronormativity. As Huey Newton once said, "And maybe now I'm now injecting some of my prejudice by saying even a homosexual can be revolutionary. Quite the contrary, maybe a homosexual could be the most revolutionary" ("A Letter from Huey" 282). Consequently, the more sexual boundaries the Bad Man/Nigga and Queen B(?) cross, the badder (more transgressive and revolutionary) they become. The Bad Man/Nigga and the Queen B(?) set up folkloric sexual values and aesthetics in real life and cultural texts of Black lower-class culture that counter racialized sexuality and the heterosexualization of desire found in critical theoretical discourses of Black America. Despite that this text is primarily concerned with African American female culture, reconsiderations of the Bad Man/Nigga's gender and sexuality are also crucial to considerations of the Black female, since those reconsiderations destabilize binary gender conceptions. Yet folklore and vernacular traditions are not typically seen as referential models of discourse African Americans turn to for discussions of sexuality. Before Black folkloric analysis of sexuality can be discussed, other discourses in Africa America that have been used to disseminate information of sexuality, analytical models, need some explication.

Racialized Sexuality and the Heterosexualization of Desire

It has never been easy to create a critical agenda on Black sexuality, specifically queer sexuality. *Mutha*'s introduction explored the ramifications of nationalism on the study of African American folklore. In the case of sexuality, certain versions of nationalist rhetoric have hindered discussions of queerness and race. Object choices for sexual desire are often the conflicting foundations of these restrictions in nationalism. Afrocentric critics such as Molefi Asante and Frances Cress Welsing have demonstrated how uncritical African American critics would like to remain on the issue. Asante's most notorious claim was that "homosexuality doesn't represent an Afro-centric way of life" (66). Asante's words suggest tensions of homophobia in Afrocentric thought. Since Afrocentric thought has been defined as "literally, placing African ideals at the center of any analysis that involves African culture and behavior" (2), Asante basically asserts that a group of people connected through historical experiences of race and cultural lineage would all have similar sexual desires, no, similar object choices for their sexual desires. Not alone in his assessment of homosexuality and the African diaposra, Welsing was once lambasted by Essex Hemphill for her theory on Black male homosexuality as genocide introduced by white Western society (Hemphill, *Ceremonies* 57). Though Asante's and Welsing's concepts are continental in theme, their approach is nationalist. Sadly, a model of rhetoric created to liberate one faction of people often time lapses into a type of policing of the same group.

In "Black Nationalism and Black Common Sense," Wahneema Lubiano argues that "black nationalism is plural, flexible, and contested: that its most hegemonic appearances and manifestations have been masculinist and homophobic; that its circulation has acted both as a bulwark against racism and as a disciplinary activity within the group" (232). Though Lubiano classifies nationalism as a complicated and reactionary force that has supported (white) male supremacy, she also notes it as dangerously effective in mobilizing specific groups of Black people. Nationalism has the potential to unfetter oppressed people by organizing them around a common goal and a utopian narrative, but neither the goal nor narrative can be sustained if it becomes limited by one particular facet of a group's identity. As seen from Asante's comments on homosexuality, conflicts of gender, sexuality, or class remain in jeopardy of being dismissed or subordinated by activists for the greater good of "the Black nation," understood to be the developing heteronormative Black family.[2] The major problem with this approach is that the use of nationalism, by any group of people, risks becoming a tool of imperialism. Cedric Robinson notes in *Black Marxism* that nationalism "a second 'bourgeois' accretion, subverted the socialist creation . . . a mix of racial sensibility and the economic interests of the national bourgeoisies, was as powerful an ideological impulse as any spawned from these strata" (3). Robinson, in exploring why Marxism was so influential for key African diasporic leaders, makes an argument that demonstrates how nationalism, as perpetuated by the state, is in the interest of Western hegemony.[3] Robinson is not the only scholar to offer interrogations of nationalism helpful to this reassessment of sexuality.

In *Nationalism and Sexuality*, George L. Mosse focuses on the middle class and their obsession with respectability to expose the flaws of nationalism. Mosse found that "the middle class can only be partially defined by their economic activity. . . . For side by side with their economic activity it was above all the ideal of respectability which came to characterize their style of life" (4). The middle class constructs itself based on its moral values and the maintenance of its economic assets, but it is the quest for respectability that makes their performances of class, gender, sexuality, and race different from the rich or upper class. Yet lower-class communities, which have little or no access to money, erect communities around that which cannot be initially controlled by economics—cultural assets. And as long as lower-class people can maintain control over their culture, they establish values and morals based on their own practical needs, none of which is respectability as defined by the bourgeoisie. Mosse's historical claim reveals that the middle class, characterized as frugal, devoted, dutiful, and morally restrained, would come to see itself as better than the "lazy" lower class and the "extravagant and amoral" aristocracy. As Cedric Robinson uncovered in his analysis of Black Marxism, these claims are just as relevant and applicable to Black people.

From 1920 to 1960 in Black America, Carter G. Woodson and E. Franklin Frazier also demonstrated that these concerns of respectability and normality existed in Black communities as well as modern Europe. "Lifting as we climb" and "talented-tenth" rhetoric and platitudes often fostered and encouraged ideals that supported aims of respectability and normality meant to contain the chaos of sexual passion. In the still relevant masterpiece *Black Bourgeoisie*, Frazier speaks on the mission of respectability ingrained in formal higher education agendas for the "Negro":

> The young men, but more especially the young women, were to live chaste lives. To be detected in immoral sex behavior, especially if the guilty person was a woman, meant explusion. . . . The graduates of these schools were to go forth and become the heads of conventional families. Was this not the best proof of respectability in the eyes of the white man, who had constantly argued that the Negro's "savage instincts" prevented him from conforming to puritanical standards of sex behavior. (71)

In accordance with Robinson and Mosse, Frazier argues that the Black middle class's quest for respectability stems from a need to alieviate a "deep-seated inferiority complex" caused by their disidentification with and rejection of Black lower-class culture and society, as well as from their alienation endured because of the contempt of white America (27). Though Black people in the United States are denied full citizenship participation for centuries, it is the separate and developing Black nation situated on the margins that embraces nationalism with its penchant for respectability.

For African Americans, then, nationalism does not contain a readily available and different discourse about sexual desire than other Western schools of thought. The clamor for *the* Black nation is also projected onto the flesh in ways that demonstrate the connection between nation and family. Since nation is a macrocosm of family situated around geography rather than blood, sex, as an act solely for procreation, functions as a huge factor in historical and contemporary nationalist ideologies. Family, as understood within nationalist models, could grant Blacks their desired access to respectability. As critic Roderick A. Ferguson recently found, "African Americans' fitness for citizenship was measured in terms of how much their sexual, familial, and gender relations deviated from a bourgeois nuclear family model historically embodied by whites" (20). Subsequently, it is the Western nuclear family model that replaces a non-Western, communal family model and prohibits broad ideologies of gender, sexual desire, and identity in Black America.

The preservation of the nuclear family model, according to Jon D'Emilio, influences how individuals construct sexualities and communities:

> Only when individuals began to make their living through wage labor, instead of as parts of an interdependent family unit, was it possible for homosexual desire to coalesce into a personal identity—an identity based on the ability to remain outside the heterosexual family and to construct a personal life based on attraction to one's own sex. (8)

Although industrialism and urbanization in the age of capitalism may have been responsible for the changes the Western family undergoes, it seems evident that variations in family models, especially those that don't prioritize procreation, allow for certain queer communities. For Black communities, critics such as Ifi Amadiume, Stephen O. Murray, and Will Roscoe initiated studies of families and societies in African nations that opened the door to queer perspectives.[4] Essays by Eugene J. Patron, Cary Alan Johnson, and Gloria Wekker soon followed to offer methodologies that were African diasporic and queer.[5] Traditional nationalist rhetoric was absent from these endeavors. Hence, nationalism not only subverts socialism or other economic movements, it also seeks to preserve Western canons of gender and sexuality ordered by axiologically opposed and ranked binaries. None of this is mentioned to suggest that Black cultural nationalism be abandoned, but to remind us to be aware of the inherent risks to formation of sexuality in Western cultures. On the other hand, critical inquiries that take into account nonprocreative object choices of desire as well as nationalist concerns can lead to a wealth of new insights.

Bourgeois sexuality is not the only discursive framework influencing expressions of sexual desire in African America. In an alternate reading of Michel Foucault's *The History of Sexuality*, "Sexuality on/of the Racial Border," Abdul R. JanMohamed establishes his theory of "racialized sexuality," which can be defined as "the point where the deployment of sexuality intersects with the deployment of race" (94). Of racialized sexuality, JanMohamed claims, "Racialized sexuality, unlike its bourgeois counterpart, links power and knowledge in a negative, inverse relation: the perpetuation of white patriarchy and the preservation of its self-image require that it deny a 'scientific discursive' knowledge of its sexual violation of the racial border" (103). JanMohamed's definition of racialized sexuality does not shut down conversation on sexual desire in the way bourgeois sexuality does, but it instead focuses on early interracial sexual relationships viewed as illegal and immoral. White patriarchy's open secret of violating the racial order, which suggests slaves as inhuman, influences developing sexual discourses. The slave master's repressed sexual desire thrust upon Black bodies alters or undermines the race border, and the silencing of this border crossing inhibits the building of any type of positive analytic discursive models with regards to sexuality. In addition to undermining the race border, the slave master's desire also trespasses against the border of nation building. These transgressions make null and void any claims of moral superiority in the machine of U.S. imperialism and colonization: In that regard, the desires put in jeopardy capital and cultural gains of the developing United States. The open secret must be maintained at all cost.

Incidentally, any form of Black nationalism that ignores sexuality in its rhetorical framework helps maintain the open secret of sexual transgression of the racial border. White supremacy and imperialism gain ground, even in a discourse created to destroy it, such as Black nationalist rhetoric. In addition, as sexual customs and behavior in African America evolve, open-secret logistics also make deviant and abnormal any type of sexual desire that does not uphold the values of a bourgeois nuclear mold. Subsequently, African America's reliance on monolithic nationalism creates a defensive posturing against the silence and repression at the core of racialized sexuality. The leaning toward unitary nationalism often works to counter the problems of racialized sexuality by favoring a strict adherence to the heterosexualization of desire as delineated by Judith Butler:

> The heterosexualization of desire requires and institutes the production of discrete and asymmetrical oppositions between "feminine" and "masculine," where these are understood as expressive attributes of "male" and "female." The cultural matrix through which gender identity has become intelligible requires that certain kinds of "identities" cannot "exist"—that is, those in which gender does not follow from sex and those in which the practices of desire do not "follow" from either sex or gender. (*Gender Trouble* 23–24)

Butler's point demonstrates how gender influences discourse on sexuality. In order for the logic of gender constructs to remain logical, sexual desire must follow the same pattern of binary oppositions. If man is to be man, then he must be sexually attracted to his opposite, woman. However, Butler's position needs to be developed a bit more when we take into consideration the experiences of African Americans. Whereas Butler observes that fixed gender constructs and hierarchies have to be sustained through the heterosexualization of desire, something quite different occurs for African American culture. While gender may be latently fluid, the construction of sexuality in Black culture struggles against such liminality. In African American culture, the heterosexualization of desire is not simply a result of the cultural matrix of gender identity. It is the result of a complex cultural matrix of the open secret of this othered sexuality.

Racialized sexuality has created a separate logic of intelligible gender in African American communities. Rather than destroying the Western constructs of sexuality that have consistently othered Black bodies to set off its "normative" sexual codes and behaviors and the heterosexualization of desire, Black critical discourse has often accepted and absorbed the detrimental blanching discourse. The possibility of sexual fluidity that exists because of the flexibility of gender in Black communities continues to be displaced by an agenda to present Black people as "normal" and respectable. For instance, when Asante claims that homosexuality does not represent Afrocentric thought, he attempts to preserve "authentic blackness" by maintaining the heterosexualization of desire. Such tactics revert back to the strategic silences of racialized sexuality. In taking JanMohammed's concept further, we should complicate the issue by noting that his theory begins the exploratory work on racialized sexuality by positioning it in a heterosexual matrix. Due in large part to his thoughtful analysis, we can now extend his theory to a queer matrix to explore how his conception of sexuality impacts other Black communities, as well as "heterosexual" African American communities. In the end, racialized sexuality creates an environment in which Black people's sexuality cannot evolve as a healthy and positive aspect of Black life as long as its existence rests on foundations of normality and respectability.

When we give in to the open-secret dynamics of racialized sexuality, we blind ourselves to the reason for such logic and maintain an order of gender and sexuality that oppresses. Of analytical discourse, Ferguson has proven with his queer of color analysis that "an ideology has gathered in the silences pertaining to the intersections of race, gender, sexuality, and class" (5). Arguing historical materialism and liberal ideology as the culprit, Ferguson notes that the distinctions between normative heterosexuality and nonnormative gender and sexual practices emerge from the field of racialized discourse. As a result of such binaries, as long as Black family and sexual relations remain abnormal white heteronormativity can flourish. To eliminate these ideologies, we must speak about what was once made silent. Allowing sexual desires to continuously occupy a private and intimate space, rather than a public and political space, has done more harm than good for African Americans. Here, it becomes crucial to admit the difference between public desires versus stereotypes and representations. They are not the same. Critics concerned with respectability and nation building "rescue" Black sexuality from racialized, othered, and non-heteronormative ideologies by vehemently clinging to the puritanical or the open-secret approach to sexuality and the heterosexualization of desire, which then fosters homophobia in the process.[6] Any critique on the presentation of Black sexuality must acknowledge the presence of racialized sexuality, and then acknowledge the inclination toward the heterosexualization of desire as a response to it. In order to disturb Western constructs of sexuality in African American cultural texts, cultural producers have to perform three specific tasks: overturn racialized sexuality, uproot the heterosexualization of desire, and explode the binary of hetero/homo in sexuality. The remainder of this chapter asserts that the comprehension and use of Black folklore culture allow Black female cultural producers to complete these three tasks to address the sexual desires of a wide range of Black female communities.

JanMohamed reminds us that "sexuality on the border was not a construct that could be administered through analytic discourse" (104–105). While JanMohamed's analysis of Richard Wright's *Native Son* demonstrates how one Black writer found a way to discuss racialized sexuality through less analytical and scientific discourse such as fiction, this work returns to trickster's narrative as "cosmic shit" (Vizenor 7). Vulgarity, profanity, and uncensored mode of a sexual theme characteristically return this study to the trickster as bad, bedeviled, and communal id. There is no better way to destroy the detrimental elements of racialized and bourgeois sexuality on Black female desire than to corrupt it through the very vein which it attempts to control and repress sexual desire, culture. Fiction is one discursive method African American communities use to deconstruct racialized sexuality, but African American writers all too often return to folklore traditions of trickster to do so.[7] Nationalist rhetoric may be a way of policing ourselves in regard to gender and sexuality, but folklore and vernacular have consistently provided those willing to break the social laws with a public rhetoric to call our own. For what can't be whispered of in uplifting Black culture can be shouted about to the tin roof of outlaw culture.

In African American trickster tradition, graphic and explicit sexuality is saved for the most formidable tricksters, Bad Man/Nigga and the Queen B(?). Part and parcel of the same genres of folk ballads, songs, and myths, the male tradition of the Bad Man/Nigga is better known due to the works of critics such as Roger Abrahams, John W. Roberts, Daryl C. Dance, and Robert Levine. But both these folk outlaws gained their notoriety in outlaw society and cultural venues. Toasts and trickster tales about figures such as Queen Bee and Pimpin' Sam become iconic and gain notoriety from a communal embrace toward the absence of privacy. Zora Neale Hurston's analysis of Black folk expression also rejects the terms of open-secret sexuality: "Likewise lovemaking is a biological necessity and an art among Negroes. So that a man or woman who is proficient sees no reason why the fact should be moot. He swaggers. She struts happily about. . . . Then if all his world is seeking a great lover, why should he not speak right out loud" ("Characteristics of Negro Expression" 39). Hurston's statement does not assign this boisterous attitude about sexuality to the male gender alone. Black lower-class communities refuse to exhibit the clamor for respectability, and they will not engage in the detrimental silence surrounding sexuality. This proclivity for the absence of privacy makes those who practice the art outsiders or outlaws to the overall goals of a community or nation concerned with respectability.

Still, as newly freed men and women, early twentieth-century working- and lower-class Blacks understood how silence or prudishness could be another type of bondage. Rather than reiterate sexual stereotypes about Black sexual prowess, Hurston focuses on the rhetorical modes surrounding sexual discussion in Black folk communities for good reason. The sexual bravado created from the absence of privacy counters models of sexuality explicitly derived from enslavement, particularly open-secret models. In this way, Black sexuality resists being the repressed open secret of the evolving Black nation or the taboo of white America. The folk outlaws demonstrate how sexual variation is encouraged by illegal daring in the face of nationalist policing.

Tricking the Tropes of the Bad Nigga and the Queen(B?)

Hurston's attention to public declarations of sexual prowess should not be taken lightly. It is these declarations that connect orality to issues of performance that are significant to many discussions of queerness. Annamarie Jagose's *Queer Theory* provides a discussion of queerness that enlightens the roles folk outlaw figures may play in sexually destabilizing heterosexuality in Black America:

> Broadly speaking, queer describes those gestures or analytical models which dramatize incoherencies in the allegedly stable relations between chromosomal sex, gender and sexual desire. Resisting that model of stability—which claims heterosexuality as its origin, when it is more properly its effect—queer focuses on mismatches between sex, gender and desire. Institutionally, queer has been associated most prominently with lesbian and gay subjects, but its analytic framework also includes such topics as cross dressing, hermaphroditism, gender ambiguity and gender-corrective surgery. Whether as transvestite performance or academic deconstruction, queer locates and exploits the incoherencies in those three terms which stabilize heterosexuality. Demonstrating the impossibility of any "natural" sexuality, it calls into question even such apparently unproblematic terms as "man" and "woman." (74–75)

Jagose's focus on model stability, performance, incoherencies, mismatches, and analytic frameworks occurs in institutional discourses as well as popular discourses. Though queer studies have been evolving over the last few years to do exactly as Jagose notes, to undermine Western principles of gender and sexuality, the field has only recently begun to conceptualize the way that class and race impact the issues of sex, gender, and desire for people of color.[8] Even so, we should not be completely satisfied with these efforts and continue to seek cultural artifacts that posses an agenda similar to that of queerness, but one with strong connections to Black cultural input. As Barbara Omolade acknowledges,

> Sex between black women and black men, between black men and black men, between black women and black women, is meshed within complex cultural, political, and economic circumstances. All black sexuality is underlined by a basic theme: where, when, and under what circumstances could / would black men and women connect with each other intimately and privately when all aspects of their lives were considered in the dominion of the public, white master/lover's power. (*Rising Song* 57)

These tensions of public versus private realms also shift any discussion of African American sexuality into discursive realms of queerness. Yet before the articulation of queerness, Black folklore and myth offered similar functions. By analyzing Bad Man and Queen B(?) myths, we can learn how Black America deliberately chooses to use folklore and myth, as opposed to the analytical models associated with queerness, to exaggerate incoherencies in the presumed established connection between biology, gender, and sexual desire. For Black people, the private and personal performance of race, gender, and desire remain influenced by numerous dominant public discourses. Nevertheless, African American folklore countered with its own logic meant to call into question the logic of "man" and "woman."

Animal tales once again show how to reject oppressive influences over sexual desires. For example, in "Shoot the Habit," Black America revisits its favorite animal character:

> Papa rabbit, you know, he got kinda tired. He won't for no stuff, you know. And so Papa Rabbit told Mama rabbit, he say, "Look here, honey, Screwing ain't nothin' but a habit!" She say, [very sexy, seductive tone] "Well, shoot the habit to me, Rabbit" (Dance, *Shuckin' and Jivin'* 116)

Clearly, this is not the beloved and family-oriented Br'er Rabbit tale informing Blacks on how to get over on master during slavery. However, considering the numerous intercourse euphemisms associated with rabbits and reproduction, it is very surprising to note that there is little investigation that connects such euphemisms to Black folklore tales of Br'er Rabbit.

As we have already observed in other chapters, critics are quick to point out how Br'er Rabbit and other animal tales in African American folk communities teach about everything from race and class, with no mention of gender and sexuality. Yet the short tale "Shoot the Habit," like any other animal trickster tale, offers a lesson. It stresses sexual desires of both male and females as equally important. When Papa Rabbit attempts to deflate and put off the sexual needs of Mama Rabbit, she coyly uses his own words to show that she will not be deterred. Regardless of the aims of Black political rhetoric, Black folklore records radical sexuality and its discursive mechanisms in Black communities.

Daryl C. Dance's collection *Shuckin' and Jivin': Folklore from Contemporary Black Americans* contains numerous accounts of sexual fluidity in Black folklore, especially in the section entitled "Are You Ready for This? Miscellaneous Tales" (274). Dance's well-known collection is important for preserving Black folklore that will yield a wealth of possibilities for future scholars. While Dance's collection contains dates mostly from the 1970s, the fact that some of the tales have been recorded in other folklore collections dating back to the 1910s reveals the repetitious tendency of oral culture, even in its revisions for contemporary culture. The tales are also told by male and female informants of all ages. In addition, the idioms and slang also date many of the tales in very obvious linguistic registers assigned to certain decades.

The tales in "Are You Ready for This?" are very ribald, make heterosexual assumptions, and contain noticeable homophobic sentiments. Despite some of the problematic characteristics, a number of the tales present a wide range of sexual desires and bodily functions. The specific title of the chapter in Dance's collection warns the reader not to make any sexual or moral assumptions. In one tale, we find a satirical, less judgmental tone about homosexuality and sodomy. Three men are in court and a judge looks at the first man and asks, "Well, what you here for? " The man replies, "For eatin' PEACHES!" The judge then asks the second man what he's in for, and the second man gives the same reply as the first. The judge then asks the third man, "Well, who are you?" and the third man replies, "I'm Peaches" (274). The tale operates on the basis that the reader will not make the necessary assumptions about the three men presented at the beginning. Eating peaches could refer to eating fruit, or, if we are making heterosexual assumptions, it could very well refer to the male's performing oral sex on a female whose name is Peaches. Yet those assumptions are destroyed by the third male, who reveals that he is Peaches and that same-sex desire exists in Black communities.[9]

In either case, this African American folk tale represents sexual desires that might be considered outside the norm in an illegal and outlaw domain, but it does not reprimand or negate those desires. In the language of dominant society, conveyed through laws, statues, arrests, and court cases, oral sex, and especially same-sex oral sex, are morally wrong and criminally punishable. However, Black folklore culture manages to acknowledge individual desires and community aspirations at once while avoiding the repression of sexual desire. Though these men are clearly in court on sodomy charges, no qualms exist about the presentation of three Black men as partaking in homosexual activity. The tale implies that the only crime committed comes with being caught. It is a bawdy tale of humor; the punchline and release of tension through laugher arise from the inclination to heterosexualize desire, not homophobia. The three men do not meet the expectation of heteronormativity, and that is a laugh of resistance in the face of dominant racialized and bourgeois sexual discourses. It is also interesting to note that Dance collects the oral stories without making judgments about the object choices of sexual desire exhibited by characters.

Another tale from the Dance collection reveals the idea of sexual fluidity and the evocation of homophobia in the Black communities. Ironically, "I'll Show You How Straight I Am" parodies the vain and comical inclination toward the heterosexualization of desire in African American communities. When two males are drinking one night, and one man sexually touches the other on the buttocks, the offended man argues, "I don't go for that!" The other man then replies, "Look, I'm a all-right guy cause, look, I'm married and got three kids. I'll tell you what I'll do. Sunday you come by my house, and I'll show you how straight I am" (275). This particular tale also exposes the fatalistic flaws of bourgeois assumptions about heteronormativity. The "all-right guy" really means respectable, connoting heterosexual, man. The intelligible logic behind the biological aims (breeding) and social formations (marriage) and performance of gender are supposed to align sexual desires in their appropriate boxes. When the offended party goes to the married man's house, trickery abounds. Upon arriving at the house, the single man is left alone with the man's wife, who pretends to seduce him: "She say, 'Come on.' She went into the bedroom. She took off all her clothes. She say, 'Look don't worry about 'im. Don't worry bout im. You come on. We kin get a quick one in before he ever get back'" (276).

At this point in the narrative, if the listener/reader is making any moral or heterosexual assumptions, she is not prepared for the ending of the tale, in which the "all-right guy" goes from proving how straight he is to using his wife as a strategy to appease the desires of his indeterminate sexual subjectivity. In order to prove himself, he convinces the male who proclaimed his heterosexuality to have intercourse with his wife:

> So he say, "Okay, okay." He took off his clothes and got in there [on top of her]. She put her arms around him like that [very tight embrace around his neck]; legs aroundim like that [she locks her legs tightly around his waist, holding him firmly in a position with his posterior up in the air], and then she hollered, "Okay, George—I got im! Come on an get him!" (276)

With the wife's act, the heterosexual jig is up. From the beginning of the story, the moral implications of both men might be considered flawed in mainstream society or culture. The bisexual male has an open marriage, and the heterosexual male doesn't seem to have any moral dilemmas about forsaking the sacred bonds of the stranger's marriage for his own sexual gratification. The wife's sexuality is also not clearly heterosexual or homosexual. None of this behavior would be definitively described to be heteronormative, but the tale itself serves as a welcome discourse away from Black sexuality obsessed with respectability and representations of normativity. Folklore and vernacular tradition present fewer restrictions for desire and also demonstrate society's reactions to those liberties.

However, folktales and toasts do sometimes reveal the ever-present existence of homophobia in Black communities. If the intent of their telling is to shame non-heteronormative actions, does that contradict the importance of how their very existence historicizes and explicates on queerness in communities that typically withhold such discussion in political discourses? A close reading of the previous tale also underlines several flaws with the recognized and acceptable presentation of desire and sexual orientation in African American communities. The character educates its audience about the way some men in Black America conceptualize masculinity and same-sex desire as distinctly different from sexual orientation or identity. Nevertheless, if placed in terms of orientation, the man positioned as homosexual may be seen as the stereotypical homosexual who is always attempting to trap the "normal" and "straight" man. Yet he destroys dominant stereotypes of homosexuals as highly effeminate and limp-wristed. He also destabilizes the nuclear family model of the respectable bourgeoisie. After all, marriage and family are supposed to contain any sexual desires, especially queer ones, and allow Black men and women to get their due. Yet the joke is that it does not restrain sexual desires. The real sly man on the make, who will do anything to seduce another man, is married to a "nice, fine wife" and has "nice kids. . . . three o' them" (276). The story's presentation of trickery for sexual conquest destroys preconceived notions of homosexuality and heterosexuality. The binaries are further disrupted by a wife who knows of her husband's fluid sexuality and helps him trick the man whom her husband desires. With no aspirations to achieve nuclear family modality, this married couple reconfigures its marriages to incorporate polymorphous sexual desires.

It seems important to note that these tales are presented in folklore, rather than in the analytical works of the African American community. The folk, oral, and vernacular provide a much needed and distinct commentary on sexuality and the representation of sexuality in Black communities. However, many more tales demonstrate that polysexuality has long been a theme in African American folklore, especially because of the way the discourse of sexuality and race intersect with each other. Thus, Black folklore acknowledges the racialization of sexuality and sexualization of race in ways that many written texts cannot. As JanMohammed disclosed earlier, analytical texts, especially as they concern African Americans, could never conceive of sexuality on the border. Clearly, the vernacular offers revised readings of sexuality. As Dance's chapter title suggests, we need only be ready for them.

In returning to the trickster figure's form as male and female and sexually ambiguous, we must appreciate the central figures in African American folklore that still possess those qualities of sexual fluidity. In addition to risqué animal tales, interracial sex, and tales about everyday people, stories about cultural icons such as the Bad Man/Nigga and Queen B(?) prominently figure into presentations about variation in object choices of desire for Black people. In *From Trickster to Badman*, John W. Roberts discusses how the Bad Man/Nigga tradition in Black folklore serves as the "transformation of the trickster tradition or the trickster as proto-outlaw" (185). I do not intend to argue against that point or prove further Roberts's conclusions that "trickster-like behavior became associated with black badmen" who "could offer individuals adaptive behavioral advantages in retaliating for their economic exploitation and persecution" (198). Roberts's text acknowledges how trickster-like activities deemed illegal create economic advantages that might not be possible otherwise.[10] This chapter agrees with his conclusion and moves on to discuss how Roberts's belief allows us to trick the traditional trope of the Bad Man/Nigga as it relates to sexuality.

It may seem inappropriate to include the role of the Bad Man/Nigga in this assessment of Black female culture, but it is a warranted inclusion. The Bad Man/Nigga influences the culture and lives of Black women of various genders and sexualities. Further, given the recent interest and work being done on female masculinity, if there is to be more work done on Black female masculinity, then the Bad Man/Nigga figure has to be broached. Its inclusion also allows this text to not make the mistakes of previous studies. Although trickster actions of the Bad Man/Nigga enhance the material values for Black individuals through outlaw behavior, the figure also creates a sociocultural environment in which sexual activities and expression become less shaped by the society's moral standards and conceptions of sexuality. Some critics account for the trickster's sexuality in Black folkloric figures by implying that the sexual bravado and hypersexuality of these figures remain symbolic of the trickster's original variant sexuality.[11] One of Roberts's major point in the configuration of the Bad Man as trickster demonstrates why the Bad Man/Nigga and Queen B(?) as potential disruptors of sexual boundaries in Black communities are understudied in Black culture:

> [I]n transforming their conception of the trickster to create a folk hero whose actions unfolded primarily in the black community, African Americans had to be concerned with the consequences of condoning behaviors that potentially threatened both their communal values and the well-being of its communities. (199)

Since the very notion of folk figures derives from the folk (lower class), Roberts's statement concedes that the well-being of the community acts as a significant force in the potential destruction of sexual borders. We must ask what African Americans and who defines the communal values and well-beings?

Tricksterisms only threaten the well-being, that is, the actual or potential material wealth and social status, of Black communities who embrace the values embedded in white supremacy systems of imperialism and capitalism. This possible threat to communal values explains why the existence of sexual mutability in theories of such tricksters as Eshu and the signifying monkey remains largely unaccounted for in studies of Black culture. It is imperative to ascertain how specific figures expose the flaws of these communal values in terms of broader African American communities. One major benefit of rereading the Bad Man/Nigga and the Queen B(?) tropes in Black cultural texts is the location of a cultural mechanism that moves Black art away from an agenda to represent Black people as heteronormative to other communities. As outsiders, the figures allow Black communities to question concepts of sexuality in a culturally specific manner.

One of the most crucial ways to do so comes in tricking the established heterosexual trope of the trickster in African American folk narrative, the Bad Man/Nigga—John, Stackolee, Billy, or Benny. Daryl Dance notes: "That the term Bad Nigger from its beginning had positive connotations to certain Black people and negative connotations to white people suggests its early meaning as a Black man who fought against the system" (*Shuckin' and Jivin'* 224). Dance's assessment discusses the racial implications of the Bad Nigga. Our exploration of the sexual inferences suggests that the heterosexual trope of the Bad Nigga exists because critics tie it to a heroic tradition of Black males defeating the white power structure. In addition to violent actions taken by this character, his hypermasculinity is consistently evident. The super prowess of the Black male in Bad Man/Nigga tales consistently seeks to move beyond the subordinated male identity that might come with racial oppression, which is still highly contradictory. As Dance notes, Bad Niggas "are sexual supermen, but their women are enemies to be conquered, humiliated, and controlled rather than loved" (225). The hostility and sexual aggression toward Black women presented in these tales work to highlight the heteronormative pattern of behavior by Black males. Yet many Bad Man/Nigga figures adhere to traditional definitions of trickster's polysexuality, even if the tales seems superficially devoid of the other basic characteristics, ambiguous and anomalous sexuality. We must remember that the Bad Man/Nigga exists as a trickster figure, and seriously reread him in terms of the crossing of racial and sexual boundaries by other Bad Man/Nigga figures in Black cultural texts.

Traditionally, critics assert that the system the Bad Man/Nigga fights against is simply a racist or white supremacist system of oppression. However, if we delve deeper into these tales, we realize that the Bad Man/Nigga cannot disrupt systems of white supremacy without disrupting other ideologies within those systems. Consequently, the Bad Man/Nigga, without purposely being constructed to do so, disrupts the boundaries and borders of sexuality in order to disturb the oppressive racist ideologies detrimental to his community. When the notorious Dolemite proclaims himself the Bad Man, white supremacy is not the only system running scared:

> I got a job in Africa kicking lions in the asshole to stay in shape. . . . I fucked a she elephant till she broke down in tears. . . . I could look up a bull's ass and tell you the price of butter. . . . Even fucked the same damn cow that jumped over the motherfucking moon. (*Shuckin' and Jivin'* 231)

We can be sure that wreaking havoc on bourgeois sexual values and disturbing those dominant ideologies of sexuality are other goals of Dolemite's rant. His physical strength and bravery surmount the king of the jungle. But he is not all prowess and sexual charm; he is also intelligent enough to accomplish deep scientific and logistical information. His sexual baddness moves beyond gender into species. The trickster figure Dolemite uses bestiality, over the top at that, to accentuate how badd he is, and in doing so proves that folklore incorporates an agenda of queerness into its tales. Dolemite may not appear sexually ambiguous, but he is sexually anomalous.

In "Stackolee" or "Stag-O-Lee" tales, homoerotic and homosexual behavior surface the "badder" Stackolee tries to become. Even in death, the Bad Man/Nigga's baddness ignores the established binary boundaries of sexuality. After being killed by Billy, Stackolee dies and goes to hell. In hell, he has intercourse with the devil's wife, daughter, and niece, and finally when he comes back to the devil's wife again, she proclaims, "Devil, get him down. . . . Get that motherfucker before he fucks us all" (Abrahams, *Deep Down in the Jungle* 112). Stackolee copulates with out-of-this-world, in human demons. He trumps Dolemite as the Baddest Man. The implication is that Stackolee is so badd (trangressive) that he would move beyond the established boundaries of sexuality, which suggest that he has sexual intercourse with women only, and move onto his same gender, or in the case of the devil, a being who is not even of this world. It is a credit to the power of nationalism and folkore research that this gender outlaw becomes emblematic of Black hypermasculinity and not transgenderism since the figure's actions remove it from male and female gender altogether.

In another version, Stackolee pushes the boundaries of heterosexual assumptions even more, when confronted by Billy Lyons. Billy exclaims, "You know, you bad motherfucker, I know your name is Stackolee," and Stackolee answers back, "And by the way, what's your name, look so fine?" (Abrahams, *Deep Down in the Jungle* 142). Stacklolee's comments about Billy's physical appearance cannot be dismissed. In tales about two Bad Men fighting it out, the implications is that the winner becomes the unltimate Bad Man, but the loser becomes his lesser, his subordinated woman (sweetheart). Stackolee makes such statements to provoke his competitor because he knows the provocative and taboo nature of such criticism. He uses these elements to weaken or disarm his adversary.

In other tales that Blacks tell about anonymous Bad Men/Niggas, it becomes very obvious that the sexual prowess and superiority of the Bad Man/Nigga reveals how racialized sexuality combined with the trickster's trait of hypersexuality shifts Black sexual desire beyond the borders of heterosexuality:

> A white man promised his daughter when she turned sixteen he would have her satisfied. After sending her several men who proved unsatisfactory, he finally sent up a black man who stayed and stayed. At midnight, while the father waited anxiously on the corner, his little son came down and cried out, "Daddy, daddy, you know that black man you sent home, well he done satisfied sister, sister sue, mary lou, he done packed me [had anal intercourse] and he waitin' on you, so get yo' ass down there." (Levine 333)

Criticism of this tale has explicitly focused on the Black male's supersexual stamina, while ignoring the queer implications.[12] Sexual stamina has little to do with sexual preference. Despite the othering that takes place in the tale, there is something quite compelling about the homosexual implications in the tale.

While the exaggerated sexuality of the Black male in this tale is stereotypically problematic, one cannot ignore how transgressing binary sexual boundaries attributes to the badness in the construction of Bad Man/Nigga figures. Reexamining the heterosexual troping of the Bad Man/Nigga in African American culture acknowledges these implications and the complications created from the intersections of race and sexuality. Black folk figures epitomize such knowledge. Because the Bad Man/Nigga's masculinity is a conscious performance of masculinity, hyped up as it is, the tales uncover a folkloric male gender to counter Western biological gender. This folk male gender does not adhere to the intelligible logic of gender that seeks to match object choice with "normative" models of gender. One might even argue that this folk male gender, like trickster, could easily switch to perform female gender in the same exaggerated manner it performs masculinity. Yet critical reflections of this fact in African American research have not been remarked upon. Rereading the Bad Man/Nigga in this way ensures that models of Black masculinity based on badd (good in a trangressive way) men can somehow acknowledge that gender and sexual hierarchies figure into evolving models of Bad Man/Nigga. Sylvester and RuPaul were/are some Bad Men for the way they expose gender as an illusion. Subsequently, Black drag kings can now also be figured into these discussions of Bad Man/Nigga. A female Bad Man/Nigga would certainly continue tropes established by Stag-O-Lee with noticeable revisions. After all, Black drag kings perform not only masculinity, but by virtue of their skin color offer references of hypermasculinity based on Black male bodies. Likewise, if one moved beyond the biological, one could also argue Black male drag queens as Queen B(?) figures. Remember, trickster's shape-shifting ignores gender. Though the folk tales and figures stop short of offering serious critique and criticism of the constructs of sexuality, African American writers who draw from Black folklore and oral traditions use their skills to manipulate such figures and tales to disrupt racialized sexuality and the heterosexualization of desire in their fictional texts. Manifest trickster traits allow them to do so. As a mechanism of "cultural guerilla resistance," these forms and their figures are Black people's "queer" discourse before "queer" can even be defined by the white academic masses.

According to Hynes, the trickster's trait of messenger and imitator of the Gods stems from its uncertain or impure birth between humans and gods, or gods and Gods. Subsequently, the trickster has "both divine and human traits . . . , can slip back and forth across the border between the sacred and the profane. . . . He may bring something across the line from the gods to humans—be it a message, punishment, and essential cultural power, or even life itself" ("Mapping the Characteristics of Mythic Tricksters" 40). While the Bad Man/Nigga focuses specifically on the masculinity in Black culture, this study locates its symbolic figure of folk queerness in several complementary models to the Bad Man/Nigga figure. The outlaw and illegal human tricksters in Black female culture are derivative of one major figure, the Queen B(?), for Black females.

The namesake Queen B(?) does not appear as a figure in African American culture, but the presence of Queen B(?) exists as a theoretical means of trickster-troping for Black women in many cultural contexts. Whether it's hip-hop's Lil' Kim, Gayl Jones's *Eva's Man*, Alice Walker's *The Color Purple*, Kasi Lemmon's *Eve's Bayou*, or Rudy Ray Moore's *Dolemite*, the Queen B(?) figure has been a part of African American communities for decades. However, sociological and popular discourses have named her everything from Sapphire and emasculating matriarch to welfare queen and chickenhead. Yet what these titles fail to encompass is a very specific class dynamic necessary for examining the issues of race, gender, and sexual desire. Although the Queen B(?) figure has its definitive roots in Black folklore and vernacular culture, its values and aims date back to and evolve from the historical trickery of Harriet Jacobs's designs for fulfilling and representing her own sexual desires. Where Bad Man/Nigga figures represent a revolutionary and boundary-breaking masculine tradition, the Queen B(?) serves as a parallel female tradition that exceeds the goals of the Bad Nigga tradition.

I propose that there are three intersecting tropes of the Queen B(?) figure that appear in African American culture, and these three tropes of the same figure are what differentiates Queen B(?) figures from other communities concepts of Queen Bees. The initialization of Queen B(?) allows "B" to serve as a representation of Queen Bee, Queen Bulldagger, Queen Bitch, all at once. As with the Black rhetorical tradition, the explicit meaning of Queen B(?) can only be obtained via the context in which the word is used, rather than the sound. Any use of the Queen B(?) figure as the Queen B(ee), Queen B(ulldagger), or Queen B(itch) emphasizes and embraces the destruction of white heteronormative social orders, and the dismissal of false bilateral ordering of sexuality. In recognition of this fact, spelling of the figure's title will be Queen B(?) to highlight the fluctuating position of this outlaw figure in African American culture. Before looking closely at each trope of the Queen B(?), it seems necessary to state the purpose of the Queen B(?) as I have theorized its existence in Black women's culture.

The purpose of the Queen B(?) in Black female culture is nuanced. First, Queen B(?) proposes sexuality as a work/play tactic. Yes, it's a binary, but not one with a conceptual order of ranking. Sexuality as a work/play tactic is the ideological balance of sexuality as an act of pleasure and joy and sexuality as an act of labor. Since sexuality, as Carole Vance claims, is "simultaneously a domain of restriction, repression, and danger as well as a domain of exploration, pleasure, and agency" (1), Queen B(?)'s exploration of sex as a work/play tactic is purposeful. If it suits their needs, then Queen B(?) figures can tip the balance of work/play in favor of one realm more than the other based on the particular domain she may be located in. Despite the empowering uses of the erotic and female sexuality as discussed by Lorde and exemplified by the symbolic healing of the body in Gayl Jones's *The Healing*, Black women understand that self-love and philosophical gains don't pay the bills. Thus the creation of Queen B(?) figures allows Black female cultural producers to provide a discursive constitution and improvisation of gender and sexuality to inform or change the oppressive material realities of their existence, as well as the metaphysical. Only shifts in power can do that. Understanding how sex can shift the dynamics of power within the interior of self and the exterior of society, Queen B(?) suggests that women theorize sexuality as work and play.

Even before Labelle sang the story of how a man "met Marmalade down in old New Orleans, strutting her stuff in the street" ("Lady Marmalade"), Black women were already theorizing sex as hard work! But . . . Sex is work. Period. Cynically, such statements remove all the joy and pleasure we tend to imagine sexual acts giving us. Yet from the various academics who have taken on the stereotypes of sexually wanton Black woman to the preacher's wife to sex workers on the ho-stroll, Black women have all been engrossed in sexuality as labor at some point in their lives. Our historical experiences as slaves and third-class citizens suggest that whether we are engaged in the production and distribution of sexual ideas and discursive practices, the distribution and production of sexual acts in the institution of marriage (hetero or homo), or as a form of self-employment, sex is work. With the politicization of sexual identity, sexual desire also becomes labor. With the marketing of sexual acts, sex becomes work. Queen B(?) figures exemplify that if Black women remember the shifting between sex as work and sex as play, they can create sustaining representations of the self that won't limit metaphysical and material possibilities. Queen B(?)'s use of the work/play tactic blurs the line between the two endeavors and dismantles the division between public and private discourse, an act that benefits many representation of Black female sexuality. To comprehend her sexuality as a tactic can mean unheralded opportunities, as explained by Michel de Creteau's formulation of a "tactic":

> The space of a tactic is the space of the other. Thus, it must play on and with a terrain imposed on it and organized by the law of a foreign power. It does not have the means to keep to itself, at a distance, in a position of withdrawl, foresight, and self-collection. . . . It takes advantage of "opportunities" and depends on them, being without any base where it could stockpile its winnings, build its own positions, and plan raids. . . . It must vigilantly make use of the cracks that particular conjunctions open in the surveillance of the propriety powers. It poaches them. It creates surprises in them. It can be where it is least expected. It is guileful ruse. (37)

As we will see, Queen B(?)'s construction of sex as a work/play tactic uses the cracks and poaches the borders organized by "the law of foreign power"—in this case, the terrain imposed on it and the foreign powers are racialized sexuality, the heterosexualization of desire, and the binaries of hetero/homo in sexuality. Hence, Queen B(?)'s other purpose in Black female culture.

Rather than being a promoter of strict binaries, Queen B(?) serves as a designation that other possibilities exist. Understanding the mutability of the figure, rather than fixing it in a specific heterosexual frame, allows us to understand how African American female cultural producers use it to portray various Black female sexual desires. My consideration of Queen B(?) can be deemed valid once we remember that like the Bad Man/Nigga, the Queen B(?)'s power stems from her rejection of heteronormative patterns of behavior for "women." The Queen B(?) myth alludes to baddness (imitating omnipotence and desecrating established sexual values) for Black females. The Queen B(?) folk myth presents female omnipotence through sexual desire, sexual freedom and independence, and violence carried out by deception and trickery.

The first figuration of Queen B(?), the Queen Bee myth, draws from ideas on insect mating behavior.[13] However, like many of its animal trickster tales, African American culture quite adeptly adopts the tale of the Queen Bee for its own rationalization of racialized Black female sexuality: "You know the Queen Bee kills the male after she finishes with him. That's right, use him and kill him . . . Yes, wham, bam, thank you sir" (Dance, *Honey, Hush* 24) In this brief folk tale, Black women telling the tale switch the tradition of baddness from the male to the female. The Queen Bee figure surfaces in early twentieth-century Black Harlem Renaissance social life and folk culture. Those tales relied on real-life versions of Black females.[14] Queen Bee's baddness stems from the violation of moral and legal laws. Whereas the Bad Man/Nigga unleashes his reign of illegality upon women and white communities, the Queen Bee releases her reign of baddness against all men and white power structures.

African American writers often incorporate such tales into their own fiction to further develop the mythology of the Queen Bee figure. In Gayl Jones's psychological novel, *Eva's Man*, the myth of the Queen Bee plays an important role in the search for identity of main character Eva Medina. Right before orally castrating her male lover to become a Queen Bee herself, Eva tells him: "There was a woman . . . called the queen bee. I don't even know what her real name was, but she was a real good-looking woman, too. People used to say she was marked, because she had three men, and each of them died, you know. . . . I guess she was sure too, because she met this man she was really in love with and killed herself" (73). Eva's revelation that she does not know the name of the woman called the Queen Bee supports the notion that mythical icons, while often based on real persons, displace the real with the myth over time.

Jones's Queen Bee may sound like a Black version of the Black widow, but sexual desires and the figures own end to her life differentiate it. One can't help but notice the similarities between the Queen Bee figure and Annie Christmas. The independence and assertiveness of the figures, and their acts of suicide as a solution for their indefineable subjectivity, position the two characters as one and the same. However, unlike Annie, Queen Bee's persona hinges on her ability to get many men to make love to her, knowing they would die (Jones, *Eva's Man* 53, 142). In any Queen Bee myth, sexuality becomes power to be wielded for protection, a door to independence and pleasure, and a marker of criminality and outlaw status. The potency of her sexual desire, perceived as abnormal by mainstream society, makes her murderous seductress. For Jones, the illegal act of oral sex places Eva Medina in a position to become Queen Bee. The act of sexual violence, the castration of her lover during oral sex, solidifies Eva's status with that of the mythical Queen Bee she discusses earlier.

Outside of literature, the Queen Bee figure is present in a number of Bad Man tales, though she is not always referred to as Queen Bee. She might be a prostitute, a barmaid, or a wise-cracking working domestic. Take for example the words of one Queen Bee figure in the toast "Pimpin Sam": "When you pimp me you thought you could fill me full o bull. But you can't look up a mule's asshole and see how big a load she can pull" (Dance, *Shuckin' and Jivin'* 235). Obviously, the utterance of the last sentence specifically signifies on an earlier Dolemite toast, in which that Bad Nigga figure boasted of being able to give the price of butter from looking up a bull's rear. While Bad Man/Nigga tales are filled with sexual violence and exploitation of Black females, they are also filled with Black female figures who give as good as they get. This includes sexual and violent retribution.

Queen Bee tales do tend to present the continued image of the Black female as hypersexual, and in a manner akin to that of the Bad Man/Nigga, we can see the remnants of bourgeois and racialized sexuality in one such Queen Bee folk moment:

> LeaElla and Deal were hanging out they daily wash one morning, when Deal was moved to ask LeaElla, a personal question. "Ella, I don't mean to pry. But girl, I been wondering, why did you have seven children by different mens and not marry a one o' them?" LeaElla snorted, "A man won't gonna make a fool of me twice." (Dance, *Honey, Hush* 349)

Folklore entailing Queen Bee imagery reflects the concerns of the Black female as a matriarch who has no need for the Black male. Like Annie Christmas, LeaElla seems very fertile. However, Annie Christmas's birthing of twelve sons does not contain any implications of moral judgment. For all we know, Annie could be the mother of sons fathered by the same man. Not so with Queen Bee figures. In its most denigrating critique and evolution, the Queen Bee becomes the depiction of two stereotypes: the lascivious Black woman and the welfare mother who has children by different male partners, although she never marries one.

The above tale comically depicts another Black woman's profound bewilderment over why another woman engages in such behavior. For Deal, marriage would put a stop to LeaElla's foolishness. The answer given, wrought with dry wit, compels readers to question the morals of LeaElla. Yet when we move beyond discourses of morality and heternormativity, LeaElla's response corresponds to a discussion also initiated by Hortense Spillers in critical commentary on the canonical discourses of gender: "Because black American women do not participate, as a category of social and cultural agents, in the legacies of symbolic power, they maintain no allegiances to strategic formation of texts, or ways of talking about sexual experience, that even remotely resemble the paradigm of symbolic domination, except that such a paradigm has been their concrete disaster" ("Interstices" 80). The discourse of matrimony and womanhood that deems LeaElla's behavior as wrong and immoral matters little to the life of LeaElla, primarily because of her race and class.

LeaElla's response indicates the need to exercise freedom and to establish the independence of her sexuality and body without worrying about propriety and respectability. LeaElla's response also suggests that the institution of marriage allows men to make fools of women. Men can pursue their dreams and desire within marriage, but women who do so are seen as bad wives or mothers. As we saw with Harriet Jacobs, Annie Christmas, and Harlan Eagleton, Black females' suspicion of the social contract of marriage appear very valid. LeaElla's concerns are no different. Although LeaElla was not previously married, her actions to avoid the institution offers that marriage hold no security or convenience to LeaElla or her children. Though she is the mother of seven children, LeaElla's dismissal of the validation of marriage indicates the Queen Bee's systematic rejection of heteronormative assumptions about male/female relationships and morals. Marriage for middle-class women might hold some sort of financial security, but for a poor Black woman it in no way guarantees such security. Selection of mates may be limited by a number of factors and, hardly invested in the idea of romantic love, LeaElla adheres to a Queen Bee belief that it is better to remain independent and broke rather than coupled and imprisoned. Further, if the goal is something other than financial security, such as autonomy, then a rich mate of any race might not necessarily mean true freedom.

Nevertheless, a certain amount of violence and death surrounds the Queen

Bee figure. In another tale, the trickery and sexual baddness of the Queen Bee figure lead to her downfall. In "That's Why I Poisoned Ya, Honey," a woman lies on her deathbed confessing her sins to her husband:

> She say, "But sumpin' else I want to tell you, honey. I haven't been true to you. I've had other men. Every time you'd go away in the morning, another man would come in, and he'd spend the day with me. And just 'bout time for you to come home, he'd just be leaving." . . . And the husband said, "Honey, huhn, huhn, I know that's why I poisoned ya!" (Dance, *Shuckin' and Jivin'* 149)

While the lesson of this Queen Bee tale suggests a lesson of adhering to marriage vows since the female figure dies because of her nonmonogamous lifestyle, the element of law breaking lingers. The Queen Bee representation in the folk seems as ambiguous as that of the Bad Man/Nigga. A positive view of Queen Bee figures can be ascertained by doing simple feminist readings of these tales. In each tale, the figure works to be economically and sexually independent and free. The case of violently killing the male acts as a defensive mechanism for Black females whose independence might be in jeopardy due to the ideologies of patriarchy embraced by males. Like the Bad Man/Nigga, the Queen Bee's use of the male becomes a way to retaliate for economic exploitation and persecution. As a result of the Queen Bee myth, polyamory, loving or desiring more than one husband or mate at a time, remains an underlying sexual theme in every Queen B(?) tale. Free from moral dogma ascribed by certain sects, Queen B(?) preserves trickster's variant sexuality, often defined as "excessive sexuality," for a female population. Loving and desiring without boundaries embraces a range of sexuality found to be unacceptable in some societies. Asserting a culture of polyamory allows the figure to set up a use value for sexuality that benefits the figure in every way.

The second configuration of the Queen B(?) figure is the Queen Bitch. Queen Bitch, a late-twentieth-century revision of the Queen Bee figure, mirrors characteristics of Queen Bee figures—with one exception. In most tales, Queen Bee has been either extremely comedic or perversely tragic. Queen Bee as presented in Annie Christmas tales and Gayl Jones's *Eva's Man* represents the classic tradition of a tragic Queen Bee figure. Even as such characters move from a state of victimization to empowering acts of violence to save themselves, neither is allowed to exist as outsiders in mainstream society. Annie Christmas dies, Eva Medina goes to an insane asylum, and LeaElla is represented as ignorant. On the other hand, the tale of LeaElla and the adulterous wife in "Tales about Women" found in *Shuckin' and Jivin'* represent the comical and unapologetic. Such characters remain in the Queen Bee trope, and never transition into other possibilities of the figure such as the Queen Bitch. Queen Bitch is as assertive, skeptical of monogamy, and economically independent as Queen Bee.

However, Queen Bitch does not come off as tragic or funny, but she does appear cognizantly militant and violent:

> I'm the one who can trick so fast
> Before you can wink your eye
> I pat and beat your ass
> Your know me Queen Bee
> Chicken-shit holders
> Come and get advice from me (Lady Reed, "Queen's Philosophy" album)

Queen Bitch boasts about her violent nature. The element of militancy stems from the trickster's perpetual nature of trickery. One need simply understand why trickster plays tricks to comprehend the concept of militancy in trickster tradition. As an outsider, trickster has the options of conforming or existing as a figure consistently on the defensive about its subjectivity and behavior. However, if trickster decides to avoid being placed in a position where it must prove itself to society or consistently seek approval of a specific community, the figure must combatively approach his existence. The art of trickery and deception, another manifest trickster trait, exists as a war strategy that allows trickster to always remain on the offense, rather than the defense. Playing tricks permits the figure to usurp the hierarchy of power in society on its own terms. When trickery in African American tradition is not submissive to dominant white society's regulations, like Br'er Rabbit's initial reaction to Tar Baby, it becomes militant. When it seeks to establish its own order, like the Bad Man/Nigga it militantly places the marginalized outsider at an advantage.

The Queen Bitch figure harnesses the aggressive tendencies of the Queen Bee and works to create its own social universe with it sexual desires in mind. Queen Bitch avoids being cast as the emasculating matriarch by incorporating an appreciation and understanding of male culture into her systematic dismissal and critique of that same culture. At the same time, Queen Bitch avoids the downfall of being too concerned with the constructs of womanhood and femininity: romance, dependency, chasteness, decorum, and fragility. As indicated earlier, Queen Bee, as seen in a film such as Rudy Ray Moore's *Dolemite*, serves as the comical Queen Bee. Although the figure is strong and physically overpowering, the combination of that with the comic absurdity of *Dolemite*'s exploitation aesthetics removes, or at the least inhibits, the understanding of political and social messages in such films. In addition,

Queen Bee was never the focal point of that film. As Joy James once said of blaxploitation's depoliticizing of the Black female revolutionary icon: "The image of Angela Davis as fugitive (we might also add former Panther leaders Kathleen Cleaver and Elaine Brown) became commercialized and sexualized in the Coffy/Cleopatra Jones blaxploitation films of the 1970s—the armed, revolutionary black woman as embodied by stereotypes (and phenotypes)" (124). James offers one valuable reading of how a Black feminist politic came to be negated in some of the blaxploitation films, but within some of those films we might argue that additional Black politics were offered as opposed to one limited replica.

Despite valid claims about commercialization, the sexualized revolutionary needs to be reexamined in the context of Queen B(?) myths and culture.[15] Although Coffy was the construct of a male filmmaker, Pam Grier's performance as Queen Bitch is what made Coffy different than Black female characters in other blaxploitation films. Even as some critics lambaste the presentation of sexuality with regard to these Black female characters, Coffy's dedication to her mission mixed with Grier's then revolutionary, unabashed love of her body and sexuality, signifies the very articulation of an evolving Queen Bitch figure with a work/play strategy. Again Creteau reminds us of the importance of tactic in the surveillance of the propriety powers: "It poaches them. It creates surprises in them. It can be where it is least expected. It is guileful ruse" (37). Grier's acceptance of the role and her performance sets aside a space to create a Black feminist politics that considers the play of desire as much as the political work of controlling images of that sexual desire. It also shifts Queen B(?) imagery from comical and tragic Queen Bee to militant Queen Bitch. Grier's Coffy moves beyond the Queen Bee figure to that of Queen Bitch precisely because the characters are not tragic or comic due in large part to their political mission. They are characters concerned with armed revolution in the hands of Black females. Although the characters may have been phenotypes, Grier's acceptance of the role does become an act of transgression. In the decades that preceded Coffy, Black women were asexual maids and mammies, sexual tragic mulattas, but because Grier performs the Black sexualized radical the mythical Queen Bee icon can evolve into the complex Queen Bitch persona.

Grier's roles never aligned with the conservative communal values of Black people at the time. However white America might have used the sexualized Black female revolutionary to further racial stereotypes, less conservative Black female culture intuited how this new fictional figure could impact its own culture. Grier's acceptance of her historical blaxploitation roles and her performance reveal a real-life dilemma for Black females who want to be both revolutionary and sexually open and assertive: how can these women dismiss the boundaries of private and public to fulfill and articulate their wants? As Bayard Rustin and other gay/lesbian civil rights activist showed, African American communities could not address this issue in real life, but Grier's decision to play Coffy, however monetarily motivated, forces us to. The fictional manufacturing and mythical configuration of blaxploitation Queen Bitches ask if Black females can be politically oriented and communicate sexual desires and use values of those desires outside of the heternormative aims of nationalism. The Queen Bitch figure offers a post–civil rights view of sexual freedom that was no longer on the defense, one that suggested pursuing your own individual sexual desires, whatever they may be, is political and sometimes revolutionary. As we will see in chapters 6 and 7 on contemporary Black women's music, that view carried over into the culture of another generation of young Black females in hip-hop.

As with the Bad Man/Nigga, the Queen B(?) figure occupies several spaces of sexual possibilities, but the trope of heterosexuality in the figure needs to be tricked and revised in order to use those other spaces to disrupt binaries in nonfolk discourses of gender and sexuality. The sexual liminality of the Queen B(?) figure comes from more than the presentation of exaggerated sexual prowess of Black females; it reverberates in the agenda of the Queen B(?)'s dismissal of a consistent male presence in her life to validate her existence. In any configuration of the Queen B(?) figure, male companionship does not take priority for the woman. While portraying a superficial heterosexual agenda, Queen Bee implicitly embraces a homosocial organization of community, and its subjectivity flirts with the boundaries of heterosexual/homosexual subjectivities. Further, Queen Bitch's militancy reformulates the use value of sexuality according to her material circumstances, in which the figure uses its sexuality to obtain something other than marriage or offspring.

Lucille Bogan was one of many blues women who performed this facet of Queen B(?)'s persona. In "Tricks Ain't Walking No More," Bogan sings about the streetwalker: "Times is done got hard, money's done got scarce,/Stealin' and robbin,' is goin' to take place./'Cause tricks ain't walkin,' tricks ain't walkin' no more." The Queen Bitch can easily resort to violence and sexual labor to support herself. Badd women always have options. Queen Bitch uses its sexuality for economic and political gain. Interestingly enough, perhaps these aversions to monogamous male-female relationships lead critics to also suggest that the construction of the Black lesbian serves as another evolution of the Queen B(?) in Black culture.

In another tale of a Queen B(?) figure, "At the Whorehouse," the tactic of sex as work/play expresses the morphing possibilities of Queen B(?): "Back in forty two when the poor man had nothing to do,/All the hoes had made plans/To fuck each other like a natural man" (Dance, *Shuckin' and Jivin'*

234). The phrase "fuck each other like a natural man" is a remark founded in the simplistic idea that lesbians are masculine women who desire other women. In response to possible unemployment of men, the sex workers within the tale have chosen to engage in same-sex acts for sex as play or pleasure to fulfill sexual desires. Further, ever cognizant of their financial needs they will not lower their monetary standards that men pay for sex to get the sexual play they desire. When a potential customer suggests paying "two bucks" for sexual intercourse, one sex worker exclaims, "Nigger, befo' I fuck for ten or less,/I'll cut my cock from under my dress/Hang it up on bamboo wire/Say, 'Stay there, pussy, till cock get higher'" (234). As it concerns her income, the sex worker will not lower her prices, for to do so means to compromise the power and independence she has gained from her current career. Elaborating on her sex as power, the sex worker makes a distinction between her genitalia (pussy) and her sexuality as commodity (cock). If her money-maker can't get the higher price it deserves, then her sex will not come down. The power the women enjoy comes in the knowledge that there are many opportunities made available by the tactic of sex. And lesbianism is pitched as a priceless one.

SDiane[16] Bogus's "Queen B in African American Literature" uncovers a unique and culturally relevant connection between "Queen B" and lesbianism. Bogus states, "Queen B is a euphemism for Queen Bulldagger or Bulldyker. Judy Grahn traces the linguistic and historical etymology of the word to the cunning female warrior of A.D. 61, Boudica (pronounced boo-uh-dikey-ay), a leader/Queen of the Celtic" (275). This particular queen led an uprising against Roman imperialism. Bogus then goes on to tie this etymology to the Black community by suggesting that Black cowboy Bill Picket brings the word "bulldogger," from his 1923 movie *The Bulldogger*, into Black culture. She asserts, "In time, 'bulldogger' mutated into bulldagger" (275). Queen B(ulldagger), like Audre Lorde's use of the Carricou word *zami*,[17] replaces the term "lesbian" (white female same-sex desire) with a term culturally situated in African America; one that can account for the historical experience of racism and heterosexism experienced by Black females with same-sex desires.

Bogus's research on the etymology of bulldagger in Black America is especially illuminating, but her assessment of Queen B(?) appears short-sighted because it fails to acknowledge other representations of the Queen B figure, not specified as Bulldagger, in Black folk culture. The Picket reference excludes knowledge that before 1923, there already existed in African American folk culture notions of the Queen B(?) that vacillate between heterosexual and homosexual representation. In this case, I'm specifically thinking of the Queen Bee that also surfaces during this same time. As we will see in a later assessment of Shockley's "A Meeting of the Sapphic Daughters," Bogus's Queen B etymology is a much-needed attempt to assign historical value to the representation of same-sex desire in Black female culture so as to avoid Western configurations such as Sappho or lesbian. However, as Bogus's work provides a racial framework, it still includes a Greek reference point.

This is not to suggest that Bogus's claim that the Queen B represents lesbian sexuality in the African American community is incorrect. As a matter of fact, Bogus attends to real historical Queen Bulldaggers like Bessie Smith and Gladys Bentley to explicate on her examination of Queen Bs in African American literature. Noticeably, all of these figures are singers (279–81) who disrupt the binary of sexuality.[18] Therein lies the space to extend Bogus's analysis of Queen B—Bulldagger. Queen B(?), as this text defines her, a trickster figure who cannot be bound by career borders. While we should accept Bogus's representation that Queen B—implies bulldagger/lesbianism, we must broaden our understanding of this particular figure outside of blues women and outside of the sexual binary of heterosexual and homosexual. We must also remember the Queen B(?)'s potential to deploy the sex as work/play tactic. Queen B acts as an African American oral mechanism of initializing the names or titles seen as too taboo to speak. Though Bogus's spelling of Queen "B" differs from the folk tale spelling Queen "Bee," it should be noted that in a culture based on orality and aurality, there is no difference in the pronunciations of the two titles. The sexual desires and meaning of the figure cannot be ascertained from its pronunciation; we must look toward the social context in which the figure might be located.

This text's revised reading of Queen Bee, Queen Bulldagger, and Queen Bitch figures in Black culture finds that these tricksters do not represent a fixed sexual identity for African American females. According to the trickster aesthetics of shape-shifting, the figures essentially serve as branches of a Queen B(?) figure that is meant to represent multiple Black female genders and sexualities, rather than the fixed definitions assigned by historians and located in long-established heterosexual readings of the figure. In addition, Queen B(?) remembers sexuality as a work/play tactic that can influence her material and ideological needs. Becoming the Queen B(?) means following one's object's desire even when it does not meet a society's or community's prerequisites of gender, race, or nation. Ironically, these Queen B(?) figures will disrupt racial constructs and rhetoric, in addition to sexuality and gender. For this reason, as we will see in the next chapter, Queen B(?) will consistently be deemed a race traitor, inauthentically Black, not Black enough, and the ever-popular "discredit to the race." Queen Bee, Queen Bulldagger, and Queen Bitch are three dominant militant myths and figures that operate in African American female culture. However, I suggest that they are merely factions of one huge looming trickster figure, Queen B(?), that acts as a Jungian-Radinian collective queer subconscious of Black female cultural producers who wish to remain unnnameable and unclassifiable so that they might continue to self-author their own subjectivity and sexual desires. Jung postulated of trickster's psychological function in communities:

> The figure works, because secretly it participates in the observer's psyche and appears as its reflection, though it is not recognized as such. It is split off from his consciousness and consequently behaves like an autonomous personality. The trickster is a collective shadow figure. . . . And since the individual shadow is never absent as a component of personality, the collective figure can construct itself out of it continually. Not always, of course, as a mythological figure, but, in consequence of the increasing repression and neglect of the original mythologems, as a corresponding projection on other social groups and nations. (*Four Archetypes* 177)

The existence of the three mythical figures is Black women's psyche, very conscious attempts to deal with issues of sexuality, race, and gender. As Bogus expounded, the benefits of examining blues women provides early evidence of how some Black women projected the three tropes of Queen B(?). However, the Queen B(?) figure is a reflection that notes the limitations of those single motifs due to increased repression and neglect by dominant white society and their own Black communities.

Queen B(?) serves as the in-between spaces of the representations and stereotypes of Black women. She is the trope where myth and fact meet, the shadowy existence and subconscious, and a figure meant to blur the lines between the private and public, as well as the personal and the communal. If Queen B(?)'s philosophy had to be translated from its myths and vernacular into a brief analytical philosophy situated in the language of wider communication, it might encompass the words of Luce Irigaray:

> You don't have to raise your impulses to the lofty status of categorical imperatives: neither for your own benefit nor for anybody else's. Your impulses may change; they may or may not coincide with those of some other, man or woman. Today, not tomorrow. Don't force yourselves to repeat, don't congeal your dreams or desires in unique and definitive representations. You have so many continents to explore that if you set up the borders for yourselves you won't be able to "enjoy" all of your own "nature." (*This Sex Which Is Not One* 204)

Because Queen B(?) is an outlaw she refuses to set up borders or adhere to any borders established by a majority. Queen B(?) serves as a trickster figure specifically invested in the radical play of gender expression and sexual desire. The mythological being exists to teach Black women how to enjoy all of their own nature. Queen B(?) symbolizes Black women's folkloric take on queerness. As David Halperin's *Saint Foucault* explains, "Queer is by definition whatever is at odds with the normal, the legitimate, the dominant. There is nothing in particular to which it necessarily refers. It is an identity without an essence. 'Queer' then, demarcates not a positivity but a positionality vis-à-vis the normative. . . . [Queer] describes a horizon of possibility whose precise extent and heterogeneous scope cannot in principle be delimited in advance" (62). Halperin stresses positionality as opposed to identity politics. Such representations move beyond the notion of thinking of the figures' sexual desires simply in terms of hetero or homo, but in the various ways that sexual desire can be expressed. Queen B(?)'s functional positionality makes it a perfect tool of trickster-troping for Black female cultural producers who wish to interrogate the terms and limits of binary sexual desires and create additional representations of Black females with same-sex desires.

Although this will be covered more in the next two chapters, a brief assessment of the Queen B(?) figure as a collective queer id can be gleaned by returning to the presentation of Queen B(?) in Gayl Jones's *Eva's Man*. To be certain *Eva's Man* is a psychosexual novel about the sexual abuse and emotional silences that occur in Black women's lives. The very meaning of the novel is still being debated today.[19] Set in a psychiatric prison, the institutionalized Eva Medina recounts the mythological status of the heterosexual Queen Bee figure in her childhood neighborhood. Yet in addition to the presence of that Queen Bee is the Queen Bulldagger, as made evident by Eva's cellmate, Elvira. If, as Jones postulates, through the voice of Eva, "The Queen Bee. Men had to die for loving her," then might we ascertain from the very vocal ending of Jones novel that with reference to Queen Bulldagger: Women had to live for loving her? Black women's liberating sexual representations hinge on how willing they are to integrate elements of Queen Bee, Queen Bulldagger, and Queen Bitch into their psyche and culture?

Since readers are privy to both the heterosexual and homosexual encounters that Eva has from a young girl into adulthood, and the sexual advances of Elvira throughout the text, the novel's ending with Eva's sexual submission to Elvira: "'Tell me when it feels sweet, Eva. Tell me when it feels sweet, honey' . . . I leaned back, squeezing her face between my legs. And told her, 'Now'" (177) bespeaks not a silence, but a vocal ambivalent presence that had been constructing itself throughout the text, the Queen B(?). In her mental embrace of Queen Bee and her eventual physical embrace of Queen Bulldagger, Eva embraces Queen B(?) and what the figure represents: sexual choice and freedom without abuse. Queen B(?) is the stressing of positionality over fixed identity. As a Black female, and one who was sexually abused, Eva's sexual identity was never fixed. The ambiguous narrative strategy of Jones's ending signals that Eva has not come to some finalized and essential identity while still maintaining her subjectivity. *Eva's Man* leaves Queen B(?)'s imprint.

In the end, Black women's culture hopes to continue the ultimate legacy of Queen B(?) that was left in the early twentieth century by Lucille Bogan. I turn now to Bogan not because of her career as a blues singer, but because Lucille Bogan explored this text's conception of Queen B(?) as a disruptor of the heterosexual/homosexual binary and as a facilitator of a sex as work/play tactic in many of her blues lyrics. She queered Black women's experience and captured the dynamic of their sexuality as engaged in sex as work/play tactic. In "Groceries on the Shelf," Bogan attends to sexuality as a commodity, by claiming, "My name is Piggly Wiggly, and I swear you can help yourself. . . . And you've got to have your greenback, and it don't take nothin' else."[20] Rather than compare her body to a temple, Bogan likens it to a Piggly Wiggly, a popular grocery store chain in the twentieth century. Her body remains ripe with sexual possibilities, but only if one has the monetary funds to go shopping.

Another song, "Reckless Woman," emphasizes the adventurous sexual nature of Queen B(?): "A woman gets tired, of one man all the time, Lord-Lord-Lord. . . . And don't care what you give her, you can't change her ramblin' mind." Here, reckless negates the polyamorous woman who would seek to enjoy new opportunities from time to time. Still, the classification of the woman as reckless can't take away the important belief in the freedom to love who or how many one wants to. Finally, Bogan's "B.D. Blues" laments the pejorative bulldagger's blues: "B.D. women, they all done learnt their plan. . . . They can lay their jive, just like a natural man." In a type of bluesy praise song, Bogan chooses to admire the smooth approach of certain lesbians in love games. Bogan embraced all of the tropes of Queen B(?) and helped create an archetype that other Black female cultural producers would discover for themselves.

In order to fully comprehend the trope of this figure in Black women's culture, this text's spelling and use of Queen B(?) acknowledge the initial uncertainty that comes with Black folklore's oral manufacturing of signifyin(g) through context. It also embraces Butler's "radical democratic notion of futurity," which allows the subject to remain open to rearticulations of any given identity that would shift with new political and personal contexts (*Bodies that Matter* 191). Queen B(?) seems emblematic of Black female culture's tendency to elude Western categories of gender and sexuality.

The Black and White of Queen B(?)'s Play

Emphasizing queerness as an essential and intersectional component in Black women's culture is important work, but if one wishes to be more specific and engage representations of Black lesbians within that intersectionality, the outlaw Queen B(?)'s presence and influence must be considered. While previous chapters expanded on trickster-troping as a mechanism that Black female cultural producers came to rely on to overcome silence, erasure, and invisibility, Evelyn Hammonds's question, "If the sexualities of black women have been shaped by silence, erasure, and invisibility in dominant discourses, then are black lesbian sexualities doubly silenced?" ("Black [W]holes" 303), effectively probes into the dynamics of doubling that would be incurred in attempting to produce distinct lesbian articulations and representations of sexual desire cognizant of race. Still, trickster-troping is the intersection of folklore, vernacular, and queerness, and the creative act makes it possible for queer Black women to resist passive categorizing of their sexuality and culture.

One solution posed by Sarah E. Chinn on the general invisibility of lesbians is to talk about how lesbians have sex with each other. For as Chinn argues, "If sexual connection with other women is at the core of lesbian identity, then accurately representing" lesbian "sexuality in some way is as close to a culture-making activity as we can get" (181). Although Audre Lorde's *Zami* showed how analysis of this culture-making activity offers irrefutable evidence of trickster-troping to vocalize desires that might be doubly silenced, there was also an earlier text that attempted to address the cultural representations of how lesbians have sex with each other in ways that complicate essentialist and authentic ideals of Black lesbianism or same-sex desire. This chapter examines Ann Allen Shockley's *The Black and White of It*, originally published in 1980, for the way it employs Queen B(?) figures as representations to counter the erasure of race from queerness and the devaluation of queerness in Black communities. I discuss trickster-troping as a folk process of unnaming gender, but further clarify Black lesbians unnaming of their sexuality as defined by Western models. I make use of the vernacular coding of the term "play" to further explore Queen B(?)'s sex as a work/play tactic, and I argue the presence of trickster-troping of situation-inversion and shape-shifting as the techniques used in Shockley's Queen B(?) tales to unveil the politics of racialized sexuality embedded in white lesbian narratives.

Ann Allen Shockley's "The Black Lesbian in American Literature" found that "the Black lesbian was a nonentity in imagination and reality" (83), and with her 1979 essay Shockley initiated a recovery of Black lesbian sexuality and culture with her brief analysis of pertinent texts of the time that included lesbian characters or themes. Since the essay was published before Lorde's *Zami* and only a few years after the pivotal publication of her own lesbian novel, *Loving Her*, in 1974, Shockley was dismayed and disappointed at the representations. She then suggests that African American women poets had done more for lesbian representation than African American women novelists. However, in her review of Black women's literature (1900–1970), it is apparent that the early representations of Black lesbians were shadowy figures, not simply out of shame and fear, but out of a sense of the lack of language to represent and speak about Black females with same-sex desire. Thus before Lorde finds a new spelling of her name in her biomythography, this failure of language to capture desire creates sketchy silhouettes of Black female same-sex desire. From this silhouette, Black female writers produce Queen B(?) figures, indefinite monikers, as a way to discern the modifications in analytical discourse about racial, sexual, or gendered identity that will occur over time. These figures are meant to call attention to lesbians, but also to the limited models of blackness and woman. As a way to demonstrate sexual freedom and independence, same-sex desire, and the ambiguity Black women may have felt with identifying as lesbian, Black women cultural producers consciously and unconsciously constructed Queen B(?) characters.

For example, how can we ignore the tense narrative of hesitant lesbianism in the works of Gayl Jones, specifically in her representations of Black women of all ages and backgrounds who at some point grapple with their porno-troped bodies, sexual identities, and sexual well-being? Or who could ever forget the maelstrom of controversy that occurred at Barbara Smith's lesbian reading of Toni Morrison's *Sula*? For Smith, a queer presence preoccupies that text in a way that the presence of blackness does for Morrison in American literature. Ironically, Morrison's own confession of aesthetic strategies of orality and tricksterism lends credibility to Smith's reading.[1] Silhouettes of Black lesbians existed not just in texts by so-called heterosexual Black women writers, but in the works of bold lesbian writers. In a discussion of her experience with and representation of interracial lesbian relationships, lesbian writer Judy Nicholson once noted her own personal experience with this predicament: "I do not know enough to love me, to love my blackness, and to love other black lesbians" ("Dear Sisters" 106). Positive depictions by Black women expressing same-sex desire for other Black women were infrequent. But always the Queen B(?) figure was there, if not as some character, in some idealized and utopian form or idea, like Afrekete or Zami, that writers hoped would reconfigure racial heritage, gender identity, and sexual desire. For if Black women writers were attempting to make the title "Black woman" work despite all the encodings of white womanness implicated in that, then think what a seemingly insurmountable task existed for Black women who wanted to depict and make real and honest Black females with same-sex desires.

After the publication of novels with complex Black queer women—*Zami*, *The Women of Brewster Place*, *Loving Her*, and *The Color Purple*—the need for figures who ideally allow Black women to embrace the object choice of their own desire does not disappear. The shadow or silhouette of the Black lesbian may be partially due to fear, shame, and homophobia, but it is also about an unwillingness to wholeheartedly accept and name their desires as lesbian—a white female subject with same-sex desire. In her dissection of queer sexualities, Hammonds noted two objectives that must be accomplished for exploring the intersection of queerness with Black female sexuality. The first project demands that "white feminists must refigure (white) female sexualities so that they are not theoretically dependent upon an ever absent yet-ever-present pathologized black female sexuality" ("Black (W)holes" 306). Hammonds's second point, and most important for Black women, states that "black feminist theorists must reclaim sexuality though the creation of a counternarrative that can reconstitute a present black female subjectivity and that includes an analysis of power relations between white and black women and among different groups of black women" (306). Enter the Queen B(?) as presented in Shockley's work and in her own writerly performance as Queen B(?). In Shockley's case, she uses her position as a Queen B(?) to hold white women accountable for creating a sexuality not dependent on pathologized Black female sexuality. Within her narratives, the Queen B(?) figure acts as a mechanism whereby Black women can create counternarratives about same-sex desires and reject the term lesbian. This is more evident in her lesbian collection of short stories, *The Black and White of It*.

In prefatory material from the short story collection, Shockley makes a statement about her title: "I know there are times when you have to think of the black and white of it" (1). What does that mean? The collection fictionalizes interracial lesbian relationships, but to read the short stories as simply taking on taboo topics of the time means underreading the text. *The Black and White of It* takes up the complicated interdependency of racial and sexual discourses to complete Hammond's two-fold project. Its goal is to depict Black women having sexual and loving relationships with other women, and sometimes those relationships might be with other women who are not Black. It compels readers to consider the issues of Black and lesbian authenticity. To dismantle those authenticities, Shockley relies on the characteristics of trickster. The need to avoid copying Western tradition and to present the way race might shape discussion of sexuality seems foremost in her presentations of Black lesbians. In addition to creating Queen B(?) figures who can express the shadowy silhouette of a presence felt, but not seen, writers had to create and use variant tricksterism in their texts. In five short stories, Shockley's trickster trope of unnaming showcases the importance of the Queen B(?) figure for Black female culture and its representations and depictions of same-sex desire of the past and present. While all of the characters in Shockley's short stories may not reach Queen B(?) status, it is their struggle to get there that emphasizes the limitations of naming themselves as lesbians which insists upon the need for Queen B(?) figures.

Initially, rereading Shockley's *The Black and White of It* through queer strategies of the Black trickster, the Queen B(?), demonstrates how vernacular forms become mechanisms of "cultural guerilla resistance" (Wynter 100)[2] against Western discourses on "normative" gender and sexuality. The terms and conditions of race, gender, and sexuality are always shifting with the times. When one considers the number of racial name changes that African Americans have undergone to reflect those shifts, it can be a bit overwhelming. In addition, nineteenth- and twentieth-century Eurocentric discourses on sex, gender, and sexuality have been as confusing as the constructs they spawned: man, woman, female pseudohermaphrodite, male pseudohermaphrodite, true hermaphrodite, hermaphroditic homosexual, homosexual hermaphrodite, homosexual man, lesbian woman, third sex, third gender, psychic hermaphrodites, uranians, intermediate sex, intersex, transsexual, transgendered, transvestite (Dreger 10–11). Queen B(?) encourages shape-shifting the self to keep up with the times. In each tale, Queen B(?) excels at the practice of shape-shifting. The figure follows the pattern of other tricksters who "can alter . . . shape bodily appearance in order to facilitate deception." (Hynes, "Mapping" 36). In the first edition, Shockley uses the sexual closet as a way to create a border for her trickster Queen B(?)s, and their unnaming of themselves as lesbians and their dismantling of essential blackness and womanhood. Typically, we might assign shape-shifting to a temporal fluctuation in the construction of gender and race, but Shockley assigns shape-shifting to disrupting the construction of heterosexuality in Black America. Shockley documents that when one is "homosexual" and Black, shape-shifting, a.k.a passing, becomes a necessary art. I argue that these stories are influenced by the developing Black lesbigay discourse of the early 1980s.

The publication of *The Black and White of It* occurs directly after a concerted effort to politicize sexual and gendered identities from the lesbian/gay and feminist movements of the 1970s, and after the civil rights and Black power struggle of the 1960s (D'Emilio xxvi). At the time, there is no such thing as queer nation rhetoric, but Shockley's work does engage Black nationalist rhetoric. The intersection of Black nationalist thought with same-sex desire and identity captures the unique experience of Black lesbians. Since there were many race and ethnic divisions within major social movements, queers of color became acutely aware of how the larger movements were not addressing multiple oppressions. Further, the mainstream movements often perpetuated the oppression in much the same fashion as heterosexual social orders. Shockley's short story collection illustrates that as African Americans were becoming comfortable with expressing racial and sexual politics, the politics of blackness often insinuated itself into the discussion with one repetitive question: Are you Black first, or are you queer?

According to Gregory Conerly, the politics of blackness created two avenues of expression in Black queer culture and communities, Black-identified lesbigays and lesbigay-identified Blacks,[3] the distinction being in whether race would be the primary affiliation of individual of both oppressed groups. The sources of identity conflict occur for three reasons: "cultural, social, and political institutions specifically for black lesbians and gays are rare," "racism among white lesbigays and heterosexism among straight blacks," and "lack of overlap between the mostly white lesbigay culture and mostly heterosexual black culture" (Conerly, "Are You Black First" 11). With the publication of *The Black and White of It* in the1980s, Shockley offered an examination of Black-identified lesbians who have to address these conflicts. Shockley's *The Black and White of It* provides us with a unique opportunity to uncover the way the shifts in analytical discourse can change representations, but it also allows us to see why Queen B(?)'s unnaming is and will continue to be a method by which Black female writers choose to depict their sexual desires.

BULLDAGGERS AND SAPPHOS BE DAMNED!
The Sex Work of Black Lesbians

In "A Meeting of the Sapphic Daughters," from *The Black and White of It*, Shockley addresses the convoluted dynamics of race and sexuality for

Black lesbians attempting to form a lesbian-identified community. Shockley shows the hard work that Black lesbians undertake in locating representations of themselves. The story exemplifies how same-sex desire exists for African American females, but the story continues to acknowledge that Western constructs of sexuality very often deny how the discourse of race has shaped such models. Shockley readily confronts this dilemma by creating Queen B(?) characters in her short story. Because the dilemma calls attention to the paradox of naming desire as a sexual orientation, the issue of naming and unnaming resurfaces.

When the major characters, Black lesbians Patrice and Lettie, attend a social meeting for lesbians in their (geographical) community, they become very aware of the politics of race and sexuality. Before the meeting, Patrice appears excited at the possibility of meeting other Black lesbians, but Lettie tempers her enthusiasm with "how can we when they're in the closet" (62). The subsequent exchange calls attention to the issue of naming, hypocrisy, and Eve Sedgwick's epistemology of the closet:

"Well so are we!" Patrice exclaimed in exasperation, turning to face her.
"Have we come out to our colleagues, friends—students?"
"For what? To become ostracized? It's bad enough being looked upon as lepers by whites, let alone blacks. You know how blacks feel about—*bulldaggers*." Lettie spit out the epithet deliberately.
Patrice shuddered. "I hate that word."
"So do I. But that's what our people call us," Lettie said softly. (62)

Shockley masterfully unfolds the differentiations Black people make about their sexuality. Lettie and Patrice clearly identity as Black first, as evidenced by their primary attention to racial oppression followed by sexual oppression. Further, Shockley exposes that her characters' prime affiliation with blackness happens for different reasons. As a student who integrated 1950s Alabama schools, Lettie goes on to experience her blackness in an isolating sea of white institutions throughout her life (61). Patrice, however, a product of Washington, D.C., has consistently been surrounded and involved with Black communities all her life (62). Despite their different backgrounds, Shockley makes it clear that no matter how much of a construct race is, the lived experience of Black people creates a principal attachment that would be hard to let go, even if so desired. At the same time, each character recognizes how their primary affiliation potentially limits or dismisses their sexual identity. Their use of Black vernacular becomes a chief indicator of how huge a conflict the politics of identity can be.

Lettie and Patrice's discussion of the term "bulldagger" can be seen as akin to a serious discussion on the uses of the term "nigger" by white and Black people. Both derogatory epithets are imbued with a historical sense of prejudice and hatred. However, for these two characters there is no appropriation of the word, no dropping of the "er" and replacement with "a" or "ah" to express love or solidarity, and no colloquial phrases ("What's up my Bulldaggah," "that's my bulldagga," or "bulldagga please"). Despite the fact that its etymology can be traced to Black culture, these two Black lesbian characters hate the word. Ironically, the vernacular to discuss Black lesbians allows Shockley to expose the limitations of blackness even as she exposes its potential limitless possibilities through Queen B(?). Lettie and Patrice cannot rely solely on Black vernacular's expressions for lesbian representation, but they can return to the trickster nature of African American culture to help address these identity conflicts. Through the deception and trickery of the closet, Queen B(?) begins constructing her own dimensions of same-sex desire as influenced by race.

When Lettie asserts "we" (Patrice and Lettie) cannot meet other Black lesbians because "they" are in the closet, she reveals a peculiarity of the closet influenced by race. What is the definition of being in the closet? Lettie initially discounts their living arrangements as closeted because they accept and identify as homosexual. However, Patrice's response parallels Eve Sedgwick's analysis of "the closet" years later: "Even at an individual level, there are remarkably few of even the most openly gay people who are not deliberately in the closet with someone personally or economically or institutionally important to them" (*Epistemology of the Closet* 67–68). Yet Lettie and Patrice's sexual closet is vastly different from the closet of white lesbians. Lettie and Patrice's skin color suggests a varying organization of ideals in shaping their closet. As two women living together as lovers and partners, they don't fit the definition of bulldagger in Black America. As once defined by Maya Angelou in her self-assessment of why she was not a lesbian, bulldagger acts as minstrel evocation of Black female same-sex desire: "After a thorough self-examination, in light of all I had read and heard about dykes and bull-daggers, I reasoned that I had none of the obvious traits—I didn't wear trousers, or have big shoulders or go in for sports, or walk like a man or even want to touch a woman" (272). Such stereotypes suggest that bulldaggers are loners, masculine, and lecherous women, conceivably always on the make. In the end, bulldaggers would not choose to live as they have chosen to live, as two women in love and who express that love in a domestic space that reworks the parameters of gender and sexuality for their era.

Despite the cowardly notions of the closet, as Sedgwick has argued, it does serve a purpose. In the case of Shockley's Queen B(?) characters, the closet enables the tricksters' shape-shifting so that they may avoid classification as fixed representations. For trickster's shape-shifting has been known to involve the occasional need for closets: "Relatively minor shape-shifting through disguise may involve nothing more than changing clothes with another" (Hynes, "Mapping the Characteristics of Mythic Tricksters" 37). Lettie and Patrice's closet contains sexual outfits that are outdated, no longer fit, or are no longer useful, but that same closet may hold space for new sexual outfits. In accordance with these closet politics of shape-shifting, Shockley's story implores that there is a matter of greater concern for Queen B(?): vernacular unnaming. No matter how pro-Black they are, Black lesbians will not be confined to identifying as bulldaggers.

The nature of Black lesbian experience is one that encompasses triple oppressions of race, gender, and sexuality. Given the way SDiane Bogus historicizes the term "bulldagger," in addition to other stories in Shockley's collection,[4] where bulldagger is defined as a very tough and masculine, usually butch woman, Lettie and Patrice deplore the word for its derogatory history, but also because it does not seem to represent the way they view themselves. Lettie and Patrice's unnaming of themselves, a sexual disidentification, provides them with a way to reformat the powerful stereotype into their own considerations of Black female same-sex desire.[5] In the process of creating representations of themselves, we know, from their hatred of the word "bulldagger," that they wish to dismiss traditional African American readings of their desire. However, their literal unnaming as bulldaggers and their symbolic unnaming through "the closet" exposes how identification "always includes multiple process of identifying with. It also involves identification as against" (Sedgwick, *Epistemology of the Closet* 61). As identity is a process, Lettie and Patrice are constantly dealing with the "intensities of incorporation, diminishment, inflation, threat, loss, reparation, and disavowal of various representations to form their identities" (61). Attempts to name that identity with a term that expresses the experience of oppression prove as difficult as overcoming the oppression. Since bulldagger has negative connotations, Patrice and Lettie must locate their sexual community and name for it elsewhere. They both cautiously hope that a meeting of the Sapphic Daughters will provide them with a community and a name.

Yet upon their arrival at the meeting, they are the only women of color. They spend the evening listening to Trollope Gaffney, a white woman in her mid-forties, speak about building *a* lesbian community: "We have to assert ourselves—build. Identify ourselves to each other—this great army of lesbian women, because we are all sisters-s-s. We are all one in the beauty of Sapphic love-e-e" (*Black and White* 65). As the meeting progresses, Patrice and Lettie learn that the community Trollope speaks of is an all-white community. The acknowledgment of the absence of women of color and the goal of building a lesbian community prompts Lettie to muse on forming a separate community: "Who needs one? If I'm going to build a separate community of any kind, it'll be a *black* one!" (65). Historically, sapphic love has specific connections to ancient Western culture and whiteness, and it makes absent blackness in present communities of lesbians that adopt the name and culture. Indeed, Shockley plays with the idea as to whether there were any Black lesbians on the island of lesbians when one white lesbian, Wendy, proclaims, "We've never had any black lesbians here before" (66). At the time the story is set and written, bulldaggers are a caricature of Black female same-sex in African America, and Black lesbians may be invisible or as mythical as unicorns in lesbian (white) culture and communities. In both racial communities, Lettie and Patrice could potentially cross over into being sideshows or freaks. Yet, each Queen B(?) takes these predicaments in stride and continues to unname herself.

When Trollope asks the more vocal and radical Lettie what she thought of the speech, she replies, "There doesn't seem to be anything in any lesbian literature on the lesbian movement addressing itself to helping the black lesbian to become free from racism—especially inside the lesbian community" (67). Aside from Trollope being flustered by Lettie's comment, other white women around them become uncomfortable, even trying to reposition themselves as allies though sexual relationships. After Lettie's proclamation on the status of Black women in lesbian communities, Wendy blurts out another inappropriate comment, "I had a black lover once," and Lettie replies, "It's easy to be liberal between the sheets" (67). Lettie's comments are crucial to putting into perspective the irony of the title, "A Meeting of the Sapphic Daughters." The story is concerned with if and how lesbian political and cultural struggles incorporate dimensions of racial oppression into their discourse, movements, and representations. Correspondingly, it is helpful to see how these questions have been broached in queer studies. In a really smart assessment of Sedgwick's canonical question about sexuality and politics: "What does it mean—what difference does it make—when a social or political relationship is sexualized?" (*Between Men* 5), Mason Boyd Stokes suggests that we "reshape Sedgwick's question, then, or more accurately, to provide its antecedent" (*Color of Sex* 69). Before asking what difference it makes, Stokes proposes that when a social or political relationship is sexualized, we must first ask "what the terms of the 'social' and 'political' are. And if the answer is that the social and political are defined primarily by race . . . the sexualization of these relationships will depend not so much on relations of gender but on relations of color" (69). Stokes's comments connect to the way that race is being privileged in Shockley's text without undermining the importance of sexual politics.

Sexual solidarity does not necessarily erase racial differences and oppression in the same way that racial sameness does not and should not expunge gender and sexual differences. How can the Greek Sappho, the Celtic Boudica, or the Eurocentric lesbian symbolize and be representative of Black females with same-sex desire who endure oppression based on race, as well as sexuality and gender? Through Lettie's words, Shockley convinces readers that thematically she is very concerned with disrupting discourses of feminism, lesbian politics, and race relations. As Lettie makes clear, one can still be a racist and pursue sexual relations with someone of another race. The dilemma of the Black "lesbian" articulates the point that sexual freedom without racial freedom offers no true liberty, and racial equality without sexual liberations allows the tenets of white supremacy to maintain the inequalities born out of racism.

Historically, the experiences and the representations embedded with the term "lesbian" cannot serve as a comparable substitute. Lettie and Patrice go to the meeting hoping to find a way to name themselves, and in the process realize that they must keep unnmaing themselves. Shockley uses the sexual closet as a way to create a border for her trickster Queen B(?)s, and their unnaming of themselves as lesbians, their dismantling of essential blackness, and their critique of womanhood. They can continuously work and play with their sexual identity and desires until they find a solution that works best for them. Although Shockley does not resolve the political conflicts of the closet, she does ensure that Lettie and Patrice are recognized as Queen B(?)s to help further representations of Black lesbians. At the end of the tale, Lettie and Patrice lie in bed pondering the realizations of the day:

> Lettie asked sleepily: "Now, has your curiosity been satisfied about the Sapphic Daughters . . ."
> "Maybe someday, we might find that silent legion of black lesbians. But until then . . . we stay in the closet," Patrice mumbled, moving closer to her.
> "It would be nice to know—others."
> "Perhaps we do. And possibly one of these days, they'll let us know," Lettie said. (*Black and White* 68)

Though Lettie sees the existence of Black lesbians as something that could be proved by the breaking of silence, the women's decision to stay in the closet resists such a notion. For the question is not whether Black women who love other Black women exists, but whether they choose to call themselves Black lesbians. As Lettie notes, they may already know some women who love and share themselves sexually with each other. Their attendance at the meeting and the exasperation that follows showcases why communities of same-sex loving Black women would unname themselves. By choosing to "stay in the closet" in terms of naming their desire, but still pursue a queer relationship, these Queen B(?)s can shape-shift their way to a self-authored representation of their identity and subjectivity. In accordance with Lorde and Dhairyan, Shockley presents her story as not particularly interested in the white social construct of Black female same-sex desire—the lesbian (white) darkened to "Black lesbian." Shockley's narrative, based on the trickster mechanisms of shape-shifting and situation inversion, stipulates that such fixed models cannot exist in her narratives. And while it attempts to avoid the fatal flaws of creating essentialist or authentic Black lesbian representation, Shockley's work uses Queen B(?)'s potential ability to shape-shift as a tool in other stories to help readers think more perceptively and initiate changes about representations of Black female queer representations.

Homey Don't Play That: Playing Black, Playing Queer

After asserting that there is virtually no gay person who is not in the closet to at least someone in his or her life, Sedgwick provides us with further perspectives as to how to understand the way Shockley employs the closet as her Queen B(?)s unnaming themselves as lesbians. Segwick argues that "'the closet' and 'coming out,' now verging on all purpose phrases for the potent crossing and recrossing of almost any politically charged lines of representations, have been the gravest and most magnetic of those figures" ("Epistemology of the Closet" 71). In the context of this work, we could possibly read every closeted gay/lesbian individual as a trickster figure, for Sedgwick is speaking of sexual borders and margins: tricksters live in the margins. Yet the closet still would seem to prohibit the culture transformations that trickster is known for. The remedy for these prohibitions would be for cultural producers to make a show of exaggerating the division between public and private spheres. I am most concerned with what this means for Black lesbian characters in *The Black and White of It*. Shockley has already exposed the way Black lesbians define and dismiss the epistemology of the closet on the one hand, and advocate its open-secret situation on the other. By creating closeted lesbians, Shockley demonstrates the difficulties of being out, but she also reflects on the limitations of political identities and the infinite possibilities of desire.

The title of the next short story, "Play It, But Don't Say It" returns me to Queen B(?)'s work/play tactic. The title is a pun on sexual passing deliberated on in African American vernacular. Further, the themes in the story explore race as a performance in the same way that other artists explore gender and sexuality as performance. In the context of this work, playing Black relies on

E. Patrick Johnson's discussion of the dialogic relationship between blackness and performance that "is not always self-constituting" (2). Playing Black could be appropriating "the theatrical fantasy of the white imaginary that is then projected onto black bodies," or the inexpressible yet undeniable racial experience of black people—the ways in which the "living of blackness becomes a material way of knowing" (8). As we saw with "A Meeting of the Sapphic Daughters," playing queer entails being in or out of the closet. Simultaneously, playing Black and playing queer means more rigorous work for Queen B(?). In order to fully comprehend the Queen B(?) nature of this story we must acknowledge the various meanings that the word "play" has in African American discourse:

> 1) To be involved in affairs outside of one's main relationship. 2) To deceive someone; to put something over on people, to outsmart them. "We all got played" . . . 3) Attention, special favor, signals of interest, in the romantic or sexual sense. "When I first met her, she gave me a lil play, so I decide to call her." 4) Acknowledgement, endorsement, support. (Smitherman, *Black Talk* 230)

Furthering the meanings of play is "play like," defined as to pretend. In "Play It, But Don't Say It," Shockley depends upon each Black vernacular meaning of play to allude to performances of sexuality that name and unname Black female same-sex desire, as well as continue the proliferation of trickster's shape-shifting mechanisms. Although some critics have accused Shockley's work as lacking in blackness for its lack of vernacular, Shockley, time and again, queerly engages strategies of Black vernacular for her purposes.[6] I don't say this to authenticate Shockley's work as authentically Black, but to situate the way in which she invokes both race and queerness as performances. She cleverly relies on performative acts of blackness to queer Black females in a culturally relevant way. The short story's title lays the foundation for what Judith Butler theorizes as performative power:

> Performative acts are forms of authoritative speech: most performatives, for instance, are statements that, in the uttering, also perform a certain action and exercise a binding power. . . . Implicated in a network of authorization and punishment, performatives tend to include legal sentences, baptisms, inaugurations, declarations of ownership, statements which not only perform an action, but confer a binding power on the action performed. If the power of discourse to produce that which it names is linked with the question of performativity, then the performative is one domain in which power acts as a discourse. (*Bodies That Matter* 225)

Naming and unnaming are performative acts. In the case of "Play It, But Don't Say It," what the Queen B(?) says (a performative act) and what the Queen B(?) does (a performance) can be in accord with each other or can run counter to each other. The instabilities of these performances grant power as a discourse to Queen B(?). Queen B(?) figures who embrace trickster's performative power gain access to limitless prospects for representations of self and desire.

In "Play It, But Don't Say It," Shockley offers, through her characterization of a passing (sexual) Black lesbian political figure, Mattie B. Brown, and her politically active lover, Alice, the complex negotiations Black women make in reference to same-sex desire and politicizing sexual identity. Mattie and Alice represent Queen B(?)s for very different reasons. As a politician and as a Black woman passing as heterosexual, Mattie is already a trickster figure. Mattie's actualization as a Queen B(?) figure happens because of the way she insists on unnaming her sexual identity, for her object choice is that of power. She plays dominant society before it can play her. Alice functions as Queen B(?) because of the way she interrupts notions of racial authenticity and sexual identity. Shockley's characterization of Mattie B. Brown as a congresswoman climbing the political ladder allows her to dissect the ideological effects of binary oppositions of the public and private with regard to sexual identity. What better way to expose the clashes of political identities than to make your protagonist a politician? It also reveals moves necessary for Queen B(?) liberation: "But crucial to a sexually radical movement for social change is the transgression of categorical distinctions between sexuality and politics, with their typically embedded divisions between public, private, and personal concerns" (Berlant and Freeman 154). With Mattie and Alice's relationship, Shockley offers a glimpse into the transgressions between such categories.

Here, the story uses trickster tropes of unnaming, border transgression, and deceiver/trick player to dissect the distinction some African American women make concerning sexual practice and sexual identity. Identity is political, and practice is behavior dictated by apolitical desire. To name the non-heteronormative behavior is to accept an identity that seems anti-Black. In this story, the main characters' "mutual constructing/deconstructing, avowing/disavowing, and expanding/delimiting dynamic that occurs in the production of blackness is the very thing that constitutes 'black culture'" (E. Johnson 2).[7] Yet it is also this dynamic that queers blackness and makes possible representations of Black same-sex desire, that is, the Queen B(?)'s desires, through several depictions. What is said or unsaid is destabilized by a character's actions and the reversal can also be true.

The protagonist Mattie B. Brown, whose very namesake emphasizes a main link to color/race, is not a Black-identified lesbian, but her lover, Alice, is a Black-identified lesbian. Early in the narrative, a description of a billboard divulges to readers that Mattie may have successfully won her seat in Congress based on her successful performance of blackness supported by a Black nationalist platform: "Vote for Mattie B. Brown—U.S. Congresswoman, Third District—Voice of the Black People. Two flags surrounded her, one the red, green, and black liberation banner, and the other red, white, and blue" (*Black and White* 25). Mattie's very public political ambitions become tangled in nationalist discourses, Black and American, that have at their core foundational concerns of respectability and controlled heteronormative sexual urges. As Wahneema Lubiano expressed earlier, despite nationalist platforms that spoke of eradicating gender and sexual oppression,[8] few ever did so. The Black queer nation was nonexistent.

In addition, in order for Mattie to satisfy her political ambitions, she cannot simply be pro-Black politically, she must appear as authentically Black as possible. Shockley juxtaposes descriptions of Mattie, "short, black hair in tightly curled ringlets peaking above a broad, brown face" (26), with descriptions of Alice: "Alice was lighter in complexion than her mother. . . . Alice reminded her of those supposed-to-be black dolls that she used to get for Christmas as a child—the ones with keen features, straight hair, and painted brown" (27). Mattie is presented as more racially authentic because of her physical features. Alice's social and political work in various and numerous Black organizations combined with her lack of physical authenticity alerts us to her status as the Queen B(?) trickster figure for the Black community. Her political work comments on essentialist notions of blackness that don't consider the play of sexuality, while Mattie is the Queen B(?) for dominant culture and Black community for her sexual passing.

Shockley's narrative presents the opposition of public and private discourse and the gap between the expression of sexual desire and racial identity. After a hard day, Mattie and Alice settle in with each other. Mattie kisses Alice and tells her, "Babes—why don't you go and get comfortable for me?" (29). While the two dining together had initially been presented as if it could have been two female roommates sitting down to dinner (28), the intimate contact and innuendo highlight Mattie and Alice's relationship as something other than familial and platonic. Mattie and Alice are lovers. Soon thereafter, a discussion of their first meeting discloses performativity and play of two Queen B(?)s, and how they function in the text. Mattie fondly remembers:

> "That was my first formal introduction to the black co-mune-ni-tee-e, as my fired up young black activists call it," she laughed. "I gave some speech, didn't I? It was on a Black Woman's Search for Justice. . . . Later, I got a spread in *Ebony*—Black Female Lawyer in the Ghetto." (29)

In terms of appearances, Mattie can't get any blacker in the above passage. She self-authenticates and aligns with Black nationalist thought with the subject of her speech. The Black (bourgeoisie) press authenticates her. Within the article, the location of the Black female lawyer, the ghetto, authenticates her as ultra-Black, despite what might typically have been perceived as an elitist job for Black people, a lawyer.

However, Mattie and Alice's relationship disturbs traditional heteronormative presentations of blackness that both are very aware of, and their relationship also enforces the patterns of tricksterism that Queen B(?) figures return to:

> Clad in black silk pajamas, Mattie lay on her side, off-handedly stroking Alice's breast, as she talked in what amounted to a monologue: "I'm going to set that capitol on fire when I get there. Those white male congressmen are goin' to know who *this* black woman is inside six months. And the black me-en-n ain't never gonna see-e-e a more black bitch of a woman than this ole Sapphire." (30)

In this brief passage alone, Mattie has referenced every facet of Queen B(?) possible. Her physical attentions to Alice mark her as the Queen Bulldagger, her self-reference as a "more black bitch" refers to her Queen Bitch status, and her likening of herself as Sapphire hearkens to the Queen Bee figure. Yet the very fact that Mattie understands the roles she plays or will play, and how her performances can lead to rewards and punishments highlights her as the Queen B(?) who won't be limited by anyone else's boundaries. Mattie may be as pro-Black as the next Farrakhan, but her gender and her hidden desires destabilize that blackness. So she can't merely be racially Black and think like a good Black. Mattie has to play Black. Within that performance, Mattie has to play down (deception and trickery to outsmart) her lesbianism so that she can get a lot of play (support) from Black voters. As a woman seeking political office, it's not enough for her to physically be Black; she must continuously perform and authenticate blackness.

Mattie understands that as a Black woman in a country ruled by white men, she remains invisible. She also comprehends that, for Black men, she represents a threat of emasculation. She relishes being and manipulating those representations and the power they provide her. Because she plays those roles against each other, she can share a life with Alice and be a "somebody" (27). That play is also what makes her a Queen B(?). However, as Audre Lorde notes of her own life, playing up to those representations entail risks of eliminating other aspects of her self: "With respect to myself specifically, I feel that not to be open about any of the different 'people' within my identity, particularly the 'mes' who are challenged by a status quo, is to invite myself and other women, by my example, to live a lie. In other words, I would be giving in to a myth of sameness which I think can destroy us" ("Interview" 100). It is the status quo and the myth of sameness that Alice challenges in her exchanges with Mattie.

Because Mattie has ingested the restrictive views of blackness, she limits herself. Mattie's repetition of herself as the "evil Black woman" who succeeds where Black men don't is then coupled with homophobic remarks about her past political opponent, Ike Smith: "I sure beat the hell out of that little fag" (31). When Alice questions how Mattie knows Ike is gay, Mattie provides a description of Ike as "going round all prim and prissy . . . so neat and clean . . . polite as an undertaker" to prove her point (31). Alice then chastises Mattie, "You shouldn't call him that, Mattie" and later "Suppose . . . somebody called you—" (31). Alice cannot finish the sentence without harsh reprimand: "'Called me what?' Mattie stopped her angrily, sitting upright in the bed . . . 'I dare you to say it!' she challenged, forgetting the ambiguity of it all embedded in her precious ruinations on genteelness versus speaking your piece" (31). Alice wanted to show Mattie the problems with status quo stereotypes of what it means to be gay or lesbian. Alice's unfinished point is that if Mattie could see Ike's mild-mannered approach as a sign of homosexual tendencies, then her balls-to-the-wall approach would implicate Mattie as a lesbian, or bulldagger, to parallel the language Mattie uses to describe Ike. Mattie would not want either term affixed to her image. However, Mattie's threat to Alice and Alice's challenge to Mattie reinforces the different interpretations that each woman has with regard to their relationship. Such interpretations are established early in their interactions.

After sleeping with Mattie for the first time, Alice says, "I guessed it all along. That's why I wanted to meet you, to find somebody in this god awful secret black lesbian world with whom I could at least be myself—"(31–32). Alice's comment reveals the limitations placed on their love. The secretive community of Black lesbians acknowledges same-sex desire, but it comes with its locks. While Alice can be herself with Mattie, Mattie denies Alice the right to name both of them Black lesbians:

At those words, Mattie had pushed her away hissing: "What are you talking about?"
 "About you-me-us," Alice repeated, a trifle frightened.
 "There is nothing to say about us . . . As long as we are together like this—I don't want to discuss it. In other words, don't *say* it." (32)

Hence, Mattie and Alice can play at being lesbians in love, but the work entailed as politically identifying as a Black lesbian is not something that Mattie will ever say she wishes to do. Mattie's words are a threat to Alice, an ultimatum meant to eliminate the fear of naming her desire. To name her desire means politicizing it in a way that would open her up to public scrutiny that might end her quest for political power. Though the results are different, unnaming here still acts as a powerful political tool for Mattie in the same way it did for Harriet Jacobs and Sojourner Truth. The distinction about representations of sexual desire that is being made here is typical of the Queen B(?): Once you name something, you accept an identity that may restrict your desires.

Mattie takes "the love that dare not speak its name" to the extreme. Ironically, the silence the phrase implies is not sustained, because their living arrangements say more than words ever could. It is no small feat for two Black women to live as two women in love with each other. If tricksters change societies from the outside in, then these Queen B(?)s, from their closet (a border or margin), do exactly that. Each and every day together forces them and others who know of their love to revise their ideas of blackness and queerness. Even Alice's statement acknowledges that fact. Finally, when Alice has had enough of Mattie's denials, she ignores Mattie's previous warnings and exclaims to her, "You play it; you might as well say it" (32). Alice hones in on Mattie's simultaneous playful performance of same-sex desire and the work she has done to unname that desire. Mattie strikes back with physical violence. The exchange between Mattie and Alice allows Shockley to focus on an issue of naming in African America that merits more discussion. What barriers or rhetoric must be engaged or disengaged for Black women to identify as lesbians, or Black females with same-sex desire?

When Mattie refuses to name her desire as lesbian, a reminder of the conflict between her political ambitions and her same-sex desire surface at the wrong time. When Cathy Storm of the *Gay Free Press* asks Mattie if she plans to "support legislation in favor of homosexuals that would be especially beneficial to the triple jeopardy associated with black lesbians," Mattie offers a response that brings to the forefront the limits of representation of Black female same-sex desire and the conflict with naming: "This is not my concern. You see, there are no such black women" (35). In trying to "play" mainstream society, Mattie gets played by the press. Subsequently, the press uses the statement to mock her. Mattie's unnaming and Alice's naming emphasize the tensions of naming and representation in African American culture, but play it, don't say it is a revision of the open circle that Black gay culture has been using for centuries. As Richard Bruce Nugent once proclaimed of the Harlem Renaissance, "People did what they wanted to do with whom they wanted to do it.... Nobody was in the closet. There wasn't a closet" (18).

Although Alice preaches the virtues of naming with her insistence of labeling them as lesbians, her understanding of Black female same-sex desire is more complex than that. After Mattie's faux pas with the gay press, Alice offers her lover this tidbit of wisdom:

> Sure, I know some black lesbians and so do you. Only the nice middle-class black women who are won't admit it. Careers, hiding behind husbands and social status are more important in black life than admitting a same sex preference.... Besides, in the long run, what good would it do? Coming out of the closet is more significant to white lesbians. That's why that white woman asked you the question. (36)

What does Alice mean when she says coming out of the closet is more significant to white lesbians? It doesn't mean that Black queer people are less in the closet, or that they don't care about not being oppressed because of their sexuality. Alice's statement demonstrates the way race marks the experience of gays and lesbians as different from that of their white counterparts. In this case, racial oppression is prioritized over sexual oppression. Because race appears to be a more visible marker for oppression than sexuality, it gets prioritized. And because white gays and lesbians can enjoy certain privileges of whiteness, they can prioritize their sexuality. The Black minority seeks to become a part of the majority, while members of dominant white majority attempt to construct their community as a sexual minority.[9] Alice's point returns to Shockley's earlier notions of the closet for Black women. Yet, this Queen B(?)'s assessment of closet time is very different than Patrice and Lettie's theorizing of their closeted sexuality in "A Meeting of the Sapphic Daughters."

Alice reads Queen B(?)'s shape-shifting in and out of the closet as Black lesbian identity not being politicized:

> We black women in our struggle against racism planted the seeds for the white women's movement. Now, I guess it's time for them to do us a favor. Liberate the so-called sex crazy black woman from her own hang-ups. Making it so that if she's a lesbian, she won't be afraid to say or feel deep within her that it is as good as shouting "black is beautiful." (36)

In some sense, Alice's words return to Segwick's question about social or political relationships being sexualized. And just as we saw with "A Meeting of the Sapphic Daughters," race matters when posing this question. In this case, it is not a black/white dynamic, but Mattie's idea of what it means to Black and political versus what it means to Black and political for Alice. Because

Mattie accepts nationalist formations of blackness based in authenticity, she sees no way to politicize her sexual identity. Alice talks of politicizing her sexual identity, but her considerations of sexual identity are just as problematic as Mattie's because she views white lesbian models as the correct way to be a Black lesbian. Patrice and Lettie in "A Meeting of the Sapphic Daughters" already expose the flaws of such thinking. Both Alice and Mattie see only binary possibilities (sexually repressed Black woman/liberated white woman, public/private, political/unpolitical). When Mattie asks Alice to stay behind when she moves to D.C., it is an action that Alice sees as the end to their relationship. Shockley's ending insists that both Queen B(?)s must continue to play the field if they are to evolve beyond rhetorical binaries. Although Shockley uses interracial dynamics to explore the emulation of white lesbian life and culture, impressing matters of race in universal queerness, she also unveils white society's consumption of the Black female body to create lesbian gender and identity in her short story "The Mistress and the Slave Girl."

The Performative Racialization of Butch/Femme

The second edition of the *Black and White of It* includes two new stories, "The Mistress and the Slave Girl" and "Women in a Southern Time," in addition to the previously published stories that move beyond exploring the predicaments of Black lesbigays. In the new stories, Shockley weaves tales about white mistresses and employers engaging in sexual relationships with Black female slaves and housekeepers. Through situation inversion and shape-shifting she imagines these mistress/employee and slave/housekeeper as racialized butch/femme performances. For the purposes of this text, I will only be exploring the portrayal of butch/femme dichotomies in the "Mistress and the Slave Girl." Shockley relies on racialized sexuality and the race border to explore the intersection of race with sexual discourse to document the historical limitations of the term "lesbian." She complicates the issue by then incorporating the trickster element of situation inversion—connecting the taboo of interracial sexual relationships to her shape-shifting agenda. In this way, Shockley can address racialized heterosexuality, homophobia of the Black community, and the less depicted racialization of homosexuality.

The last story to be read through trickster contains moments of unnaming, Queen B(?) figures, racialized sexuality, and gender expression and sexual desire through butch/femme performances. As we continue to understand how identity politics figures into Black lesbian relationships, I wish now to return to Chinn's statement about how lesbians have sex with each other, especially with regard to erotic sex *play*. As we have seen with animal and human trickster tales, some tricksters do tend to enjoy a significant amount of erotic play. In addition to using Queen B(?) characters to address identity politics conflicts stemming from race and sexuality, Shockley's collection also uses Queen B(?) to dabble in desire and identity politics within sexual communities. Attempts to broach all of these issues is no small feat, but Shockley does so by deploying the trickster tropes of shape-shifting and situation inversion with the representation of interracial lesbian erotic play in "The Mistress and the Slave Girl."[10] The shape-shifting that happens in this short story looks less like turtle women transforming into real women and more like the emerging shape shifting that occurred in lesbian spaces in the 1950s and 1960s. I am speaking of butch/femme roles and erotic play. African American folklore allows Shockley to make her assessment especially relevant to Black communities. Although African American folklore is filled with heterosexist and homophobic stories of butch women, Shockley relies on the outlaw temperament of human trickster figures to devise her creation of a Queen B(?) who can inscribe Black female desire, especially that which plays with gender and object desire, into African America without being reduced to copying one raced gender over another, or eliminating object choices that don't align with racial or sexual preference. The most suitable way to do this is through an investigation of gender outlaws who make us inquire as to the possible connection between racial discourse and butch/femme performances.

During the 1890s "butch" referred to a female butcher who was a "hard-fisted woman of the people" (Linton 598). Since sexologists defined lesbianism as a mannish invert, femme identities didn't receive public representation until the 1950s and 1960s in Black and white lesbian cultures.[11] However, butch women became invisible again during second-wave feminism, which argued the butch/femme polarity as unhealthy and politically useless. The works of queer theorists soon argued for it as a positive part of lesbian erotic expression. In *A Lure Knowledge*, Judith Roof argues that butch/femme roles are more "complex, contradictory, and diverse" than some queer and feminist theorists have assumed (245).[12] Adding race into theories further complicates erotic expression. Despite Halberstam's groundbreaking work on race and the drag king scene, how race informs butch/femme expressions has been less discussed.

When Michelle Gibson and Deborah T. Meem edited *Femme/Butch: New Considerations of the Way We Want to Go*, a collection of essays that delved into the butch/femme phenomenon, they noticed something peculiar. Within the collection that touted various theoretical approaches and perspectives, a discussion of race was missing. The editors of the collection acknowledge the absence of race with the following statement:

> How about the relationship between race and butch-femme? Here a difficulty arose for us. . . . As two white women, we acknowledge that the problem might well have been some kind of oversight in the call for papers, or perhaps our way of representing the discussion revealed our limitations. We simply don't know why we were not able to encourage women writing about race to submit articles; what we do know is that it didn't happen and we regret that—partly because the lack of discussion of race diminishes this collection, but perhaps more important, also because we believe that examination of the relationship between race and lesbian gender is a project that needs to be pursued. (6)

Gibson and Meem wisely preface the absence of coverage on the issue as others before them had done.[13] Ironically, the collection does have an essay by Hoz-Sze Leung on lesbian genders in contemporary Chinese culture and features commentary by Karen Williams, an African American woman professing her love for butch/femme roles. We know from Lorde's biomythography that the examination of the butch/femme in African American lesbian communities existed in the 1950s and 1960s. And anyone who partakes of club nightlife in major metropolitan cities will see how invested Black lesbian communities are in butch/femme play. However, the relationship between race and lesbian gender is a project that has been under pursued by all stretches of the imagination.

However, in her discussion of Harriet Jacobs and the sexual abuse and desires of the Flints, Hortense Spillers intuits the dynamics of one possible relationship between race and lesbian gender that would have proven helpful for Gibson and Meem and that solidify the importance of Shockley's "The Mistress and the Slave Girl." Of Jacobs's unwanted sexual triangle, Spillers found that the triangle of the master as gendered male, mistress as gendered female, and slave as ungendered female "demarcates a sexuality that is neuter-bound. . . . Since the gendered female exists for male, we might suggest that the ungendered female—in an amazing stroke of pansexual potential—might be invaded/raided by another woman or man" ("Mama's Baby" 273). Thus to pursue the relationship between race and lesbian gender means to disclose the possible function of white patriarchal supremacy within that gender and the limited functions of that gender over time. Though it may not be a positive disclosure, it is one that must be discussed all the same. In an ironic twist, such explication also reveals the potentiality of ungendered females to disrupt and destroy the order of white patriarchal supremacy.

In addition, to discuss the relationship between race and butch/femme means acknowledging politically incorrect and taboo interracial lesbian relationships. Such relationships interrupt Black nationalist rhetoric and factions of womanhood. Nevertheless, since the trickster Queen B(?) exploits the tensions of taboos and the taboos, she serves as a thoughtful apparatus to dissect the influence of white patriarchy and supremacy in constructions of white female same-sex desire, the possible intrusion and defeat of white supremacy in Black female same-sex desire, and a viable means to explore desires that do not correspond to nationalist agendas. Though substantial gains have been made by Black lesbians in representations of their sexuality, with greater ones to be made, those gains have always been connected to idealized references to representations of Black-on-Black lesbian love.[14] By returning to the site of criminalization or deviation of interracial relationships, slavery, Shockley investigates the relationship between race and butch/femme, as well as returns to how Black women may pursue their object's desire and its representation outside of Black heteronormative paradigms and Eurocentric homosexual narratives. She then creates and historicizes the Queen B(?) as a representation of Black female same-sex desire and expression.

If Queen B(?) parallels the tradition of the Bad Man/Nigga, then she also manipulates similar taboos. In African American folklore, there exist numerous tales that show that the most transgressive Bad Man is one who pursues and sleeps with white women, since the cost of breaking rules of social segregation and laws was often imprisonment or death.[15] Subsequently, a Black female who engages in an interracial sexual relationship with a white woman poses a threat to a unified Black community based in heteronormativity and a unified Black lesbian community based in racial exclusivity. The outlaw mold continues to transgress against identity politics that threaten to limit one's options. Further, the writer responsible for representing those transgressions is as much a Queen B(?) as the characters she creates.

"The Mistress and the Slave Girl," set in the pre-emancipation South, is a complex short story that elicits initial reactions of surprise, anger, discomfort, confusion, and curiosity. "The Mistress and the Slave Girl" is a fictional account of Heather, a white woman who returns to the South to take over her father's plantation. Upon Heather's return home she "falls in love" with a Black female slave, Delia. In order to pursue her "love" for Delia, Heather purchases and "rescues" the slave from the horrors she might receive at the hands of male slave owners. On the surface, the story is about a white female slave owner falling in love with a female slave. However, the inversion of situation implied in the title moves readers from dominating models of master and slave to mistress and slave. The inversion signifies subversion of gender and sexuality in haunting narratives of slavery. Shockley's "The Mistress and the Slave Girl," through trickster devices, successfully disrupts the constructs of racialized sexuality and the heterosexualization of desire. In *Colonial Desire*, Robert J. C. Young emphasizes that "nineteenth-century theories of race did not just consist of essentializing differentiations between self and other: they were also about a fascination with people having sex—interminable, adulterating, aleatory, illicit, inter-racial sex" (181). Shockley uses her trickster revision of the white construct of lesbian to make way for Black female same sex-desire in a way that recognizes imperialist politics and the interlocking of racial and sexual discourses.

Though there are no obvious oral aesthetics of Black culture in this particular tale, there is the presence of tricksterism. Shockley inverts every dynamic of slavery and Black slave narratives that we have come to know. Female-centered politics replace the maleness of plantation-era representations, and mistress displaces the master as the head and owner of land. Ironically, though one of the major characters is the Black female slave, Delia, we cannot recover Delia's story as a type of slave narrative. Shockley presents the story through a focus on the white female slave owner, Heather:

> After her father passed six months ago, she had come back to Virginia. More liberal minded towards women and slaves than most of the surrounding planters, he sent her to be educated in the north. Years of being away had made her virtually a foreigner to this place where she was born.... In a pleading letter, their family lawyer had beseeched her to return, or the plantation would be put up for sale because of mismanagement. (105)

Shockley revises the pattern of Black writers who address the institution of slavery using the slave as the major voice or character. Using third-person narration, rather than the traditional first-person account in slave narratives, Shockley presents the mistress, Heather, as the main character and "protagonist." Delia merely serves as a secondary character, but she is still a Queen B(?) figure.

Why does Shockley, a Black lesbian writer, choose to focus more on the white female character? By making Heather her thematic focal point, Shockley moves the open secret (desires of whites) further into the public domain. Because she does so, white practices of secretly fulfilling desire through the racialized body is no longer the slave's shame and abuse, and Shockley's strategy becomes a damning critique of, in addition to the institution of slavery, the criterion of "normal" sexuality. Shockley constructs Heather as a liberal white Southern woman who believes in women's rights and emancipation. However, as Shockley reveals, there is a contradiction. Heather's schooling is paid for by the labor of the slaves her family owns. Her privileges come via the slave economy. Heather's return to manage, or stop the plantation from being sold, is in clear conflict with her abolitionist philosophies. Shockley's tricksterism of situation inversion enables her to reveal the destruction of self and morals for the slave owner.

A second strategy in the short story involves the reversal of dominance and exploitation. Readers are accustomed to thinking of men sexually abusing women in the institution of slavery.[16] Shockley exposes how white women sexually exploited and dominated Black females for their own ends. The overturning of such models seeks to disrupt ideologies of racialized sexuality. Upon returning home, the libertine and feminist Heather stops at a slave auction, where she witnesses men bidding to purchase Delia. When the auctioneer wants to raise the bids, he makes Delia the sexual specter: "'Come now, surely she is worth two thousand!' the auctioneer challenged. Abruptly he bared a breast, exposing a perfectly molded mound with a brown tip. . . . 'See . . . A fine specimen'" (106). The auctioneer's actions remind us of another incident in which a Black female's breasts (Sojourner Truth's) are bared to signify her value as the physical and sexual specter of femaleness. However, this scene is lacking the "feminist" background of the actual historical moment of Truth's incident. Herein lies the incongruity of trickster behavior that Shockley uses as a writerly resource: Delia is the object and Heather the spectator. Shockley's text acknowledges the position of power white women maintained over Black females.

As previously noted, the transgression of racial borders makes illegal and false any claims of love made between the enslaved and her master/mistress. In addition, racialized sexuality distorts the labor position of the Black female slave. As determined by bondage laws of the time, the African child's status as a free Black or a slave depends upon the mother's status. In U.S. patriarchal society, it is clear that this law begins the detrimental myth of Black females as emasculating matriarchs. Further, the institution of slavery, in order to benefit from the myth in a commodified form, places the sexuality of the Black female at the border. Shockley manages to reconfigure these ideologies by inverting the situation. Though both the mistress and the slave girl exist in a patriarchal institution of slavery, the labor and social community established between the two is meant to be matriarchal. Where the tendency has been to expose racialized sexuality by explaining how it makes abnormal the Black family in slavery, either through notions of emasculation or the defilement of Black womanhood by white males, Shockley takes an alternative approach with issues of same-sex desire.

When Heather witnesses the auctioneer's tactics for selling Delia, the author presents to the reader two separate accounts of her reactions. Within the omniscient narrator's account of Heather's thoughts lies the polyphonic discourse that can capture the complex tensions at the intersection of race, gender, and sexuality: "Something about the girl fascinated Heather as she took in the pink silk dress hugging the curves of her body. . . . Heather swallowed hard as she experienced a familiar sharp sensation piercing warmly through her" (106). In addition, Heather's decides to buy Delia after the auctioneer highlights Delia's physical attributes by baring her naked breast (106). Shockley's description of the auction scene and its impact on Heather as shown by her being fascinated, haunted, and physically excited by Delia makes one question, if not invalidate, the omniscient narrator's account of Heather's actions thereafter: "Anger flared within her at the sight. Reaching over, she shook her brother awake. 'Ralph, come!' she ordered, climbing hurriedly out of the carriage, 'I'm going to buy that girl'" (106). Shockley's doubled narrative represents a true trait of trickster discourse: double-voicedness. Shockley uses this particular narrative strategy in the way that returns us to Jung's theory of trickster as a parallel of an individual shadow:

> Since this shadow frequently appears in the phenomenology of dreams as a well-defined figure, we can answer this question positively: the shadow, although by definition a negative figure, sometimes has certain clearly discernible traits and associations which point to a quite different background. It is as though he were hiding meaningful contents under an unprepossessing exterior. Experience confirms this; and what is more important, the things that are hidden usually consist of increasingly numinous figures. (*Four Archetypes* 177)

The interiority of Heather's thoughts are juxtaposed with her actions and voice of indignation. Heather is not the Queen B(?), but Shockley, as the author, takes up the tasks of the Queen B(?). Her narrative strategy exposes the ongoing theatrical fantasy of the white imagination projected onto the Black body. In one paragraph, Shockley presents the reader with two very distinct reactions. The first focuses on Heather's thoughts, which by no means allude to any type of social/political feminist empowerment or woman-to-woman solidarity. The sharp sensation, piercing and warm, appears to be a strong pronouncement of desire and Heather's primary and true reaction to Delia. Shockley emphasizes Heather's desire over her rising anger. Heather's thoughts, then, make invalid the next part of the narration aimed at showing the moral outrage of Heather. Shockley finds a subtle way of showing how the open secret works in less heteronormative ways. This doubled narration allows the reader to see that Heather's motive for purchasing Delia should be viewed as ambiguous. Heather does not buy Delia to rescue her from the clutches of evil men; she does so to fulfill her own wants. Heather's attentions show a transgression of the racial and gendered order. Even the title of the story comes to remind us of the need to constantly dislocate racialized sexuality. "Mistress" replaces the dominant image of "Master" in the representation of slavery. Shockley's presentation reveals that the institution of slavery could further corrupt even those white women who perceived themselves as liberal minded.

The introduction of lesbianism into the slave setting is a pertinent one because it permits Shockley to investigate perhaps one of the most complicated issues in lesbianism and race, the relationship between scientific racism and the homosexual body. In *Queering the Color Line,* Siobhan Somerville discusses how scientific racism is used to argue that homosexuality is deviant. Somerville demonstrates that biological notions of sexuality and race shift from a focus on the body to psychological theories of desire in the twentieth century: "One way in which they overlapped and perhaps shaped one another was through models of interracial and homosexual desire. Specifically, two tabooed sexualities—miscegenation and homosexuality—became linked in sexological and psychological discourse through the model of 'abnormal' sexual object choice" (251). Somerville argues that physicians and sexologists like Havelock Ellis and Edward Carpenter conceptualized the emerging models of homosexuality on the Black body presented in scientific racism (254).

In order to solidify her argument, Somerville includes Margaret Otis's "A Perversion Not Commonly Noted" written in 1913 to record the widespread lovemaking between the white and Black girls in all-girl institutions of reform and boarding schools: "One white girl . . . admitted that the colored girl she loved seemed the man, and thought it was so in the case of the others. . . . The difference in color, in this case, takes the place of difference in sex" (113). Somerville's analysis of this article found that Otis reverts to "stereotypes established by earlier anatomical models," and that "she used a simple analogy between race and gender in order to understand their desire: black was to white as masculine was to female" (252). Clearly, the Black body plays an important role in discourses of homosexuality in regard to sexual deviance and queer erotic play. Somerville's analysis makes it difficult to believe that we can continue to ignore issues of sexuality, specifically homosexuality, in discussing African diasporic culture.

Perhaps this is why "The Mistress and the Slave Girl" becomes such an important story to reread. Shockley's portrayal of Heather and Delia does not serve as an exact account of lesbian relationships as expressed by Margaret's Otis's report on interracial relationships in all-girl institutions. Shockley, unlike Otis, does not rely on stereotypical anatomical models but real historical conditions. However, the performance of butche/femme roles introduced by Otis does occur in "The Mistress and the Slave Girl" with noticeable differences. Otis's account shows how Black women are usually positioned as butches and white women as femmes in interracial relationships. However, this dynamic hardly subverts dominant ideologies of the gendered positions of the women based on their races. White women form the very basis of femininity in the West, with women of color projected as something other than femme. As Queen B(?), Shockley inverts the racial assignment of butch/femme based on the actual power dynamics of the time. As Spillers and Gayl Jones illustrated, white women, like men, could exploit Black female bodies for domestic labor, as well as consume those bodies for sexual labor.

By setting her story during the period of antebellum slavery, Shockley can use this issue of consumption and butch/femme play to show the constructions of genders, sexual identities, and expressions within lesbian communities. After getting Delia home, Heather, in attempting to determine Delia's position on the plantation, inquires as to her skills. Upon learning that Delia is educated, can sew well, and is pretty, Heather proposes, "You will be my personal servant, Delia" (108). As if it needed to be enforced any more, Heather's naming of Delia as her personal servant serves two purposes. First, since "gendering takes place within the confines of the domestic, an essential metaphor that then spreads its tentacles for male and female subjects over a wider ground of human and social purposes" (Spillers, "Mama's Baby" 266), Heather's choice to place Delia in the house rather than the fields is huge in the creation of her own white lesbian identity. In the fields or in the house, as a captive body, Delia's sexuality remains neuter-bound. However, Heather's domestic use of Delia begins the process she needs to gender herself as butch. Had Delia been assigned to the fields, Heather's gendering as butch would be impeded.

Second, in terms of the desire of the gender that is being constructed, the domestic space reiterates Heather as a top and Delia as a bottom. Because Delia's labor will take place in the house as opposed to the field, Shockley can explore the domestic spheres of women's interracial relationships. From here on, Delia's presence as Queen B(?) becomes prominent. She concurrently refutes representations as the asexual Mammy and the sexually licentious Black woman. In addition, the domestic space, while allowing Heather the performative space to become butch, also brings to the forefront racialized sexuality's severing of the captive's body from her motive will and desire. According to queer theorists, "Butch" (and femme) are about gender identification/presentation and sexual desire (Epstein 51). Shockley's trickster narrative reveals all of these elements. In a discussion of butch-identified lesbians, Butler argues, "If butchness requires a strict opposition to femmeness, is that a refusal of an identification or is this an identification with femmeness that has already been made, made and disavowed, a disavowed identification that sustains the butch, without which the butch qua butch cannot exist?" (*Bodies That Matter* 115). In "The Mistress and the Slave Girl," Heather needs to set up an environment in which her disavowed identification of femmeness can sustain her. By projecting Delia, her house slave/servant, as the femme, she can continue to disavow femmeness and identify as butch. She literally and figuratively eats her femmeness and keeps butching up herself through Delia's servitude to her.

The consumption of the Black female body hints at issues of object choice and subjectivity in exchanges of sexual relationships for both Black and white women. In her autobiography, *Lady Sings the Blues*, Billie Holiday comments on white women's consumption of the "other" and reveals how same-sex desire became a taboo and lesbianism a white thing for Black women. Telling of the attentions a rich white woman gave her, she explains:

> She came around night after night. She was crazy about my singing and used to wait for me to finish up. I wasn't blind. . . . It wasn't long before I knew I had become a thing for this girl. . . . It's a cinch to see how it all begins. These poor bitches grow up hating their mothers and having the hots for their fathers. And since being in love with our father is taboo, they grow up unable to get any kicks out of anything unless it's taboo too. (86–87)

Billie Holiday may not have had a degree in psychology, but she was on to something, despite the inflammatory nature of her comment. If little white girls could not have sex with their fathers, as Freud says, or could not have sex with their white mothers, as French feminists claim, then, according to Holiday, Bad Man/Niggas and Queen B(?)s were quite possibly the next best thing. Although African American critics are quick to read Mammy as servile, subservient, and asexual, Black writers have been challenging that myth for years.[17] Shockley's creation of Delia further probes the sexual possibility of domestic workers as tricksters. With her story of torrid interracial lesbian relationships, Shockley capsizes white women's childish consumption of the maternal Black woman into the taboo sexual desire it may represent. By pursuing that taboo object choice, white women can then become the lesbians they always dreamed they could be. Yet Shockley does not stop with white women's sexual subjectivity; she then allows Black females to use that desire to write their subjectivity as Black sexual subjects.

Joan Nestle's *The Persistent Desire* proposes butch/femme as "a lesbian-specific way of deconstructing gender that radically reclaims women's erotic energy" (14). The reclamation of erotic energy may be through the same means of butch/femme, but it does not mean that the illustration of the means will appear universal. There are all kinds of erotic play within the butch/femme category distinguished by cultural and personal yearnings: femme top, femme bottom, butch top, butch bottom, stud and lady, Mommy/Daddy, girl and boy, Tomboy and Tomboy-girl, stone-butch/stone-femme, high femme, power femme, kiki, and so on. The very fact that more terms and categories are being added as this text is being written and published demonstrates the shifts in sexual identity and representations of desire, as well as why Queen B(?) works in reading such demanding erotic play. Since "butch and femme are gender constructions that arise from a sexual definition of lesbianism" (MacCowan 306), then at some point race, ethnicity, or class are going to intrude on those constructions. Thus, "The Mistress and the Slave Girl' symbolizes another branch of the butch/femme tree of lesbian expression, an S/M expression, no less. Heather certainly qualifies as the butch. Heather and whiteness are associated with whiteness's dominant position and blackness's subordinated and "feminine" position. The interesting way that race and sexuality function in the dissemination of same-sex desire and the disfiguration of gender cannot be missed. In a traditional heterosexual trope, Heather would be the weaker sex, but same-sex desire and race allow Shockley to play with gender hierarchies. Like the animal trickster tales that opened this work, this human trickster tale more readily reflects the reality of racialized sexuality.

The reversal of racialized sexuality, moving it outside the domain of heterosexuality, exposes how the racialized Black body is used to construct a homosexual identity, not necessarily for Delia the Black female, but for Heather the white woman. In the story, Heather can explore her lesbian desire through her ownership rights to Delia's Black body. She uses Delia, her legal property, to assert her lesbianism in a society that forbids her to do so in any other way. This is not to say that same-sex desire does not exist for Black females, but that the social construct of lesbian, like that of woman, is inadequate for framing such desires. As the narrator indicates, Heather has associated with free Black females in the North. In noting the less subservient personality of Delia, Heather is reminded of them: "The girl was definitely not servile in her speech or appearance. An air of dignity emanated from her in the stately way she stood. Heather was reminded of the Negroes with who she attended private school in Boston, daughters of free Black men, and the southern white slave owners whose consciousness pricked them to educate their illegitimate daughters" (107). Heather notices the Sojourner Truth–like qualities of Black female subjectivity, but like real-life women suffragists, she uses that Black female subjectivity to validate and create her own identity. Heather attended all-girl schools with Black females, but she still does not consider them as equals, as exhibited in her ownership of Delia. Heather's purchase of Delia allows readers to ascertain that Heather means to use Delia for her own purposes—to assert herself as a lesbian, butch, through exploiting the Black body. Shockley exposes white women's participation in white supremacy, even as they attempt to dismantle white patriarchy through fulfillment and expressions of their queer sexual desires.

As Heather and Delia continue to learn about each other, Delia reveals that her mother was a free woman. Heather, understanding the significance of this detail, exclaims, "Then, you were free" (110). Despite learning that Delia was a free woman who was kidnapped and sold into slavery (110), Heather maintains the mistress/slave dynamic of their relationship. Ordinarily, in white feminist thought, Heather might be championed as something of a radical and exceptional woman. She seems very liberal minded when she proclaims, "What I would really like to be is an abolitionist. Free the slaves, sell the plantation, and go back to the north to live" (109). She owns land and property, she acknowledges her same-sex desire, and according to the townspeople, she's "got a mind like a man's for business" (107). However, Shockley concerns herself with a much more complex agenda, the penetration of white Eurocentric discourses into the Black female body. In one scene, Shockley convincingly presents how the white woman uses the Black body to construct her sexuality:

> Turning to Delia, she questioned: "Have you ever cut hair before?" When the girl answered in the negative, Heather handed her a pair of scissors. "Let's give it a try."
> As the cut tresses lay scattered on the floor by the chair, Heather scrutinized the effect in the mirror. She resembled Ralph more than ever now without his moustache and sideburns. . . . "Don't cut yours," she said, reaching up to finger Delia's hair. (109)

Hair has consistently been a way to mark or articulate one's queerness in various queer communities.[18] In Heather's private world of the plantation, she can transgress borders. The cutting of her hair symbolically captures the character's cutting off societal constraints of gender and desire.

The environment of dominance and submissiveness that slavery presents promptly reveals the irony of interracial relationships and lesbian relationships, and the presentation of both as "deviant" behavior. The institution of slavery fosters an atmosphere in which the social constructs of female same-sex desire, the butch and the femme, must rely on exploitation rather than free expression of sexuality. As Shockley shows, these ideologies of role-playing can then expose the collusion of racialized sexuality and scientific racism in constructing ideologies of homosexuality. Heather's actions mirror the dehumanizing efforts of white heterosexual men as slave owners. The twist of female-on-female sexual exploitation reveals that heterosexuality is not any less "deviant" than homosexuality. Going beyond this realization, we note all too quickly that Western canons of sexuality present troubling definitions for sexuality.

Upon seeing Heather's new hairstyle, her brother Ralph notes, "So you've cut your hair . . . another link to wearing pants and buying a slave girl. . . . What role are you trying to play, dear sister?" (109). Heather denies playing a role, but clearly she does: She wears pants, she cuts her hair, she thinks like a man, and she desires like a "natural man," according to the logic of intelligible gender and the antebellum South. Yet butch/femme, as Roof observes, produces "a systematic challenge to the necessary connection between gender and sexuality while appearing to reaffirm heterosexuality" (Roof, "A Lure of Knowledge" 245). At the outset, it might seem that Heather's performance as butch interrupts the discourse on gender of man/woman, but Shockley's trickeration goes even further in that interruption because she implements the break through race. Because whiteness is personified as femininity, the only way Heather can engage her masculine play is to align femininity with blackness.

Hair, traditionally a pivotal physical feature in considerations of the feminine for Black and white women, is the first way that she can butch up her white body and femme Delia in the process. While Delia remains less vocal, she participates in Heather's performance by cutting the hair. She understands the role she is playing. Heather's insistence that Delia not cut her hair signifies the roles of butch and femme in some lesbian relationships, and it is further altered by the fact the Delia is a slave who is legally bound to be submissive to Heather. Shockley utilizes the institution of slavery to show the literal representation of the problem with current canons of sexuality. Critic Jill Dolan suggests that without critical queries, the Western canon of sexuality (homosexuality/heterosexuality) and gender hierarchies are reinforced all the more in the actualization of the lesbian (white female with same-sex desires):

> Reconstructing a variable lesbian subject position that will not rise like a phoenix in a blaze of essentialism from the ashes of deconstruction requires emptying lesbian references of imposed truths, whether those of the dominant culture or those of lesbian radical feminist communities which hold their own versions of truth. The remaining, complex, different referent, without truth, remains dependent on the materiality of actual lesbians who move in and out of dominant discourse in very different ways because of their positions within race, class, and variant expressions of their sexuality—dragging at the margins of structure and ideology. (53)

Sexuality becomes fixed and limited as a result of whiteness needing to remain in a dominant position of power. When we ignore the way race shapes the construction of lesbian, we limit both white and Black female same-sex desire. The Black subject continues to be object and fetishized, while the white female remains locked in heteronormative genders. Because butch/femme has been touted as a third gender, Shockley provides readers with lesbians who have conflicted relationships with dominant ideologies of race and sexuality. Historically, implicit in white women's nineteenth-century gender liberation and twentieth-century sexual liberation is the way it consumes Black female bodies for its own agenda. In ways that we might ignore in representations of butch/femme in white-only or Black-only same-sex relationships, the tensions from the taboos of interracial butch/femme lesbian relationships embolden us to keep revising and altering our perceptions of lesbian identity and butch/femme desires away from essentialist models.

For instance, when Heather further asserts her lesbianism during sexual contact (rape) with Delia, several factors are revealed. When Delia comes to Heather's room, she is invited to sleep in the bed with Heather. In bed Heather informs Delia: "You know, some women can feel about one another the way men and women do" (112). Delia's response is an admission of same-sex desire, not necessarily hers: "I know now" (112). As Shockley did with Mattie and Alice or Patrice and Lettie, she positions the white lesbian as a type of lesbian archetype that needs to be broached and then disavowed for some women. Why? Because of race. Delia's same-sex desire is problematized by her status as slave/servant. Even if Delia freely desires Heather, she is not free, and Heather continues to use their unequal status as a way to create her sexual identity.

As Heather lies in bed with Delia, she clearly takes on the dominant role as butch and mistress: "Slowly, Heather began to remove Delia's gown. 'I want to see your beautiful body.' . . . Lightly, Heather caressed Delia's breast and stomach" (112). Throughout the entire scene, readers barely know what Delia is saying, thinking, or wanting. Despite her silence, Delia remains the Queen B(?) trickster figure of the text, specifically when we take into account the descriptive nature of trickster in Brian Streete's reflections on Zande tricksters: "Although he has not himself developed a model of the 'meaningful' to the audience and shown how it developed and is continually being developed out of the meaningless, the amorphous. By acting at the boundaries of order the trickster gives definition to that order" (101). As previously outlined with attention to the way Delia's presence allows Heather to be butch, Delia's silence continues to establish a distinct order by acting at the boundaries of the governing order of race and sexuality. Her silence signals her acceptance of their lovemaking as an act about the fulfillment of their same-sex desire. However, when Delia does speak it is at the request of Heather, and a miscommunication ensues that divulges more situation inversion from the writer-as-trickster, Shockley: "Delia, say my name," Heather whispered, nibbling on her earlobe. Delia, in turn, replies, "Mistress—" (112). The function of any trickster is to create chaos so as to disrupt conceptual orders. Shockley's use of the "say my name" sex play might be comical were it not a reiteration of the way vernacular naming and unaming functions.

"Say my name" is vernacular play or sex game. In the context of Shockley's story, the phrase functions in two ways that explore the ramifications of race and sex identities. The phrase enjoys a coded meaning in sexual relations that signifies issues of power, submission, pleasure, responsibility, and authority. Who is giving you this pleasure, who is making you surrender, who else can make you feel this way? Or the reversed position: I know who is giving pleasure, I choose this particular person, and I acknowledge that fact by naming them. Despite the position of power that Heather enjoys as mistress, she needs Delia to unname her as mistress so that she can become lesbian and validate her desires. Halberstam reminds us that the butch's transgression of gender is "often filled with fear, danger, and shame rather than heroic satisfaction" ("Between Butches" 59). Images of butch women are further revised when we consider the way race functions here. As a white woman who seeks to make herself butch through the privilege of white supremacy, it seems ironic that she cannot reach the third gender state she longs for as long as she continues to participate in the order of white supremacy instituted through chattel slavery. If Delia says Heather's name instead of acknowledging her status, she may alleviate the butch's fear and shame, as well as disentangle her from the detrimental influence of white supremacy.

I am not implying some ridiculous Hegelian notion of slaves as empowered. Delia is not all powerful because she is still a slave. However, as Hammonds has argued, the historical white constructions of lesbian needs the Black female body. Shockley's work suggests that in order to find less problematic models of sexuality, women must move away from Western categories of gender and sexuality. They must open themselves up to the chaos and disorder of the trickster. If lesbians (white) need Black female bodies to construct lesbian identity, what does that mean for Black females with same-sex desire? It is as if "The Mistress and the Slave Girl" were a fictional tale concocted to answer a probing question asked by Hammonds, "How does the structure of what is visible, namely white female sexualities, shape those not-absent-though-not-present sexualities that . . . cannot be separated or understood in isolation from one another" (306). Obviously, the existence of Mattism in African nations offers that the white female body isn't as essential to same-sex relationships and desire in the African diaspora. But in African America, the exploration of homosexuality as a political identity, not as a sexual practice or behavior, does entail white women in the way that Shockley's collection, including "The Mistress and the Slave Girl," has been implying all along. Shockley's work adheres to a major mission of queer theory: "Queerness should challenge and confuse our understanding and uses of sexual categories" (Doty, *Perfectly Queer* xvii). She continues to work on resolving the silence on issues of class, race, and biology that occurred in early Black lesbian fiction.

Whereas Heather seeks to construct her lesbian self through her consumption of the Black female body, Delia constructs herself as the Queen B(?) by participating in Heather's desires. If Elizabeth Grosz is correct when she says, "Desire is a fundamental lack, a hole in being that can be satisfied only by one 'thing'—another(s) desire. Each self-conscious subject desires the desire of the other as its object. Its desire is to be desired by the other" (64), then Delia's silence and actions throughout the story can be read as a way to create subjectivity. Because society defines her as an inanimate piece of property, Delia's fundamental lack can be read as the need to be seen as a human subject. However, if and when Delia desires the desire of the other as its object, in this case Heather, she controls the writing of her subjectivity. Shockley writes Delia as a trickster operating between two discursive worlds. For the mythical tricksters, those two worlds were divine and human, but for the Queen B(?) in Shockley's time the two worlds are discourse communities ordered by race and sexuality. Because Delia has been free and educated, she perceives the world differently than those born into slavery, but she also realizes her limitations as a house slave. In Delia's case her lack arises from what she once had, as opposed to what she wishes she could have. This minor detail informs the way she will go about obtaining the object of her desire, herself. Delia's actions showcase her performance as trickster writing radical Black female subjectivity by manipulating white woman's lack.

Though not summoned to, Delia comes into Heather's room, and she places herself as equal to Heather by revealing her status as formerly free. For Delia to name or unname Heather as Mistress influences her very subject position, as well as Heather's. For if Heather is Mistress, then Delia will always be slave. If and when Delia decides to call Heather by her name, rather than her status and position, we will know that Delia has become a lover and not a sex slave. We will know that Delia has made herself into a subject as opposed to the object. Despite the bonds of slavery, Shockley, like Truth and Jacobs, uses unnaming to imply that Black women must accept responsibility in creating their subjectivity through willful or imagined acts of desire. Delia's insistence on calling Heather Mistress is Shockley's way of reminding readers that she is aware of the othering that occurs in interracial lesbian relationships. Though Heather assures Delia that she is not her mistress but her lover, the point is made. Delia, about whom we know little, perceives their affiliation as what it is, a mistress exploiting a slave. The fact that Delia does not call Heather by her name signals Delia's comprehension that their relationship is far from equal, much less based on love.

While Heather may not want to be called Mistress because of its intended ties to the institution of slavery she supposedly despises, she doesn't mind using her position as a mistress to find a way to assert herself sexually as a lesbian. Such a reading of the story is not to suggest that lesbianism is deviant. It means to surmise that Shockley's short story is able to disrupt and question discourses on sexuality, race, and their connectedness. Shockley completes her turn as trickster, for as D. Alan Aycock has argued: "The 'trick' played is to transcend ordinary reality by violating it in such a way . . . that society is simultaneously disrupted and renewed" (124). The story truly depicts Abdul JanMohamed's concept of racialized sexuality, while at the same time avoiding a strictly heterosexual matrix. Shockley's appraisal of sexual desires locates other open secrets, beyond the white male desiring the Black female, within the institution of slavery. Western groupings of gender and sexuality made it so that the wretchedly violent and disgusting institution of slavery serves as the secret space where nonmonogamous relationships, interracial sexual relations, homosexuality, sadomasochism, bondage, role-playing and other nonheteronormative sex could be practiced. Shockley's trickster tale reveals that, in addition to economic benefits for white people in the United States, slavery afforded them other benefits. Shockley, as the situation inverter, demonstrates that sexuality remains more than a binary construct. She also demonstrates the impact of these open secrets toward any future relationships within and between the races. Yet the rest of the narrative suggests ways around that.

Shockley's story submits that the Black woman's genderless position and potential pansexuality can destroy the foundations of racism and patriarchy in the West. In the end, as Shockley writes it, Delia does become subject by unnaming her slave status when she says, "Lover. Heather," at her mistress' prompting (112). In doing so, she enables Heather to become butch and herself femme. Following the unnaming, Delia's sexual climax assures her surrender to Heather. Yet the subversions of gender that happen as a result are not the end of the way butch/femme roles interrupts logics of gender. Ann Cvetkovich points out the irony of butch sexuality: "That the butch who 'takes erotic responsibility' for her partner's sexual pleasure could, in her eagerness to tend to another's desires, as easily be considered feminine as masculine" (159). In shape-shifting the roles assigned to them by society, Heather and Delia revise and remake gender and sexuality.

Shockley's narrative is clearly controversial given the historical importance of rape in African American history and narrative. However, "reconfiguring gender requires reconfiguring the institutional and discursive conditions that structure and are structured by regulatory norms, but also reconfiguring interiorities, and, in particular, distributions of power, autonomy, attachment, and vulnerability" (Martin 74). The story forces us to return to Harriet Jacobs's reading of her decision to sleep with a white man who is not her master. Jacobs saw that act as one of humanizing liberation. Could she realistically say no to any white man who desired her during slavery? Perhaps not, but the illusion that she could pivotally shapes how she sees herself and impacts her decision to pursue freedom. Likewise, as a slave, Delia was never classified as a woman, and that position enables a transition into a possible third gender situation. Delia's sexual subjectivity isn't reached because she surrenders to and accepts a white woman's demands on her. She reaches sexual subjectivity because she attempts to control the sexual construction and identity of herself and her white mistress.

The question that the text invokes is how much of a surrender this is for Delia, who is a slave. As a piece of property, she has no real free will. Is the subjectivity obtained through the unnaming process valid if Delia is still a slave? Shockley attempts to resolve those contradictions with a romantic happy ending: "Months later, Heather freed the slaves and sold the plantation . . . moved to Boston, taking Delia with her" (113). The narrator notes that Heather frees the slaves, and the implication is that Delia is included. Hence, as a free woman Delia moves to Boston with Heather and lives with her as a lover. The story's ending implies that once we move beyond systems of captive bodies and limited rhetoric of genders, new models of liberation may be possible. Whether readers accept this ending at face value depends on whether we accept the trickster-troping of Shockley and her presentation of Delia as Queen B(?). If readers reject the ending based on the historical implication implied in racial discourses, then we also erase the lesbian history Shockley is fictionalizing. We discount the way lesbianism has been constructed through race. We ignore the viability of Black female same-sex desire: same-sex desire that could be butch or femme. And that is the tricky nature of Shockley's Queen B(?) tale.

Inevitably, Shockley's short story reveals how racialized sexuality should be taken into account for the fulfillment of Black sexual desires in post-emancipated eras. In "The Mistress and the Slave Girl," Shockley provides readers with a solid exploration of why Queen B(?) and her mutability proves to be so necessary in a reconceptualization of same-sex desire for Black female communities. Returning to racialized sexuality's ideological beginnings—slavery—Shockley announces just how awkward the constructions of homosexuality and heterosexuality are for Black peoples by showing how "as its embodiments of whiteness attests, heteronormativity is not simply articulated through inter-gender relations but also through the racialized body" (Ferguson 5). Through her depiction of slavery and lesbianism in "The Mistress and the Slave Girl," Shockley shows why Black females with same-sex desires cannot simply rely on Eurocentric classifications of sexuality used in her other stories. Finally, Shockley's entire text offers readers a Queen B(?) who can "reconstruct a tenable lesbian subject position . . . somewhere between deconstruction and essentialism" (Dolan 53).

6

Queen B(?)'s Queering of Neo-Soul Desire

Caught up in the anticipation of sexual desire and the throes of sexual ecstasy, people can rediscover and reinvent themselves time and again. From the moment we begin the process of acting on and fulfilling desire, we accept ourselves as liminal subjects. Desire is a personal narrative that can be revised and edited. Sexual desire is a song with lyrics, notes, movements, beats, rhythms, pitches, and timing. Different vocalists and musicians can dramatically alter the song's sound, mood, and meaning. Though the basic framework is still present in the lyrics, the song is never the same. Sexual desire is a song; the body, its lyrics; the spirit, its music; and the mind, its arranger. It can be remade, sampled, and remixed for the needs of the performer and the audience. Black music represents this philosophy in a manner especially germane to Black bodies that have been sexually enslaved and colonized. It offers multiplicities of sexual desire as varied as its genres and forms.

Black music is spirituals, gospel, chain gang tunes, blues, jazz, rock and roll, R&B, soul, neo-soul, disco, reggae, dance-hall, go-go, and hip-hop. Black music produces a chain of evidence that denies the existence of an essential blackness. For even in the few genres listed above, there are differences and distinctions within lyrical content and instrumental attributes that are influenced by geography, class, gender, sex, sexuality, and simple individual quirks. And while contemporary analysis of trickster has showcased it as a divine linguist, this chapter continues to propose that trickster also acts as cosmic player or entertainer for divine beings and humans alike. During Black people's involuntary and voluntary residing in this New World, Black music has consistently produced some of the most phenomenal modern-day tricksters and trickster culture. Each and every time, trickster's performances and aesthetics crossed new boundaries, created new genres, and helped our frail human bodies transcend their preconceived limitations and lifted our spirits to new heights. Trickster lives on in Black music: writing its own music, producing tracks for self and others, and making guest appearances on musical projects. When trickster is reincarnated for contemporary African American cultures, it refashions blackness, discombobulates gender, and revises sexuality in ways that make us giddy, uncomfortable, critical, joyous, breathless, exasperated, hesitant, and exhausted.

In his discussion of Black music in *The Black Atlantic: Modernity and Double-Consciousness,* Paul Gilroy's clarification of music and performance offers an explanation as to why Black music serves as a lucrative arena for the evolving trickster in African America: "Music and its rituals can be used to create a model whereby identity can be understood neither as a fixed essence nor as a vague and utterly contingent construction to be reinvented by the will and whim of aesthetes, symbolists, and language gamers" (102). Gilroy's point alludes to music's fortes of liminality and performance. As we will see, music allows the theoretical liminality of trickster to materialize either in performance or within the cultural product. Since Black women exhibit a concern with praxis and theory within their lives,[1] music offers creative artists and critics the option of trickster-troping to address ideological and material needs. By revealing the trickster-troping that occurs in the music of Meshell Ndegeocello and Lil' Kim, this chapter and the next examine Queen B(?) strategies in Black women's music for sustaining indeterminacy, exploring and expressing sexual desire, and maintaining a path of self-determination for Black female culture.

I've already observed how some Black female culture makers annihilate gender and articulate queer desires while calling into question the traditional limitations of blackness. This chapter proposes that we learn to read the actualization of desires and genders that refute those binaries in African American women's culture. Lesbian sexualities may be dependent upon a theory of Black women's sexuality, but as Evelyn Hammonds argues, "Black queer female sexualities should be seen as one of the sites where Black female desire is expressed" (311). This chapter and the next reveal the Queen B(?) as a positional site of queerness that allows producers of Black female popular culture to overcome the insistent hushing of their desires by middle-class modes that prioritize a heteronormative model or an assimilative homosexual model of Black female sexuality deemed acceptable to governing society. Queen B(?)'s queerness also allows her to antagonistically voice her sexual desires in opposition to patriarchal modes that insist upon making deviant the very articulation of such desires through linguistic signs of "hos," "gold-diggers," "bulldykes," and "bitches" for men's pleasures and constructions of masculinity.

In the case of Meshell Ndegeocello and Lil' Kim, acts of unnaming aligned with queerness that is not fixed as homosexual or heterosexual permit them to maintain autonomy over the process of self-authoring in regard to identity and desires. Merl Storr's "The Sexual Reproduction of 'Race'" clarifies what knowledge can be gained in the broadening of queerness:

> The proliferation of "queer" identities and practices in the current *fin de siècle*—not just homosexual (or indeed heterosexual) queer but bisexual, transgender, rubber, leather, SM, piercing, fetishist, polyamorous, butch, femme, and other formations—should alerts us to the possibility that homo/hetero binary is not the only force at work in the production and regulation of sexual subjects. (76)

Storr reiterates the importance of object choice in desire as a major consideration of sexualities. If one does not desire a man or woman, but a fabric, a sensation, a metal, or a paddle what then do we call that sexuality? Music by African American women has often made similar theories about object choice that are only recently being acknowledged. Although vastly different in stylization and methods, Queen B(?) figures Meshell Ndegeocello and Lil' Kim rely on shape-shifting and the sensibilities of outlaw culture in their music to usurp traditional binary forces at work in the production and regulation of sexual and racial subjects. As I will show, Ndegeocello's trickster-troping occurs through revisions on the trope of flying African, the use of soul as a hermeneutic to imitate erotic goddesses/priestesses, conceptualizing bisexuality as a narrative, and the construction of a lesbian phallus displaced by the pleasures of the vulva.

Ndegeocello: The Trope of Flying, Shape-Shifting, and Sexual Freedom

That Harriet Jacobs chose to write about her decision to engage in a relationship with a white male other than her master bespeaks the importance of choice and freedom to any human being. She deftly joins together narratives of free will and the body. Early slave narratives and autobiographies showcase a dual understanding of the body that directed ideologies of freedom for Black America: the body as imprisoned within the institution of slavery and the body as a prison for the spirit or consciousness. Once delivered from bondage, Black women, like Jacobs, soon realized that Black codes, Jim Crow, and sexism would dictate the extent of their freedom as something other than the escape from chattel slavery. Yet through racial and gender passing, some Black women learned that it wasn't the body that imprisons spirit and consciousness, but women's unwillingness to disturb the languages and laws that seek to regulate and confine bodies marked by race and gender. Meshell Ndegeocello provides one example of a Queen B(?) figure in music quite willing to instruct us in such lessons. Ndegeocello's music represents the vanguard of expanding blackness so that it accepts queer desires, while still maintaining the vernacular aesthetics that have been attributed to distinguishing Black cultural products as different from other culture. That in and of itself would be enough to qualify her as a trickster figure. Yet in addition to those aspects, Ndegeocello's openness about her bisexuality coupled with her musical genius is able to infiltrate the misogynist and homophobic world of hip-hop, as well as insert the lesbian phallus into Black America's Quiet Storm lovemaking music.

As a teenager struggling to accept her bisexuality in a profoundly religious family, Ndegeocello felt isolated because of her sexual orientation. She also felt unattractive and invisible.[2] While her music became a way to explore her emotional turmoil, her physical appearance came to reflect her internalized acceptance of her sexual desires. She shaved off all of her hair at the age of sixteen, and she had been going bald until very recently (Hilburn 23). Like Clotel and Ellen Craft, Ndegeocello changed her appearance to pursue her freedom—sexual freedom. For this reason, I will be examining all performative aspects of Ndegeocello and her work, including her appearance. However, before ascertaining the depth of her methods, we must first understand that Meshell Ndegeocello was once Michelle Johnson, and that Meshell Ndegeocello is also Tyrone "Cookie" Goldberg.[3] Like Toni Cade Bambara, Ndegeocello unnames herself at specific moments for the purpose of eluding classification and appositionally of all aspects of her identity and desires. After Ndegeocello's initial introduction to the music scene in 1993, *Essence* writer McClean Greaves described Ndegeocello as a "close-cropped, openly bisexual single mother . . . stretching the definition of the Black female R&B artist to funky new heights" (98). Clearly, the unnaming signals that Meshell Ndegeocello is meant to accomplish what Michelle Johnson might have been unable to do. Free from the expectations of Michelle Johnson, Meshell Ndegeocello can bend musical genres, be out and open with regard to sexuality, reconsider the spiritual aspects of desire, and provide critical commentary about race. Or in the words of the artists herself: "It's about being able to grow, be different . . . change" (Wiltz, "Meshell Ndegeocello Breaks Step with Pop" N01).

This unnaming is especially useful for a Black bisexual musician who positions herself as radically pro-Black and sexually open. For as E. D. Daumer has argued, "Because bisexuality occupies an ambiguous position between identities it is also able to shed light on the gaps and contradictions of all identity, on what we might call the difference within identity" (159). Bisexuality, then, has the potential to dismantle finite manifestations of blackness, gender, and sexuality. One might also claim that it acts as a means of unnaming. Bisexual activist Paula Rust has also noticed critics' ineffectiveness in defining bisexuality: "When the question is raised, the answer is usually that bisexuals come in 'all shapes, sizes, and colors.' And that bisexuality therefore defies definition" (234). Although Ndegeocello's sexuality may not be the sole reason for her unnaming of self, the act does coincidentally embrace the parameters of bisexuality as previously defined. Further, Ndegeocello exhibits a preference for the liminality that the concept of bisexuality incorporates. From there, she infuses her music with an aesthetic model based in trickster's linguistic and sexual fluidity.

Ndegeocello's first unnaming remains an important one. The surname Ndegeocello means "free as a bird" in Swahili. Since tropes of flying Africans and metaphors and symbols of flying have been used quite frequently by African Americans attempting to cope and deal with their lack of corporeal freedom, we should emphasize that Ndegeocello's literal unnaming stresses the continuation of unnaming for freedom's sake. As if in response to the powerful words from Halle Gerima's film *Sankofa*, "Spirit of the dead rise up, spirit of the dead rise up, and possess your bird of prey," Ndegeocello embraces the mythological importance of flying in African America to embrace and represent her trickster subjectivity. These claims might be read as far-fetched were it not for Ndegeocello's impressive regard for orality, myth, and folklore as stated in the makeup of her own work. The titles alone of her music novels, CDs, suggest an informed analysis of orality, vernacular, and myth in the African diaspora: *Plantation Lullabies* and *Cookie: The Anthropological Mixtapes* are the major compositions that expose her knowledge.[4] She has even said of herself: "I'm like the shaman."[5] In the process of inventing herself and carving out a space for that subjectivity through folklore and vernacular, she evolves the tropes of flying Africans from that of one concerned with racial homeland to that of one interested in sexual freedom.

Like Br'er Rabbit, Signifying Monkey, and Tar Baby, myths about flying Africans, buzzards, and Sankofa birds can be read as trickster tales. Olivia Smith Storey argues that "traditions of flight in Africa, such as shape-shifting, continue into the present" ("Flying Words" 2). Storey equates flight and shape-shifting as one and the same in certain African American myths. Indeed, Virginia Hamilton's *The People Who Could Fly* narrates the story of flying Africans only to reveal a myriad of tricksterisms. In that tale, an African shaman is captured and bought to the southern United States. He knows the words that will transform his people into humans who can fly. After a young woman has learned the shaman's words, she says them aloud and takes flight: "She flew clumsily at first. . . . Then she felt the magic, the African mystery, she rose just as free as a bird. As light as a feather" (169). The tale incorporates a complex negotiation between the importance of language, expanding the function of corporeality, and tricksterism. Because the slaves need not abandon their bodies to fly and be free, the tale resists the ranking of spirit over flesh in obtaining freedom. Further, it clarifies that it is language, either the lack of or knowledge of it that can shift the body into a space where it can be free.

Despite the lessons about the body and language that the tale teaches, African American criticism views flight in a culturally specific structure of collective consciousness marked by the sole experience of racial identity.[6] The dispossession of land is one reason African American people become committed to flight in regard to race and home, but it is not the reason it continues to be used, specifically with regard to Black cultural producers like Ndegeocello. Following in the path of Freud, critic John Henderson connotes flight as a metaphor that points to "man's need for liberation from any state of being that is too immature, too fixed or final" (Henderson 121). Ndegeocello's unnaming in flight attempts to eliminate the threat of existing as a state of being that is too immature and too fixed. That the woman who has been described as a "blackwomanbisexualbassplayersentientbeingGramscianintellectualandrevolutionarysoulsinger"[7] chooses to unname herself as akin to a species that appears to be unbound, nomadic, and free exposes the function of Ndegeocello and her work. Ndegeocello becomes a mythical persona whose purpose is to pass on the words that will produce flying Africans, or literally Black identity that reflects liminal subjectivity. While many recent artists in hip-hop and neo-soul practice the art of (un)naming, Ndegeocello returns to the slave's classical technique of unnaming to resist the continued onslaught of sexual colonization.

Like the shaman in the folklore of flying Africans or Turtle Woman myths, Ndegeocello possesses magical words that she can teach that will allow Black women to shift into beings who can liberate themselves from the immature and finite Western system of gender and sexuality. These symbols of flight can also be seen as further expression of her attempts to establish liminal subjectivity. In *Black Women, Identity, and Cultural Theory*, Kevin Quashie continues to theorize about Black women's liminal subjectivity. He postulates a notion of the "liminal divine" that allows us to see why this symbol of flight is so crucial to Ndegeocello's surname:

> What is tender, undeniable, fluid, like winter, memory, or hunger: this practice of pairing with an/other and oscillating between states of (dis)identification yields a liminal identity, a subjectivity that is material and corporeal but which

also transcends the limits imposed by corporeality, visual culture, and colonization—a selfhood that challenges normative constructions of "self." (78)

The surname is typically called the last name. It is supposed to be final, but the symbolic meaning of Ndegeocello's name is not finite. Through the purposeful action of unnnaming oneself a being engaged in flight, Ndegeocello creates a mythological version of selfhood that challenges the normative constructions of her other self, Michelle Johnson. As Meshell Ndegeocello or Tyrone "Cookie" Goldberg, she ensures her transcendence of the limits imposed by corporeality, visual culture, and colonization. Under the tutelage of Ndegeocello, we can learn valuable lessons about freeing ourselves from the discursive cuffs and leg irons of gender, race, class, and sexuality.

Trickster-Troping with Soul: Queen B(?) as Imitator and Messenger of Erotic Goddess/Priestess

Queen B(?)'s dedication to a work/play ethic allows her to chart new grounds. She can either reflect the elements of bee, bulldagger, or bitch, or she can find herself in a whole other sphere. The (?) emphasizes the tensions between secular and sacred spaces of Queen B(?) as a trickster to produce more possibilities. That is the point of the unknowable referent (?), and as Jacques Derrida alluded to earlier, there is something sacred, divine, and godlike about unknowable and unnamable referents. Furthermore, it is no coincidence that what is unknowable and unnamable is also very queer. Gods are queer, and the role of the erotic priestess is to teach humans this mind-blowing lesson. When Robert Pelton takes the time to admire trickster as a demigod, he alerts us to how trickster's joining of sacred and profane aesthetics elicits change in universal orders: "How amazingly large that order is, how charged with both danger and delight, how opposed to the mindless tinkerings with mystery so fashionable to the secularized West, the trickster reveals, ironically: as he grasps the ungraspable and spells out the unsayable, he shows forth divination's power to redraw in the plain earth of daily life the icon of all that truly is" (*The Trickster* 289). In regard to Ndegeocello, she uses her music to perform the work of blurring the line between the secular and sacred. Her literal play(ing) of music increases insights as to how some Queen B(?)s possess other viable ways to dismantle and reassemble society to make space for their gender and sexual desires. However, the return to the African concept of sacred sex for political reasons configures the work as the militant efforts of a Queen B(?).

Because Ndegeocello invents herself out of the tropes of flight and flying Africans, I return now to the divine nature of such myths. There are several myths about flying Africans, and Hamilton's version, which depicts the shaman and his use of magical words, exists in many variations.[8] Because shamans are often described as engaged in the art of divination, tropes of flying Africans signify the trickster trait of messenger and imitator of gods as well as the art of shape-shifting. Other versions speak of transformation into buzzards and a practice of magic and witchcraft.[9] These particular retellings of the flying Africans consider the figures within the tales as imitators of the gods. The Africans who transform rely on traits of a divine nature. Their transformative power, like that of trickster, comes from higher gods.

There are also alternative versions that don't speak of a shaman and those that creatively revise the importance of flying within the tales. These imaginative revisions in retelling the myth expose how the role of the messenger and imitator of gods is transferred from the tales to the tellers. Oral storytelling and mythmaking are as much habits of creation as is the creation of worlds for supreme beings and gods. In *Black Folktales*, Julius Lester documents a version of the flying Africans entitled, "People Who Could Fly": "Some of those who tried to fly back to Africa would walk until they came to the ocean" (148). Paule Marshall revises this version for her novel *Praisesong for the Widow*. In Marshall's version, the Ibos walked on water to get back to Africa. From Lester and Marshall, we can determine that some Black communities looked for different ways to reflect the realities of their situation with the hope offered by myth. In the absence of an African shaman or mysterious magic, tellers of some tales improvised. Because the tellers of such stories have to address the limitations of humanity and amend the stories in ways that won't make illegitimate the claims of flying Africans and freedom, the very process of revision makes these griots both messengers and imitators of gods.

In his testimony to ethnologist Miguel Barnet, former slave Esteban Montejo addresses the realities of the human body with the mythical freedom of flying Africans through a statement meant to blur the lines between reality and myth: "I know all this intimately, and it is true beyond a doubt" (43–44). Tales about flying Africans that consider the body and spirit are compelled to present these incidents as both godlike acts and human fact in order to represent the means of obtaining freedom. As an author Montejo, like Marshall, can exercise godlike control over the world he constructs in his narrative. He stands as a major authority and will not allow any other discourses to supplant his argument. The authors and oral narrators of flying African tales are as much imitators of god as the Africans who transform into birds or humans of flight in the stories. As shape-shifters, trickster admixes "both divine and human traits, he can slip back and forth across the border between the sacred and the profane with ease. He may bring something across this line from the gods to humans—be it a message, punishment, an essential cultural power, or even life itself" (Hynes, "Mapping the Characteristics of Mythic Tricksters" 40). Those who dabble in divine and human traits, or the sacred and secular (profane), bring us elements that transform culture each time. This last alternative version of reworking myths of freedom applies to the work Ndegeocello does concerning sexual freedom. Since Ndegeocello proclaims to be free as a bird, she stands as a Queen B(?) figure who comprehends the creative energies of trickster in a manner especially cognizant of trickster as imitator of god(desses) and messenger of god(desses), specifically goddesses of eros and sexuality.

Though we could easily continue to position Ndegeocello as a shaman or a griot, Ndegeocello's status as a Queen B(?) is reified because she functions more as an erotic priestess or sexual healer[10] than any of the aforementioned subjects. Queen B(?) as a sexual outlaw possesses the potential to function as an erotic priestess based on her ability to transgress and disrupt sexual borders. Critic Loraine Hutchins notes that this particular sacred figure delves into "the ceremonial uses of erotic energy for various purposes . . . to mean anything from erotic calisthenics, to enhanced partner intimacy or therapeutic spiritual and sexual healing; anything from the pursuit of better orgasms and feel good ambience, to seeking connection with the divinity within and beyond oneself" (209) The traits of shape-shifting, imitative and messenger of divine forces, and the pursuit of sexual fluidity already mark Queen B(?) as an erotic priestess, but Ndegeocello develops the characteristics and concerns through her music in a manner that exposes how much of a Queen B(?) she can be. Melisse LaFrance and Lori Burns have already offered a detailed assessment of Ndegeocello's disturbance of Christian moral logic and sexuality in "Mary Magdalene" from *Peace beyond Passion:*

> "Mary Magadelene" sees Ndegeocello rereading and rewriting the "biblical" story of Jesus and Mary Magadelene. To do so, Ndegeocello writes herself, a black and openly bisexual woman, into a cultural text whose interpretations are frequently used to legitimize sexism, misogyny, racism, homophobia, heterosexism, and the derision of bodies materialized and conditioned by the norms of femininity. (153)

Anyone who has ever listened to Ndegeocello's songs "Deuteronomy: Nigger man," "Ecclestiastes: Free My Heart," "Leviticus: Faggot," "Mary Magdalene," and "God Shiva," just to name a few, can attest to the nature of Ndegeocello's music as a type of sex work for African American communities still struggling to recover the link between sexuality and spirituality.[11] Cultural critics from Mark Anthony Neal to Robin Roberts have assessed how a great deal of Ndegeocello's work concerns all genders, as well as how Christianity influences her introspective music on gender and sexuality. However, her position as a Black bisexual woman doing the work through Black vernacular form propels her further into the trickster realm of Queen B(?). For this reason, rather than focusing on the Christian narrative in Ndegeocello's work, this text reflects upon the alternative influences within her narrative structures and themes. The unconventional authoritative narrative that also shapes Ndegeocello's commentary on spirituality and sexuality is the sacred/profane trait of trickster epitomized by Queen B(?) as erotic priestess.

Spiritual connections to sexuality seem to have been a gray area for U.S. Black communities over the last two centuries. According to Cornel West, "black families, churches, mosques, schools, fraternities, and sororities" were institutions that affirmed blackness, and that these "institutions refused to engage one fundamental issue: black sexuality" (304). If neither Christian nor Islam institutions, arguably the two pervasive religions for U.S. Blacks, were engaging sexuality, what Black institutions were? As Gilroy assessed earlier, Black music becomes an institution that, if it chooses to, can address Black sexuality with ease. And while gospel, spirituals, blues, and jazz were the institution's earliest means, soul serves as a more suitable vehicle for further analysis of Ndegeocello's Queen B(?) work. Ndegeocello has never been one to support the pigeonholing of her music into a specific genre of music. Indeed, her music relies on jazz, funk, go-go, reggae, hip-hop, blues, acoustic, and yet-to-be-classified styles of music.[12] Still something about her artistic persona and her work fits with the moniker of soul. Ndegeocello's unnaming toward flight, liminal subjectivity, and fluid sexuality allies with definitions of soul that recapture the connection between spirit and flesh, and it deconstructs the separation of soul and body created by colonization.

In his definition of soul as created by Ray Charles, Nelson George pays attention to the dramatic workings of the music form: "By breaking down the division between pulpit and bandstand, recharging blues concern with transcendental fervor, unashamedly linking the spiritual and the sexual, Charles made pleasure (physical satisfaction) and joy (divine enlightenment) seem the same thing" (70). In the tradition of Charles and, later, Marvin Gaye, soul acts as a genre in the institution of Black music dedicated to the sexual decolonization of African diasporic people. Those professors of soul, the singers and songwriters, are trickster figures engaged in acts of trickster-troping which include sacred/profane nullification, imitating gods, and serving as messengers of a higher power. There is no doubt that Charles stands as a trickster figure concerned with a process of sexual decolonization for his time. Contemporary scholarly investigations into soul explain how the concept is adopted by a Queen B(?) who functions as an erotic priestess.

In the edited anthology about soul, *Soul: Black Power, Politics, and Pleasure*, Richard C. Green and Monique Guillory work to determine the meaning and aesthetics of soul: "While we acknowledge 'soul' as it is applied to food and music, a particular moment in the history of African America, or a style or aesthetic that is thought to be endemic to black America, at the same time we question the myth of black cultural unity that imbues blacks with a certain quality of being by their race alone" (3). Their discussion of soul positions it as a postmodern movement that recognizes race but also the differences that may exist within racial communities. In a cultural vein similar to Charles and Gaye, Ndegeocello stands as a cultural demigod taking up the work of soul as it has been defined by George, Guillroy, and Green.

On the nature of any erotic priestess work, Hutchins asks a question that relates directly to this chapter's discussion of Ndegeocello: "What does this phenomenon of women as erotic priestess and sexual healers, particularly bi women as sexual healers, mean for all people in this culture, especially in the context of increased interest in holistic, mind-body integration, and efforts to harmonize sexuality and spirituality?" (208). Although Hutchins is concerned with less specific and universal understandings of the erotic priestess in U.S. society, I am interested in uncovering how a Black bi-woman constructs herself as an erotic priestess or sexual healer in Black female culture and what that means for the culture. As I have been conceptualizing, soul as formulated by the Black music institute is how she constructs herself as an erotic priestess and delivers her message.

Despite Queen B(?)'s savvy insight into sexuality as a tool for power and pleasure, the figure is not a shallow ego. Trickster is, after all, a divine being. As such, Queen B(?) can be quite soulful when she wants to be. Beyond her unnaming, Ndegeocello's motivation for sexual freedom guides her to a concept that can express her racial pride and sexual fluidity: soul. Ndegeocello's music may not reflect the soul stylizations of Aretha Franklin, Donnie Hathaway, or James Brown, but her music does echo the comprehension of creation and boundary breaking exemplified by those figures. It mirrors their insistence upon music as a method upon which the soul can be temporarily released from the body. Her music also exemplifies soul as a political and social concept, and soul as it has been discussed allows Ndegeocello to go about the work of representing her sexual identity as a Black bisexual woman. Because soul's foundation is rooted in African beliefs in the unification of the spirit and body, Queen B(?) turns to alternative avenues of spirituality to determine sacred sexual freedom.

Take for example Ndegeocello's *Comfort Woman*, released in 2003. The project is decidedly different from her aforementioned projects, in which

Christianity was a force of repression immobilizing efforts aimed at sexual liberty. *Comfort Woman*, however, seeks sexual self-determination through unconventional spiritual means. When we examine *Comfort Woman* as a music narrative with chapters composed of songs about pleasure, a signifying CD title and song titles, symbolic CD cover art work, and purposeful images of the author within that art work, we can ascertain a narrative that positions sexuality as concerned with a broad configuration of spirituality, as opposed to being committed to monotheistic religious sects of Christianity, Islam, Hebrew, Catholicism, and so on. The artwork for the music text situates us in the realm of space. Page after page, music fans are confronted with pictures of galaxies, solar systems, stars, nebulae, and suns. On the first page, Ndegeocello's headshot stands as a profiled image against a backdrop of the blackness of space. The artwork insinuates Ndegeocello as a goddess amongst the stars, a being who has surpassed the pull of earthly forces. Ndegeocello's musical opus exposes her imitation of a mythical god/goddesses at work creating man, or in this case, a "comfort woman." Ndegeocello no longer wears the cropped or shaved hairstyle, but instead sports thick cornrows, makeup, and a lone looped gold earring in one ear. Like her unnaming, her change in appearance signals the embracing of another facet of her identity, one in which a single identity discourse does not have to dominate over another. Her mythological work details a creation myth about a "comfort woman," one who centers her life in her desires and dreams. Ndegeocello conveys her mythology through an interesting visual use of sun, moon, and stars informed by Black folk legends of flight. But the visual elements that are used in her imitations of erotic goddess are surpassed by trickster's dedication to orality.

In addition to these visual collages, several selections from *Comfort Woman* capture the CD's theme of space intersecting with and revising myths of flying Africans. "Liliquoi Moon" relates the story of a father who yearns to fly coupled with other distinctive patriarchal legacies of the tropes of flying Africans. In recounting what her fictional daddy would say to her mother, Ndegeocello sings the words spoken by the father: "I can't promise you love, and I can't promise you me. In my heart of hearts I yearn to fly, and death will come fast. I wanna be free and closer to sky." The father expresses his need for flight to get to freedom, but as the song continues it is the mother who suffers and cries tears of regret at his leaving to pursue that freedom. The song makes an implicit connection between gender, freedom, and the pursuit of dreams through the symbolics of flight. Gay Wilentz's analysis on the trope of flying Africans argues that gender impacts Hamilton's tale in comparison to others ("If You Surrender" 23). Wilentz pays particular attention to the role of mothering as the distinguishing feature that reveals the importance of gender in shaping dialogues about freedom in metaphors of flight. The fact that one version tells of Sarah flying back to Africa with her child in her arms, while tales of men represent their transformation into flying African as a solitary and individual act insists that women create their own myths based on their experiences.[13] Ndegeocello integrates these tensions into "Liliquoi Moon." Though Ndegeocello's song focuses on the father's words, it begins with an examination of the mother who thinks little of dreams and love because they remind her of the man who left her to pursue his own dreams. Since Ndegeocello's song is about a woman who, rather than see her own dreams symbolized by the gift of flight, surrenders to the notion that flight is a masculine privilege, we should note that a revisionist attention to gender in the trope of flight within the song. The myth is revitalized for the comfort woman that the Queen B(?) is constructing.

"Liliquoi Moon" addresses the roles of gender and flight in an approach similar to that of Hamilton's collection. Unlike the mother, the singer-daughter does not judge or negate flying by ignoring dreams or discussions of flight. On the contrary, "Liliquoi Moon" expresses what the child/singer learns from her parents: that love, dreams, or desires bounded is not freedom. The implication is that love from another is not as lasting, enduring, or as liberating as flying. The lyrics hint at a need to return to the divine nature of self. Because romantic love has the tendency to become entangled in contracts and moral responsibility, the freedom it offers is displaced by the way various social institutions turn it into a matter of possession and ownership. According to the building mythology of the comfort woman, she must perceptively avoid the imprisoning of her soul.

As a Queen B(?), Ndegeocello reinvests in the notion of flight as being a means to freedom regardless of sex. The title of the song functions in opposition to narrative about the mother turning away from or dismissing the power of flight. For the moon in "Liliquoi Moon" serves as another creative alcove for women to remember their dreams, freedom, and how to fly. By taking flight away from the earthly world to that of space, flight can be imagined in womanly terms. Mythology about the moon centers on the female body, sexual desire, and fertility. Even the Dahomean trickster god Mawu-Lisa is both the sun and the moon. Mawu represents the moon. The flying African evolves into the "Liliquoi Moon." The daughter can pursue her dreams and desires without feeling as if it is masculine privilege. Ndegeocello's imitation of goddesses in this chapter is complete, but her function as erotic goddess continues in other songs from *Comfort Woman*.

"Love Song #2" continues Ndegeocello's revision of gender in tales about flying Africans and in terms of exploring sexual liminality: "Born on a black star I've come so far. . . . Beyond the stars is where I'm from. . . . We can fly. Butterflies." In this song, the flying African has flown beyond Earth's blue skies into the nether regions of space. Humanity's knowledge of space is small, and our fear of it has been even greater. Yet based on the cover of *Comfort Woman* and the lyrics from the songs, Ndegeocello's image sits and dominates the backdrop of space, almost as if to signal her divine trickster nature. Her words also reimagine flight from that of a bird to one of a black star or butterfly. When she later calls herself the sun, her nouveau representation of a flight is complete. Ndegeocello's neo-trope of flight becomes that of celestial bodies that are less bound to the gravitational forces of the earth. This form of movement is otherworldly flight. Still, the singer returns to traditional motifs for flight such as the butterfly to ensure that we understand that her concern with the sun and butterflies is about transformation and change that should lead to freedom.

In another song from the same CD, "Andromeda and the Milky Way," Ndegeocello implicitly sings about flight and queer desires: "Take me down to your river. I wanna get free with you. Take me down . . . I wanna get free." The river, or the water contextualized by specific bodies in space, returns us to motifs of flying Africans who walk on water before flying. Further, water symbolizes spiritual rebirth in many communities. Because water is a liminal element that can be vaporized, frozen, or returned to its original liquid state it serves as a succinct metaphor for the spirit/soul bound by the earth's river banks, man's technology, and most notably the human body. It's the potential of water to somehow escape encapsulation that makes it a dangerous threat and a healing life force. In both cases, its potential for freedom parallels and corresponds to that of flight. Through "Andromeda and the Milky Way" Ndegeocello can depict a spiritual rebirth through traditional imagery of water. However, the river also symbolizes a feminine force that offers a sexual rebirth. Although the song is about an infinite love unbound by space and time, signified by the presentation of Andromeda and the Milky Way as involved in a relationship and a love written in the stars, the connotation of sexuality is there. Though gender is not mentioned, both Andromeda and the Milky Way have roots in female myths.[14] These two feminine celestial bodies symbolize a spiritual refashioning of same-sex desire.

Luce Irigaray provides an enriching theorization of women's sexual desires that proposes river imagery as a consideration of gender and sexuality that displaces the hardness of the phallus as ultimate sexual signifier:

> You remain in flux, never congealing or solidifying. What will make the current flow into words? It is multiple, devoid of causes, meanings, simple qualities. Yet it cannot be decomposed. . . . These rivers flow into no single,

definitive sea. The streams are without fixed banks, this body without fixed boundaries.... Between us, "hardness" isn't necessary. We know the contours of our bodies well enough to love fluidity. (215)

Both Ndegeocello and Irigaray envision female sexuality as bodies of water. Because Ndegeocello is a woman singing about being taken to a river, same-sex desire takes center stage. The title reinforces queer desire in the song. Andromeda and Milky Way become personified female bodies. Since Andromeda and Milky Way are vast and almost immeasurable entities in space, the two subjects symbolize the unlimited possibilities of pleasure embedded in female bodies. The female body offers symbolic fluidity that can free those engaged in an exchange of love and desire. The love Ndegeocello espouses a yearning for is not devoid of sexual desire or spirituality. In a manner that reminds us of Ray Charles's gift for soul, Ndegeocello replaces the sentiments of the Negro spiritual, "take me to the water to be baptized," with her own: "take me down to your river, I wanna be free." The phrase creates a space for spiritual rebirth and sexual freedom. Since mainstream society positions same-sex desire as deviant, Ndegeocello's use of the river to symbolize female sex and her allusion to baptism as an act of lesbian lovemaking represents the colliding of sacred spiritual beliefs with "profane" notions of sexuality. The collision is trickster's imitating god with the hermeneutic of soul. The Queen B(?) erotic priestess turns to the sublimity of soul as defined in African diasporic terms to create tropes of flying Africans who may be queer. Such a trickster-trope demands more from configurations and performances of blackness.

Paul Gilroy, in an interview with Guillroy and Green, sets up this particular paradigm for soul. According to Gilroy, soul "stands for black sublimity... It also stands for the dramatic, oppositional moment where the processes of fragmentation and commodification begin [to], if not exactly break down, then at least lose some of their totalizing power ("Question" 252). What is the imagined (w)hol(l)y unified Black nation if not a commodification of racial identity to the exclusion of all other facets of identity, but soul exposes the classification without dismissing the political benefits of such racial solidarity. The totalizing power of blackness bends to acknowledge the Queen B(?)'s same-sex desire. Ndegeocello's subtle reference to a spirituality located in Black oral customs and "pagan" myths is a challenge to Black spiritual traditions that ignore sexual desire in their considerations of blackness and spirituality. While she seeks sexual freedom, she constantly expands blackness. In addition, because so many of the songs from *Comfort Woman* rhythmically rely on reggae music, the limited ideals of soul for Blackness are reconfigured in the Black-Atlantic exchanges of music as a cultural product. So while the beat reflects Caribbean influences, the lyrics refer to U.S. Black influences of soul music. That said, Ndegeoceollo provides further trickster-troping with the division between the sacred and profane.

Ndegeoceollo's references to space are not only about Greek mythology, but they also reference the spiritual school of astrology. As one continues to unfold the CD pages of *Comfort Woman*, other images of space are uncovered. An astrological chart floats amid the nondescript stars in the artwork. Because astrology exists in many cultures carried out through different means, Ndegeocello has gravitated toward a spirituality that can express difference without concerns of hierarchical struggles for power. It acts as a wonderful act of trickster-troping. Communities create their forms of astrology from studying mysticism and its influence on signs, constellations, planetary elements (water, fire, air, earth), and polarities (Omarr 24–28). As we know from 1970s poster culture, there was an interesting intersection between soul, sexuality, and astrology that occurred in Black popular culture. During this time, a series of posters was initiated from one main poster entitled "The Afronomical Ways." In a soulful reinterpretation of the Kama Sutra, this poster depicted the twelve signs of the zodiac through specific sexual positions said to align with each sign's traits. The human figures were painted in neon and drawn with afros and other physical features that signified blackness for the time period. The poster then spawned a series of posters that graphically enlarged each sexual zodiac sign. "Afronomical Ways" represents a modern pop culture moment of Black people attempting to recapture their belief in the connection between the body and soul lost during enslavement and colonization. In a similar manner, Ndegeocello's inclusion of an astrological chart contributes to the creation of her comfort woman that exists in the stars: a comfort woman who practices the reconnection of body and soul displaced by slavery and imperialism.

In "Love Song#1," Ndegeocello sings about a divine love based in intellectual, physical, and spiritual attraction: "I adore you. Your mind, body & soul. . . . You're deeper than love. Deeper than blood." As she did with "Liliquoi Moon," Ndegeocello insists upon a notion of love that exceeds the notion of quixotic love. Whatever she has found, it is deeper, more meaningful than the very concept of love. Likewise, the reference to a force deeper than blood signals that the object of her adoration also exceeds the borders of lust sometimes confused with love. She posits the existence of a feeling and state of being that is more than spirit (divine love) and flesh (blood). The Queen B(?) works hard to begin the process of sexual healing. However, rather than leave listeners with asexual thoughts on love, she remains true to trickster's ability to integrate the physical components of the sexual into the spiritual.

Although she chose in "Andromeda and the Milky Way" to mask sexual acts with images of women's sexuality as a river, "Love Song #1," like the neon coloring used in the "Afronomical Ways" poster, speaks more colorfully and boldly about a divine love, as well as explicit sensuality: "Stir it up. Move your body nice and slow. . . . All around. Touch your body, baby." The body does not remain absent in Ndegeocello's vision of spirituality and sexuality as a conjoined force. Though gender of the love object can only be inferred in this song, the previous ethereal symbolics in "Andromeda and the Milky Way" has been replaced with fleshy representations of rhythmic gyrations, autoeroticism, and voyeurism as another way for trickster to maintain the fluidity of desire. In the song, the narrator's spectral position might typically be seen as implicitly male since in U.S. patriarchal society there's a tendency for only women's bodies to be watched or commanded like that. Yet as we continue observing the markers of trickster-troping, Ndegeocello grants us even queerer insights than that of a woman appropriating a masculine spectral position. She is a Queen B(?), and as such this trickster figure returns to goddess foundations of specter and spectator. Those gods and goddesses of numerous creations myths that humans position in the sky as all-knowing and all-seeing supplant man as voyeur and commander of sexualized bodies. These expositions of trickster reveal the false separateness of sacred and profane. The wall between the two binaries is not present in divine figures and discourse, but It is placed in the metaphysical world of humans. Within the exchange of bodies, desire moves from being an ethereal suggestion to a more active energy that demands divine pleasure and joy that does not have to be relegated to a specific race, gender, or sexual orientation. Queen B(?) continues to trust soul's incorporation of the body to pull off such antics.

In extolling the difference between soul and funk, Gilroy mentions the importance of the body within soul: "The thing about soul which distinguished it from funk was its relationship to the idea of embodiment and its very particular attachments to notions of bodily performance, where the voice is the dominant aesthetic issue, not the rhythm" ("Question" 253). These ruminations on soul serve Queen B(?) well in her work as erotic priestess and sexual healer so that when she has finished dealing with divine love, it is not such a jolt to go into the depths of godly desire. Sexual acts become the bodily performance of the expression of spirits, and that is soul. The Queen B(?)'s use of soul becomes an imitation of divine power, a message about divine power, and a report on human needs and wants. Queen B(?) moves between the plane that separates man and gods and expounds on the benefits of fluidity in sexual representations and desires symbolized by trickster's polysexuality.

Queen B(?) Playing with Bisexuality as Narrative

Trickster has been characterized as a sexually anomalous figure. Willing to decenter the phallus, if only momentarily, Carl Jung observed of the figure: "Even his sex is optional despite its phallic qualities: he can turn himself into a woman and bear children. From his penis he makes all kinds of useful plants. This is a reference to his original nature as a Creator, for the world is made from the body of a god" (Jung, *Four Archetypes* 169). If trickster's sex is optional, then object choice certainly can change for any trickster's desire. Thus, the liminal trickster figure is a mythical personification of bisexuality. E. D. Daumer speaks of bisexuality as

> not merely a problem of an unrecognized or vilified sexual preference that can be solved or alleviated through visibility as a third sexual option. The problem of bisexuals are social and political ones. . . . I propose, therefore, that we assume bisexuality, not as an identity that integrates heterosexual and homosexual orientations but as an epistemological as well as ethical vantage point from which we can examine and deconstruct the bipolar frame work of gender and sexuality. (159)

If it is true that trickster's midway point between man and god makes her a cultural transformer, then a Queen B(?) figure positioned as bisexual—Ndegeocello, for instance—is doubly engaged in cultural transformation. Though soul work allows the Queen B(?) to dismiss the separation of the spirit from the flesh, it is Queen B(?)'s proclivity for play that allows her to interject bisexuality into the politicized identities such as race, gender, and class. With Ndegeocello, Queen B(?) as engaged in a sex as work/play tactic continues in a very different manner than that of Queen B(?)s discussed in the previous chapters. Ndegeocello finds a delicate balance between projecting sex as work and play. Having already addressed the soulful work of Ndegeocello as Queen B(?), I turn to the playful nature in which she engages sexual desire and racial identity through her music. Her performance appears to be rooted in aesthetics of Black vernacular and a historical understanding of the way bisexuality has functioned in her personal life and within the larger African American community.

Because of the way African American gay and lesbian studies have claimed and reclaimed specific queer figures for itself, I'm not certain whether it is necessary to locate a cultural history of bisexuality in African American women's culture. It exists and is there. From the open performances of bisexuality by Bessie Smith to the speculative notions of Lorraine Hansberry as bisexual, to deliberate claims that the liminal space of bisexuality marks one as a go-between or fence-sitter, bisexuality in African America has been broached and oftentimes dismissed. At least that is what critic Gregory Conerly proclaims in "The Politics of Black Lesbian, Gay, and Bisexual Identity":

> The choices for African American bisexuals are more complex because our society sees sexual orientation as an either/or homosexual/heterosexual proposition.... Therefore, they are often forced either to emphasize a preference for one gender over the other and socialize in those cultural spaces that support that gender preference or to go back and forth between straight and lesbian or gay communities. African American gays and lesbians usually have the option of socializing in a community where their specific sexual identity is centered, where as bisexuals frequently do not. (134)

Though Conerly's presentation on the predicament of Black bisexuals accurately reports the position of Black bisexuals in Black America, not all Black bisexual figures have gone the way of the tragic mulatto. Some have become rebellious outlaws who refuse to submit to the oppressive orders. I read Black bisexuals as trickster-outlaws made so by their desires. Bisexuals, especially men, stand as social pariahs who, because of ignorant assessments, elicit fear and loathing, while consistently signifying the destruction of every social rule of gender and sexuality.[15] Black bisexual men and women threaten both racial and sexual communities, but what moves certain bisexual figures from social pariahs to bad-ass sexual outlaws is their openness about their sexual orientation.[16] The music of Black women has often managed to disallow dominant or interior social regulations from impinging on how sexual desire is articulated. Open bisexuality in Black female culture stands as an aggressive and militant act representative of a Queen B(?) figure. Indeed, Ndegeocello's disclosure of her sexuality to the public and her musical skills enable her to provide Black women everywhere with new models of Queen B(?) trickster culture that can translate and represent changing sexual desires.

Influenced by Ndegeocello's example, rap artist Queen Pen was one person who heard and comprehended the early lessons of Ndegeocello as Queen B(?). As we will see, Queen Pen's "Girlfriend" musically serves as Daumer's theoretical mission of bisexuality as an epistemological and ethical framework that can deconstruct bipolar frameworks of gender and sexuality. Further, because the production of the rap song is essentially influenced by Ndegeocello, the singer/songwriter's Queen B(?) status in Black music is solidified. In addition to being a hot dance track for its percussive beats and sexually explicit lyrics, Queen Pen's rap single "Girlfriend" boasts of fluid desires and one woman stealing the affections of another woman away from a man. From the song's lyrical opening, the conflict of fluid desires and the moral and social constraints of society are highlighted: "Now how you just gon' be playa hatin' on me cause I got mad bitches just wantin' me. And i got mad niggaz just checkin' for me." In the case of bisexuals, the playa hatin' being done takes place in normative discourses of gender and sexuality that maintain the conceptual order of ranking differences into either/or categories. Yet Queen Pen uses street vernacular to remove listeners from normative models of gender by displacing women with "bitches" and men with "niggaz." When she later speaks of both in terminology of capital and consumption, she refers to each as her "stock," she furthers her non-heteronormative approach to desire in a way that queer of color critique critic Roderick Ferguson might find significant. Rest assured that Queen Pen knew exactly what she was doing, even if she may have overstated her contribution to the discursive measures she chose to engage.

In an article for the *New York Times*, Laura Jamison proclaimed Queen Pen as a "feisty female rapper (who) breaks a hip-hop taboo" in reference to the way Queen Pen depicted same-sex desire on her hip-hop anthem (337). And though Queen Pen imagined herself as "the first female to bring the lesbian life to light on wax,"[17] students of Black music know differently. Of Queen Pen's boasting of her lesbian prowess, Lucille Bogan might say that Pen has play "like a natural man." Though she picks up where Ma Rainey, Bessie Smith, and Lucille Bogan left off, Queen Pen's "Girlfriend" is made possible by trickster-troping begun by Ndegeocello's funk-filled release "If That Was Your Boyfriend (He Wasn't Last Night)":

> Now I'm the kind of woman
> I'll do almost anything to get what I want
> I might play any little game
> Call me what you like but you know it's true
> ... So if that's your boyfriend he wasn't last night!!!
> Boyfriend, boyfriend, yes I had your boyfriend.

Ndegeocello's song is about the polyamorous nature of herself as trickster. As a trickster, deception and trick playing remain the most productive way to achieve the fulfillment of desires not sanctioned by individuals or specific societies. Remember the Queen B(?), through any of its permeations of bee, bulldagger, and bitch, is polysexual! As an effort that trickster engages in most widely to challenge and change, play as expressed by Ndegeocello is romantic efforts, and it also coincides with Robert Pelton's argument of play with regard to the mythical trickster: "Thus the trickster incarnates in every culture the oxymoronic imagination at play, literally 'fooling around' to discover new paradigms and even new logics. As such, he reveals man's freedom to shape the world just because it actively offers itself to him—even if he must trick it to make it come across" (*The Trickster* 272). The trickster in the song fools around with another woman's partner, and she also assists the boyfriend in his playing of his partner. Through the remainder of "If That Was Your Boyfriend," as well as the legacy of the song in contemporary Black music, the trickster's (Ndegeocello's) fooling around in love and music yields new logics and paradigms that some may not find agreeable.

The mention of playing games to get what one wants leads the speaker into a precarious outlaw position as Queen B(?). As such, the Queen B(?) in the song has endured some name-calling. Though we don't have the specific name(s) that are associated with the boyfriend stealer, one can imagine that they are terms that have been used to denote such women as bad and immoral. However, this text refutes such connotations and upholds these women as Queen B(?)s. Trickster refuses to recognize borders for desires, and monogamy stands as a border of monotonous sexual desires. Ndegeocello's openness about her bisexuality at the release and subsequent play of the song, contributes to the trickster's play to knock down gender roles and sexual walls through gamesmanship. Not one to crumble under righteous indignation, this trickster prefers cajoling and boasting to apologies.

"If That Was Your Boyfriend" represents a remarkable demonstration of sexual signifyin(g) at its best. While its content focuses on gender and sexuality, its aesthetics remain mindful of Black vernacular traditions. The Queen B(?)'s signifyin(g) in the song means to respond to some form of signifyin(g) done by the emotionally injured woman. Caught up in a verbal game of wits, the boyfriend stealer is called out of her name, and rather than engaging in name-calling, the singer prefers directive signifyin(g). Thomas Kochman argues that "when the function of signifyin(g) is directive, and the tactic which is employed is one of indirection . . . , the signifier reports or repeats what someone has said about the listener; the report is couched in plausible language designed to compel belief and arouse feelings of anger and hostility" (257), Ndegeocello does exactly as Kochman outlines. Rather than keep the attention focused on herself, the accused Queen B(?) turns to an analysis of both the boyfriend and the jilted woman using information gained from phone conversations. Throughout the remainder of song, the Queen B(?) figure calls into question the stability of the couple's relationship, the male's affection for his proclaimed girlfriend, and the woman's sexual knowledge and appeal. Her reports are couched in plausible knowledge gained from phone conversations involving all parties. Most of the song endorses directive signifying that uses indirection. Despite accusations that might place all of the blame on one person, cheating does require the participation of more than one party. In the process of rescuing herself from derogatory womanhood created by name-calling, the Queen B(?) also exposes relationship commitments as something for the trickster-impaired population of humanity. In direct signification, the singer has the last word when she proclaims, "Call me what you like while I boot slam your boyfriend tonight." While one woman, the girlfriend, is caught up in the social mores of womanhood, the other woman manages to fulfill her desires rather than society's desire for her body. Again, Queen B(?) could does not aspire to normative sexual behavior represented by monosexual object choices.

Finally, in a move that mirrors the militant implications of trickster, Ndegeocello deftly allows her music to stands as a cultural product that offers evidence of bisexuality as a narrative. Critic and bisexual movement activist Marjorie Garber argues that "bisexuality is not an 'identity' (or a figure or a trope) but a narrative, a story. Yet the practical necessities of politics require making bisexuality into an 'identity,' at the same time that bisexuality itself, or bisexualities themselves, put into question the viability of a 'politics of identity' at all" (87). Ndegeocello's sexual fooling around (the affair) and her vernacular fooling around (signifyin[g]) lead to a song that can reflect bisexuality as a narrative. Within the song itself, the accused's constant defense of her actions proves that fooling around is admonished by normative models of society. Nevertheless, other artists found Queen B(?)'s playing around as a required example to emulate in their own models of sexual transgression. When female rapper Queen Pen proposed to her producer Teddy Riley to do a song about lesbian drama and romance, she based her song on Ndegeocello's signifyin(g) song "If That Was Your Boyfriend."

Moving beyond the dozens, the orientation of Ndegeocello's "If That Was Your Boyfriend" in Queen Pen's "Girlfriend" reveals a nuanced type of signifyin(g) influenced by gender; one that is understood and comprehended by Queen Pen who takes the refrain "If That Was Your Boyfriend, He Wasn't Last Night" and changes it into "If That Was Your Girlfriend, She Wasn't Last Night." Both Queen Pen's use of Ndegeocello's work and Ndegeocello's musical appearance on the single for vocals and bass playing alert us to a gendered form of signifyin(g). Their collaboration invokes the praxis of what Marcyliena Morgan has commented on as the two major characteristics of Black female language communities: "(i) pointed indirectness—when a speaker says something to someone that is either of no relevance to current or prior contexts, and/or not obvious from the prepositional contents and (ii) baited indirectness—when a speaker says something general which is taken by the audience to be specific or addressed to someone because of contextual evidence" ("Indirectness" 440).

"Girlfriend" begins as a rhythmic conversation between two Black women clearly invested in the major characteristics of Black female language communities. At the first thumping line of the song, when Queen Pen utters, "Meshell Ndegeocello, play it for me, come on talk to me," she establishes that they are about to engage in some very serious pointed indirectness about same-sex desire. Ndegeocello's reply also displays a type of pointed indirectness that hinges on Ndegeocello's status as openly bisexual and Queen Pen's sly queer sexual positioning in the song. As opposed to denying rumors of their queerness, Queen Pen and Ndegeocello sing and rap the refrain, and the song about same-sex desire and cheating signifies all over Black heterosexuality. Their signifyin(g) lays the groundwork for bisexuality to seep into hip-hop, a cultural product and discourse that normally prohibits nonhomophobic discussions of queerness.

Pointed indirectness occurs because the refrain first uttered by Ndegeocello, and revised by Queen Pen, is already about fluid and non-heteronormative sexuality (polyamory). The pointed indirectness in Queen Pen's single isn't for a specific individual but for the misogynistic and homophobic sphere of hip-hop communities that purport that same-sex desire is either of no bearing to current or prior context of sexual boasting and romantic game. It threatens the domination of the Black phallus in hip-hop. As the song points out, when "he can't control how you throw your pussy," women lose their fear of being associated with the pejoratives of unchaste or queer female sexuality: whore (ho) or bulldagger. From there, the potential to gain access to power previously denied to them is greatly transformative for the female subject and threatening to a society structured on woman as lack. The pointed indirectness unveils how, despite their performances in separate music traditions and genres, Black vernacular acts as a powerful weapon to dismantling gender and sexual systems of oppression for Black women. Queen Pen emulates every vernacular strategy of Ndegeocello, while Ndegeocello's voice musically centers her revision of the lyrics. When Ndegeceollo asks Queen Pen where she met her new lover, the two tricksters move from pointed indirectness to baited indirectness.

Even if listeners of Black music chose to ignore the sexuality of Ndegeocello as they listened to "If That Was Your Boyfriend," perhaps in a strictly heterosexual vein, they cannot do so in the baited indirectness of Queen Pen's song. Since the song's original context is derived from Ndegeocello's lyrics, and because the context is reimagined as a conversation between Queen Pen and Ndegeocello, same-sex desire can no longer be marginalized. As a Black bisexual, Ndegeocello keeps finding ways to revise her sexuality and self in ways that are specifically Black-identified.[18] Ndegeocello's very presence on "Girlfriend" is a nod to her Queen B(?) trickster status of situation-invertor for whom "no order is too rooted . . . that it cannot be broached or inverted" (Hynes, "Mapping the Characteristics of Mythic Tricksters" 37). Because

Ndegeocello allows Queen Pen to sample her lyrics and project her image as open bisexual, she offers a continuation of a narrative that some might have assumed was completed and finished on "If That Was Your Boyfriend." But because bisexuality is also a narrative that can be rewritten so that it never ends, her original narrative, "If That Was Your Boyfriend," is not fixed or final. Ndegeocello has found a way to make Black music do for her sexuality what Ralph Ellison defined as a particular function of jazz in regard to identity:

> There is a cruel contradiction implicit in the art form itself . . . Each true jazz moment (as distinct from the uninspired commercial performance) springs from a contest in which each artist challenges all the rest; each solo flight, or improvisation represents . . . a definition of his identity. . . . Thus, because jazz finds its very life in an endless improvisation upon traditional materials, the jazzman must lose his identity even as he finds it. (*Shadow and Act* 234)

In jazz, improvisation and challenges to monolithic identity is acceptable, indeed welcomed for the sake of the splendid product. Though Ndegeocello is not a jazz man, in a *One World* interview, she did make a statement that situates her sexuality and music as a conscious functionality akin to jazz: "There's some neophytes in the vibe, but basically, hip-hop being counterculture, underground culture, that's sorta dead. That's not going down. And it's all mainstream. It's just a bunch of pop music. . . . No one's striving to be Miles Davis. And, you know, I wanna be like Miles Davis" (Moore, "Last Woman Standing: Interview"). Her creation of "If That Was Your Boyfriend" and her work on "Girlfriend" realize the endless improvisation of her sexual identity that can be expressed through music. As opposed to being like Miles Davis, Ndegeceollo functions as a Queen B(?). The (?) of Queen B(?) symbolizes the improvisation of identity. As Queen B(?) personifying sexual fluidity, she chooses to lose her identity even as she finds it in and through her music. Her object choice changes as she changes, and her music offers her the opportunity to showcase the improvisation of sexual desires. She formulates trickster's trait of shape-shifting for the next millennium in Black culture.

Queen B(?)'s Lesbian Phallus

Queen B(?)'s configuration of bisexuality as a narrative leads Ndegeocello to other methods of trickster-troping that involve the trait of situation inverter. In the end, Ndegeocello's playing with bisexuality as a narrative also allows critics to examine her play with masculinity, femininity, same-sex desire, and race. Before speaking specifically about the drag king scene in her work, Judith

Halberstam explains that "lesbians produce wildly divergent masculinities in many different cultural arenas" ("Mackdaddy" 117). I submit that bisexuals produce outrageously differing masculinities and femininities in many different cultural arenas. As it concerns Ndegeocello, I argue that her instruments, especially the bass guitar, in conjunction with lyrical content allow her to produce these divergent masculinities and femininities without being trapped by the logic of intelligible genders. I argue that because Queen B(?) figures incorporate trickster's hypersexuality, Ndegeocello's fluidity in desire and object choice for her desires insists upon the inclusion and/or dismissal of a lesbian phallus to confront the conflicts that may arise from identity politics that might prohibit expression of desire.

Trickster is a contortionist that denies the three dimensions of the body for additional unseen dimensions that would surely dismantle biological reasoning were it not a myth. Imagination allows her audience to sometimes bend that reality. Take, for example, the sexual symbolics implied in Bill Leigh's article, "Meshell Gets Real":

> "It's true," chuckles Meshell Negeocello. "I can't reach the tuning pegs on my bass when it's strapped on." Here's evidence that size doesn't matter. Though she stands only five feet tall, the bandleader's giant sense of groove is only a small part of her stature as a creative musical artist. (44)

Leigh's comments reflect upon the sexual symbolics associated with Ndegeocello's instrument and her physical stature as a woman. The implications for sexual transgression are made obvious by the "size doesn't matter" phrase. Like trickster, Ndegeocello uses her musical imagination to bend reality. Ndegeocello has consciously acknowledged the sexual transgression the bass allows her with women during an interview, "Sybil of Soul," with Alison Powell:

> MN: Girls are the same way. I mean, you could be ugly, but as long as you play the guitar or something . . . guitar players and sax players really do O.K.
> AP: But the bass is sexy, right?
> MN: I don't know. I think just because I'm up front I get a little bit more . . . I get more attention. [laughs]
> AP: Well, the bass is sexy. It's so pelvic and deep.
> MN: Yea, in fact, the uterus is very responsive to bass tones. It's the low frequencies. Go to a party or to big shows and watch how girls love to sit on the woofers. (510)

Ndegeocello's phenomenal stage presence derives from her own body and the instrument so prominently affixed to it. Like most successful artists,

Ndegeocello's appeal to her audiences reflects her ability to hone in on the desires of all sexes, in addition to her amazing skills as a singer, songwriter, and musician. Together, her body and her bass grant Queen B(?) the visual means to align with her symbolic disorder for sexuality. Ndegeocello's wielding of the bass guitar and her mastery of it construct a hermaphroditic symbolic body consisting of the vulva and lesbian phallus that serves as a site of desire, and these desires displace heterosexual agendas that may become embedded in Black music.

As this text has taken great effort to decentralize the phallus in trickster studies in general, the matter of now imagining the lesbian phallus in Black trickster culture should be seen as a part of that decentralization. Legba and the Bad Man/Nigga, the tricksters most associated with phallic glorification in the African diaspora and phenotypes for dual gendered or performative gender, potentially possess this lesbian phallus. Of the lesbian phallus, Judith Butler insists, "of interest here is not whether the phallus persists in lesbian sexuality as a structuring principle, but how it persists, how it is constructed, and what happens to the "privileged" status of the signifier within this form of constructed exchange" (*Bodies That Matter* 85). Because Ndegeocello is bisexual and has been projected as a Queen B(?) figure in this text, our goal is to learn how the phallus persists in trickster's narratives of desire, how it is constructed, and what happens to the signifier in her work. Yet the primary site of the phallic privileging in African diasporic trickster tales reveals its own mythological creation story about the lesbian phallus.

In a retelling of the Fa myth about Legba, Herskovits and Herskovits record the tale of Legba's hypersexuality and the privileging of the phallus. After learning of her trickster son's (Legba's) deception in having sex with a mother and daughter, Mawu orders him to undress and "as he stood naked, Mawu saw how his penis was erect and said, 'You have lied to me, as you have deceived your sister. And since you have done this, I ordain that your penis shall always be erect, and that you may never be appeased'" (*Dahomey* 205). Though the penis is privileged in this particular trickster tale, it does not have to be so with other tricksters, especially with Queen B(?). For even as Legba is already erect, it is the mother, the feminine side of Mawu-Lisa, Mawu, that creates the imaginary, always erect penis—the phallus. Until she does, Legba merely possesses a penis that could, at any moment, become flaccid and devoid of the symbolic masculine power. Further, since Mawu's phallus means that Legba will never be appeased, the trickster's object choice is far from fixed and does not have to adhere to any particular models of logic with regards to gender, species, etc. As the tale reveals, after his punishment, Legba proceeds to sexually accost his own sister.[19]

As Butler has questioned in her psychoanalytical meanderings of the masculine and the lesbian phallus, "the question, of course, is why it is assumed that the phallus requires that particular body part [the penis] to symbolize, and why it could not operate through symbolizing other body parts. The viability of the lesbian phallus depends on this displacement" (*Bodies That Matter* 84). By making us aware that ownership of a penis is not necessary for the way we imagine the phallus' function in ideals of sexuality and gender, Butler echoes Pelton's sentiments about trickster and phallic models before her: "His phallus symbolizes his being the limen marking the real distinction between outside and inside, and the wild and the ordered, even as it ensures safe passage between them" (*The Trickster* 108–109). Pelton and Butler speak of the symbolic and imaginary signification of the phallus and both insist upon its potentiality for liminality. So while Legba's phallus is constructed via the penis, other tricksters might turn to other means. Queen B(?) prefers a variety of options in lieu of the single penis.

Butler explains how the Queen B(?)'s lesbian phallus would function as different than that of tricksters such as Eshu, Legba, and the Bad Man/Bad Nigga:

> Consider that "having" the phallus can be symbolized by an arm, a tongue, a hand (or two), a knee, a thigh, a pelvic bone, an array of purposefully instrumentalized body-like things. And that this "having" exists in relation to a "being the phallus" which is both part of its own signifying effect (the phallic lesbian as potentially castrating) and that which it encounters in the woman who is desired (as the one who, offering or withdrawing the spectacular guarantee, wields the power to castrate). That this scene can reverse, that being and having can be confounded, upsets the logic of non-contradiction that serves the either-or of normative heterosexual exchange. In a sense, the simultaneous act of depriviliging the phallus and removing it from the normative heterosexual form of exchange, and recirculating and repriviliging it between women deploys the phallus to break the signifying chain in which it conventionally operates. (*Bodies That Matter* 88)

Thus, even though trickster is already transgressive, the Queen B(?) could keep reinventing the very concept of transgression in wily ways that shirk off anatomical destinies. What this means for Black women's cultural communities, then, is that the heteronormative inscriptions of blackness could be dismissed, along with the racialized priviliging of whiteness in matters of gender and essentialist notions of sexual orientation, when a Queen B(?) decides to unveil her lesbian phallus through some representation other than the penis.

However, what remains missing in these configurations of the lesbian phallus is a consideration of how the symbolic phallus constructed via the penis distinguishes itself through acts of penetration. In order to penetrate, the phallus must remain hard. That is why the phallus becomes a much more potent marker of masculinity than the penis, and because of its relentless potential for penetration we imagine anything not like it as lacking. However, if hardness of the phallus is not about penetration, and Butler's various means of having a lesbian phallus, suggest that it is not, why do we need to imagine and construct it anyway? Power, of course, but it continues to be a pertinent question to pose and obscure if we insist on conceiving of a lesbian phallus, even if it is strictly a symbolic imaginary. In addition to answering that question, more radical explorations of lesbian phalluses would address the way pleasures of the vulva displace the phallus. The phallus (lesbian or not) must maintain rigidity not for penetration but for stimulation of the vulva area that insists upon movement, friction, and pressure for pleasure, transformation, and agency. Yet even then the multifarious nexus of the vulva, via acts of tribadism, could change at any moment so that it too becomes a powerful symbolic imaginary not based in erection or penetration, once again displacing the privileging of the penis as well as the symbolic importance of the phallus. The hermaphroditic possibilities of the vulva and lesbian phallus as symbolic imaginary offer further compelling analysis of Nedegeocello music as Queen B(?)'s trickster-troping.

Ndegeocello's bass as a visual moniker and as a compositional foundation for most of her music should be read as the vulva/lesbian phallus. It is clear from Leigh's review that the bass affixed to her small body becomes exotically fetishized in the minds of some critics and fans. Her live performances with bass in tow allow us to reimagine the guitar away from its imagery as an extension of the male penis to a more fluid representation as both lesbian phallus and instrumental vulva. Because the playing of a guitar and its various chords' locations plucked in deliberate ways is what produces music, such instrumental work could be seen as mimicking sexual contact with a woman's vulva. In acts of sexual instrumentation, the parallel seems obvious. The touching of inner and outer lips, the clitoris, clitoral hood, skin, and hair with various points of pressure become strings that could produce any possible responses or sounds at the skillful or unskilled hands of its player. One might say that Ndegeocello's instrument reflects both the potential for vulvic and lesbian phallic possibilities. In terms of her own use of the instrument, she tends to also fit into a mode of presenting her guitar as an extension of female sexuality that must be strummed, plucked, and picked in a rhythmic crescendo that reverberates back onto itself repetitively until the final release. In Queen Pen's "Girlfriend," this is the double entendre of the line Queen Penn coos to Ndegeocello: "play it for me, come on talk to me." It isn't just the visual image that positions Ndegeocello's use of the bass as vulvic instrument, it's the aural effect. Queen Pen's words could explicitly mean play that bass for me, or, as they are signifyin(g) on same-sex desire, play that sex for me.

Ndegeocello, as the Queen B(?) figure, unveils her lesbian phallus when she plays with the ideology of bisexuality as a position and a narrative. Ndegeocello's lesbian phallus also materializes through her stage presence as a singer and bass player. For some time, the guitar has acted as a way of visually exaggerating masculinity in many ways. Depending on the way one holds it or places it in a tactical spot on the body, it could appear to be an extension of the penis. In the music movie *Purple Rain,* Prince struts around on stage with a guitar, stroking it up and down in simulation of a male masturbatory act. In the finale of the movie, he strokes and caresses the instrument into a blinding wave of musical excitement and beauty that results in a literal climax all over the audience. The guitar was specially designed to shoot out (ejaculate) water in ways that add to the exaggeration of masculinity. Ndegeocello's bass guitar serves as one possible way for the Queen B(?) to remove the penis from such considerations of power. As Butler argued earlier, instrumentized bodylike things could be central to having a lesbian phallus. Yet projecting the bass as a lesbian phallus is not the only way appearance of the Queen B(?) multiplies her genders and sexualities. Because she has already shown a penchant for writing bisexuality as a narrative, the symbolic imagery of her bass guitar as an extension of her body positions the artist and her work in a transgendered space of hermaphroditic imaging. Though visually manipulating the corpus is one way Queen B(?)'s hermaphroditic body endowed with lesbian phallus and vulva is introduced into Black culture, some of Ndegeocello's songs provide a trickster soundtrack to the images.

In one song, "Barry Farms," Ndegeocello can both refer to the trangressive power of the lesbian phallus and use the vulva to displace the lesbian phallus so that it does not establish conceptual order. The bass controlling the rhythm of the song represents the lesbian phallus, while the lyrics allow Ndegeocello to complete her disruption of the symbolic phallus. In this way, the trickster's lesbian phallus allows the singer to comment on sexual shame and politicize desires in ways that Butler ascribes as a function of the lesbian phallus, the breaking of the phallus's signifying chain. However, it also allows the vulva to triumph because of its penchant of producing multiple pleasures. "Barry Farms" begins with go-go mastermind Kiggo Wellman claiming, "So go-go music is party music." With Wellman's introductory lesson about go-go music, Queen B (?) establishes her foray into playing again. However, go-go music is especially well-suited to these claims of bass as a lesbian phallus for Ndegeocello. Go-go music relies on percussive elements of heavy bass (drums and guitar).[20] While Ndegeocello's voice is flirtatious, feminine, silky, and deliberately soft, the beat is a rigid, hard, and prominent counteraesthetic. As the song continues, Ndegeocello offers a story about herself and another woman during their teenage years. While the two young women, as girls, enjoy an intimate bond and harmless sexual flirtation, the manifestation of sexual desires has been ignored until the two decide to move beyond the heteronormative boundaries of physical contact for women:

> But one night she wanted to see
> Just how far it could go
> Just how far I would go
> Hahaha
>
> Oh yeah
> She couldn't love me without shame
> She only wanted me for one thing
> But you can teach your boy to do that . . . Yeah
> Can you love me without shame?

Early on Ndegeocello warns female listeners that she is about to "wind up" women or bring up a taboo subject: lesbian sexuality. Yet the reason lesbianism is taboo remains falsely complicated, as highlighted by the way youthful innocence of desire in the song contradicts with the adult constrictions on desire. In her revelation about a teenage love affair, Ndegeocello speaks candidly about her own open desires and another female's closeted desires. The shame and closeted sexual desires expose the truth of Butler's comments about examining how the phallus persists and is constructed in lesbian sexuality. Its absence and its unacknowledged presence in the fabrication of lesbian identity are important. Lesbian sex, typically deemed nonprocreative, receives part of its shame from its inability to produce human life. Reproductions of lesbian sexuality in cultural texts predicate their representations on the absence of the male penis, privileging the vulva as the center of sexual desire. Yet as the song implies, the hierarchical ranking of the penis over the vulva persists, and such privileging results in one of the parties feeling ashamed. If the young Ndegeocello's fictional friend could find a way to displace the phallus perhaps shame would be unnecessary in the articulations of her same-sex desire.

Still, the early narration of the song raises another question, what is the one thing the ex-girlfriend wants that Ndegeocello suggests she teaches her boy to do. Here, Ndegeocello continues constructing her symbolic lesbian phallus. As Butler notes, "the phallus will thus always operate as both veil and confession, a deflection from an erotogenicity that includes and exceeds the phallus, an exposure of a desire which attests to a morphological transgression and, hence, to the instability of the imaginary boundaries of sex" (*Bodies That Matter* 88). Whatever the act, Ndegeocello hints that it might be a substitute for the penis in the endeavor to construct a symbolic lesbian phallus and vulvic displacement of that phallus within the song, but I am jumping ahead. As we continue to examine the song, we see how Queen B(?) constructs her lesbian phallus by signifyin(g) through lyrical content and through the music itself. Here, the lesbian phallus unveils itself. It allows Queen B(?) a rather unique way of signifyin(g).

Of course, when Gates said that "signifyin(g) is black double-voicedness because it always entails formal revision and intertextual relation," he was speaking of the way multiethnic masses in society "draw on 'arbitrary substitution' freely, to disrupt the signifier by displacing its signified in an intentional act of will" (*The Signifying Monkey* 51). Yet Ndegeocello as the Queen B(?) conceives of signifyin(g) in a more radical way. Ndegeocello draws on the Black double-voicedness of trickster tradition. However, she changes this Black double-voicedness into a polyvocality. She freely makes arbitrary substitutions between her voice, lyrics, and the go-go beat, an especially Black cultural production, to create a lesbian phallus to disrupt the signifier, the phallus, in a specifically Black context. Comparable to the imagined phallus, the beat pulsates throughout the subconscious of the narrative. The phallus, as Butler has noted, "constitutes an ambivalent site of identification and desire that is significantly different from the scene of normative heterosexuality to which it is related" (*Bodies That Matter* 85). Part of what allows Ndegeocello to invert the parameters of shame and sexual freedom is the way the go-go beat functions as a lesbian phallus within her musical composition.

Although Kiggo Wellman claimed go-go as party music, what he later says in "Barry Farms" about go-go imagines it as an object that one can employ in the creation of a phallus, "When I play, I watch the crowd. I watch the women, women party." Wellman's statement conjures a scene in which women's bodies and their exchanges of pleasure become a spectral fantasy for the male musician. Despite that the go-go beat replaces the male's penis, and becomes a phallus of sorts that can be inserted and removed between one woman or many women, women still remain objects to be signified upon while the male and his penis remain the primary signifier. Yet, go-go can also serve as a lesbian phallus in the context of "Barry Farms." All go-go does not function as a lesbian phallus, but Ndegeocello's text, her commitment to bass-driven songs, and the way she uses the music to underwrite her lyrics and voice enforce go-go as an ambivalent site of identification and desire. Because the Queen B(?) Ndegeceollo assumes the place of Wellman as the creator of music; she then becomes the one watching the women and their chain reaction. As I noted earlier, Ndegeocello makes the site of spectral fantasy even queerer.

Her creation and playing of go-go beats remove the scene of normative heterosexuality. She can choose to either place her feminine voice, symbolic of the vulva, alongside those women, or she can insert her lesbian phallus, the go-go beat predicated on bass, into the heteronormative voyeurism of the go-go master narrative established by Wellman. She chooses to do both and breaks the signifying chain. As we learn from further narration in the song, this disrupting of the signifier is necessary for those involved in same-sex relationships and exchanges of desire. For the two women to fully immerse themselves in same-sex desire without fear, guilt, or shame, the privileging of the penis and its subsequent projection of heteronormativity must be disturbed. In heterosexist traditions, the shame would be placed on the queer female, but Ndegeocello, as a trickster, has used go-go to invert the logic of heteornormativty so that the shame falls on the "straight" girl. And while the lyrics do a suitable job of projecting the complications of desire and homophobia, it is the combination of the lyrics and a go-go beat that thrust the lesbian phallus forward into the narrative of secret love.

As the song continues, listeners learn of how the two women enjoyed an amorous relationship that depended on secrecy. When rumors or gossip spread about the relationship, the object of Ndegeocello's desire calls off the affair. However, what the go-go beat has been insinuating the entire time, Ndegeocello fully explains when she runs into her old flame some years later. The ex-lover proclaims that she has missed Ndegeocello, whereby Ndegeocello asks what it is that she misses. The go-go beat pauses for a half note in anticipation of the ex-lover's answer: "Can't nobody eat my pussy the way that you do." Ndegeocello's former lover serves as the heteronormative context throughout the song. In additional lyrics from the song, the singer mentions how the boyfriend of her ex-lover purchases gifts and items for the woman. These lyrics allow Ndegeocello to establish the historical capitalist base of heterosexual and romantic relationships in the West. As Ferguson argued earlier, the performance of heteronormativity could increase or decrease one's wealth depending upon the success of such acts. The ex-lover has clearly given great performances, but those performances, or the material gains from such facades, do not quell the non-heteronormative desires. Although both understand the longing, the ex-girlfriend still situates that want in a sphere of deviance rather than difference. Again, Ndegeocello's musical accompaniment and her voice render this fact.

It is significant that all music pauses for a half note in a rhythm organized in 4/4 time before Ndegeocello whispers her lover's confession about the importance of cunnilingus in the closeted relationship. The pause signifies on the previously coded lyrics—"she only wanted me for one thing" and "you can teach your boy to do that there." Now decoded, oral sex, like the bass go-go beat, uproots the penis as the root nature of the imagined phallus. The prominence of oral sex in the song argues that the tongue is capable of displacing the penis in reading the phallus as primary site of pleasure and order. The striated organ now becomes the manifestation of a lesbian phallus alluded to by Butler and the vulvic interrupter as discussed in this work. The tongue is an organ capable of pressure, penetration, fluidity, and hardness. Thus once it is established as a lesbian phallus the symbolic order of the phallus is destroyed by the demands of the vulva. Penetration, according to the ex, was not enough.

The lesbian phallus veils through coding, but it offers confession through the music and whisper in the ear. The profession also reveals that the ex-girlfriend cannot simply teach her boy to do the one thing, and that there is something specific about the way her female lover makes her feel. In the end, the capitalist regime's dominance of money can't buy love, and it can't supplant the power of non-heteronormative sexual desires. The admission depicts that the lesbian phallus as constructed in the text has operated within its set parameters: "[T]he lesbian phallus signifies a desire that is produced historically at the crossroads of these prohibitions, and is never fully free of the normative demands that condition its possibility and that it nevertheless seeks to subvert" (Butler, *Bodies That Matter* 86). It is not merely the act of oral sex that becomes tantalizing, but the prohibition of the act between the two women. Such an understanding highlights the tendency to eroticize lesbian sex without politicizing it. In speaking of loving without shame, desire moves from the realm of the private to that of the public. The double meaning of the statement questions if the two women can love freely, and if they could love freely without the taboo-ness of the desires, would they both choose to. In this song, the privileging of masculinity is thwarted over and over again, and the political authenticity of lesbian sexuality is interrupted by the queerness of closeted sex.[21]

Butler asks pertinent questions that connect Ndegeocello's role as a Queen B(?) to a site that makes room for same-sex desire in a context that is not specifically lesbian:

> [W]hat happens if the law that deploys the spectral figure of abject homosexuality as a threat becomes itself an inadvertent site of eroticization? If the taboo becomes eroticized precisely for the transgressive sites that it produces

what happens to . . . sexed positionality, to the fast distinction between an imaginary or fantasized identification and those social and linguistic positions of intelligible "sex" mandated by the symbolic law? (*Bodies That Matter* 97)

While the ex-girlfriend is imprisoned by the expectations of heteronormativity, the Queen B(?) finds a way to speak her desires and act on them in any political, social, or individual circumstance. Since the Queen B(?) can disrupt heteronormative and capitalist paradigms of gender and sexuality, it also reveals how Ndegeocello's lesbian phallus occurs in this work, as well as in her fragmented narratives in Black music that are for a detailed heterosexual audience. When Ndegeocello moves her work into a specifically heterosexual format, the bass also stands out as a lesbian phallus. Ndegeocello's adept skill at revealing bisexuality as a narrative in her music allows her to briefly be a disturbance in the heterosexist and homophobic forces in hip-hop music. Nevertheless, hip-hop is not the only genre in Black music that has hypermasculinity and heterosexuality at its core.

During the blaxploitation era, Black musicians created a cultural commodity that drew from African American music of the time (soul, R&B, funk) to form its own genre. I am speaking of the movie score and soundtrack genre. And for some time, this genre was heavily dominated by Black male artists such as Isaac Hayes and Curtis Mayfield, to name a few. Though Ndegeocello has yet to be responsible for producing and performing an entire motion picture soundtrack, her work has been included on numerous soundtracks for movies in which Black love and relationships are at the center. Ndegeocello's bisexuality and hermaphroditic vulva/lesbian phallus ruptures the precise and inconclusive heterosexual context of Black films such as *Love Jones, The Best Man, Love and Basketball, Brown Sugar,* and *How Stella Got Her Grove Back* just to name a few. What does it mean when Ndegeocello's bass-driven (queer melodies) are strategically placed with heterosexual love scenes? It means the Queen B(?) has found a way to rewrite the bourgeois and racialized narratives of sexuality in Black America. These fragmented songs, a reflection of the artist's queer trickery, resituate queer desire in Black heterosexual communities and exchanges. So even if Hollywood won't make a movie about Black queer love and desire, it can't prohibit the influence of it. Despite the inability of Black heterosexual communities to critique their own hypocrisy and homophobia, trickster manages to do so for them and have a nice laugh about it. As a musician who has rarely received any major airplay from Black (and white) radio stations, Ndegeocello's singles produced for soundtrack enjoy an enormous amount of popularity. While critics and fans have insisted that male artists such as Luther Vandross, Teddy Pendergrass, Al Green, and others produce music made for lovemaking or baby making, the Queen B(?)

has cleverly penetrated the straight bedrooms of Black America's Quiet Storm music tendencies to prove how she can transform society at her whim and showcase how queer desires can be just as procreative as heterosexual desires.

Meshell Ndegeocello repeats and revises queer music trends by Black women with a noticeable difference, an incorporation of spirituality. Ndegeocello as Queen B(?) practices what she preaches—liminality as the key to freedom. She uses her music to construct bisexuality as an epistemological framework and devises the lesbian phallus/vulva as an ethical vantage point so as to examine and deconstruct the bipolar frame of gender and sexuality. Finally, she uses soul and go-go to complete her trickster-troping in a racially cognizant manner.

7

Representin' for the Bitches

Queen B(?) in Hip-Hop Culture

There seem to be some contradictions in anti-vernacular theories when we examine the product of vernacular art forms through the lyrics and music of Black female musicians and rappers such as Ndegoecello and Queen Pen. If the vernacular is limited to the genres of blues and folklore, or exclusionary to most of the Black female population, how are those two women able to sing or rap so succinctly and unabashedly about mutable sexual desires in a way that showcases folklore's and vernacular's values of flexibility and transgressing false social borders as they relate to gender and sexuality? The previous chapter briefly gleaned the connection between hip-hop and Queen B(?) through the provocative lyrics of Queen Pen. However, to really appreciate the way female folklore and myth continue the evolution of the Queen B(?), we need merely examine the work of Kimberly Jones, a.k.a. Lil' Kim. This chapter suggests that rather than read Lil' Kim as a stereotype of the hypersexualized Black woman, we should read her as a performative satire on the conflation of white feminine beauty and the twentieth-century cult of heteronormative Black womanhood that still persists and polices today's Black women. Lil' Kim's trickster troping happens as a result of her performing Queen B(?)'s trait of sexual militancy and queerness, corporeal posing that exaggerates the threat of Black women's sexuality, and the ritualization of sexual violence exhibited by many tricksters. Once we explore Lil' Kim's work, as well as that of others like her, through the trickster's expanded definition of queer, we can enjoy new readings of texts that she and other Queen B(?) figures in hip-hop produce. Such presentations are weapons of choice against the devaluation of Black female bodies.

There is a war on Black female bodies, and strategies for the fight have been marred by reducing approaches to turning bad girls into good girls instead of making men and women change their limited notions of gender and sexuality. *Essence*, the self-proclaimed Black women's magazine, made it official when it took a break from its impersonation of white women's magazines and briefly mustered a different editorial agenda for 2002:

> We recognize that the war against our girls is just as insidious, potentially deadly and capable of compromising the lives of innocent victims as the one that currently obsesses our government. We also know that its casualties are far more likely to go unchampioned. (Villarosa)[1]

Ever since the inception of *Essence* there has been a war against little Black girls, but what allows the magazine to take its contemporary talented-tenthish philosophy of "lifting as we climb" is the assumption that the victims—the girls—are going unchampioned. However, as part of the historical conglomerate of the Negro Press of the 1950s, Johnson Publications, *Essence*'s agenda remains subject to its inferiority complex as discussed by E. Franklin Frazier's examination of the Negro Press:

> The Negro Press . . . is the chief medium of communication which creates and perpetuates the world of make-believe for the black bourgeoisie. . . . Although the Negro press declares itself to be the spokesman for the Negro group as a whole, it represents essentially the interests and outlook of the black bourgeosie . . . is concerned primarily with opportunities which will benefit the black bourgeoisie economically. (146)

Essence should be commended for its attempt to take on the war on girls, but the insidious way in which editors project their agenda as solely about the voiceless and silenced girls remains a problem once when we examine elements and aspects of Black female culture that the magazine seeks to invalidate or ignore.

As Gwendolyn Pough's explanation of "bring wreck" in her assessment of women and hip-hop culture describes, somebody has been championing the girls: the girls themselves:

> Bringing wreck . . . is a rhetorical act that has close ties to various other speech acts that are often linked to Black womanhood: talking back, going off, turning it out, having a niggerbitchfit, or being a diva. Each of these actions has simultaneously been embraced by some Black women as a marker of unique Black womanhood and renounced as the stereotypical Black woman stance by others. (78)

While rap from hip-hop culture has been a huge target for those interested in doing traditional feminist work that focuses on sexism and misogyny, Pough's work showcases the different approaches Black women have taken and responses to their approaches. Many of the female rappers in hip-hop begin their careers when they are girls, and many of them also feel that they are speaking for themselves and other females. While MC Lyte, Bahamadia, Lil' Kim, Salt-N-Pepa, the Real Roxanne, Queen Latifah, Queen Pen, Foxy Brown, Trina, TLC, and others are discussed in this chapter, the analysis is not meant to write these female rappers as role models. Rather, the point of the analysis is to explore how they have, in their own distinct ways, participated in the war and championed the little girls that they once were. Very often it is the way we choose to read their performances, or the lens we view them through, that influences whether they can be deemed valid, invalid, or unchampioned. *Essence*'s claim of giving a voice to the voiceless proves the type of "well-intentioned" policing that the politics of sexuality fosters. It's not that these women and girls can't champion themselves, but, as this chapter later explores with its specific and detailed analysis of female rap artist Lil' Kim, it is more likely that the way some females choose to defend themselves in the war against Black girls won't meet the "appropriate" codes of conduct. Given the numerous possibilities for gender and sexualities, isn't it time for discursive models capable of explaining them? Queen B(?)'s everywhere voice a resounding "Hell, yes!"

BITCH: The Death of Wifeable Women and a Queer Intervention

Had Annie Christmas not been reared in the rural South, ruled by the levee, or committed suicide, she'd be the present-day manifestation of Black female trickster urbanity, the Queen Bitch, but as this text prefers, Queen B(?). The tone and insistence of sovereign bodies found in Black female rap performances signal an assertion not to be denied. When producers of Black female customs forgo representations of victimization and self-sacrificing women for something more human and flawed, like a Queen B(?) model, transformations seem boundless and too complicated.

One of the well-known controversies in debates about hip-hop, Black women, and language is the use of "bitch," a word that Lil' Kim and several female rappers frequently use. The word means female dog in heat, but it is spoken as a way to refer to females, males, objects, and places. Few of these debates attempt to really understand why its usage is so pervasive in female hip-hop culture, as much as they argue for its erasure in the name of love. Yet female hip-hop's ambivalence about the word is telling. Though Queen Latifah won a Grammy for her song "U.N.I.T.Y.," in which she asks a male, "Who you calling a bitch?" she has been careful to avoid policing women's use of the term to discuss themselves. Indeed, many of the actual women in hip-hop culture, comedians Monique, Adele Givens, and Sommore, as well as musicians Missy Elliott, Salt-N-Pepa, TLC, and a host of others have either used the word or have commented on the word in ways that refuse to regulate and make deviant those women who would use it or want to use it. While one cannot easily dismiss Pough's engagement with debates about the word and her valid concerns about self-respect and self-love, there should also be room to examine the word for its potential disruption of gender and sexual binaries. Female use of the word and its personification of the word in Black women's hip-hop are about total annihilation of gender hierarchies.

In "Are the Revolutionary Techniques Employed in *The Battle of Algiers* Applicable to Harlem?" Francee Covington's claim that "revolution—the overthrow of a government, form of government, or social system with another taking its place—is not an easy task" (245) suggests why it is not so easy to replace current models of gender and sexuality. Perhaps one of the reasons it is not easy is that there is simply no single way to achieve such a radical action. It takes both political and cultural movements to replace one social system for another. Take for example the way both political and cultural moves solidified the changing of the word "black." In general, the meaning and use of "black" exposes the inconsistencies of language to express self-respect and self-love. If the various dictionaries and reference tools constitute legitimate assessment of meaning, the use of "black" by many Black Americans is an appropriation of a negative term. How does a term that connotes negativity and absence on the one hand become a cultural representation of love and power? If we dismiss appropriating measures, then "Black is beautiful" is an oxymoron. But rather than accept Eurocentric definitions of "black," Black people, politically and culturally, appropriate the word and successfully replace Western meanings of "black" with their very own values. This attention to language use reveals the truth of revolutionary techniques in regard to radical Black female sexual subjectivity. If usage and nonusage of the word "bitch" is really a question of self-love and self-respect, then I also return to a question that this text has been asking all along: Why do Black females continue to use damaging words like "woman" and "lady," which are all words constructed by white Western discursive models that attempt and fail to describe and connote Black female subjectivity? Why is this appropriation of words deemed acceptable, but the appropriation of other words by some Black females deemed wrong? Aren't we all involved in reappropriation of terms and words at some level, unless we come up with new terms for Black female subjectivity and identity? The use of "bitch" by women in hip-hop appears to be another way to unname gender, impolite as it may be, and logistically is not any less valid than other means.

The use of the word acts as some Black women's trickster-troping to overthrow the passive agenda of Black womanhood with a new social system, a queer system. The appropriating gesture that occurs with women's usage of "bitch" makes it a queer word. Its usage in contemporary Black culture has evolved to be somewhat gender flexible. It can refer to a weak man or woman, as well as a strong, assertive, and vocal woman. Dependent on context and user, the word connotes positive, negative, ugliness, beauty, good, bad, and badd. It's versatile, and it has been used and appropriated by heterosexual, gay, lesbian, and trans communities. Its use in Black women's hip-hop culture have surely reflected both its problematic demeaning of women, as well as the queer possibilities for non-heteronormative Black female subjects. Yet in any hip-hop context, the word has come to be less about a female dog and more about women who do not fit proscribed notions of womanhood. The word will never be associated with wifeable women, and, depending upon what type of revolution one is really seeking, representing one's self as a Queen B(?) is not necessarily a bad and self-loathing thing. Whereas Gayl Jones's unwifeable woman becomes a healer, hip-hop's unwifeable woman is the Queen B(?).

The use of "bitch" in hip-hop is also a queer intervention meant to remark on the overabundance of rhetoric and the absence of militancy and selfishness (self-preservation) in Black feminism, womanism, and even hip-hop feminism. Unfortunately, none of these schools of thoughts has really devised a way in which radical Black female sexual subjectivity comes first. Whether it's the fear of being deemed a traitor to the Black (male) nation, the threat of being called a lesbian, or legitimate concerns over how mainstream systems dehumanize Black women, none of the aforementioned branches of thought have made it possible for Black women to desire themselves or express their object's desires in ways that are revolutionary. Hip-hop women's use of the word attempts to create a space of selfishness that has been missing from woman, womanist, and feminist.

When bitch is used as an affirmation of assertive and aggressive women, it places Black women's desires first and foremost. And the philosophy of putting "ladies first" has been a marker of Black women's hip-hop culture from its birth. Laura Jamison's "Ladies First" renders a worthy womanist histography on the legacy of women in hip-hop, and gender remains the main issue of analysis for the critic. Jamison offers a declaration from Ms. Melodie, a female member of the Boogie Down Productions crew, that brings legitimacy to her historicist piece: "It wasn't that the male started rap, the male was just the first to be put on wax. Females were always into rap, and females always had their little crews and were always known for rockin' house parties and streets, school yards the corner, the park, whatever it was" (178). "Ladies First" provides a critical account and record of female hip-hop, but it fails to connect this tradition to remnants of other Black female popular culture.

Notably, female rappers' use of "bitch" is unavoidably retro in its nod to 1970s radical Black female subjectivity. Francee Covington said it best when she stated, "When someone says 'Freedom by any means necessary' and someone else suggests that the earnings of prostitutes be used for procuring guns—that's by any means necessary" (245). A traditional and contemporary feminist response would heave at the thought of women using their bodies in such a way, but a Queen B(?) would comprehend its objective of self-preservation in the face of enormous odds. This is not to suggest that freedom is the aim of every female rapper who uses "bitch," but the use of the word does aim to carve out a discursive niche that legitimizes Black women's "selfish" attempt to achieve one's heart's desire by any means necessary. A militant stance of self-preservation and the desire toward a better quality of life in that self-preservation marks Black women's hip-hop culture as different than any other women's empowerment movement. While some Black women choose to take up the mantle of womanhood, there are those who choose to pick up themselves. Covington's statements are phenomenal and relevant to this text's task of emphasizing that the complete and total destruction of Western categories of gender and sexuality is what should be encouraged. After all, there is a war being waged, and trickster figures play pivotal roles in social and cultural wars of the oppressed.

As a trope of trickster, bitch, or Queen Bitch, serves as a symbolic site of identity that relies on the force of desire to propel marginalized individuals to cross established boundaries to satisfy the self, in spite of what the consequence may mean for a dominant community/society. As with most post-emancipation human tricksters, the Queen B(?) seeks an appropriate expressive location for direct confrontation, as opposed to the ambiguity and guile of Tar Baby and Br'er Rabbit tales. In the past, "antebellum animal tricksters had never been beyond murder to accomplish their ends, but they had almost always murdered trough trickery. Now they frequently did so in direct confrontation with their more powerful adversaries" (Levine 383). Accordingly, when social circumstances change, trickster models change. Hip-hop culture serves as the most recent Black oral form to provide the most rigorous vehicle for tricksters who would violate taboos and borders through violence and sexuality, or sexual violence. Although this has been a widely acknowledged fact, few have broached these elements in a specifically female hip-hop culture. As indicated by tales discussed in this book, a wide majority of trickster tales (African and African American) are extremely violent, and "sexual exploits abound in most trickster myths" (Hynes, "Mapping the Characteristics of the Trickster" 43).

However, violence has been projected as an ends to a means necessary for survival in many trickster tales. In animal tales and early slave tales, murder occurs through coincidental trickery. Yet the "crucial change marking black folklore after emancipation was the development of a group of heroes who confronted power and authority directly, without guile and tricks, and who functioned on a secular level" (Levine 386). Black female culture adapts the philosophy of the greater Black community to its own situation. In jook joints, via the Hurston-defined element of Black idiom, other elements of Black expression flourished: the absence of the concept of privacy and myths of cultural icons. In the greatest tradition of tricksterism, Zora Neale Hurston's conception about the absence of privacy evolves into the deliberated use of excessive or overt sexuality in Black female culture. It serves as a strategic rejection of conformity to any nation's limitation and binding of individual sexuality and expression of sexual desire. It provides sexual militancy in a sphere threatened by the excessive forces of colonized regimes.

As Cornel West once noted: "White fear of black sexuality is a basic ingredient of white racism ... black sexuality is a taboo subject in America principally it is a form of black power over which whites have little control" (305). Arguably, West is partially correct: post-emancipated Black sexuality is a form of Black power. As seen in the narrative of Harriet Jacobs, as well as texts by other slave authors, enslaved Black people never enjoyed control over their sexuality. After the decimation of chattel slavery, it is the loss of control over Black sexuality by white America that producers of Black culture very often work to exploit and manipulate to their own advantage. This chapter is concerned with such strategies in regard to taboos of Black female sexuality and Black female urban culture. Trickster's goals of taboo breaking picks apart the Black nation's goal of normative sexuality, as well as white America's fear of Black sexuality. Since the dominant myths of Black female sexuality in Black and white America can be categorized as "Jezebel (the seductive temptress), Sapphire (the evil, manipulative bitch) or Aunt Jemima (the sexless, long-suffering nurturer)" (West 301), then modern trickeration occurs in gaps between the performances or depictions of these types by Black females.

There are culturally historic reasons, outside of hip-hop culture, as to why female rappers are drawn to and continue to use Queen B(?) performances. As opposed to the 1960s asexual strategy of crossover-happy Motown, the dominant themes of love, relationships, and explicit sexuality from the classic blues era were reborn in soul, R&B, and disco music of the 1970s. One need only heed the words and voice of Millie Jackson to appreciate how the Queen B(?) figure morphs from generation to generation: "Don't start something you can't finish, frustration ain't no fun . . . got to be an all the way, all the way, all the way loverrrr." Like true second-wave post-emancipation tricksters, Jackson, Donna Summer, and others moved away from subtle connotations onto blunt proclamations of their sexual desires. Recently, female rappers such as Da Brat, Lil' Kim, and Jackie O have claimed to be influenced by the 1970s idols. Jackson's work serves as the necessary link to understanding how female rappers and MCs unconsciously took up the Queen B(?) role for their own generation.

The remainder of this Queen B(?) chapter seeks a complex negotiation between the genres and values of various popular culture forms informed by urban vernacular. As suggested by the opening section, these are not safe spaces but tabooed open secrets of Black popular culture. Black female hip-hop artists reveal the complexities of the QueenB(?) figure and what it can offer to disturb the continuities of established sexual boundaries. The transgressive behavior negatively described as sexually promiscuous and lascivious in popular criticism offers an alternative version to the clean sanitized representations of Black sexuality offered up by the Black bourgeoisie. Sexuality has ties to eroticism and the uses of the erotic, but it has also been used as currency in various cultures. What urban Black female culture manages to do is to simultaneously explicate on sexual desire as part of eros and sexuality as currency, and it exploits the instability of the terrain in which Western society tries to define and limit sexual desires. When we examine urban Black female culture, we find the liminal Queen B(?) negotiating the fine line of currency and eros, moving back and forth between Queen Bee, Queen Bulldagger, and Queen Bitch but never fully relinquishing the unfixed Queen B(?) subjectivity.

In a genre of music heavily based on Black masculinity and masculine culture and where Black women are typically relegated to the margins (as they are in U.S. society in general), female rappers rely on and manipulate the threat of female sexual desire to their advantage. As Queen B(?) figures, they have trickster-troped all over their assigned roles as asexual butches and hypersexualized femmes in hip-hop by blurring the philosophies of normative gender and desire to get rich, reconfigure the margins of hip-hop, and offer mechanisms for exploring unpoliticized desire in Black female culture. Through an examination of the gritty lyrics and personas of selected female rappers, we will learn how Black female culture employs Queen B(?) philosophy to usurp traditional binary canons that split sexuality in terms of homosexual/heterosexual, good/evil, sacred/profane, use value/abuse value.

While Jamison documents the songs and artists of as many female endeavors as possible, cultural critic Tricia Rose, in her "Never Trust a Big Butt and a Smile," offers a more critical assessment not only of the music genre and gender, but about the critics who have attempted to analyze hip-hop culture. Piece by piece, Rose examines the output and production of female hip-hop culture and its importance in discussions of gender and sexuality. In addition, she readily connects her analysis to Angela Davis's work on blues women, "Black Women and Music: A Historical Legacy of Struggle." Perceptively, Rose's work encourages us to move beyond comparative boy/girl frameworks and issues of status and hierarchy along gender lines to complete a more sustained analysis of sexuality and Black females in hip-hop culture. Such a study reveals that verbosity about sexuality acts as a form of militancy necessary for the survival of the Queen B(?). Without sexual militancy delivered through trickster performances, Black females and their culture remain either a lesser demonstration of greater blackness (male), mimetic mirror of "the woman," or an endangered "other."

While today's hip-hoppers enjoy the verbal battles between 50 Cent and The Game, Nas and Jay-Z, Benzino and Eminem, and Tupac and Biggie, some people still remember a playing field that suggested that female MCs could be as bold and cold as their male counterparts, and the issue of sexuality (sexual desires) created this level playing field. In 1985–86, whether you were in New York, Los Angeles, or some inner city in the Midwest or the South, if you had an urban radio station to listen to you became embroiled in the soap opera appeal of a battle that pit males against females in a way that has yet to be seen ever again: U.T.F.O. versus the Roxannes versus the other Roxanne-like female rappers. In terms of bravado and exaggeration, these battles were reminiscent of the lion and the monkey, Br'er Rabbit and Tar Baby, and Sis Goose and Fox! Lyrical wit mattered more than male privilege.

As Jamison notes: "The firestorm started when an unsuspecting trio of male rappers, U.T.F.O., cut a song called 'Roxanne, Roxanne' about a stuck-up girl who had the nerve to resist their charms. Suddenly out of nowhere, a record featuring a 14-year-old with a high voice and a debilitating wit slammed U.T.F.O: She was Roxanne Shante" ("Ladies First" 179). Roxanne Shante's response, "Roxanne's Revenge," to UTFO's rap provided a narrative that suggested that females were not simply game to be pursued by warrior males on the mike. In spouting her rap, Roxanne Shante placed herself on the offense and suggested that she had choices/options as to how to fulfill her own desires:

> You thought you was cute, yeah, you thought you was a prince
> You're walkin' down the block, holdin' your jock. But everybody knows that you're all on my yacht I'm just the devastatin,' always

rockin,' always have the niggas clockin.' Everybody knows it's me, yeah, the R-O-X-A-N-N-E, yeah . . .

Clearly, the fourteen-year-old girl did not need someone else to champion her. Roxanne responded in a way in which she did not have to defend her sexuality because to do so would weaken her position. Instead of rapping about if she was "stuck-up" or sexually promiscuous, she chose instead to deconstruct the performance of hypermasculinity by young Black males. This tactic reveals that more powerful than male bravado is the self-control she could exercise over her sexuality. Further, Roxanne's lyrics set a precedent for use of Queen B(?) skills of rhetorical exaggeration, direct baiting, and confrontation used by Black females in hip-hop culture to dismiss and handle Black male sexism and misogyny.

In the end, this game of the dozens initiated by three young men and one little girl spawned one hundred Roxanne-related records to be released over urban airwaves, a feat that mirrors the proliferation of various trickster tales, as well as productions of numerous Bessies and Mas by the Race Records era after the initial success of Bessie Smith and Ma Rainey. Trickster culture evolved with its original blueprint still intact. In the hands of a young female MC, the hip-hop generation revises the Queen B(?) figure. While her style and demeanor may have changed, Queen B(?) trickery still protects the female's need for self-definition, independence, self-preservation, and voicing of sexual desires. It is no coincidence that the subject of these early urban battles was sexuality. Despite the negative criticism that some female rappers receive for using exaggerated sexuality, today's performers all accept that aggressively asserting control over sexuality, as exemplified via the Roxanne records, gave birth and longevity to female rap artists in hip-hop culture. The Roxanne battles showed that rap thematically concerned with sexuality makes it impossible to ignore Black females, takes away the gendered master narratives, and levels the playing field.

Rose dissects male fear about leveling the playing field in the production of male hip-hop culture, hence her title "Never Trust a Big Butt and a Smile." She includes rapper Ice Cube's comments on the power of female sexuality: "I mean the power of sex is more powerful than the motherfuckers in Saudi Arabia. A girl you want to get with can make you do damn near anything" (239). A female rapper who raps about sexuality places the male MC or rapper in a vulnerable position because she can undermine the legitimacy of just about any boast or toast that he makes, and as blues women demonstrated, concerns about propriety need not be obstacles in the way of dominating the mike. Rose rightly assesses that Ice Cube's comments reflect a male fear and "that many men are hostile towards women because the fulfillment of male heterosexual desire is significantly checked by women's capacity for sexual rejection and/or manipulation of men" (239). If that is the case, why put female sexuality in check or chains? Rose's piece, published in the early 1990s, had a much easier task of critiquing sexuality in female rap since its focus was on acts such as Salt-N-Peppa, MC Lyte, and Queen Latifah. These acts fit well into Rose's notion of traditional love and relationships as the driving force behind sexual themes in female rap music.

Yet as a diversity of women on and off the mike became front and center in hip-hop culture, certain critics seemed totally incapable of understanding the negotiation female rap artists make concerning sexuality. In briefly addressing the likes of Foxy Brown and Lil' Kim, Joan Morgan's *When Chickenheads Come Home to Roost: My Life as a Hip-Hop Feminist* negates power that might evolve from exploiting such fear by calling women who choose to explicitly use sexual power to gain social position or economic gains "chickenheads."[2] *When Chickenheads Come Home* accepts the presentation of overt sexuality simply as denigration, or as females being co-opted by a male system, all the while implying acceptance of social regulations of women's sexuality through notions of romantic love and marriage as systems less denigrating to women. It also misses the evidence afforded us by important historical moments like the Roxanne battles. Fortunately, Suzanne Bost's "Be Deceived If Ya Wanna Be Foolish" offers a more complicated analysis of female hip-hop culture. Focusing on Da Brat, Ursula Rucker, Dana Bryant, and Sarah Jones, Bost explodes Morgan's simplistic framework of skeeza, hoochies, whores, and freaks versus the good girls by focusing on fluidity, manipulation of the whore image, and theorizing about excessive bodies as a counter theory to commodified contained bodies.

While some female rappers address more traditional themes of love and relationships, some consciously write lyrics or create images with the manipulation of sexual power in mind, and that is what moves them from the realm of female rapper to trickster Queen B(?) icon. The Black female rapper who performs Queen B(?) uses sexuality as a weapon because sexuality is one of the trickster's weapons of choice: "In both ritual actions and artistic depictions, the trickster sometimes carries a phallus or phallic club" (Hynes, "Mapping the Characteristics of Mythical Tricksters" 43). In the absence of a phallus or phallic club for Queen B(?), we can substitute the presence of her deliberate decision to harness the use value of female sexuality for her own purposes and goals, rather than society's intended uses of simply wife and mother.

The harnessed female sexuality (phallic club) connotes and correlates with a theme of sexual violence seen in human trickster tales. Traditionally criticized from a non-folklore viewpoint, the elements of violence and explicit sexuality make it difficult to grasp gestures of rebelliousness of certain female rap artists in the way of trickster. Queen B(?)'s sexual militancy derives from trickster's hypersexuality. Lil' Kim is a Queen B(?) figure who, in very distinct ways, harnesses the use value of sexual desire and makes her depiction of that desire a weapon to be wielded in the struggle to maintain control over Black women's identities, lives, and images. Like Gayl Jones's fictional Harlan Eagleton, who must realize the transformative power of her Turtle Woman heritage, cultural performances by female rappers allow them a fluidity of sexuality almost impossible in other spheres of Black popular culture.

Queen B(?)'s—Queer Desires and the Sexual Militancy of Lil' Kim

Lil' Kim is not gay, but as her dual iconic status in hip-hop culture and homosexual culture (not necessarily separate all the time) suggests, her performances are rather queer. But only those interested in less-than-heteronormative ideologies could really appreciate the significance of how her queer work dismantles binary systems of gender and sexuality. Yet heteronormativity continues to dominate the minds of select Black women. On the April 2003 cover of *Essence*, the magazine advertised the titles of stories included in the issue. The most troubling title and story was "What White Women Think of Us," meaning what white women think of Black females. This particular title and subject matter encompasses every point that E. Franklin Frazier warns against when it comes to the Black bourgeoisie: "Among the women of the black bourgeoisie there is an intense fear of the competition of white women for Negro men. . . . Both men and women among the black bourgeoisie have a feeling of insecurity because of their constant fear of the loss of status" (180). Ironically, only Black middle-class women have status to lose. Moreover, status does not necessarily mean equality. Throughout the years, *Essence* magazine has profited from bourgeois insecurity and constant fear of status loss. The magazine has always been geared toward middle- and upper-class Black females, as well as females interested in those same class values, and the magazine presents the perfect example as to why Black females continue to need the militancy presented in Black female vernacular culture.

In "Deconstructing Lil' Kim," an article from an October 2000 edition of *Essence* magazine, Akissi Britton writes a commentary intent on deconstructing the hip-hop artist: "The whole world is watching Kimberly Jones. So why isn't anyone telling her what she needs to know?" (112). Britton then launches into a discussion as to whether Lil' Kim can be read as feminist or antifeminist. This conversation had also been broached by Joan Morgan and continued with Rebecca Walker's *One World* interview with Kim. *Essence* had also published other articles, letters, and editorials about female rappers like Lil' Kim. All of the articles commonly assume an insecurity about the loss of status and heterosexual context in their discussions of Black women's sexuality as presented in hip-hop.[3] Yet the question remains as to how Black women can lose status that they never had, and what about actual social and economic equality. The Britton piece garnered a wide variety of responses, many in defense of Lil' Kim. As one fan articulates, *Essence* and its author know too little about deconstructing and much about hypocrisy: "You say '[W]e are bombarded by images that show women as only token pieces, to be sported like jewelry.' Yet in the same magazine these words are written are numerous ads, and articles, that support the objectification of women and the use of women's sexualized images to sell a product." (Hairston). As the fan observes, Kim was not the only one harnessing the uses of sexuality, but she was the only one being negatively constructed in the discussion. Subsequently, the selling of *Essence* to Time Warner certainly implicates a certain amount of hypocrisy in regard to *Essence*'s concern for Black female representation. What remains clear is that sexuality and use value of sexual acts remain very personal and individual things, and the guise of feminist discourse cannot change that.

Although there have been many critiques about the stereotypical sexually licentious Black female in the last three decades, there have been very few dissections of the way the construction of the "other" has inhibited Black female sexual desire. Lil' Kim's brash lyrics and image remain a crucial factor in opening such dialogue. She is neither feminist nor antifeminist because her work engages tricksterism. In a discussion of ambiguity and inversion in language and ritual associated with trickster, Klaus-Peter Koepping offers one characteristic relevant to accepting Lil' Kim as Queen B(?) trickster. Koepping found that the elements that designate trickster across all cultural variations were the figure's "cunning form of intelligence and the grotesqueness of the body imagery used to indicate the inversion of order" (194). Lil' Kim, or Kimberly Jones, is one Queen B(?) figure who demonstrates this belief by establishing a type of sexual militancy. As a true Queen B(?), Lil' Kim's lyrical prowess and her presentation of aggressive and excessive sexuality mirrors trickster's intellect and grotesque body imagery. What has been classified as offensive and vulgar in Lil' Kim's lyrics and image might have roots in the very serious cause of cultural transformation through radical inversion of social demeanor. Lil' Kim's Queen B(?) approach attacks ideologies of normative and racialized sexuality in Black U.S. culture today.

Hip-hop's, and specifically Lil' Kim's, embrace of the term "Queen Bitch" has nothing to do with the misogynist contextualization of the term, and everything to do with Queen B(?)'s original folk presence in Black culture. After Annie Christmas dies, she can later be heard singing on the big river. According to the tale, she isn't singing an ode to Miss Ann, pondering the wonders of Mr. Charlie, or trying to figure out how she could get John Henry or Stag-O-Lee to marry her; she is singing a river tune to the thunder sky. She is reveling in her own important self. As exhibited in the Annie Christmas tale, there were few positive depictions left for Black females who did not fit or aspire toward a goal of respectable and chaste womanhood. After all, Black females were inclined to be chaste and more virtuous because of the stigma laid upon them by a society economically and politically invested in racialized sexuality of the African race. As Annie Christmas shows, physical suicide was one option. Succumbing to the model of feminine virtue was the other. Today, the options remain more of the same: assimilation, death, or total rejection. Queen B(?) opts for rejection of normative sexuality.

In her song, "Suck My Dick," Lil' Kim exclaims: "Queen Bitch! What bitch you know can thug like this? Imagine if I was a dude and hittin' cats from the back with no strings attached." Kim's lyrics emphasize that she is no "bitch," contextually an attribute ascribed to weak or passive females who don't go after what they want. Yet, in the same way that the Bad Man/Nigga in the folk manipulates his noncitizenship in the United States to ignore society's laws, the Queen B(?) figure works to do the same with the constructs of womanhood. As Lil' Kim vocally harnesses her sexuality as a weapon, metaphorical allusions to a phallic club disappear. She asks listeners to place her outside the traditional realm of woman, but not in the space of man either. Lil'Kim strategically performs Queen Bitch. She makes a distinction between the two by asking what ordinary female ("bitch"—females struggling to fit themselves into the model of womanhood) can transgress established boundaries (thug) like she (the Queen Bitch) does. She creates an alternative discourse practice for herself in her proclamation as the Queen Bitch. "Bitch" in either context is at the same time condemned by bourgeois and feminist critics alike. Queen Bitch becomes a separate category of gender that does not have to adhere to the logics of intelligible gender. In answer to feminist critics who would reprimand her for her refusal to submit to their standards of what defines revolutionary discourse for Black female subjectivity, she retorts with the title of her rap song, "Suck My Dick." It is clear that Lil' Kim removes herself from the social and biological markers of gender, not only with her vocal reclamation as a Queen Bitch, but also in projecting her female body as endowed with a phallus.

In returning to Britton's discussion of Lil' Kim as feminist or antifeminist in "Deconstructing Lil' Kim," one clear statement emerges as antithetical to the trickster-troping of Black female culture but indicative of what has typically been considered a priority in "respectable" Black female culture: "But I'm having a problem when all these voices are being classified as empowering and feminist. . . . Feminism is about embracing our power without reducing it to what's between our legs" (112). The major problem with Britton's statement is that the vagina, the pussy, the cunt, the imagined phallus of Lil' Kim's rap, or the unspeakable "what's between our legs" is, as Francee Covington alluded to earlier, a part of the power that a number of Black females don't access or won't access out of concern for normality and loss of imaginary status. Lil' Kim's personae and lyrics may not be feminism, but they do connect to something older and more powerful than that particular discourse: trickery, deception, indeterminacy, polyvalence, and situation inversion. If not for trickster, how else would we continuously be conscious and aware of negotiating the illusions and the real of individual Black female genders and sexual desires?

Queen B(?)'s Signifyin' Pose

In order to fully deconstruct Lil' Kim and see her as trickster practicing sexual militancy, we have to be willing to deal with the issue of sexual desire, as opposed to false gender identifications. Most of the deconstructing being done around Lil' Kim has been devoted to preserving heteronormativity and heterosexist ideologies about desire and gender. For example, Lil' Kim's dismissal of feminine virtue, straight sex, the sanctity of marriage, and her progressive acceptance of sexuality for personal pleasure and economic gains act as the most dominant and harshly critiqued ideology of female hip-hop that explicitly details sexual desire. If the critiques dealt solely and completely with sexuality, it would look less like the feminist reading presented by the previously mentioned writers, and more like the polysexual culture of trickster. As Hynes notes of the trickster trait of sacred/lewd bricoleur: "The trickster traffics frequently with the transcendent while loosing lewd acts upon the world" ("Mapping the Characteristics of Mythic Tricksters" 42). Lil' Kim tinkers with and transcends the sacredness of female virtues, Black normalization, and heterosexual power by releasing "lewd" acts upon the world in a public forum.

As already noted in this text, when critics have looked at a trickster such as Eshu or the Bad Man/Nigga and conceived of a trait of hypersexuality, they focused specifically on the erect penis, the phallus. Rather than focusing too explicitly on a phallocentric reading, we must remember that trickster's sexuality is not simply hyperactive but polysexual. In images of Eshu, the erect penis takes precedence. In addition, depictions and posturing of Bad Men in folklore and contemporary urban culture, vocal and self-groping replace the naked penis. Male crotch shots in hip-hop seemed an undeniable part of the bravado. In that same sense, over the span of Lil' Kim's career there has been a consistent pose that graces the covers and stories on Lil' Kim—the legs-wide-open pose.[4] As with the Bad Man/Nigga's phallus, Kim's spread-eagle pose drips with symbolism of trickster's proclivity for grotesque body imagery.

Lil' Kim's persona as a trickster invested in sexual militancy earns credence once the symbolism is interpreted. The cause that moves Lil' Kim's aggressive sexuality from the realm of vulgarity is the consciousness behind it. One of the first ways that young girls learn about the power of their sexuality is when they are taught to always sit with their legs closed. Whether they're donning pants, a dress, or a skirt, sitting with one's legs open has always been perceived as some kind of nasty threat. A female with open legs is a threat to herself, but more importantly, to men. Keeping the legs crossed or closed maintains a sense of control over that threat to men, while simultaneously serving as a reminder to females that to open the self in such a way is to ask for harm or sexual violence. So the simple etiquette of closed or crossed legs becomes a focal point of Lil' Kim's trickster performance—her club. Open legs typically imply wantonness, invitation, abandonment, but in Lil' Kim's case it means overwhelming power, a loaded gun ready to be fired.

On the cover of *Hardcore*, Lil' Kim's first album, she kneels before the camera with her legs spread. While other female rappers such as Foxy Brown and Trina have denied their role in constructing their image and fallen into rhetoric of victimization by a male-dominated industry,[5] Lil' Kim accepts responsibility for her image by dogmatically acknowledging that she takes full control over her career and image: "What happens is that I come up with a concept of how I want to look . . . I try to find out who is shooting me, and I come up with how I want to look" (*One World* interview 63). The pose seems to be very much a part of the Queen B(?) arsenal. It's a hostile facade that connects with the lyrics concocted by Kim. It seeks to topple and trick with every fear about sexuality, including racialized sexuality.

As a way to promote her third CD, *La Bella Mafia*, Lil' Kim appears on the cover of *King* magazine in June 2003, in which she is also interviewed. Lil' Kim poses bent down at the knees with her legs spread open as a cross falls between her barely covered breasts to land right above a thong covering her genital area. These are very subversive messages being sent. Lil' Kim's excessive and overt sexuality allows her to maintain a disarming position of blatant power and aggressiveness meant to threaten males and females who would attempt to define or limit her desires. They will not be contained or controlled by anyone except their owner. On the cover, she subverts religious dogma about sexuality by mixing the sacred and "profane." The pose mocks the Virgin Mary. In Christianity, the separation of body and spirit depends upon the immaculate conception of Jesus; Mary's legs must have surely remained closed. However, in various non-Western cultures, creation myths detail various copulations of earth with tricksters or of man with tricksters. Chaotic desire replaces controlled immaculateness in the creation and recreation of man. In Lil' Kim's threatening pose, the unacknowledged master narrative of sexual value—Mary's birth without intercourse and without body—is countered with all body and desire for pleasure rather than reproduction.

In that same magazine, above the layout interview, Lil' Kim sits in a chair, legs spread wide open, breasts spilling from under a black tank top that reads "Got Dick?" The shirt utilizes the vernacular strategy of the uncensored mode with a deliberate trickster pose to create a greater threat. She signifies on bourgeois values. Initially, we might be inclined to believe that the "Got Dick?" phrase, in addition to the stance, means that Lil' Kim wants penile intercourse. It may mean that, but there is also another subtext to that particular picture. The second picture does not have only one meaning when we take into consideration the entirety of Lil' Kim's work. Once we do that, the meaning is no longer a heterosexual privileging of the phallus and not simply a case of objectification and vulgarity. As with other Queen B(?)s in Black culture, Lil' Kim reveals an admiration for Black masculine culture of hypermasculinity while rejecting it with trickster's hypersexuality that refuses patriarchical gendering.

Queen B(?)'s Scatology:
Trickster and Ritualized Sexual Violence

Perhaps it is her donning of blue, green, yellow, and blonde wigs with colored contacts that distracts many critics away from the way Lil' Kim's trickery has mildly queered hip-hop. Though she does not follow in Ndegeocello's path of deploying the lesbian phallus, Lil' Kim does resort to queer trickery to vocalize sexual desires. On her first three disc releases, Lil' Kim alludes to dethroning the phallus in some form, be it a challenge to the flaccid male penis, real actualization of the wonders of the clitoris, or the uses of a dildo, Lil' Kim's lyrics work to topple traditional power dynamics that privilege the male phallus as the ultimate sexual power. In "Suck My Dick," Lil' Kim spits out: "Niggas ain't shit but they still can trick/All they can do for me is suck my clit." Lil' Kim shows an appreciation of the way males manipulate their power and control over women, but won't allow her admiration to take away from her elevation and valuing of her self. On "Queen Bitch," she warns:

"Get off my dick, kick it bitch." And in the underground *Streetsweepers* disc, she venomously declares: "Hatin Ass Niggas/Treat you like a bitch/strap on a dick and stick you where you shit." The harsh language and violence in these lyrics are purposeful. While traditionally it may be difficult to fathom that Lil' Kim moves from object to subject with her poses, there is no doubt that her lyrics inherently project fantasies of trickster's penchant for violence and gender-bending antics as a sexualized practice. These antics are meant to reflect another aspect of trickster. Koepping asserts of trickster's turn to violence that "the violence (whether rape or murder or even cannibalistic devouring) inherent in such acts places them in an ambiguous, ambivalent category, which may be . . . codified in a 'ritualization of violence'" (192–93). This ritualization of violence happens so as to reveal the mask of politeness covering up the hypocrisy of a community. For Lil' Kim, then, African American society has been too quiet and reserved on matters of Black female sexual desire. Trickster antics, she suggests, may literally disturb the peace.

Lil' Kim's lyrics invert the sexual mores of our time. As opposed to focusing on vaginal intercourse between man and woman, Lil Kim's attention to the sexual taboo of anal sex enables her to rebuke racialized sexuality and shift from a discussion of heteronormativity. In Lil' Kim's lyrics, the heterosexual construction of the licentious Black woman falls to the side, as well as the Black female striving for womanhood. What remains are queer desires and practices. Lil' Kim's Queen B(?) strategy provides a form of cultural representation for Black females who express queer desires and practices. Just as Bessie Smith did so long ago, Lil' Kim uses her performative space to topple binaries. The projection of queerness derived from Lil' Kim's words contextually conflicts with critiques that Lil' Kim fulfills all the stereotypes about Black females. The sheer aggressive nature of the act toward men differs from imagery of wanton and ready to be used females waiting to be filled and made whole by the phallus. Lil' Kim's appreciation for the dildo also allows her to recoup the forceful and destructive nature of the phallus for a discussion of her own personal sexual desires. Like Ann Allen Shockley's Queen B(?), Lil' Kim inverts situations and shape-shifts for her own gain. In Lil' Kim's lyrics, female sexuality becomes ripe with power, but more flexible than the phallus. Her trickster strategy of shape-shifting occurs when she alludes to female genitalia in a way that interchanges the clitoris with the phallus (dick), and she trickster-tropes on desire to create a hip-hop narrative on female pleasure that parallels and rivals white sexologists.

In recent discussions about the implications of dildos in sexual acts, sex critics Tamsin Wilton argues that the power of the phallus is not merely a power specifically for men:

> [Penises] come attached to male people and demonstrate a troublesome tendency to resist both the burden of the phallic power (they may become soft and flaccid at the most inconvenient moments) and the imposition of disciplinary power (they are not easily controlled or directed by their "owner"), it is not hard to see that dildo's may be perceived as superior. (303)

Wilton observes the limitations and inconsistencies of male genitalia by exploring the rhetorical distinctions that critics make in discussions of male genitalia. Society distinguishes between the two by referring to the unerect and flaccid member as the penis, as opposed to referring to the erect member as the phallus. Yet Lil' Kim's rhetorical interchanging of the clitoris and phallus (dick) in her lyrics exposes the infinite possibilities of female sexuality. Moving beyond the act of being penetrated, Lil' Kim asserts that female sexuality is so fluid that it cannot be limited by two gonadal forms alone.

The narrative she creates avoids being entangled into binary schemas for desire. Lesbian, straight, bisexual, or polysexual females benefit from her narrative. From Lil' Kim's lyrics, we can see how the clitoris no longer appears as a passive body part waiting to be coaxed from its soft hood. In this way, Lil' Kim asserts female sexuality as an entity unlike the revered phallus. The clitoris exceeds the limitations of the phallus because in its most exciting moments it can be erect and soft at the same time. The flexibility/variety of female sexuality and pleasure is then pushed a step further with the imagery of Lil' Kim strapping on a dildo to penetrate man. The tool allows the Queen B(?) to playfully exaggerate her resistance to traditional categories of gender. Although the focus on the phallus may lend itself to a heterosexist appeal, the hostility of the images evoked by Lil' Kim's words suggests that she is taunting male suitors with the liability and limitedness of their male member in contrast to her female genitalia. Further, in theorizing female masturbation with a dildo, Sarah Smith suggests that the female "steps outside the male/female, active/passive framework. During the sex act she is both the penetrator and penetrated, so there can be no question of losing autonomy. The dildo 'resists its interpretation as an agent of heterosexuality'" (303).

As the Queen B(?), Lil' Kim reimagines female genitalia and positions herself on the margins of binary sexuality so that her sexuality does not become fixed or located in the remains of racialized sexuality. The reimagined clitoris and the decision to strap on allow Lil' Kim to resist being an agent of heterosexuality and racialized sexuality. Rather than conforming to the heterosexualization of desire dominant in early Black culture, Lil' Kim turns to what has been deemed homosexual practices, sodomy and strap-ons, to project individual sexual power. Of her sexual prowess, she boasts: "Kim got 'em in a zone beating they dicks/Even got some of these straight chicks rubbing their tits/What? I'm loving this shit" ("Suck My Dick"). Lil' Kim not only embellishes the biggest taboos associated with divine and animal tricksters—excrement and blood—she also exploits the taboos of human trickster such as the Bad Man/Nigga. The transgression of sexual boundaries present in Lil' Kim's persona of the Queen B(?) refuses any final acceptance of the binary constructs of gender or sexuality. In Lil' Kim's world, the male becomes female and the female become male. When she speaks explicitly of sexuality through body parts of "dicks" and "tits," Lil' Kim imagines herself as sexually appealing to both sexes, and dodges the heterosexual trope of the Queen Bee figure. As the Queen B(?), Lil' Kim remains not only capable of being entered as a female in the act of sexual intercourse, but of entering a male from behind, and of being male and female at once. Her sexuality is changeable and in the end undefineable.

Lil' Kim's lyrics also remind listeners that the militancy of Queen B(?)'s sexuality remains about maintaining individual control over sexuality, as well as refuting any ideologies that suggest that Black female sexuality be ignored in discussions of Black liberation. Moving beyond the erect uses of the phallus, Lil' Kim then situationally inverts ideologies about sexual ejaculation and incorporates ejaculation into her theories on sexual desires. In "Queen Bitch II," Lil' Kim contemplates the importance of ejaculation in the representation of powerful sexuality: "And I'm a picky one I like my dicks rock hard /. . . Oh something missing, the shower pissing/All up in your mouth. What? You think I'm kidding?" Once again, Lil' Kim takes sexual desires out of the realm of homo/hetero to avoid making any one position permanent. Unlike the victim, the wanton woman, the virginal woman, Queen B(?) is hardly ever represented as waiting for her pleasure or pain to be thrust upon her. To the contrary, Queen B(?) thrusts her pleasure onto others. Lil' Kim's cursory nod to the queer practice of water sports also acts as an early acknowledgment of Lil' Kim's appreciation for female ejaculation. It reflects both a folkloric and feminist comprehension of the act. When trickster acts as the sacred/lewd bricoleur, "gastronomic, flatulent, sexual, phallic, and fecal feats erupt seriatim. Yet, the bricoleur aspect of the trickster can cause any or all of such lewd acts or objects to be transformed into occasions of insight, vitality, and new inventive creations" (Hynes, "Mapping the Characteristics of Mythical Tricksters" 42). Lil' Kim, like numerous tricksters, returns to taboos of the body. As opposed to blood or fecal matter, she engages tricksterism on the taboo of fluids evidentiary of sexual desire.

Further, in ways that many feminist critics could not, Lil' Kim reincorporates female pleasure via the clitoris back into mainstream consciousness:

> I keep my pussy fresh like Dudley; watch the show
> as my flow bubble over like Mo's and Cristal's
> Ain't scared to bust my pist-al, sippin' hard on Cristal
> I be, flirtin' for certain, wearin' short skirts
> But ain't no dicks insertin' see, that's the difference
> between me and other bitches, they fuck to get they riches
> I fuck to bust a nut. ("Fuck You")

Critics have failed to realize the significant absence or dismissal of vaginal penetration in the lyrics of Lil' Kim. It's significant because Lil' Kim's dismissal of vaginal penetration signals the trickster strategy of situation inverter at work. Asserting herself as Queen B(?), Lil' Kim maintains a stance that female pleasure does not have to be tied to male entry to the female body. Further, her "flow" that bubbles over, her courage in busting her pistol, and busting a nut, all exist as rhetorical strategies to reorder the uses of female sexuality. Lil' Kim's strategic use of ejaculation undermines any argument that she uses her sexuality strictly for economic gains. It is an implicit statement about the use of female sexuality in institutions such as marriage, as well as prostitution. Lil' Kim asserts that personal pleasure remains the least discussed and most misunderstood aspect of articulating Black female sexuality. In this case, pleasure acts as a militant weapon.

As she grew bolder and more militant in her persona, Lil' Kim wreaked more havoc on binary sexuality when she announced that she's the "Mike-beater, back-beater, the pussy-skeeter" ("Chinatown"). Determined to complete her rhyme, assert her vicious mike skills, and still pay homage to her sexuality, Lil' Kim chooses her words carefully. Pussy-skeeter explicitly refers to the act of female ejaculation. The vernacular allows Lil' Kim to express how the act of female ejaculation discounts the notion of ejaculation as a male-defined act of sexual release and reproduction. In sexuality studies, the act of ejaculating has consistently been used to explain the reason for nonmonogamy among males: Males must spread their seed to ensure human survival. In being the pussy-skeeter, Lil' Kim sets up a logic of reasoning that situates her in a position to usurp female monogamy. Her logic does not represent ejaculation as a means to reproduction but as a solidifier of how infinite female sexual pleasure can be. In doing so, her work becomes intimately connected with the legitimacy of female pleasure obtained without the phallus. Once accepted as a normal part of female pleasure, female ejaculation has since been fetishistically perceived as abnormal.[6] Yet Thomas Laqueur's *Making Sex* documents, in the one sex model, how scientists and doctors conceived that females and males had the same genitals and genital function even if reproductive organs differed. The female's clitoris located on the inside was not as visible as the man's protruding phallus located outside. Shannon Bell's "Liquid Fire," explains that "female ejaculation is one route back to a potentially nonhierarchical one-sex/one-flesh model" (334) because

> [t]he female body, free from limitations of the one-sex model which posited the female as an inversion of the male body, reveals physiological difference within anatomical symmetry. The female body can ejaculate fluid from thirty or more ducts and with stimulation can ejaculate repeatedly. It can ejaculate more fluid than the male body and can enjoy a plurality of genital pleasure sites: the clitoris, uretha, vagina, the vagina's entrance, the roof of the vagina, the bottom of the vagina, and the cervix. (339)

Female ejaculation supercedes male ejaculation. The phallus, often associated with violent imagery of guns due in large part to its ability to ejaculate, loses its place of privilege. If we take into consideration Lil' Kim's sexual pose and her attention to female ejaculation, Lil' Kim's Queen B(?) sexuality becomes particularly militant. If male ejaculation is a .45 pistol, female ejaculation becomes a machine gun or many guns capable of backing up revolutionary words with action. If this is what her sex can do, then why should it be bound and limited to one person, or closed off from herself? Queen B(?)'s revolutionary coup happens while consciously incorporating the body into its arsenal, rather than omitting it in the way that bourgeois Black nationalist thought asserts that we do. Trickster's overt or excessive sexuality provides an option that interrupts the discourse of "normativity" in liberation narratives.

I'm not suggesting that Lil' Kim reads books by nineteenth- and twentieth-century sexologists to understand the importance of ejaculation and the phallus in ideologically lessening the status of women, especially Black females. I am suggesting, however, that through some folklore and vernacular culture, Lil' Kim learns to theorize about the importance of female ejaculation and plants that in her rhymes. The previous chapters have already provided us with representations of tricksters who cuss, fart, play sexual tricks on other tricksters, have sex with nonhumans, and so forth. Female ejaculation is this Queen B(?)'s tool of bodily expression meant to disrupt from the margins. As a student of Black music, Lil' Kim, like many teenagers of the 1980s, had to have been privy to the (im)modest lyrics of Apollonia 6 on this very topic: "I'm a sex shooter/Shootin love in your direction/Come on play with my affections/Come on kiss the gun." These lyrics, cowritten by a trickster in his own right (Prince) and his female protégée (Apollonia), provide a more metaphorical take on the plurality of female pleasure and ejaculation while still maintaining the tongue-in-cheek fun that downplays the militancy of the act as expressed by Lil' Kim. Lil' Kim moves beyond Apollonia's tongue-in-cheek representation of female genitalia and extracts the militant nature of such images.

In addition to folklore and music, Black pornography serves as the vernacular culture that influences Lil' Kim's trickster-troping. In "Big Momma Thang," Lil' Kim provides bibliographic evidence of research for her theories: "Handle it like a real bitch: Heather Hunter, Janet Jack-me." When she recites the names of notable Black female adult film stars, Lil' Kim shows how the vernacular works. In pornographic videos filled with images of men, and most recently females, ejaculating with and without phalluses, Lil' Kim recognizes a power dynamic stemming from the ability to ejaculate. Despite previous implications of the dildo, for greater recognition of female sexual power, Lil' Kim returns to female genitalia and its varied responses to sexual stimuli. In her canon of work, she prefers to think of her sexuality as the soft-erect core militantly responding with force, rather than the dependent canal clutching the more powerful and independent phallus.

Continuing a process of unnaming that began with gender, Lil' Kim's persona of Queen Bitch harkens back to the folk configuration of the Queen B(?) figure in Black culture. Queen B(?) provides the model needed to develop a way to construct a Black female sexual self in the hip-hop nation. The Queen B(?) figure allows Black female subjectivity, in regard to gender and sexuality, to remain indefinable as it evolves from one generation to the next. Unafraid of moving beyond the pristine prism of discourses on female sexuality, Lil' Kim's dependence on supposed "vulgarity" and its aesthetics allow her to discuss the full range of her sexuality as a Black female. She conceives of a sexuality that will not be bound, controlled, or imprisoned by words and representations, one that is as visually deceptive as trickster and just as aggressive and transgressive. Other hip-hop culture and artists have embraced different factors of the Queen B(?) to do the same.

What does any of this mean to hip-hop culture? Although this chapter only addressed female artists who presumably are heterosexual, it seems clear that tricksterism becomes the major way to incorporate an understanding of queerness into urban vernacular culture. Lil' Kim has made considerable use of her undefinability to express personal desires and make economic profits. Furthermore, the growing underground homohop, or queer hip-hop, movement and its artists in urban areas such as Oakland, San Francisco, Atlanta, and New York suggest that trickster strategies discussed in reference to Ndegeocello, Queen Pen, and Lil' Kim may be the most useful way to liberate the Black community from its homophobic and heterosexist genocidal tendencies.[7] It's not the form that inhibits a proliferation of sexual identities in the hip-hop community; it's the Black community's homophobia. Alternative hip-hop groups such as Deep Dick Collective and Rainbow Flava have learned that if Queen Pen and Lil' Kim can manipulate Queen B(?) strategies for themselves, then homohop can too. If lesbian artists such as Miss Money and Mizz Platinum out of Atlanta can follow the philosophies of early rap Queen B(?)s and manipulate this fear of sexuality, then perhaps the closed doors of the music recording industry will matter less than the social good that can come from their trickster efforts.

Remembering Queen B(?)'s original folk roots of being a transgressor of societal boundaries makes it possible to reread "badness" in Lil Kim's overt and exaggerated sexuality. Her work can be read as a militant stance to move hip-hop culture into overcoming its learned homophobia and heterosexualization of desire. Subsequently, when we continue to read through trickster, we can see how popular culture in Black women's communities offers a wide array of methodologies for articulating desires of radical Black female subjectivities.

Conclusion

Trickster's Gift
A Language of Sexual Rights through Polymorphous Erotics and Voluptuous Black Women's Sexualities

How can I attempt to end dialogue about a figure that transcends time and space, when even as this conclusion attempts to conclude what cannot be concluded, new theories of tricksters are waiting to be written? For this reason, I turn to the words of Cheryl Clarke, a poet who has not received the attention she deserves, but who has demonstrated how well she comprehends the workings of a trickster in her poem "Morgan Harris": "The poetry poured out of her when she cross-dressed.... To her, poetry is the smallest thing, her greater depth" (*Experimental Love* 14). As Cheryl Clarke's "Morgan Harris" implies, poetry is a suitable temporary epilogue for *Mutha Is Half a Word* because it is a queer art form based on indiscretions of time, space, categories, and uncontrollable urges. Rather than concluding, Clarke's poetry enables me to give a final acknowledgement of trickster's gift to Black female culture.

Twenty years ago African American assessments of trickster tales in Black culture reduced the tales and figures to graphs, mathematics, equations, and charts,[1] as if trickster were a formula to be solved. Such theories froze trickster. Joyce A. Joyce bravely attempted to broach this issue in 1987 with much controversy when she said that "it is no accident that the Black post-structuralist methodology has so far been applied to fiction, the trickster tale, and the slave narrative. Black poetry—particularly that written during and after the 1960s—defies both linguistically and ideologically the 'poststructuralist sensibility' (295). As if in agreement with Joyce, Cheryl Clarke's "Morgan Harris" alludes to poetry as a form that is a small space capable of expressing greater depth, and those expressions are tied to transgressions against boundaries, definitions, classifications, and categories. While poststructuralist sensibilities may not be able to handle cross-dressing configurations of Black poetry, the polyvocality and multifarious cultural elements of trickster can.

Out of respect for Joyce's words, I hope that *Mutha' Is Half a Word* has moved beyond viewing trickster, folklore, and vernacular culture as "linguistic events" or "complex networks of linguistic systems" (Joyce 296). Rather than figuring trickster out, I hope to have made trickster more undecipherable. As opposed to totally dismissing the connection of trickster to language, I hope that I have shown that trickster culture provides African America with discursive strategies on sexual desires and sexual culture that we will need for the remainder of the twenty-first century. *Mutha Is Half a Word* was written with the intent of reinvesting in the radical nature of folklore, broadening the landscape of how we examine gender and sexual desire in African American female culture, and revealing how precarious the categories of race and gender could be in the fulfillment and presentation of those sexual desires. Oddly enough, what led me to this project was the possible destabilization of all those social categories by one particular writer.

In November of 2000, I began conducting research for an essay on Black lesbian pulp fiction. One of the widely known writers in this field was Red Jordan Arobateau. Arobateau's novels were the focus of my essay because they exhibited a concern with the contradiction of the white bourgeois construct of lesbian as it concerns Black female same-sex desire. During the 1970s, Arobateau was a writer outcast from the mainstream literary community. The Black literary community also dismissed Arobateau's pop fiction because it was written in Black vernacular and concerned queer people from Black underclass communities. I'd chosen Arobateau because her self-published lesbian dime novels appealed to my purpose of finding a way to discuss the fluidity of Black subjectivity as influenced by sexuality, gender, and especially class. As a lesbian, biracial writer living in the urban ghettoes of Oakland and San Francisco, Arobateau seemed to be a comparable fit with my work concerning Black sexual culture.

As I worked to solidify my theory of Arobateau's work, I had to face how unprepared I was, as was the field of African American studies, for discussing the fluidity of gender and sexuality in Black culture. In a response to an e-mail asking for an interview, Arobateau e-mailed me with the following revelation: "Dear L.H. Stallings, I'd be glad to cooperate with your interview. Some bio: I identify as mixed race heritage of African American/black descent. I no longer identify myself as butch dike but ftm (female to male transexual) a transman" (November 4, 2000). Initially, I proceeded with uncertainty. My reading of the author's work was being written with the understanding of Arobateau as a (permanent) lesbian writer who wrote about Black lesbians in urban Black female culture. I knew that my project would be a failure if I did not move beyond this view. Surely I would now have to examine the canon of Arobateau and his work in light of the gender reassignment. But how could I do it? How could I broach the complex dynamics of false societal gender constructs and fluid sexual desire, and still offer a critique on how class and race impacts it all in a way that would do justice to Arobateau's work?

As I reconsidered my notes for the project, I realized that Arobateau's use of vernacular culture was the main reason I had come to formulate that there could be a distinguishing feature and culture of lower-class Black female same-sex desire. In the end, I returned to Audre Lorde's theoretical models of mythology. Myth, folklore, and vernacular culture provided its own theoretical terrain for discussing gender and sexuality, a terrain critically aware of class and race. I simply needed to try to develop Lorde's theory beyond fixed sexual identities. Arobateau's e-mail forced me to see the limited span of my early project, and it gave me my initial vision of trickster politics for this venture. I had already begun to lock myself into an established dichotomy of seeing gender as strictly male/female and sexuality as heterosexuality/homosexuality. Such a strategy would have been very antithetical to my current work on trickster-troping in Black female culture. Polyvalence and mutability served as a starting point. In the end, the extended written narratives, stand-up comedy, and music seemed to be a nice beginning and middle, but poetry provides the best way to conclude this study.

Poetry has always been an important part of Black vernacular culture, and in Black female culture it becomes a genre very capable of translating desire through various trickster mechanisms. Pulitzer Prize–winning poet Rita Dove extols the benefits of poetry as a form or genre that offers a way to articulate one's identity and desires, even when those two things may conflict with each other. Dove asserts, "Poetry connects you to yourself, to the self that doesn't know how to talk or negotiate. We have emotions that we can't really talk about, and they're very strong. . . . I really don't think of poetry as being an intellectual activity. I think of it as a very visceral activity" (xxvi). Clarke stands as another poet who intuits the benefits of folklore, vernacular, and queerness to discuss her identity as a Black lesbian and her sexual desires. In her collection of poetry, *Experimental Love*, Clarke's visceral activity turns to trickster. Clarke's poems serve as a narrative on how love and desire would form and be represented were individuals able to break the bonds of social categories, rules, and norms. In the process Clarke becomes a trickster who rebels and rescues: "To question everything in society would lead to anarchy; to preserve everything would lead to stagnation; the conflict is presented, and the balance achieved, in the trickster tales which so many societies possess. And in all of them a universal feature of the trickster is his role as both revolutionary and savior" (Street 97). Clarke avoids becoming fixed in the role of savior by rebelling in ways that contradict dominant ideologies. Her role as trickster is that of revolutionary and minor god who must delicately balance creativity and destructiveness.

Clarke's "Space Invocation" begins the experiment of representing love and desire without categorization. In the poem, trickster and its strategies abound in the title, stanza, and every metaphor connected to space:

> I must get to those spaces
> black space of throathole
> brown space of asshole
> red space of cunthole
> sex space of no turning back
> Stomach
> take me to them
> and lead me in a good song. (*Experimental Love* 8)

Clarke's poem offers a reading of sexual desire embedded with a doubled context that fits the model of many trickster narratives. The first context positions the body as an astronomical innerspace, comparable to the astronomy of outerspace that contains black holes. But the innerspace, which she designates as a sex space, brims with fleshy holes that offer various possibilities for those invested in sexual fluidity. The holes or orifices of the body signify pleasure points which may or may not align with heteronormative desires. Hence, "Space Invocation" observes that experimental love (queer love) must be an expansive and unyielding field that people should boldly explore. The fluttering of desire makes the stomach a metaphorical spaceship that Clarke sees as her guide in exploring and singing the pleasures of the body.

The second context for "Space Invocation" hinges on reading space as either a measurement of time or a positioning within major texts that manages to invoke trickster. As opposed to speaking of trickster and trickster-troping in terms of strictly outside the text, Clarke allows us to perceive of trickster as not physically at the margins, but rather another contextualized minor entity of the text. Clarke's poem clearly delves in trickster-troping as it uses orality and sexuality to create its poetic narrative. Because trickster (or tricksterism) has been classified as a "state of ambivalence that can create a shift in the value of objects" (Spinks 7), trickster shares a common motivation as that of space in language and culture overall. Whether spoken or written, what fits in between words, notes, or colors are the spaces. These spaces are the beats, pauses, the hesitations, the empty canvases, and the voids. Nevertheless, they are chasms for change. These spaces can alter the meaning of an entire cultural narrative, in any form, to suit individual needs or wants. When Mary Douglass considers trickster as the "category between categories" (365), the connection to space cannot be ignored. This second reading observes that experimental love occurs in the spaces of larger narratives. Thus, Clarke's poem engages trickster in her theories as to what experimental love might look like.

Lee Jacobus explains of poetry that "to some extent it is mysterious, linked as it is in prehistory with religious chants and mystic prayers" (549). In this particular poem, Clarke includes this spiritual connotation of poetry as ceremony. Invocation is "the action or an act of invoking or calling upon (God, a deity, etc.) in prayer or attestation; supplication, or an act or form of supplication, for aid or protection" (*OED Online*). It has also been "the action or an act of conjuring or summoning a devil or spirit by incantation; an incantation or magical formula used for this or a similar purpose; a charm, spell" (*OED Online*). Who better represents the spirit of space that Clarke calls upon than trickster? The act of conjuring the space deity by incantation is the poet's method of trickster-troping. And for this study, space invocation is especially relevant to sexual desire. In Clarke's case, queer desire can be located in the space invocation.

Clarke creates a ceremony about spaces, but not just any spaces. She invokes spaces of the body associated with waste, filth, and messiness. She creates a physical chant thematically invested in oral cavities designated for sexual and nonsexual activities. The ambivalent meaning behind invoking theses cavities stems from the unknown of what spaces can mean at any given time. In this way, Clarke connects orality and sexuality in very physical but metaphorical ways. The use of profanity in this spiritual chant allows Clarke to confuse the sacred and the lewd, as well as move away from the scientific realm of sexuality that embraces ordered classification. In choosing to use profanity in the sacred invocation, the author suggests that the language of the social sciences or the rhetoric of propriety remain incapable of fully exposing the depths of being a Black sexual subject, rather than an object. Hence, vernacular words that are just as messy and controversial must be used.

However, unlike Clarke, the utter insanity produced in the history of sexuality as it concerns Black people has left many mute. Years earlier Clarke made an especially compelling argument as to how this happened:

> Like all Americans, black Americans live in a sexually repressive culture. And we have made all manner of compromise regarding our sexuality in order to live here. We have expended much energy trying to debunk the racist mythology which says our sexuality is depraved. Unfortunately, many of us have overcompensated and assimilated the Puritan value that sex is for procreation, occurs only between men and women, and is only valid within the confines of heterosexual marriage. . . . [B]lack folk have to live with the contradictions

of this limited sexual system by repressing or closeting any other sexual/erotic urges, feelings, or desires. ("The Failure to Transform" 199)

Somewhere between being sexual savages and struggling for "normalization," many Black people lost the ability and language to speak about their own sexuality. As the representative of everyone else's queer sex, an astounding confusion manifests itself in Black culture about individual sexuality. Hence, the key, as Clarke makes clear, comes through using space instead of language, invoking space gods, and then singing the appropriate song. Only then can we realize our erotic power. Will it be free from influences of assimilation, colonization, and self-hatred? Hardly. But the spaces and the borders are where we can confront the contradictions and conflicts.

What Is an Authentic Black Lesbian?

Where Audre Lorde used her biomythography to establish the lesbian figure in African disaporic literatures, Clarke, as well as Lorde, has often used her essays and poetry to dismiss sexual authenticity in nationalist rhetoric. In concluding "Space Invocation," Clarke details that spaces and holes have shades and color as they exist in various locations in the body. That the body has spaces solidifies that it is never whole, never fixed, and always mutable. What we choose to fill and not fill those holes with changes the body, subverts gender, fulfills or denies sexual desires. The release of materials from those holes and spaces changes the body. These spaces imply that despite sharp prisms of scientific reasoning, the boundaries of the body are infinite. Where there is space there is infinity. Where there is space there is the possibility of transformation. The spaces, the metaphors, the unspeakable, and the latent take form in trickster and trickster narratives. In those spaces, the things we know become the unknown. For years now, Clarke has been a master at discussing wants and needs that exist in the borders and margins of binary sexual categories. As seen in another poem from the collection, "Living as a Lesbian at Forty-Five," Clarke notes the lack of control over the force of those spaces of desire:

> Oh, it's a frequent dream:
> He (He?) comes home hot
> and wanting to.
> .... even though he knows you're a lesbian
> there are those times

he still loses his crotch
in the part of your ass through your dress. (*Experimental Love* 68)

Clarke's incredulity, symbolized by the parenthetical "he" followed by a question mark, captures the uncertainty of her object choice as a self-identified lesbian. As with Arobateau, Clarke notes that there really is no intelligible logic of gender or desire. As she continues to consider the complexities of lesbian desire, Clarke highlights the tensions between desire and identity politics in a mode that Jewelle Gomez claims as revolutionary:

> For me the erotic tension of being a lesbian lives in that place where expected elements come together: the stone butch woman who knows how to turn a hem, or looks like a little girl when she laughs. Or the high femme with her skirt hiked up as she changes a tire. The tension of when the unexpected comes together is what makes being a lesbian a political act. That spilling over into the categories women are not meant to occupy is the transgressive behavior that can break down the barriers to personal and political liberation. ("Femme Erotic" 106)

Never shy about politically engaging the repression of sexuality in essay or poetic form, Clarke lays bare the foundation of her own poetic mission. Whether she's prophesizing about experimental love or living as a lesbian, Clarke's work reminds us that same-sex desire should also exist without boundaries:

> Dykes are hard to date.
> A dyke wants commitment,
> romance without abatement,
> and unrelenting virtue. . . .
>
> Dykes should break loose and put off
> monogamy, pregnancy, and permanency
> Pack your rubber, latex, and leather
> And go on the make
> I know we'll hook up somewhere. (*Experimental Love* 66)

"Dykes Are Hard" addresses the way gay/lesbian models of resistance moved too far to the center in terms of seeking to prove, much in the same way that Black political discourse did, the normalcy of gay and lesbians in regards to courting rituals. In her attempts to expose the elaborate nature of a nonassimilative queer sexuality, Clarke writes not only in the margins of dominant narratives, but in the spaces of marginalized narratives. Just when it seems that trickster might fit into society, she shifts toward another position. Clarke refuses to defensively object to the notion of homosexuals as promiscuous. She shirks off the notion of politically correct representations of sexual desire. At each movement in the poem, Clarke makes it clear that dykes are hard, as opposed to reductive and simplified models that can easily adhere to superficial categories. The key to navigating those conflicts lies in finding that place to hook up and figure out that most complex problem: what Black lesbians want. How do Black females who desire Black females construct their desires in ways that traverse the waters of racialized sexuality? They ignore everything else and focus on what they want.

Before she became a practitioner of experimental love, Clarke found herself morphing lesbian identity to reflect the fluidity of desire. In another collection of Clarke's poetry, *Living as a Lesbian*, she extols the benefits of trickster multiplicity. Throughout the anthology of poetry, Clarke demonstrates that she identifies specifically as lesbian. However, in an approach that inherently draws from trickster subjectivity, *Living as a Lesbian* testifies that her political identification with the category of lesbian does not fix her desires into a strictly homosexual classification. Trickster plays with cultural categories and highlights "the arbitrary nature of cultural rules and categories by constantly reminding the narrative culture that there is much beyond its own perspective and understanding" (Spinks 8). In her poem "Sexual Preference," Clarke amuses herself and readers with the lesbian cultural narrative: "I'm a queer lesbian./Please don't go down on me yet./I do not prefer cunnilingus./ (There's room for me in the movement.)" (*Living as a Lesbian* 68). As lesbian sexual practices have been portrayed to be especially orally/gentially situated, Clarke risks the very stability of lesbian identity with her spoken aversion to oral sex. She uses queer to signify on what the lesbian experience and sex act is supposed to be about. The poetry in the entire collection compels us to really consider what it means to "live" as a lesbian. Since living or life is a process that is not static, then perhaps living as lesbian or a female with same-sex desires is also less static.

Clarke's focus on living should be reunited with a Black gay vernacular phrase that it is surely meant to invoke, "in the life." When Joseph Beam used the phrase as the title of his groundbreaking collection on Black gay male identity and culture, *In The Life*, he explained why he chose it with the following statement:

> The word-of-mouth, oral tradition of the African American community

often makes it difficult to locate the etymology of a word or phrase. *In the life,* a phrase used to describe "street life" (the lifestyle of pimps, prostitutes, hustlers, and drug dealers) is also the phrase used to describe the "gay life" (the lives of Black homosexual men and women). Street life and gay life, at times, embrace and entwine, yet at other times, are precise opposites. (12)

E. Patrick Johnson explains that "the emergence of gay vernacular into popular discourse challenges the naturalization of the heterosexual sex as 'representative' of 'normal' sexual citizenship" (77). For Beam, Clarke, and many other Black queer people, these expansions of Black outlaw vernacular culture expose the intersections of racial and sexual discourse. They also challenge the heterosexualization of blackness as representative of real racial citizenship and the naturalization of whiteness as "representative" of "typical" nonheterosexual identity. Being in the life, or living, as Clarke uses it, displaces the sexual closet. As opposed to an epistemology of the closet, African American gay vernacular offers an "in the life epistemology" that submits a view of queer sexual desire as both positional and identity based.

Because a life or living changes human beings, placing emphasis on accepting one permanent identity seems harmful to any process of self-representation. As we have seen, African American women understand this fact. The vernacular "in the life" returns the queer subject to the libertory model of queer liberation, as opposed to the ethnic model.[2] Using life as a metaphor for queer sexuality adheres to the early liberationist models for gay liberation that sought a complete destruction of binary systems of gender and sexuality. In documenting the transitions in social moments from the liberationist model to the ethnic model, Steven Seidman found that "liberation theory presupposed a notion of an innate polymorphous, androgynous human nature. Liberation politics aimed at freeing individuals from the constraints of a sex/gender system that locked them into mutually exclusive homo/hetero and feminine/masculine roles" (110). Being in the life means existing outside established social orders that insist upon mutually exclusive or oppositional roles. A closet is part of a greater superstructure, and its function is limited by its dependence on the house as a superstructure of order. A life, however bound by time, has so much more possibilities. It exists as its own entity. "In the life" or living as a lesbian has more potential to disrupt heteronormative social order, and avoid assimilationist agendas exemplified by the current ethnic model. In her understanding of the established social order as corrupt, Barbara Smith asserted: "Nobody sane would want any part of the established order. It was the system—white supremacist, misogynistic, capitalistic and homophobic—that had made our lives so hard to begin with. We wanted something new . . . and more than a few of us . . . were working for a revolution" ("Where's the Revolution" 180). Clarke offers up trickster's love for chaos to uproot what has become planted and fixed.

Living as a Lesbian includes five poems that share the collection's title with minor differences: "living as a lesbian on the make," "living as a lesbian in the journal," "living as a lesbian underground: a futuristic fantasy," "living as a lesbian rambling," and "living as a lesbian at 35." The specially titled poems show the shifting of subjectivity and desire for women who identify as lesbian. Clarke creates trickster tales and her poetic lesbian representations act as tricksters created to foil the authentic or real lesbian created by contemporary gay and lesbian discourse. In the poems, Clarke's agenda is clear: subvert finite homosexuality.

In "living as a lesbian on the make," the voice is that of a lesbian in a straight bar: "straight bars ain't so bad/though filled with men" (21). When a woman comes into the bar, the voice declares, "I was lonely and knew she was looking for a woman. . . . I almost followed her out but was too horny to leave the easy man talking loud shit for a seduction I'd have to work at" (21). Being on the make, regardless of sexual orientation, is about the fulfillment of sexual desire through sexual acts. Although it seems that when it comes to fulfillment of same-sex desire, some women are just lazy, Clarke keeps expressing how difficult it is to identify as lesbian and perform that identity through the more explicit practices of fulfilling desire. In other words, desire (horniness as Clarke names it) outweighs identity politics. "living as a lesbian in the journal" and "living as a lesbian rambling" reflect private thoughts, while "living as a lesbian underground: a futuristic fantasy" truly embodies the outsider and insurrectionary nature of trickster, in addition to offering an apocalyptic revolution dictated by sexual identity.

In ways that mainstream Black political nationalists detest, Clarke queers Black civil rights and liberation through Black symbols of revolution and spirit:

> in basements
> attics
> and tents
> fugitive slaves
> poets and griots
> seminoles from songhay
> vodun queens—
> all in drag . . .
> dodging state troopers behind shades (73)

When Clarke imagines a future of queer dissent, she imagines it so that it connects back to African diasporic mythology and orality. Vodun is a derivative practice of Yoruba religions of the Dahomey as practiced in Nigeria, Brazil, and the United States. As we have seen from the beginning of this text, well-known West African trickster gods come from Oyo Dahomey. Like Lorde, Clarke connects to the queer possibilities of those gods and goddesses. Those vodun queens in drag have a cosmological legacy of violating and transgressing social borders. Though tricksters may move from world to world, their assignment remains the same: make and remake worlds through chaos and confusion. Clarke makes it clear that no matter how fluid her desire may be her self-identification as a lesbian is a political action that incites wars against those who would seek to disenfranchise queers. She does not stop at using African and African diasporic references; she contemplates imagery from other people of color who have suffered the pains of imperialism and colonialism. By creating an underground community based on sexuality, Clarke returns to trickster as an interloper of landscapes and borderlands. The fugitive queer slave migrates from one city, state, or country to another's borders. This experience symbolically resembles trickster's mythological presence in communities of humans and gods: exile and outsider.

Seven years later, in *Experimental Love*, Clarke continued to develop the experience of "living as a lesbian underground, ii":

> I was on my way underground when
> uniformed children blondish forcing
> my door nearly seized my journal
>
> Around the time little Stevie Wonder's songs
> were banned in the Bantustans, a harried editor looked
> up at me from my grazed manuscript,
> Shaking his head, said:
> "Maybe in thirty years we can anthologize an excerpt." (11)

In addition to pursuing social equality, the revolutionary lesbian poet now must contend with censorship of words and experiences. The role of white supremacy, emphasized by the allusion to Nazism and Adolf Hitler that is personified by uniformed blond children, in erasing the diversity of human life and culture takes center stage. Those who would censor do not differentiate between the public songs, manuscripts, and the personal thoughts of journals. In this lesbian underground, the lesbian poet becomes a different kind of fugitive whose crime is not only escaping master, but writing against master narratives. Words and writing can lead to death in highly politically charged times of sexual colonialism. This could mean a literal death, or a figurative death, of the lesbian writer who is not recognized by mainstream presses, publishers, or critics because of what and how she chooses to write. The poet who lives as a lesbian deliberately violates too many taboos and social mores. She risks enduring the literal and figurative death to declare her sexual desires.

When a prostitute who'd been caught and raped on a daily basis told the poet, "This word can get you violated" (11), she cannot resist her subversive nature. While on the run she encounters a fascist soldier who advises her against writing: "Hey, poeta, hope you have a good memory. Memory is your only redemption" (9). With well-conceived abandon, the lesbian poet ignores the words of both the prostitute and gestapo when she uses the undisclosed word:

> I wrote the word over and over . . .
> I wrote it in my left hand
> As well as my right.
> I recited it every time I wrote it.
> Played with my sex
> as I wrote it
> over and over.
> And said it as I came
> Over and over (13)

Like Legba's sexual defiance to Mawu's curse of the erect phallus, or the use of uncensored mode in Black female hip-hop, the poet defiantly writes the word in an act that furthers the inventions of self and fulfils the self's desire. On the one hand, paper and manuscripts can be censored, erased, burned, and shredded. Since ideas are less susceptible to those acts of destructions, memory might be considered the only redemption. However, what good is memory if it is not passed along in some form? The word must be conveyed in writing, speech, or experienced through intimate bodily contact. Clarke demonstrates that inscriptions of desire occur prominently at the intersection of orality and sexuality. Memory alone is not enough because it is the dissemination of memory that sparks insurrections. Each of the "living as a lesbian underground" poems explores the demarcation of self and national identity and provide witness to figures who are invaded or cast out in the name of nationalists agendas. As much as the poems reflect back to trickster's subject position between man and god, these futuristic imaginings of revolutionary lesbians embrace sexuality as a vital part of civil and human rights.

Defining sexual rights as not only a civil rights issue, but more globally as a human rights issue, is one of the most important contributions GLBT discourse has made to U.S. society and culture. It is a language that Black female culture has embraced in artistic venues. While some Black poets have used the art form to promote the repression of non-heteronormative sexuality, Clarke sees poetry, a less bourgeois mode of writing, as a way "to imagine a historical Black woman-to-woman eroticism and living—overt, discrete, coded, or latent as it might be. To imagine Black women's sexuality as a polymorphous erotic that does not exclude desire for men but also does not privilege it. To imagine, without apology, voluptuous Black women's sexualities" ("Living the Texts *Out*" 224). Creativity and imagination are the keys to delivering a diversity of mechanisms for trickster-troping. From postnationalist readings of the folk and unnaming to exposing the possibility of sexual fluidity in Queen B(?) narratives and poetry, the implications of trickster-trope readings insist on a refashioning of discussions on Black female sexuality.

Concerned with teenage pregnancy and the transmission of sexually transmitted diseases, former surgeon general Joycelyn Elders argued that sex education classes should teach the benefits of masturbation along with abstinence. Elders did what any original outsider would do; she sought to mix the sacred and profane as a viable solution to a real problem. Her suggestion spoke volumes on the sexual rights of teenagers. However, I was more impressed with what it signified for Black females. Elders brought Black female rhetorical models on sexuality full circle. The beginning of the twentieth century may have been about the quiet dignity of womanhood, but the end of the century optimistically leaned toward creating a space for the sexual and political. Elders utilized an approach that ignored the detrimental concerns of normativity to speak of sexual desires in a way that suggested that we all have inalienable sexual rights that should not be infringed upon in any way that might cause irreparable harm or damage to our lives.

I hope that *Mutha' Is Half a Word* helps foster an unabashed cultural environment where various discourses of desire in regard to Black female culture can be explored. Discourses of desire lead to languages of sexual rights that Black females need to know and embrace for their own sake. Cultural representations that protect and provide an environment for the discourse of desire should be heralded as significant. These intersections of folklore, vernacular, and queerness illuminate that fact. *Mutha Is Half a Word* cannot serve as a complete and full analysis of the work to be done on Black culture and Black female desire, but I hope it adds to and continues a conversation that began centuries ago in various trickster tales. In her assessment that argues against the way Western scholars have read trickster, Anne Doueihi notes:

> If trickster stories tell us about anything, it is about the difference between, and the undecideability of, discourse and story, referential and rhetorical values, signifier and signified, a conventional mind and one that is open to the sacred. It is only by missing such differences, by taking trickster narratives solely as stories, that scholarly readings have regarded them as "obscene," "immoral," and "profane." (200)

Doueihi's statement coincides with what I have attempted to suggest about Black women's culture that has typically been read as immoral, obscene, and profane. By positioning their cultural manuscripts (folklore, novels, short stories, comedy, music, poetry) as trickster stories, I hope that we can be motivated to read wild women and their culture as "inhabiting the space between story and discourse" (Doueihi 193) so that we don't miss the differences that can further liberate Black women. Instead of disregarding works that might be considered vulgar or profane, we should observe them closely for their strategies of creating radical Black female sexual subjectivity and a discourse for that subjectivity. Trickster-troping throughout the cultural collective of Black female communities suggests that to do so will prove pivotal in our survival and growth.

Notes

Preface

1. June Jordan's voice from "A Couple of Words on Behalf of Sex (Itself)" influences the title of this preface and the following introduction.

Introduction

1. I am referring to Barbara Omolade's assessment, "The black man moved toward the black woman, clothing her raped and abused black body with the mantle of respectable womanhood, giving protection, and claiming ownership of her" (258).

2. On p. 48, bell hooks reminds us that a figure who breaks the rules but has no conscious politics and does not connect it to the struggle to be self-defining focuses simply on the journey and not on the self that is being invented. In the end, such a reactionary act eliminates the possibility of plural identities for another fixed space.

3. Dorothy Roberts's *Killing the Black Body* alters discussions of reproduction and race, while Cathy Cohen's *The Boundaries of Blackness* explores how limited Black political ideologies and movements have been in regard to issues of sexual health. Angela Davis has taken on the prison-industrial complex movement, paying attention to gender within her own discussion.

4. These entertainers of the highly sexualized disco era have repudiated their previous bad-girl performances as sinful and harmful and never learned the lesson of ranking axiologically opposed binaries.

5. Hammonds discusses both of these historical accounts. Deborah Gray White's *Too Heavy A Load: Black Women in Defense of Themselves 1894–1994* argues that "black women persistently spoke on their own behalf on issues of race leadership, negative stereotypes, woman's suffrage and women's rights, and civil rights and civil liberties" (16). As Darlene Clark Hine noted of White's examination, those Black women were inevitably involved with a feminism rooted in the "noble" cause to "defend their name and to 'uplift the race'" (review). Not to undermine or make light of the 1890s club organizations of Black women, 1920s National Association of Colored Women, or the history of other Black women's organizations from the mid-twentieth century to the present, but such defensive posturing has typically led to the quieting of non-middle-class and non-heteronorma-

tive/nonheterosexual women that Black female critics like Hammonds have frequently discussed. Were all Black women silent? What about women uninvolved in those organizations or not associated with a specific middle-class contingency? Were there no instances of culture where Black women, heterosexual and queer, were not silent?

6. In *A Voice from the South: By a Black Woman of the South*, Anna Julia Cooper joins the ranks of W. E. B. Dubois and Martin Delaney in their assessments of Black womanhood at the beginning of the twentieth century. Cooper's popular phrase about Black women's social and political entry comes from the following passage: "Only the black woman can say 'where and when I enter, in the quiet undisputed dignity of my womanhood, without violence and without suing or special patronage, then and there the whole Negro race enters with me'" (31). And so the protection of Black womanhood is further incorporated into agendas of Black nationalism.

7. In addition to DuCille, there have been a number of critics who have addressed the limited and essentialist use of vernacular criticism. See Hazel Carby's "Ideologies of the Black Folk: The Historical Novel of Slavery," Diana Fuss's *Essentially Speaking: Feminism, Nature, and Difference*, and Robin D. G. Kelley's "Notes on Deconstructing the Folk."

8. Other writers who have expressed similar sentiments are Devon Carbardo, Cathy Cohen, Dwight McBride, bell hooks, Essex Hemphill, and Barbara Smith.

9. In *Yearning*, hooks speaks of postmodern blackness as a politic of difference that would "incorporate the voices of displaced, marginalized, exploited, and oppressed black people" but that would also "break with the notion of 'authority' as 'mastery over'" as simply a rhetorical device (25).

10. Jonathan Culler's *On Deconstruction: Theory and Criticism after Structuralism* reveals the importance of difference: "The term différance, which Derrida introduces alludes to this undecideable, non-synthetic alteration between the perspectives of structure and event. The verb differer means to differ and defer. Différance sounds the same as difference, but the ending -ance, which is used to produce verbal nouns, makes it a new form meaning 'difference-differeing-deferring.' Différance thus designates both a 'passive' difference already in place as the condition of signification and an act of differeing which produces differences" (97).

11. So sayeth Erik Davis, John W. Roberts, Robert Pelton, and Isaac Hayes.

12. The initial inquiry into the difference between the two is discussed in Samuel Delany's "The Rhetoric of Sex/Discourse of Desire," 3–41.

13. I refer back to Anna Julia Cooper's *A Voice from the South*.

14. See Susan T. Hollis and Linda Pershings's *Feminist Theory and the Study of Folklore* for general discussions of gender in folklore. Essays from the collection expose issues of genre and gender as well as nation and gender.

15. On p. 49, Gates's theory of signifying relies on Derrida's work in *Positions*. Derrida notes, "We can extend to the system of the signs in general what Saussure says about language: The linguistic system (*langue*) is necessary for speech events (*parole*) to be intelligible and produce their effects, but the latter are necessary for the system to establish itself" (39–40). Likewise, Derrida shows that signifiers do not produce signified, they produce more signifiers. As a less oral culture, writing becomes privileged in the West. The conceptual order of written over orality is created primarily because of the binary oppositions we have imposed on language, and rather than creating true meaning we create signifiers that must rely on each other to even obtain meaning. Gates's theory of signifyin(g) attempts to reverse this order.

16. Roberts connects the animal tales of Br'er Rabbit to the tales of John and Old

Master, John (a slave driver), human possessing all the traits of Br'er Rabbit, but his trickery is more sophisticated and complex. Br'er Rabbit leads to the establishment of a heroic tradition in America.

17. See Roger Abrahams's *Deep Down in the Jungle: Negro Narrative Folklore in the Streets of Philadelphia,* Harold Courlander's *Negro Folk Song U.S.A.*, and Joel Chandler Harris's *Uncle Remus: His Songs and Sayings.*

18. Years later, Kimberlee Crenshaw's "Whose Story Is It Anyway? Feminist and Antiracist Appropriations of Anita Hill" examines the narrow view of Black women's sexuality. She notes that within feminist contexts rape and the rape trial serve as the dominant tropes of as a central site of the oppression of women. She then argues that lynching narrative is the trope of antiracist discourse (405). In both discourses, the Black body's desires remain absent and without expression.

19. Ifi Amadiume's *Re-Inventing Africa: Matriarchy, Religion, & Culture* and Nkiru Nzegwu's "Cultural Epistemologies of Motherhood: Refining the Concept of Mother" really expose the flaws of the way the West's version of motherhood limits concepts about women and mothering in general, but African women in particular. Both works find a way to disconnect motherhood from Western concepts of womanhood in ways that delimit gender.

20. Harris's valuable contributions to the connection between Black female literature and folklore are exhibited in her critical works: *Fiction and Folklore: The Novels of Toni Morrison* and *The Power of the Porch: The Storyteller's Craft in Zora Neale Hurston, Gloria Naylor, and Randall Kenan.*

21. See Carby's "It Jus Be's Dat Way Sometimes: The Sexual Politics of Women's Blues."

22. Though this text does not examine mothering and motherhood, critics such as Sheri Parks, Yvonne Atkinson, and Marlo David have already started much-needed and serious critical conversations about the representations of mothering and motherhood, gender, and sexuality in African American women's popular culture.

23. According to linguist Geneva Smitherman's book *Black Talk,* muthafucka very rarely refers to someone having sex with one's mother, and in the case of tradition Black mothers having consensual sex seems not worthy of discussion.

24. Though they don't engage issues of sexuality strictly in terms of desire, recent scholarship of motherhood and reproduction is amazing and wonderfully educational. I am specifically enamored with Michele Mitchell's *Righteous Propagation: African Americans and the Politics of Racial Destiny after Reconstruction* and Jennifer L. Morgan's *Laboring Women: Reproduction and Gender in New World Slavery* for their dissections of the way Black women's sexuality, during slavery and shortly after emancipation, has been used for the developing United States and the Black nation within the United States.

25. See Carl Jung's *The Archetypes of and the Collective Unconscious* for his well-known discussion of trickster as the id of a community.

26. She speaks solely of desire and not trickster. I invoke her words here and elsewhere as a way to show trickster as a non-Western metaphor for desire.

Chapter 1

1. Ideas about the matrilocal structure of Black families can be found in texts concerned with the predicament of Black women in slavery. See Paula Giddings's *When and Where I Enter: The Impact of Black Women on Race and Sex in America,* Eugene D.

Genovese's *Roll, Jordan, Roll: The World the Slaves Made*, John Blassingame's *The Slave Community: Plantation life in the Antebellum South*, Herbert Gutman's *The Black Family in Slavery and Freedom*, "The Moynihan Report" in Lee Rainwater and William L. Yancy's *The Moynihan Report and the Politics of Controversy*, and Herbert Aptheker's *American Negro Slave Revolts*.

2. I am now borrowing from Spillers and taking her model to the necessary extreme in examining Janey's naming.

3. Spillers explains that such captive bodies focus "a private and particular space, at which point of convergence biological, sexual, social, cultural, linguistic, ritualistic, and psychological forces join. This profound intimacy of interlocking detail is disrupted, however, by externally imposed meanings and uses" (259–60).

4. For example, early Black nationalists adopted the use of African for slaves and exslaves, but when the Colonization Society began a movement to take Blacks back to Africa, a growing number of Black people avoided the term (Stuckey 202). Likewise, African and Colored were discontinued as some Black nationalists sought to avoid calling attention to the difference of race as Blacks sought to integrate into American society (207). Unnaming, then, engaged the ideological and institutional means by which Black people might accomplish complete liberation in the United States. (208).

5. Even the gender-neutral *alaafin* (Yorùbá word for ruler) becomes mistranslated into king or queen and ranked accordingly in Western order.

6. The very way in which Black men argued for the right to vote in terms of a masculine right at the end of the nineteenth century, and the way Black nationalism positioned Black masculinity in the fight for civil rights has already proven that dominant Black male communities prefer gender naming to gender unnaming so that they might access power through patrilineal lines.

7. Harold Courlander's *A Treasury of Afro-American Folklore* describes the number of songs and legends about John Henry as epic. Levine calls this figure the slave trickster (389), and John Roberts claims it as the John and Old Maser Trickster Cycle (44).

8. Michelle Cliff's wonderful novel *Free Enterprise* makes use of both versions of Annie Christmas. She writes a narrative about female abolitionists buoyed by the water.

9. I borrow this term from the introduction of Oyêwùmí's *The Invention of Woman*.

10. There are several works that demonstrate such a belief. I have already acknowledged Stepto's *From behind the Veil* and Gates's *The Signifying Monkey*. Other texts contain the same thematic focus: Houston Baker's *Blues, Ideology, and Afro-American Literature*. Gates's critical introduction to *The Slave Narrative* and *Figures in Black* (xxii), William Andrews's *To Tell a Free Story: The First Century of African American Autobiography, 1760–1865*, Houston Baker's *The Journey Back: Issues in Black Literature and Criticism*, and Valerie Smith's *Self-Discovery and Authority in Afro-American Narrative*. Ronald Judy argues that the theory of the slave narrative as a product committed to Enlightenment and Kantian ideas of being and humanism is debatable, and he presents Bontemps's foreword from *The Slave Narrative* (xx) as a pro-Kant view of being and the slave narrative.

11. In the foreword to *(Dis)forming the American Canon*, Wahneema Lubiano previews a specific problem with Judy's text as it concerns gender (xxii).

12. See also Judy's discussion of Kant: "Kant's problem is how to think about the Negro, not as a phenomenal appearance, or undetermined object of empirical intuition, but as an intellectual concept, a derivative of the concept of 'Man'" (*(Dis)forming the American Canon* 110–15)). It is in this particular discussion that Lubiano feels Judy could have also considered the critique of gender itself as it relates to race or the Negro.

13. Robert Stepto's *From behind the Veil* and Gates's *The Signifying Monkey.*

14. "Sign" in the *Encyclopedia of Contemporary Literary Theory* also notes that "a sign implies not only a system, however simple, within which a sign can signify, but also a sender and receiver" (623).

15. Muñoz discusses the process of disidentification as one that "scrambles and reconstructs the encoded message of a cultural text in a fashion that both exposes the encoded message's universalizing and exclusionary machinations and recircuits its workings to account for, include, and empower minority identities and identification" (31).

16. See Denise Riley's *Am I That Name: Feminism and the Category of "Women" in History* (158–60) and Constance Penley's *The Future of an Illusion: Film, Feminism, and Psychoanalysis* (179). Riley's work attempts to understand Truth's subjectivity by signifying on Truth's famous statement, changing "Ain't I a Woman" to "Ain't I a Fluctuating Identity" (1). Penley asserts that Truth's statement acts as "two ideas or strategies . . . important to feminism . . . 'epistemological' and 'metaphysical;' the other—represented by Truth—is 'political'" (179). Deborah McDowell's *The Changing Same: Black Women's Literature, Criticism, and Theory* provides prudent criticism of these two critiques of Truth's importance:

> Riley's move to appropriate Sojourner Truth introduces a subtle racial marker that distinguishes between Truth's original words and Riley's displacement. . . . That Truth's declarative question . . . might be read as political and epistemological simultaneously seems not to have occurred to Penley, partly because she manipulates both these categories . . . to conform to an already polarized and preconceived understanding. (159)

17. Accounts on the Crafts' speech published in the *Liberator* suggest that William becomes the primary speaker on the lecture circuit with Ellen speaking as directed, all as a protective measure to ensure Ellen's status as a virtuous woman.

18. William narrates the dilemma:

> On reaching my wife's cottage she handed me her pass, and I showed mine, but at that time neither of us were able to read them. It is not only unlawful for slaves to be taught to read, but in some of the States there are heavy penalties attached, such as fines and imprisonment, which will be vigorously enforced upon any one who is humane enough to violate the so-called law. . . . So, while sitting in our little room upon the verge of despair, all at once my wife raised her head, and with a smile upon her face, which was a moment before bathed in tears, said, "I think I have it!" I asked what it was. She said, "I think I can make a poultice and bind up my right hand in a sling, and with propriety ask the officers to register my name for me." I thought that would do. (34)

19. There is a sustained discussion of the moral implications of Ellen's passing in the text (30, 35).

20. One tale, "All God's Chillen Had Wings," suggests that "once all Africans could fly like birds; but owing to their many transgressions, their wings were taken away" (Hughes and Bontemps 62).

21. Valerie Smith's work and her theory of garreting support thinking of Black female subjectivity as trickster-like. When Smith discusses the way garreting allows Jacobs to move in and out of the discourses of domesticity in her American Studies Association presentation "Loopholes of Retreat," later thematically revisited in her introduction to *Incidents in the Life of a Slave Girl* by Harriet Jacobs and her critical work *Self-Discovery and Authority in Afro-American Narrative*, Smith uncovers another method of trickster-troping enacted by Jacobs

to unname. Samira Kawash elucidates further on Jacobs's use of the garret in her argument about the garret and loopholes of retreat in *Dislocating the Color Line: Identity, Hybridity, and Singularity in African American Narrative*. See also Jean Fagan Yellin's Introduction to another edition of *Incidents in the Life of a Slave Girl: Written by Herself* by Harriet A. Jacobs.

22. See the introduction to Charles H. Davis and Henry L. Gates Jr., eds., *The Slave's Narratives*.

23. Robert Stepto's *From behind the Veil* claims that the two pregeneric myths of African American literary tradition are freedom and literacy. However, that theory rarely takes into account differences based on gender, class, or caste status on the plantation.

24. See Gates's *The Signifying Monkey*.

25. Bruce Mills's "Lydia Maria Child and the Endings to Harriet Jacobs' *Incidents in the Life of a Slave Girl*" offers an opposing view of the conclusion of Jacobs's narrative. He turns to the influence of Lydia Maria Child as Jacobs's editor and argues that Jacobs's original ending included John Brown's raid. He suggests that Child encouraged Jacobs to change it to include a statement on marriage and freedom and potential joys of such domesticity as a way to calm rather than agitate her readers (257). Mills argument supports my reading of Jacobs's need to trickster-trope throughout the text. However, I further assert that even if Jacobs submits the alternative conclusion of marriage as a substitute for her more radical commentary on John Brown's raid, she continues trickster-troping to unname gender and sexuality by exposing marriage as practiced in her time as a lesser version of slavery for women.

26. In "Ties That (Un)bind: Feminism, Sisterhood and Other Foreign Relations," Oyèrónké Oyěwùmí dismisses Lorde's trickster-troping for the way it and U.S. Black female critics appropriate African culture to explore non-Western configurations of gender and sexuality for their construction of a Black lesbian nation. Though her commentary on appropriations is very valid, the direction of her assessment makes one wonder what the cause of dismissal would be had it been an African lesbian critic who had done the same thing. Or as critic Greg Thomas has noted of Oyěwùmí's critique on the invention of woman in the West: Can a critic who so easily and thoroughly dismantles the Western concepts of gender hierarchy in her own work really expect that limited concepts of sexuality would also remain intact?

27. Though she does not speak of trickster, Mae G. Henderson's canonical work, "Speaking in Tongues: Dialogics, Dialectics, and the Black Woman Writer's Literary Tradition" exposes how, even without a Mawu to give them seven languages, Black women writers possess a tradition in regard to subjectivity and language that rivals Fa.

28. See Oyěwùmí's discussion of aurality and orality in *The Invention of Women*. In further explicating on the mistranslation of gender by Western culture, she explores the weight given to the visual over the oral (30).

Chapter 2

1. The biomythography does not provide a final ending. However, Lorde's own life offers a valiant example of the power of the erotic and trickster's imprint. Alexis DeVeaux's biography of Lorde attempts to fill in gaps not covered in *Zami*.

2. See Trudier Harris's "From Exile to Asylum: Religion to Community in the Writings of Contemporary Black Women" and "This Disease Called Strength: Some Observations of the Compensating Construction of Black Female Characters," Gay Wilentz's *Healing*

Narratives: Women Writers Curing Cultural Dis-ease, and Valerie Lee's *Granny Midwives & Black Women Writers*. Each work documents, through historical analysis of critical analysis of the literary character of the healer, society's ideas about black women as healers, the known characteristics attributed to black women healers who are either exiled or outcasts from their communities, asexual and nonthreatening women, and all explore the healer's effect on those coming to be healed or being healed.

3. See Claudia Mitchell-Kernan's "Signifying as a Verbal Art," and Geneva Smitherman's *Talkin' and Testifyin': The Language of Black America*.

4. Herskovits's *Dahomean Narrative* provides great details about how the Fon view Fa as the writing Mawu uses to create each person. This is why Gates's project with poststructuralism connects so easily to trickster (207–208).

5. In *Corregidora*, Ursa Corregidora is a blues singer who gives witness through her singing gift. Her witnessing/blues singing acts as a communal way of healing African Americans. Her mythical legacy is "the important thing is making generations. They can burn the papers but they can't burn consciousness" (14). The repetitive and recursiveness of this phrase in the text makes the statement mythical in the life of Ursa and in turn impacts how she will live her life. Although one must wonder, since three of the major concerns of Corregidora are gender conflicts, sexual dysfunction and inability to love without hurting or allowing one's self to be hurt, if Ursa's return to Mutt is the beginning of her healing or a denial of it.

In Jones's *Eva's Man*, statements about the gypsy, great-grandmother Medina and the Queen Bee become important factors in shaping how Eva Medina sees herself and guides her life actions. Eva's witnessing to the life and myth of the Queen Bee and her actions of orally castrating Davis's penis serve as testimony for the traumatizing abuse black women can experience. The novel's endings are so ambivalent that past and current criticism of each text has yet to end debate as to whether either woman ever heals herself. However, unlike Ursa, Eva does not possess the tools to begin a healing process to heal herself or others, for she has lost her inability to connect through her community. At least with Ursa, there is always the possibility that healing has or will happen. In both novels, readers mostly see how witnessing and testifying have negatively impacted the protagonists' lives. We briefly receive glimmers of how the communality of oral traditions might positively affect the community and the individual. However, in *The Healing*, Jones finally provides us with that crucial and vital component of the oral, communality.

6. See Glen Schwendemann's "Nicodemus: Negro Haven on the Solomon," *Kansas Historical Quarterly* 34 (1968): 10–31.

7. However, given that sickness and ailment entail a certain amount of pain, I am certain that someone could examine African American women's trope of healers as an exploration of S/M. But this text is more interested in pleasure.

Chapter 3

1. Ross's "Camping the Dirty Dozens: The Queer Resources of Black Nationalist Invective" is an amazing assessment of the "potential interplay between the dozens as a mode of street-smart verbal jousting affiliated with urban, working-class, supermasculine (i.e., avowedly heterosexual) African American culture since at least the early twentieth century and camp as a mode of in-the-know verbal repartee usually affiliated with underground urban *European*-American homosexual male enclaves since at least the early

twentieth century and before the emergence of militant gay liberation" (291).

2. There are two major works by black female critics, Trudier Harris and Elise A. Williams, that will be mentioned throughout this chapter that in various ways discuss the breaking of taboos by Moms Mabley. Williams's *The Humor of Jackie Moms Mabley* provides a detailed and interesting book-length critique on the career and life of Moms Mabley.

3. In *Lettin' It All Hang Out* and an interview at NYshow.com, RuPaul explains how his mother love of Page affected him and his love for the comedienne.

4. Though there are few biographical entries on Page's career before *Sanford and Son*, Jason Buchanan's biosketch of Page included in the *New York Times* and All Media Movie Guide Database offers these gems about Page's early career. Watkins's text also contains some tidbits about the comedienne.

5. In *Bodies That Matter*, Butler remedies her attention to race and performance of gender and desire with a complex interrogation of Nella Larsen's *Passing*, but Halberstam perceptively observes the importance of vernacular in Black women's performance of masculinity.

6. In their song "I Wanna Hot Dog for My Roll," Susie and Butterbeans play off the sexual innuendo with lines such as "Listen, I want a dog without bread, you see" and later "Because I carries my bread with me" (Dance, *Honey, Hush*, 319)

7. Some theories that draw on the idea that the fact that Christ was a man suggests that he engaged in sexual relations with a prostitute, and this relationship resulted in them having children.

8. Bill Cosby was the most vocal critic of the show.

9. The audience member was making reference to Givens's previous act on *Def Comedy Jam*, where she makes a joke about the size of her lips and the act of fellatio. The joke presents this memorable gem for audience members of Queen of Comedy: "My big ass lips, his little ass dick it'd be like tryin' to give a whale a tic-tac. That shit wouldn't work!"

10. See Spears's discussion on black culture and class conflicts, p. 229.

11. According to Claudia Mitchell-Kernan, pp. 310–28, signifying incorporates indirection, remarks laced with taboo terms, and contextual embeddedness of meaning.

12. Troy Patterson's review of the *Queens of Comedy* stated it "might as well be called 'How Stella Got Her #@*! Back.'" 'The performers try both to foster a vibe of sisterly respect and to talk about the sex act in the least self-respectful way possible. (*Entertainment Weekly* 23). In *Apollo Guide Video Review* of Queens of Comedy, Ryan Cracknell also voiced an inability to understand: "A lot of the jokes don't generate laughs for me, simply because I don't find them funny. I guess I just didn't get it. This film is geared primarily toward a female audience. It talks about the dirty little secrets that men often prefer to avoid and experiences that exclude men because of their anatomy. . . . Ultimately, these self-proclaimed 'Queens of Comedy' are reminiscent of a band of cackling court jesters that refuses to go away."

Chapter 4

1. The very definition of queer made it possible for critics such as Pat Califia ("Gay Men, Lesbians, and Sex: Doing it Together,"), Jan Clausen ("My Interesting Condition," 11–21), and David Halperin (*One Hundred Years of Homosexuality and Other Essays on Greek Love*) to begin theorizing the various dimensions of sexual desire that expands the definition of object choice in discussions of sexual orientation.

2. Although I am focused on the more pervasive masculine and homophobic presentations of black nationalism, Lubiano's assessment can also be corroborated by Huey P. Newton's "The Women's Liberation and Gay Liberation Movements." While Newton asserts a stance to unite black power movements with women and gay liberation movements, he also acknowledges that "there has been some uncertainty about how to relate to these movements. . . . sometimes our first instinct is to want to hit a homosexual in the mouth, and want a woman to be quiet" (387). Clearly, the founder of black power recognizes how homophobia and sexism has manifested itself in Black nationalism, and this recognition further substantiates my claims.

3. In an especially damning critique of Marxism and national liberation movements, Robinson demonstrates how nationalism becomes conflated with racialism. His argument reveals that periods of nationalism in Europe are really imperialism (44–68).

4. Despite the way Ifi Amadiume's *Male Daughters, Female Husbands: Gender and Sex in African Society* displaces the heterosexual nuclear family model, she dismisses thoughts of lesbianism in Africa. Nevertheless, Stephen O. Murray and Will Roscoe provide a much-needed edited collection of essays on the subject with the publication of their *Boy-Wives and Female Husbands: Studies of African Homosexualities.*

5. Their essays can be found in Delroy Constantine-Simms's *The Greatest Taboo: Homosexuality in Black Communities.*

6. Cathy Cohen's groundbreaking text *The Boundaries of Blackness* has already examined the impact of the issues in the era of AIDS and its detrimental impact on black people.

7. In *Sula* and *Paradise*, Toni Morrison utilizes the sacred and the profane aspects of tricksterism to propel her novels forward. Paule Marshall's *Praisesong for the Widow* and John A. William's *The Man Who Cried I Am* often utilizes trickster references to help their protagonist return to a healthy use of the body and the erotic in their physical and spiritual lives.

8. In addition to the earlier efforts of James Baldwin and Audre Lorde, writers and critics such as Ann Allen Shockley, Red Jordan Arobateau, Essex Hemphill, James Earl Hardy, and E. Lynn Harris interrogate notions of gender and sexual constructs for black peoples. See also Roderick Ferguson's *Aberrations in Black;* a special edition of *Callaloo*, "Gay, Lesbian, Bisexual, Transgender Literature and Culture"; Charles I. Nero's "Toward a Black Gay Aesthetic: Signifying in Contemporary Black Gay Literature"; Winston Napier, ed., *African America Literary Theory: A Reader*, 399–420; Siobhan Somerville's "Scientific Racism and the Invention of the Homosexual Body"; Oscar Montero's "Latino and National Identity"; and Merl Storr's "The Sexual Reproduction of 'Race.'"

9. Marlon Ross's "Some Glances at the Black Fag: Race, Same-Sex Desire, and Cultural Belonging" observes that we must "bring into view the cultural role of the black faggot" (501).

10. For example, Roberts moves from discussing a slave's theft from his master (199) and a conjurer named Railroad Bill (200) to Stackolee and John Hardy (203–209). These figures serve as outlaw heroes who employ their lack of citizenship in the United States to ignore the prescribed social morals of their time. Though they often break white society's laws, they enhance the quality of life for themselves or other blacks through their trickster actions (214–215).

11. See Laura Makarius's "The Myth of the Trickster: The Necessary Taboo Breaker" (66–86) and Lawrence Levine's *Black Culture and Black Consciousness* (332–34) for a discussion of the body and tricksterism. Levine briefly explores sexual stereotypes of black

sexual superiority in black comedy and laughter derived from slave culture (racialized sexuality).

12. Levine, who records this tale from North Carolina, does not make an attempt to explain or explore the significance of homosexuality in this text (333).

13. As is the case in all colonies of social bees, the only sexually mature female honeybee is the queen. When she flies away from the nest to mate, she gives off an odor (a pheromone) that the drones find irresistible, and they follow her. The streamlined queen flies faster and higher than the majority of the short, stocky drones. As she soars upward, many of them give up the pursuit. From the few drones that can follow her as she continues on a rising, whirling flight, she chooses one to couple with. After mere seconds her mate falls dying to the ground, and she chooses another (*Britannica Online*).

14. For years, one of New York's Black newspapers in the 1920s, *Inter-state Tattler*, carried a column specifically centered on stories on female polygamists, wives caught cheating, etc.

15. Years later, Angela Davis, whom these blaxploitation character were constructed from, had to endure immense scrutiny about her sexuality after she publicly expressed dissatisfaction with the separatist agenda of the Million Man March. This was not a situation of life mirroring art, merely a reiteration that the debate around political correctness of characters, stemming from an unresolved issue of sexual desires and political agendas in the African American community.

16. This is not an error. The author spells her name exactly as I have recorded it.

17. See Sagri Dhairyam's "Racing the Lesbian, Dodging White Critics" for an insightful discussion of black female same sex desire and the Western and Eurocentric construction of lesbianism. Like Lorde, Dhairyan questions the category of lesbian and suggests that renaming it creates controversy among white gay and lesbian critics.

18. Bogus explicitly says that the "Queen B aspires to be and generally succeeds as a singer whose music contributes to and influences the world in which she lives" (279).

19. Biman Basu's "Public and Private Discourses and the Black Female Subject: Gayl Jones' *Eva's Man*"; Sally Robinson's *Engendering the Subject: Gender and Self-Representation in Contemporary Women's Fiction* (160–88); Melvin Dixon's "Singing a Deep Song: Language as Evidence in the Novels of Gayl Jones"; and Keith Byerman's "Intense Behaviors: The Use of the Grotesque in *The Bluest Eye* and *Eva's Man*." Basu contests Dixon's earlier claims about Jones's novel.

20. In 1933 Bogan also recorded another song that positions her sexuality as commodity, "Barbecue Bess": "I got a sign on my door, 'Barbecue for Sale,'/I'm talkin' 'bout my barbecue, only thing I crave,/And that good doin' meat, gon' carry me to my grave. /I'm sellin' it cheap, 'cause I got good stuff."

Chapter 5

1. In the case of Gayl Jones, a recent comprehensive collection on Gayl Jones, Fiona Mills and Keith B. Mitchell's *After the Pain*, does take into consideration Jones's deconstructions of binary sexualities. As For Toni Morrison, in a number of interviews collected in *Conversations with Toni Morrison* she likens writing to a type of modern-day divination and insists on revisions of trickster narratives with her fictional novels *Sula*, *Tar Baby*, and *Song of Solomon*. And since trickster has been described as queer in this work and sup-

ported as such by many works before my own, Smith's lesbian reading of *Sula* isn't the work of some critic gone mad. Were that the case, it would invalidate Morrison's own dissection of the Africanist presence in American literature that she speaks about in *Playing in the Dark*.

2. See this essay for a full discussion on the place of the bourgeois concept of the novel in black culture versus the place of folk and oral culture.

3. Psychologist M. L. Johnson creates the terms "Black-identified lesbigays" and "gay-identified lesbigays," but Connerly's essay exposes the depth of how this politic of identity shapes the emerging black queer nation.

4. In "Women in a Southern Time," secondary character Louella classifies bulldagger as a Black woman with "short, wavy hair slicked back" and who wears "a man's starched white shirt opened at the collar and gray, pegged pants with a zipper in front." The main character, Eulah Mae, after initial curiosity, invites the woman over to her table to join her (119–20). Eulah Mae later sleeps with her white female employer, presumed to be less butch, who presents a comfortableness with her same-sex desire that Eulah Mae cannot have in her southern black community of the 1940 and 1950s.

5. Muñoz discusses a similar type of disidentification with queer women of color doing anticolonial work that must inevitably broach Fanon and readings of him as homophobic and misogynistic (9).

6. Frank Phillips in his review in *Black World* and Jewelle Gomez in "A Cultural Legacy Denied and Discovered" perceive of Shockley's work as a denial of blackness.

7. Both E. Patrick Johnson and Roderick Ferguson discuss the ramifications of projecting the black body as abnormal or deviant in the context of whiteness as the queering of blackness.

8. In the appendix of *Liberation, Imagination, and the Black Panther Party*, the "Revolutionary Peoples" Constitutional Convention September 1970, Philadelphia Workshop Reports, shows that some black nationalist had included gender and gay and lesbian issues of self-determination into liberation agendas.

9. Annamarie Jagose describes the ethnic identity model that gay culture adopted in the 1990s over the liberationist model of the early gay liberation 1970s era.

10. Jaded views of bisexual women in "The Play" and a continuation of butch/femme role-playing in "Women in a Southern Time" are two of Shockley's other tales that move beyond hetero/homo binaries of sexuality.

11. While there are a number of works on butch/femme in early white lesbian communities, the collected papers of Ira Goodson at the Schomburg Center for Black Culture and the documentary *Ruth Ellis: Living with Pride* provide close attention to Black lesbian communities.

12. Madeline Daivs, E. L. Kennedy, and Joan Nestle, all early advocates and critics of butch identity, have reprinted and new essays in *The Persistent Desire: A Femme-Butch Reader*. Also see Sue-Ellen Case, "Towards a Butch-Femme Aesthetic"; and Judith Butler's "Imitation and Gender Insubordination." Butler, Roof, and Ellen-Case all argue in various ways that butch/femme offers a critique of binary heterosexuality.

13. Teresa de Lauretis in *The Practice of Love: Lesbian Sexuality and Perverse Desire* discusses the limited ways that gay and lesbian studies ignores race: "Thus as an equally troubling question in the burgeoning field of 'gay and lesbian studies' concerns the discursive constructions and constructed silences around the relations of race to identity and subjectivity in the practices of homosexualities and the representations of same-sex desire" (485).

14. The insistence for a community of Black lesbians whose objects of desire are black has, historically and in the fiction and analytical works of Black lesbians, always been the ideal. Even as Smith, Lorde, and others formed coalitions and relationships of various ethnic and racial backgrounds, the ideal was still there. Today, this is still the case. For example, when ULOAH (United Lesbians of African Heritage) has their annual event to celebrate lesbian communities it asks possible participants that only Black women attend, even as they also make a statement saying that they acknowledge and support Black women's choice to love and have relationships with whomever they desire.

15. Daryl Cumber Dance's "The Black Man and the White Woman" in *Shuckin' and Jivin'* contains many tales about Black men pursuing white women and the costs of such pursuits. In addition, the legacy of lynching and anti-miscegenation laws upheld throughout the United States meant that Black men who did not stay away from white women would be punished.

16. While there are various slave narratives of white women verbally and physically abusing their Black female slaves, fictional accounts have been more detailed and graphic about white women's sexual abuse toward Black female slaves. Gayl Jones's *Corregidora* explores this issue. In addition, same-sex sexual abuse of black males is discussed by Harriet Jacobs in her slave narrative and Charles Clifton's groundbreaking speculative essay, "Rereading Voices from the Past." Toni Morrison fictionalizes such abuse in *Beloved*.

17. For instance, Trudier Harris's "From Mammies to Militants: Domestics in Black American Literature," and E. Patrick Johnson's *Appropriating Blackness* reread the Mammy. Ishmeale Reed's fictional Mammy Barracuda in *Flight to Canada* also aligns Mammy and Uncle Tom with militant traditions and views her as a sexual object.

18. The historical use of wigs for drag queens, the changing of hair for drag kings, or the length of hair for representing butch/femme roles in lesbian relationships indicates how huge a factor hair can be in representations of queerness.

Chapter 6

1. I am referring to Joyce A. Joyce's "The Black Canon: Reconstructing Black American Literary Criticism" and Barbara Christian's "The Race for Theory" and "The Highs and Lows of Black Feminist Criticism." The work of both critics spawned subsequent responses that exposed ideological splits about the use of "high" theory in African American criticism.

2. Teresa Wiltz's "Meshell Ndegeocello Breaks Step With Pop" records Ndegeocello's commentary on her adolescent identity crisis with this statement about how she used her sexuality as a unsuccessful coping mechanism: "giving it to every Tom, Dick, Harry, Jane and Su, so . . . I could feel like I was really here."

3. According to *Ice* magazine's interview with Ndegeocello's manager, Kofi Taha, Ndegeocello comes up with name Tyrone "Cookie" Goldberg as a way to separate the creative and business sides of herself on the *Cookie* CD project.

4. In addition to CD titiles, song titles reflect that same knowledge: "6-Legged Griot," "I'm Diggin You (Like an Old Soul Record)," "Bla, Bla, Bla, Dyba, Dyba, Dyba," and many others.

5. When talking about her recent project *Dance of the Infidel*, she positions it as her musical collective, the Spirit Music Jamia. Wiltz observes that "Jamia," meaning a gather-

ing or meeting, serves as the perfect word for Ndegeocello's organizing of all star musicians that play and sing music she writes and produces.

6. In addition to the works discussed in this chapter, see Marilyn Sander Mobley's *Folk Roots and Mythic Wings in Sarah Orne Jewett and Toni Morrison: The Cultural Function of Narrative*, Kenneth Porter's "The Flying Africans," Michael Gomez's *Exchanging Our Cultural Marks*, and Nadia Elia's "'Kum Buba Yali Kum Buba Tamba, Ameen, Ameen, Ameen': Did Some Flying Africans Bow to Alla?" Arguably Black creative efforts have yielded the trope in a similar manner. Fictional works include Richard Wright's *Native Son*, Toni Morrison's *Song of Solomon*, Paule Marshall's *Praisesong for the Widow*, Ishmael Reed's *Flight to Canada*, and Ralph Ellison's short story "Flying Home." In addition to *Sankofa*, other films that incorporate the trope are *Daughters of the Dust* and *The Last Supper*. Lest we forget Black popular music, which at times broadens the trope: Lionel Hampton's "Flying Home," Sam Cooke's classic "I'll Fly Away," and the Commodores' "Zoom."

7. See Mark Anthony Neal's "Revolutionary Soul Singa," in which he coins the long but appropriate term for Ndegeocello's postmodernist identity as a soul musician.

8. See J. Mason Brewer's *American Negro Folklore*, Petronella Breinburg's *Legends of Suriname*, Richard M. Dorson's *American Negro Folktales*, and the Savannah Unit Georgia Writer's Project's *Drums and Shadows: Survival Studies among the Georgia Coastal Negroes*.

9. See Melville and Frances Herskovits's *Rebel Destiny* and *Suriname Folklore* for African songs and tales about buzzards, flight, and magic that makes its way through the African diaspora.

10. Since the nineteenth century, African Americans have often taken up this type of sex work. In my project on Black sex culture, I examine how Paschal Beverly Randolph creates an entire career from his theory of sex magic in the late nineteenth century. And we should not forget the various love and sexual potions created by conjurers such as Kitty Brown, Marie Leveau, and others.

11. All of these selections come from Ndegeocello's *Peace Beyond Passion*. The CD thematically centers around issues of sexual colonization carried out through a specific religious institute, Christianity. She takes on issues of religion, homophobia, self-hate because of sexuality, the limitations of gender roles, and finding god in self.

12. Not to mention her forays in doing so-called non-Black music. She's performed and worked with John Mellencamp; she covered an old Dolly Parton classic for a collection to celebrate the artist; and she has performed live with the Rolling Stones, Madonna, Alanis Morissette, and Lenny Kravitz.

13. In "If You Surrender to the Air: Folk Legends and Flight and Resistance in African American Literature," Wiletz dissects the difference of the myths in the novels of Toni Morrison and Paule Marshall.

14. In Greek mythology, Andromeda is the goddess daughter of two other supreme beings. *OED Online* states that etymology of the name as *andros* (man) and *medesthai* (to be mindful of). Given the etymology and the myth of Andromeda being rescued from a unwanted marriage to a sea god, being mindful of man could lead to other possible subjects for desire. Milky Way connects to lactation and the milk of the female.

15. Both the growth of AIDS among heterosexual Black women and the misrepresentations of bisexuals as sexually promiscuous and unsafe have increased suspicion and misunderstanding of Black bisexual men. Rather than being projected as a legitimate sexual identity, Black bisexual men have been demonized as "down-low" brothers.

16. Before her death, June Jordan was a bad-ass trickster outlaw who exemplified my claim.

17. In her article, Jamison quotes the rapper as positioning herself as breaking new ground (339).

18. In her cover of the Bill Withers's soul classic "Who Is He and What Is He To You?" Ndegeocello continues her performance of bisexuality as a narrative by not changing the pronouns in the song to align with normative gender designs of her position as a female singer. She questions a female lover's infidelity.

19. In *Dahomey*, Herskovits' recording of the tale recounts: "Legba began at once to play with Gbadu before their parent, and when reproached merely pointed out that since his organ was always to be erect, Mawu had herself decreed such conduct from him. This is why Legba dances: he tries to take any woman who is at hand" (205–206).

20. A student of go-go from an early age, Ndegeocello joined a go-go band called Prophecy in her native Washington, D.C. She's also played with Little Bennie and the Masters and Rare Essence. As Wiltz notes, Ndegeocello represented a rare female presence in the male-dominated go-go scene.

21. Butler argues that "when the phallus is lesbian, then it is and is not a masculinist figure of power, the signifier is significantly split, for it both recalls and displaces the masculinism by which it is impelled" (*Bodies That Matter* 89).

Chapter 7

1. Pretensions aside, the article could possibly be seen as informative for those who did not know the difficulties facing young Black women today.

2. The very notion of a hip-hop feminist seems not all that solid given that female hip-hop culture, while concerned with female empowerment, constructs itself as an antithesis to white and bourgeois female culture in the United States. But it is a solid marketing tool for those interested in discourses of feminism and the culture of hip-hop.

3. In addition to the previously cited Viallrosa piece, in 2002 *Essence* published articles like "The War on Girls: Sex, Lies and Videos" by Joan Morgan and "Lunch with Latifah: Seven Teens, One Queen and an Afternoon of Straight Talk." It can't get any straighter.

4. *Hype*, a short-lived sketch show on WB in 2000, once mocked the forcefulness of the pose by performing a skit that was to be a commercial for Lil' Kim's breakfast cereal. As the actress imitating Kim pitches the breakfast cereal, she makes sure that the camera captures the legs-wide-open pose by sitting on tables, chairs, and counters in a way that positions her crotch prominently before the camera. Notably, the box of cereal sits between her legs with each shot.

5. See Chuck Creekmur's "Trina Says Men Controlled Her Image" or Vanessa Satten's "Up Close and Personal" for Foxy and Trina's shirking of responsibility for controlling their images in videos and magazines.

6. See Richard von Krafft-Ebing's *Psychopathia Sexualis*, 265. Krafft-Ebing's discussion moves female ejaculation from the norm to being associated with a deviant social population.

7. In addition to Web sites by homohop groups such as Rainbow Flava and Deep Dick Collective, here are several articles that discuss the movement: Billy Jam, "Hip Hop Shop: The Queer Report"; Indigo Escobar, "Homos in the House, Gay Rappers Morplay Are Down and [Out]"; and Doug Norman's "The Identity Politics of Queer Hip-hop."

Conclusion

1. In the edited collection *Black Literature and Literary Theory*, essays written by Gates and Jay Edwards took an overly formalistic poststructuralist approach to trickster and trickster tales. Produced during the onslaught of structuralist and poststructuralist criticism, there were really impressive charts and awe-inspiring graphs included within their essays from the collection, as well as in non-trickster-related essays in the collection.

2. Annamarie Jagose's *Queer Theory* charts the development of gay and lesbian political movements. As she charts the changes over the last forty years, Jagose shows how the mainstream gay and lesbian movement moved away from a liberatory model, which included an annihilation of gender and sexuality as we know it, to an ethnic model that imitates and uses strategies from the civil rights movement.

Works Cited

Abel, Barbara Christian, and Helene Moglen, eds. *Female Subjects in Black and White: Race, Psychoanalysis, Feminism.* Berkeley: University of California Press, 1997.
Abrahams, Roger. *Deep Down in the Jungle. Negro Narrative Folklore in the Streets of Philadelphia.* Chicago: Aldine, 1970.
———. *Talking Black.* Rowley, MA: Newberry House Publishers, 1976.
Achterberg, Jeanne. *Woman as Healer.* Boston: Shambhala, 1990.
Achterberg, Jeanne, and G. Frank Lawlis. *Bridges of the Bodymind: Behavioral Approaches to Health Care.* Champaign, IL: Institute of Personality and Ability Testing, 1980.
Amadiume, Ifi. *Re-Inventing Africa: Matriarchy, Religion, & Culture.* London and New York: Zed Books, 1997.
Andrews, William L. *To Tell a Free Story: The First Century of African American Autobiography, 1760–1865.* Urbana: University of Illinois Press, 1986.
Angelou, Maya. *I Know Why the Caged Bird Sings.* New York: Random House, 1975.
Apollonia 6. "Sex Shooter." *Apollonia 6.* Warner Bros., 1984.
Aptheker, Herbert. *American Negro Slave Revolts.* New York: International, 1983.
Arkward, Michael. *Negotiating Difference: Race, Gender, and the Politics of Positionality.* Chicago: University of Chicago Press, 1995.
Asante, Molefi. *Afrocentricity: A Theory of Social Change.* Buffalo, NY: Amulefi, 1980.
Atherton, Michelle. "Feminine and Masculine Personnas in Performance: Sade Huron: A Drag Queen with a Dick." In *Acts of Passion: Sexuality, Gender and Performance*, edited by Nina Rapi and Maya Chowdhry, 227–35. Binghamton, NY: Harrington Park Press, 1998.
Aycock, D. Alan. "The Mark of Cain." In *Structuralist Interpretations of Biblical Myth*, edited by Edmund Leach and D. Alan Aycock. New York: Cambridge University Press, 1983.
Bailey, Beryl. *Jamaican Creole Syntax.* Cambridge: Cambridge University Press, 1966.
Baker, Houston A. *Blues, Ideology, and Afro-American Literature.* Chicago: University of Chicago Press, 1984.
———. *The Journey Back: Issues in Black Literature and Criticism.* Chicago: University of Chicago Press, 1983.
Bakhtin, Mikhail. *Rabelais and His World.* Trans. Helene Iswolsky. Bloomington: Indiana University Press, 1984.
Bambara, Toni Cade. *The Black Woman.* New York: Signet Press, 1970.
———. "How She Came By Her Name." In *Deep Sighings and Rescue Missions: Fiction,*

Essays, and Conversations. New York: Pantheon Books, 1996.

———. "On the Issues of Roles." In *The Black Woman: An Anthology*. New York: Signet Press, 1970.

———. *The Salteaters*. New York: Random House, 1980.

———. "Searching for a Mother Tongue. Salaam Interview with Toni Cade Bambara." *First World* 2, no. 4 (1980): 47–50.

Barnet, Miguel. *Biography of a Runaway Slave*. Translated by W. Nick Hill. Willimantic, CT: Curbstone Press, 1994.

Basu, Biman. "Public and Private Discourses and the Black Female Subject: Gayl Jones' *Eva's Man*." *Callaloo* 19, no. 1 (Winter 1996): 193–208.

Beam, Joseph. *In The Life: A Black Gay Anthology*. New York: Alyson, 1986.

Bell, Shannon. "Liquid Fire: Female Ejaculation and Fast Feminism." In *Jane Sexes it Up: True Confessions of Feminist Desire*, edited by Merri Lisa Johnson, 327–46. New York and London: Four Walls Eight Windows, 2002.

Benston, Kimberly. "I yam what I am: The Topos of (Un)naming in Afro-American Literature." In *Black Literature and Literary Theory*, edited by Henry Louis Gates Jr., 151–74. London: Routledge, 1984.

———. "Performing Blackness." In *Afro-AmericanLiterary Study*, edited by Houston Baker and Patricia Redmond, 161–84. Chicago: University of Chicago Press, 1989.

Berlant, Lauren, and Elizabeth Freeman. "Queer Nationality." *Boundary* 2, no. 19 (1992): 149–80.

Blair, Sara. "Feeling, Evidence, and the Work of Literary History: Response to DuCille." *American Literary History* 12, no. 3 (Fall 2000): 463–66.

Blassingame, John W. *The Slave Community: Plantation Life in the Antebellum South*. New York: Oxford University Press, 1972.

Bogan, Lucille. "Barbecue Bess." 1935. *Shave 'Em Dry: The Best of Lucille Bogan*. Sony, 2004.

———. "B.D. Blues." 1935. *Shave 'Em Dry: The Best of Lucille Bogan*. Sony Music, 2004.

———. "Groceries on the Shelf." 1933. *Shave 'Em Dry: The Best of Lucille Bogan*. Sony Music, 2004.

———. "Reckless Woman." 1934. *Shave 'Em Dry: The Best of Lucille Bogan*. Sony Music, 2004.

———. "Tricks Ain't Walkin' No More." 1933. *Lucille Bogan: Complete Recorded Works, Vol. 2*. Document Records, 1993.

Bogus, SDiane. "Queen B in African American Literature." In *Lesbian Texts and Context: Radical Revisions*, edited by Karla Jay and Joanne Glasgow, 275–90. New York and London: New York University Press, 1990.

Bornstein, Kate. *Gender Outlaw: On Men, Women, and the Rest of Us*. New York: Vintage Books, 1994.

Bost, Suzanne. "Be Deceived If Ya Wanna Be Foolish: (Re)constructing Body, Genre, and Gender in Feminist Rap." *Postmodern Culture* 12, no. 1 (2001): 1–38.

Botkin, B. A., ed. *Lay My Burden Down: A Folk History of Slavery*. New York: DeHa Books, 1994.

Breinburg, Petronella. *Legends of Suriname*. London: New Beacon, 1971.

Brewer, J. Mason. *American Negro Folklore*. New York: Quadrangle, 1968.

Britton, Akissi. "Deconstructing Lil' Kim." *Essence* 31, no. 6 (October 2000): 112–117.

Brooks, Sara. *You May Plow Here: The Narrative of Sara Brooks*, edited by Thorndis

Simonsen. New York: Norton, 1986.
Brown, William Wells. *Clotel*. In *Classic Slave Narratives*, edited by Henry L. Gates Jr. New York: Penguin, 1989.
Butler, Judith. *Bodies That Matter: On the Discursive Limits of Sex*. New York: Routledge University Press, 1993.
———. "Desire." In *Critical Terms for Literary Study*, edited by Frank Lentricchia and Thomas McLaughlin, 369–86. Chicago and London: University of Chicago Press, 1995.
———. *Gender Trouble: Feminism and the Subversion of Identity*. New York and London: Routledge, 1999.
———. "Imitation and Gender Insubordination." In *Inside/Out: Lesbian Theories, Gay Theories*, edited by Diana Fuss, 13–32. New York: Routledge, 1991.
Byerman, Keith. "Intense Behaviors: The Use of the Grotesque in *The Bluest Eye* and *Eva's Man*." *CLA* 25 (1982): 447–57.
Califia, Pat. "Gay Men, Lesbians, and Sex: Doing It Together." *Advocate* 7 (July 1983): 24–27.
Carby, Hazel V. "Ideologies of the Black Folk: The Historical Novel of Slavery." In *Slavery and the Literary Imagination*, edited by Deborah E. McDowell and Arnold Ramperstead, 125-43. Baltimore: John Hopkins University Press, 1989.
———. "It Jus Be's Dat Way Sometimes: The Sexual Politics of Women's Blues." In *Feminisms: An Anthology of Literary Theory and Criticism*, edited by Robyn R. Warhol and Diane Price Herndhl, 754–55. New Brunswick, NJ: Rutgers University Press, 1991.
———. "The Politics of Fiction, Anthropology, and the Folk: Zora Neale Hurston." In *New Essays on Their Eyes Were Watching God*, edited by Michael Awkward, 71–93. Cambridge: Cambridge University Press, 1990.
———. *Race Men*. Cambridge, MA: Harvard University Press, 1998.
———. *Reconstructing Womanhood: The Emergence of the Afro-American Woman Novelist*. New York: Oxford University Press, 1987.
Case, Sue-Ellen. "Toward a Butch-Femme Aesthetic." In *The Lesbian and Gay Studies Reader*, edited by Henry Abelone, Michelle Aina Berale, and David Halperin, 294–306. New York: Routledge, 1993.
Charles, RuPaul. *Lettin' it All Hang Out*. New York: Hyperion, 1995.
Chinn, Sarah E. "Feeling Her Way: Audre Lorde and the Power of Touch." *GLQ: A Journal of Lesbian and Gay Studies* 9, no. 1–2 (2003): 181–203.
Christian, Barbara. *Black Women Novelists: The Development of a Tradition*. New York: Pergamon Press, 1985.
———. "The Highs and Lows of Black Feminist Criticism." In *Reading Black, Reading Feminist: A Critical Anthology*, edited by Henry Louis Gates Jr., 44–51. New York: Penguin-Meridian, 1990.
———. "The Race for Theory." In *Making Face, Making Soul. Haciendo Caras: Creative and Critical Perspectives by Women of Color*, edited by Gloria Anzaldua, 335–45. San Francisco: Aunt Lute, 1990.
Clarke, Cheryl. *Experimental Love*. Ithaca, NY: Firebrand Press, 1993.
———. "The Failure to Transform: Homophobia in the Black Community." In *Home Girls: A Black Feminist Anthology*, edited by Barbara Smith, 197–208. New York: Kitchen Table: Women of Color Press, 1983.
———. *Living as a Lesbian*. Ithaca, NY: Firebrand Press, 1986.

———. "Living the Texts *Out:* Lesbians and the Use of Black Women's Traditions." In *Theorizing Black Feminisms: The Visionary Pragmatism of Black Women*, edited by A. Busia and S. James, 214–27. New York: Routledge, 1993.

Clausen, Ian. "My Interesting Condition." *Out/Look Natinal Lesbian and Gay Quarterly* 7 (Winter 1990): 11–21.

Cliff, Michelle. *Free Enterprise.* San Francisco: City Light, 2004.

Clifton, Charles. "Rereading Voices from the Past: Images of Homoeroticism in Slave Narratives." In *The Greatest Taboo: Homosexuality in Black Communities*, edited by Delroy Constantine-Simms, 342–61. NewYork: Alyson, 2000.

Cohen, Cathy. *The Boundaries of Blackness: AIDS and the Breakdown of Black Politics.* Chicago and London: University of Chicago Press, 1999.

Collins, Patricia Hill. *Black Feminist Thought: Knowledge, Consciousness, and the Politics of Empowerment.* New York and London: Routledge, 1990.

———. *Black Sexual Politics: African Americans, Gender and the New Racism.* New York and London: Routledge, 2004.

Combahee River Collective. "A Black Feminist Statement." In *All the Women Are White, All the Blacks Are Men, but Some of Us Are Brave: Black Women's Studies*, edited by G. T. Hull, P. B. Scott, and B. Smith, 13–22. New York: Feminist Press, 1982.

Commodores. "Zoom." *Commodores: Anthology.* New York: Motown Music, 1972, 2001.

Conerly, Gregory. "The Politics of Black Lesbian, Gay, and Bisexual Identity." In *Queer Studies: A Lesbian, Gay, Bisexual, &Transgender Anthology*, edited by Brett Beemyn and Mickey Eliason, 241–61. New York: New York University Press, 1996.

———. "Are You Black First or Are You Queer?" In *The Greatest Taboo: Homosexuality in Black Communities*, edited by Delroy Constantine-Simms, 7–23. New York: Alyson, 2000.

Constantine-Simms, Delroy, ed. *The Greatest Taboo: Homosexuality in Black Communities.* New York: Alyson, 2000.

Cooke, Sam. "I'll Fly Away." *Greatest Gospel Gems.* Hollywood, CA: Speciality Records, 1971.

Cooper, Anna Julia. *A Voice from the South: By a Black Woman of the South.* 1892. Reprint, New York: Oxford University Press, 1988.

Courlander, Harold. *Negro Folk Song U.S.A.* New York: Columbia University Press, 1963.

———. *A Treasury of African American Folklore.* New York: Marlow, 1996.

Covington, Francee. "Are the Revolutionary Techniques Employed in *The Battle of Algiers* Applicable to Harlem." In *The Black Woman: An Anthology*, edited by Toni Cade, 244–52. New York: Signet, 1970.

Cox, Ida. "Wild Women Don't Have No Blues." *Ida Cox: Essential.* Classic Blues Label, 2001.

Cracknell, Ryan. "Queens of Comedy: Review." *Apollo Guide,* February 23, 2001. http://apolloguide.com/mov_fullrev.asp?CID=2927&Specific=839.

Craft, William, and Ellen Craft. *Running a Thousand Miles for Freedom; or, the Escape of William and Ellen Craft from Slavery.* London: William Tweedie, 1860.

Creekmur, Chuck. "Trina Says Men Controlled Her Image." BET.com-Music, September 13, 2002. http://bet.com/Music/Archives/BET.Com+Trina+Says+Men+Controlled+Her+Image+529.htm

Crenshaw, Kimberle. "Whose Story Is It Anyway? Feminist and Antiracist Appropriation of Anita Hill." In *Race-ing Justice, Engendering Power: Essays on Anita Hill, Clarence Thomas and the Construction of Social Reality*, edited by Toni Morrison, 402–40. New

York: Pantheon, 1996.
Creteau, Michel de. *The Practice of Everyday Life.* Berkeley and Los Angeles: University of California Press, 1984.
Culler, Jonathan. *On Deconstruction: Theory and Criticism after Structuralism.* Ithaca, NY: Cornell University Press, 1982.
Cvetkovich, Ann. "Untouchability and Vulnerability: Stone Butches as Emotional Style." In *Butch/Femme: Inside Lesbian Gender*, edited by Sally R. Munt, 159–170. London: Cassell, 1998.
Dance, Daryl. *Honey, Hush: An Anthology of African American Women's Humour.* New York: W.W. Norton, 1987.
———. *Shuckin' and Jivin': Folklore from Contemporary Black Americans.* Bloomington: Indiana University Press, 1987.
Daughters of the Dust. Julie Dash (director). New York: Kino International Video, 1992.
Daumer, E. D. "Queer Ethics: Or the Challenge of Bisexuality to Lesbian Ethics." In *Bisexuality: A Critical Reader*, edited by Merl Storr, 151–62. New York: Routledge, 1999.
Davies, Carole Boyce. *Black Women, Writing and Identity: Migrations of the Subject.* London and New York: Routledge University Press 1994.
Davis, Angela. "Black Women and Music: A Historical Legacy of Struggle." In *Black Feminist Cultural Criticism*, edited by Jacqueline Bobo, 217–32. Malden, MA: Blackwell Publishing, 2001.
———. *Blues Legacies and Black Feminisms: Gertrude "Ma" Rainey, Bessie Smith, and Billie Holliday.* New York: Pantheon, 1998.
———. *Women, Race & Class.* New York: Vintage Books, 1981.
Davis, Charles H., and Henry Louis Gates Jr., eds. *The Slave's Narrative.* New York: Oxford University Press, 1985.
Davis, Erik. "Tricksters at the Crossroads: West Africa's God of Messages, Sex, and Deceit." *Gnosis* 19 (Spring 1991): 37–46.
Davis, Madeline, and E. L. Kennedy. "'They Was No One to Mess With': The Construction of the Butch Role in the Lesbian Community of the 1940s and 1950s." In *Persistent Desire: A Femme-Butch Reader*, edited by Joan Nestle, 62–79. Boston: Alyson, 1992.
Davy, Kate. "Fe/male Impersonation." In *The Politics and Poetics of Camp*, edited by Moe Meyer, 130–49. London and New York: Routledge, 1994.
Delany, Samuel. "Desire." In *Shorter Views: Queer Thoughts and the Politics of the Paraliterary*, 3–41. Hanover and London: Wesleyan University Press, 1999.
deLauretis, Teresa. *The Practice of Love: Lesbian Sexuality and Perverse Desire.* Bloomington: Indiana University Press, 1994.
D'Emilio, John. Foreword to *Out of the Closets: Voices of Gay Liberation*, edited by arla Jay and Allen Young. London: Gay Men's Press, 1972.
Derrida, Jacques. *Margins of Philosophy.* Translated by Alan Bass. Chicago: University of Chicago Press, 1982.
———. *Positions.* Translated by Alan Bass. Chicago: University of Chicago Press, 1981.
Dhairyam, Sagri. "Racing the Lesbian: Dodging White Critics." In *The Lesbian Postmodern*, edited by Laura Doan, 26–39. New York: Columbia University Press, 1994.
Dixon, Melvin. "Singing a Deep Song: Language as Evidence in the Novels of Gayl Jones." In *Black Women Writers (1950–1980): A Critical Evaluation*, edited by Mari Evans, 236–48. New York: Anchor/Doubleday, 1984.
Dolan, Jill. "'Lesbian' Subjectivity in Realism: Dragging at the Margins of Structure and

Ideology." In *Performing Feminisms: Feminist Critical Theory and Theater*, edited by Sue-Ellen Case, 40–53. Baltimore: Johns Hopkins University Press, 1990.
Dorson, Richard M. *American Negro Folktales*. Greenwich: Fawcett, 1956.
dos Santos, J. E., and D. M. dos Santos. *Esu Bara Laroye: A Comparative Study*. Ibadan, Nigeria: Institute of African Studies, 1971.
Doty, Alexander. *Making Things Perfectly Queer: Interpreting Mass Culture*. Minneapolis: University of Minnesota Press, 1993.
Doty, William, and William Hynes. "A Lifetime of Trouble Making." In *Mythical Trickster Figures: Contours, Contexts, and Criticisms*, edited by William Doty and William Hynes, 46–65. Tuscaloosa: University of Alabama Press, 1993.
Doueihi, Anne. "Inhabiting the Space between Discourse and Story in Trickster Narratives." In *Mythical Trickster Figures: Contours, Contexts, and Criticisms*, edited by William Doty and William Hynes, 193–201. Tuscaloosa: University of Alabama Press, 1993.
Douglass, Mary. "The Social Control of Cognition: Some Factors in Joke Perception." *Man* n.s., no. 3 (1968): 361–76.
Dove, Rita. Introduction to *The Garden Thrives: Twentieth-Century African American Poetry*, edited by Clarence Major. New York: Harper Collins, 1996.
Dreger, Alice. *Hermaphrodites and the Medical Invention of Sex*. Cambridge, MA: Harvard University Press, 1998.
Du Bois, W.E.B. "The Damnation of Women" In *Norton Anthology of African American Literature,* edited by Nellie Y. McKay and Henry Louis Gates Jr., 740–45. New York: Norton, 2003.
———. *The Souls of Black Folk*. 1903. Reprint New York: Penguin Books, 1989.
DuCille, Ann. *The Coupling Convention: Sex, Text, and Tradition in Black Women's Fiction*. New York and Oxford: Oxford University Press, 1993.
———. "Where in the World Is William Wells Brown? Thomas Jefferson, Sally Hemmings, and the DNA of African-American Literary History." *American Literary History* 12, no. 3 (Fall 2000): 443–62.
Elia, Nadia. "'Kum buba Yali Kum Buba Tamba., Ameen, Ameen, Ameen': Did Some Flying Africans Bow to Alla?" *Callalo* 26, no. 1 (2003): 182–202.
Ellison, Ralph. "Flying Home." In *Flying Home and Other Stories*, edited by John F. Callahan, 147–73. New York: Random House, 1996.
———. *The Invisible Man*. New York: Random House, 1952.
———. *Shadow and Act*. 1964. Reprint, New York: Random House, 1994.
Epstein, Rachel. "Butches with Babes." In *Femme/Butch: New Considerations of the Way We Want to Go*, 41–58. New York:Harrison Park Press, 2002.
Escobar, Indigo. "Homos in the House, Gay Rappers Morplay Are Down and [Out]." *XY*, November 2000, 10.
Evans Pritchard, E. E. "The Morphology and Function of Magic: A Comparative Study of Trobriand and Zande Rituals and Spells." *American Anthropologist, New Series* 31, no. 4 (October 1929): 619–41.
Favor, J. Martin. *Authentic Blackness: The Folk in the New Negro Renaissance*. Durham, NC: Duke University Press, 1999.
Ferguson, Roderick Antwan. *Aberrations in Black: A Queer of Color Critique*. Minneapolis: Univesity of Minnesota Press, 2004.
Frank, Katherine. "Stripping, Starving, and the Politics of Ambiguous Pleasure." In *Jane Sexes It Up: True Confessions of Feminist Desire*, edited by Merri Lisa Johnson,

171–207. New York and London: Four Walls Eight Windows, 2002.
Frazier, E. Franklin. *Black Bourgeoisie*. New York: Collier Books, 1962.
Foucault, Michel. *The History of Sexuality: An Introduction*. Vol. 1. Translated by Robert Hurley. 1976. Reprint, New York: Vintage Books, 1990.
Fuss, Diana. *Essentially Speaking: Feminism, Nature, and Difference*. New York: Routledge, 1989.
Gabbin, Joanne V. "A Laying on of Hands: Black Women Writers Exploring the Roots of Their Folk and Cultural Traditions." In *Wild Women in the Whirlwind: Afra-American Culture and the Contemporary Literary Renaissance*, edited by Joanne M. Braxton and Andree Nicola McLaughlin, 246–63. New Brunswick, NJ: Rutgers University Press, 1990.
Garber, Marjorie. *Vice Versa: Bisexuality and the Eroticism of Everyday Life*. New York: Simon and Schuster, 1995.
Gates, Henry Louis, Jr. *Black Literature and Literary Theory*. London: Routledge, 1984.
———. *Loose Canons: Notes on the Culture Wars*. New York: Oxford University Press, 1993.
———. *The Signifying Monkey: A Theory of African-American Literary Criticism*. New York and Oxford: Oxford University Press, 1988.
———. *The Slavers Narrative*. Edited by Charles T. Davis and Henry L. Gates Jr. New York: Oxford University Press, 1985.
"Gay, Lesbian, Bisexual, Transgender Literature and Culture." *Callaloo* 23 (Winter 2000): 1–498.
Geertz, Clifford. "Deep Play: Notes on the Balinese Cockfight." *Daedalus* 101 (1972): 1–37.
Genovese, Eugene D. *Roll, Jordan, Roll: The World the Slaves Made*. New York: Pantheon, 1974.
George, Nelson. *The Death of Rhythm and Blues*. New York: Plume, 1988.
Gerima, Halle. *Sankofa*. Mypheduh Films, 1994.
Gibson, Michelle, and Deborah T. Meem, eds. In *Femme/Butch: New Considerations of the Way We Want to Go*. New York: Harrington Park Press, 2002.
Giddings, Paula. *When and Where I Enter: The Impact of Black Women on Race and Sex in America*. New York: William Morrow, 1984.
Gilroy, Paul. *The Black Atlantic: Modernity and Double-Consciousness*. Cambridge, MA: Harvard University Press, 1993.
Givens, Adele. *Def Comedy Jam: All Star Vol. 1*. DVD, Time Life Video: SLBG Entertainment, 2001.
———. *Def Comedy Jam Series*. HBO. September 1992.
Goldsmith, Peter. "Healing and Denominationalism on the Georgia Coast." *Southern Quarterly* 23, no. 3 (1985): 83–102.
Gomez, Jewelle. "A Cultural Legacy Denied and Discovered: Black Lesbians in Fiction by Woman." In *Home Girls: A Black Feminist Anthology*, edited by Barbara Smith, 110–24. New York: Kitchen Table: Women of Color Press, 1983.
———. "Femme Erotic." In *Butch/Femme: Inside Lesbian Gender*, edited by Sally Munt, 101–108. London: Cassell, 1998.
Gomez, Michael. *Exchanging Our Country Marks: The Transformation of African Identities in the Colonial and Antebellum South*. Chapel Hill: University North Carolina Press, 1998.
Greaves, McClean. "Sister from Another Planet." *Essence* (September 1996): 95–96.
Green, Richard C., and Monique Guillory. "Question of a Soulful Style: Interview with Paul Gilroy." In *Soul: Black Power, Politics, and Pleasure*, edited by Richard C. Green

and Monique Guillory, 131–37. New York: New York University Press, 1998.

———. *Soul: Black Power, Politics, and Pleasure.* New York: New York University Press, 1998.

Grossinger, Richard. *Planet Medicine: From Stone Age Shamansim to Post-Industrial Healing.* Berkeley, CA: New Atlantic Books, 1980.

Grosz, Elizabeth. *Jacques Lacan: A Feminist Introduction.* New York and London: Routledge, 1990.

Gutman, Herbert. *The Black Family in Slavery and Freedom: 1750–1925.* New York: Pantheon, 1976.

Hairston, Tasha Janaya. "E-Letter." http://www.essence.com, December 6, 2000.

Halberstam. Judith. "Between Butches" In *Butch/Femme: Inside Lesbian Gender,* edited by Sally R. Munt, 57–66. London: Cassell, 1998.

———. "Mackdaddy, Superfly, Rapper: Gender, Race, and Masculinity in the Drag King Scene." *Social Text* no. 52/53 (Autumn–Winter, 1997): 104–31.

Halperin, David. "Homosexuality: A Cultural Construct." In *One Hundred Years of Homosexuality and Other Essays on Greek Love,* 41–53. New York: Routledge, 1990.

———. *Saint Foucault: Towards a Gay Hagiography.* New York: Oxford University Press, 1995.

Hamilton, Virginia. *Herstories.* New York: Blue Sky Press, 1995.

———. *The People Who Could Fly: American Black Folktales.* New York: Knopf, 1985.

Hammonds, Evelyn. "Black (W)holes and the Geometry of Black Female Sexuality." In *Skin Deep, Spirit Strong: The Black Female Body in American Culture,* edited by Kimberly Wallace-Sanders, 301–316. Ann Arbor: University of Michigan Press, 2002.

Hampton, Lionel. "Flying Home." On *Lionel Hampton: Flying Home (1942–45).* Universal City, CA: MCA Records, 1990.

Harris, Joel Chandler. *Uncle Remus: His Songs and Sayings.* New York: Penguin, 1982.

Harris, Trudier. *Fiction and Folklore: The Novels of Toni Morrison.* Knoxville: University of Tennessee Press, 1991.

———. "From Exile to Asylum: Religion to Community in the Writings of Contemporary Black Women." In *Women's Writing in Exile,* edited by Mary Lynn Broe and Angela Ingram, 151–69. Chapel Hill: University of North Carolina Press, 1989.

———. *From Mammies to Militants: Domestics in Black American Literature.* Philadelphia: Temple University Press, 1982.

———. "Moms Mabley: A Study in Humor, Role-Playing." *Southern Review* 24, no. 4 (December 1985): 765–76.

———. *The Power of the Porch: The Storyteller's Craft in Zora Neale Hurston, Gloria Naylor, and Randall Kenan.* Athens: University of Georgia Press, 1996.

———. *Saints, Sinners, and Saviors: Strong Black Women in African American Literature.* New York: Palgrave, 2001.

———. "This Disease Called Strength: Some Observations on the Compensating Construction of Black Female Characters." *Literature and Medicine* 14, no. 1 (Spring 1995): 109–26.

Hemphill, Essex. *Black Nation/Queer Nation.* Directed by Shari Frilot. New York: Third World Newsreel, 1995.

———. *Ceremonies: Prose and Poetry.* San Francisco: Cleis Press, 2000.

Henderson, Joseph. "Ancient Myths and Modern Man." In *Man and His Symbols,* 95–156. New York: Doubleday, 1964.

Henderson, Mae Gwendolyn. "Speaking in Tongues: Dialogics, Dialectics, and the Black Woman Writer's Literary Tradition." In *Changing Our Own Words*, edited by Cheryl Wall, 16–37. New Brunswick, NJ: Rutgers University Press, 1989.

Hernton, Calvin. *The Sexual Mountain and Black Women Writers*. New York: Random House, 1987.

Herron, Leonora, and Alice M. Bacon. "Conjure and Conjure Doctors." In *Motherwit from the Laughing Barrell*, edited by Alan Dundes, 359–68. Englewood Cliffs, NJ: Prentice Hall, 1973.

Herskovits, Melville J. *The Myth of the Negro Past*. 1941. Reprint, Boston: Beacon Press, 1990.

Herskovits, Melville J., and Frances S. Herskovits, *Dahomean Narrative: A Cross Cultural Narrative*. Evanston, IL: Northwestern University Press, 1998.

———. *Dahomey, An Ancient West African Kingdom*. 2 vols. Evanston, IL: Northwestern University Press, 1958.

———. *Rebel Destiny*. Freeport, NY: Books for Libraries Press, 1971.

———. *Suriname Folklore*. New York: Columbia University Press, 1936.

Hilburn, Robert. "Me'Shell Can't Hide Her Feelings." *Los Angeles Times*, August 25, 1996, 8.

Hine, Darlene Clark. "Rape and the Inner Lives of Black Women in the Middle West: Preliminary Thoughts on the Culture of Dissemblance." *Signs* 14, no. 4 (1989): 915–20.

Holiday, Billie. *Lady Sings the Blues*. London and New York: Penguin, 1956. Reprint 1992.

Hollis, Susan T. & Pershing, Linda. *Feminist Theory and the Study of Folklore*. Urbana: University of Illinois, 1993.

Holloway, Karla F. C. *Moorings and Metaphors: Figures of Culture and Gender in Black Women's Literature*. New Brunswick, NJ: Rutgers University Press, 1992.

hooks, bell. *Black Looks: Race and Representation*. Boston: South End Press, 1992.

———. *Yearning: Race, Gender, and Cultural Politics*. Boston: South End Press, 1990.

Hughes, Langston, and Arna Bontemps, eds. *The Book of Negro Folklore*. New York: Dodd, Mead, 1958.

Huggins, Nathan I. *Harlem Renaissance*. New York: Oxford University Press, 1971.

Hull, G. T., P. B. Scott, and B. Smith, eds. *All the Women Are White, All the Blacks Are Men, but Some of Us Are Brave: Black Women's Studies*. New York: Feminist Press, 1982.

Hurston, Zora Neale. "Characteristics of Negro Expression." In *African American Literary Theory: A Reader*, edited by Winston Napier, 31–44. New York and London: New York University Press, 2000.

———. *I Love Myself When I Am Laughing . . . and Then Again When I Am Looking Mean and Impressive: A Zora Neale Hurston Reader*. Edited by Alice Walker. New York: Feminist Press, 1979.

———. *Mules and Men*. 1935. Reprint, New York: Harper Perennial, 1990.

———. *Their Eyes Were Watching God*. 1937. Reprint, New York: Harper Perennial, 1990.

Hutchins, Loraine. "Bisexual Women as Emblematic Sexual Healers and the Problematics of the Embodied Sacred Whore." In *Bisexual Women in the Twenty-First Century*, edited by Dawn Atkins, 205–226. Binghamton: Haworth Press, 2002.

Hyde, Lewis. *Trickster Makes This World: Mischief, Myth, and Art*. New York: Farrar, Strauss, Giroux, 1998.

Hynes, William. "Mapping the Characteristics of Mythic Tricksters: A Heuristic Guide."

In *Mythical Trickster Figures: Contours, Contexts, and Criticisms*, edited by William Hynes and William Doty, 33–45. Tuscaloosa: University of Alabama Press, 1993.

Irigaray, Luce. *This Sex Which Is Not One*. Translated by Catherine Porter with Carolyn Burke. Ithaca, NY: Cornell University Press, 1985.

Iverem, Esther. "Review: Queens' Bring Sisterly Style to Comedy." BET.com Arts and Film Critic, January 25, 2001. http://www.bet.com/Entertainment/Archives/Bet.com+Queens

Jackson, Bruce. *Get Your Ass in the Water and Swim like Me: Narrative Poetry from the Black Oral Tradition*. Cambridge, MA: Harvard University Press, 1974.

Jacobs, Harriet. *Incidents in the Life of a Slave Girl*. In *Classic Slave Narratives*, edited by Henry Louis Gates Jr. New York: Penguin, 1989.

Jacobus, Lee. *Literature: An Introduction to Critical Reading*. Englewood Cliffs, NJ: Prentice Hall, 1996.

Jackson, Millie. "All The Way Lover." *Feeling Bitchy*. Southbound Records, 1977.

Jagose, Annamarie. *Queer Theory*. Melbourne: University of Melbourne Press, 1996.

Jam, Billy. "Hip Hop Shop: The Queer Report." *Bam*, September 12, 1997, 11–13.

James, Joy. *Shadowboxing: Representations of Black Feminist Politics*. New York: St. Martin's Press, 1999.

Jamison, Laura. "A Feisty Female Rapper Breaks a Hip Hop Taboo." In *The Greatest Taboo: Homosexuality in Black Communities*, edited by Delroy Constantine-Simms, 337–42. Los Angeles: Alyson Books, 2000.

———. "Ladies First." In *The Vibe History of Hip Hop*, edited by Alan Light, 177–86. New York: Three Rivers Press, 1999.

JanMohamed, Abdul R. "Sexuality on/of the Racial Border: Foucault, Wright and The Articulation of 'Racialized Sexuality.'" In *Discourses of Sexuality: From Aristotle to AIDS*, edited by Domna C. Stanton, 94–116. Ann Arbor: University of Michigan Press, 1992.

Johnson, E. Patrick. *Appropriating Blackness: Performance and the Politics of Authenticity*. Durham, NC: Duke University Press, 2003.

Johnson, M. L. *Influence of Assimilation on the Psychological Adjustment of Black Homosexual Men*. Ann Arbor: University of Michigan Press, 1982.

Jones, Gayl. *Corregidora*. Boston: Beacon Press, 1975.

———. *Eva's Man*. Boston: Beacon Press, 1976.

———. *The Healing*. Boston: Beacon Press, 1998.

———. *Liberating Voices: Oral Tradition in African-American Fiction*. New York: Penguin, 1991.

Jordan, June. "A Couple of Words on Behalf of Sex (Itself)." In *Some of Use Did Not Die: New and Selected Essays of June Jordan*, 59–63. New York: Basic/Civitas Books, 2003.

———. "A New Politics of Sexuality." In *Some of Use Did Not Die: New and Selected Essays of June Jordan*, 131–37. New York: Basic/Civitas Books, 2003.

Joyce, Joyce. "The Black Canon: Reconstructing Black American Literary Criticism." In *African American Literary Theory: A Reader*, edited by Winston Napier, 290–97. New York: New York University Press, 2000.

Judy, Ronald T. *(Dis)forming the American Canon: African Slave Narratives and the Vernacular*. Minneapolis: University of Minnesota Press, 1993.

Jung, Carl C. *Four Archetypes: Mother, Rebirth, Spirit, Trickster*. New York: Routledge Taylor & Francis, 2003.

———. *The Archetypes of and the Collective Unconscious*. Translated by R. F. C. Hull. 2nd

ed. Princeton: Princeton University Press, 1969.
Katz, Sue. "Drag Kings, Sluts & Goddesses: The Boston-based Lesbian Theatre Troupe Tackles Big Issues with Dance, Music and Irresistible Sexual Confidence." *Colorlines* 7, no, 4 (Winter 2004): 50–53.
Kawash, Samira. *Dislocating the Color Line: Identity, Hybridity, and Singularity in African American Narrative.* Stanford, CA: Stanford University Press, 1997.
Keating, AnaLouise. *Women Reading, Women Writing: Self-invention in Paula Gunn Allen, Gloria Anzaldua, and Audre Lorde.* Philadelphia: Temple University Press, 1996.
Kelley, Robin D. G. "Notes on Deconstructing the Folk." *American Historical Review* 97, no. 5 (December 1992): 1402.
———. *Yo Mama's Dysfunktional!! Fighting the Cultural Wars in Urban America.* Boston: Beacon Press, 1998.
Knappert, Jan, ed. *African Mythology: An Encyclopedia of Myth and Legend.* London: Diamond Books, 1995.
Kochman, Thomas. "Towards an Ethnography of Black American Speech Behavior." In *Rappin' and Stylin' Out: Communication in Urban Black America,* edited by Thomas Kochman, 145–63. Urbana: University of Illinois Press, 1972.
Koepping, Klaus-Peter. "Absurdity and Hidden Truth: Cunning Intelligence and Grotesque Body Images as Manifestations of the Trickster." *History of Religions* 24 (1985): 191–214.
Krafft-Ebing, Richard von. *Psychopathia Sexualis.* Translated by Franklin S. Klaf. New York: Stein & Day, 1965.
LaBelle, Patti. "If You Don't Know Me By Now." *Patti LaBelle: Live in New York.* MCA, 1991.
———. "Lady Marmalarde" *Lady Marmalade: The Best of Patti and Labelle.* Sony, 1995.
Lacan, Jacques. *Ecrits: A Selection.* Translated Alan Sheridan. New York: W. W. Norton, 1977.
LaFrance. Melisse, and Lori Burns. "Textual Subversions." In *Disruptive Divas: Feminism, Identity and Popular Culture,* 133–46. New York: Routledge, 2002.
Laqueur, Thomas. *Making Sex: Body and Gender from the Greeks to Freud.* Cambridge, MA: Harvard University Press, 1990.
Larsen, Nella. *Passing.* 1929. Reprint, New York: Penguin Books, 1997.
The Last Supper. Tomas Gutierrez (director). New York: New Yorker Video, 1998.
LeClair, Thomas. "The Language Must Not Sweat: A Conversation with Toni Morrison." In *A Conversation with Toni Morrison,* edited by Danielle Taylor-Gutherie. Jackson: University of Mississippi Press, 1994.
Lee, Valerie. *Granny Midwives & Black Women Writers: Double-Dutched Readings.* New York: Routledge, 1996.
Leigh, Bill. "MeShell Gets Real." *Bass Player* 13, no. 3 (March 2002): 44–46.
Lemmon, Kasi (Director). *Eve's Bayou.* TRI Mark Home Video, 1997.
Lester, Julius. *Black Folktales.* New York: Grove, 1969.
———. *Uncle Remus: The Complete Tales.* New York: Dial Books, 1999.
Levine, Lawrence. *Black Culture and Black Consciousness: Afro-American Folk Thought from Slavery to Freedom.* New York: Oxford University Press, 1977.
Lil' Kim. "Big Momma Thang." *HARDCORE.* Atlantic Records, 1996.
———."Chinatown." DJ Clue, *The Professional Part 2.* Roc-A-Fella Records, 2001.
———. Interview with Lil' Kim. *One World* 7, no. 6 (December/January 2003): 60–67.
———. "Fuck You." *HARDCORE.* Atlantic Records, 1996.

———. "Queen B@$#H." *HARDCORE*. Atlantic Rrcords,, 1996.
———. "Queen Bitch II." *The Notorious K.I.M.* Atlantic Records, 2000.
———. "Suck My Dick." *The Notorious K.I.M.* Atlantic Records, 2000.
Linton, Eliza L. "The Wild Women as Social Insurgents" *Nineteenth Century*, October 1891, 596–605.
Audre Lorde. *The Black Unicorn*. New York: Norton, 1978.
———. "Interview w/Audre Lorde." In *Black Women Writers at Work*, edited by Claudia Tate, 100–116. New York: Continuum, 1983.
———. "Age, Race, Class, and Sex: Women Redefining Difference," "Uses of the Erotic." In *Sister Outsider: Essays and Speeches by Audre Lorde*. Freedom, CA: Crossing Press, 1984.
———. *Zami: A New Spelling of My Name*. Freedom, CA: Crossing Press, 1982.
Lubiano, Wahneema. *The House That Race Built: Original Essays by Toni Morrison, Angela Y. Davis, Cornel West, and Others on Black Americans and Politics in America Today*, edited by Wahneema Lubiano. New York: Vintage Books, 1997.
"Lunch with Latifah: Seven Teens, One Queen, and an Afternoon of Straight Talk." *Essence* 33, no. 6 (October 2002): 172–79.
Mabley, Jackie, "Moms." "Grandma." *The Best of Moms and Pigmeat, Vol. 1*. Cheese Reroces, 1964. Laugh.com Records, 2003.
MacCowan, Lyndall. "Re-collecting History, Renaming Lives: Femme Stigma and the Feminist Seventies and Eighties." In *The Persistent Desire: A Femme/Butch Reader*, edited by Joan Nestle, 299–330. Boston: Alyson, 1992.
Marshall, Paule. *Praisesong for the Widow*. New York: Putnam, 1983.
Martin, Biddy. *Femininity Played Straight: The Significance of Being Lesbian*. New York and London: Routledge, 1996.
Mason-John, Valerie. "Presentation of Self as Performance: The Birth of Queenie aka Valerie Mason-John." In *Acts of Passion: Sexuality, Gender, and Performance*, edited by Nina Rapi and Maya Chowdhry, 209–20. Binghamton, NY: Harrington Park Press, 1998.
McDowell, Deborah. *The Changing Same: Black Women's Literature, Criticism, and Theory*. Bloomington: Indiana University Press, 1995.
Mills, Bruce. "Lydia Maria Child and the Endings to Harriet Jacobs' *Incidents in the Life of a Slave Girl*." *American Literature* 64, no. 2 (1992): 255–72.
Mills, Fiona, and Keith B. Mitchell. *After the Pain: Critical Essays on Gayl Jones*. New York: Peter Lang, 2006.
Mitchell, Michelle. *Righteous Propagation: African Americans and the Politics of Racial Destiny after Reconstruction*. Chapel Hill: University of North Carolina Press, 2004.
Mitchell-Kernan, Claudia. "Signifying as a Verbal Art." In *Mother Wit from the Laughing Barrel: Readings in the Interpretation of Folklore*, edited by Alan Dundes, 310–28. Englewood Cliffs, NJ: Prentice Hall, 1973.
Mobley, Marilyn Sander. *Folk Roots and Mythic Wings in Sarah Orne Jewett and Toni Morrison: The cultural Function of Narrative*. Baton Rouge: Louisiana State University Press, 1991.
Montero, Oscar. "Latino and National Identity." *Radical America* 24, no. 4 (April 1993): 16–17.
Moore, Nicole. "Last Woman Standing: Interview with MeShell Ndegeocello." *One World*, February–March 2002, 46–50.
Moore, Rudy Ray. *Dolemite*. 1974. Xenon Home Video, 1987.

Morgan, Jennifer L. *Laboring Women: Reproduction and Gender in New World Slavery.* Philadelphia: University of Pennsylvania Press, 2004.

Morgan, Joan. "The War on Girls: Sex, Lies, and Videos." *Essence* 33, no. 2 (June 2002): 120–24.

———. *When Chickenheads Come Home to Roost: My Life as a Hip-Hop Feminist.* New York: Simon and Schuster, 1999.

Morgan, Marcyliena. "Indirectness and Interpretation in African American's Women's Discourse." *Pragmatics* 1, no. 4 (1991): 421–52.

———. "No Woman No Cry: Claiming African American Women's Place." In *Re-inventing Identities: The Gendered Self in Discourse,* edited by Mary Bucholtz, A. C. Liang, and Laurel Sutton, 26–42. New York: Oxford University Press, 1999.

Morrison, Toni. *Beloved.* New York: Plume/Penguin, 1998.

———. *Paradise.* New York: Plume/Penguin, 1999.

———. *Song of Solomon.* 1977. Reprint. New York: Plume/Penguin, 1987.

———. *Sula.* 1973. Reprint, New York: Plume/Penguin, 1982.

———. "What the Black Woman Thinks about Women's Lib." *New York Times Magazine,* 22, August 22, 1971, 14–15.

Mosse, George L. *Nationalism and Sexuality: Respectability and Abnormal Sexuality in Modern Europe.* New York: Howard Fertig, 1985.

"The Moynihan Report." In *The Moynihan Report and the Politics of Controversy,* edited by Lee Rainwater and William L. Yancy, 70–101. Cambridge, MA: Harvard University Press, 1967.

Muñoz, José. *Disidentification: Queers of Color and the Politics of Performance.* Minneapolis: University of Minnesota Press, 1999.

Murray, Stephen O., and Will Roscoe, eds. *Boy-Wives and Female Husband: Studies of African Homosexualities.* New York: St. Martin's Press, 1998.

Napier, Winston, ed. *African American Literary Theory: A Reader.* New York: New York University Press, 2000.

Naylor, Gloria. *Mama Day.* New York: Ticknor and Fields, 1998.

Ndegeocello, Meshell. "Andromeda and the Milky Way." *Comfort Woman.* Maverick Records, 2003.

———."Barry Farms." *Cookie: The Anthropological Mixtape.* Maverick Records, 2002.

———. "Deuteronomy: Niggerman." *Peace beyond Passion.* Maverick Records, 1996.

———. "Ecclesiastes; Free My Heart." *Peace beyond Passion.* Maverick Records, 1996.

———. "God: Siva." *Peace beyond Passion.* Maverick Records, 1996.

———. "If That Was Your Boyfriend (He Wasn't Last Night)." *Plantation Lullabies.* Maverick, 1993.

———. "Leviticus: Faggot." *Peace beyond Passion.* Maverick Records, 1996.

———. "Liliquoi Moon." *Comfort Woman.* Maverick Records, 2003.

———. "Love Song #1." *Comfort Woman.* Maverick Records, 2003.

———. "Love Song #2. *Comfort Woman.* Maverick Records, 2003.

———. "Mary Magdalene." *Peace beyond Passion.* Maverick Records, 1996.

Neal, Mark Anthony. "Revolutionary Soul Sing: Me'shell Ndegeocello." www.seeingblack.com. July 7, 2002.

Nero, Charles. I. "Toward a Black Gay Aesthetic." In *The Persistent Desire: A Femme-Butch Reader,* edited by Joan Nestle. Boston: Alyson, 1992.

Newton, Esther. *Mother Camp: Female Impersonators in America.* Chicago: University of Chicago Press, 1979.

Newton, Huey P. "The Women's Liberation and Gay Liberation Movements." In *Black Men on Race, Gender, and Sexuality: A Critical Reader*, edited by Devon W. Carbado, 387–89. New York: New York University Press, 1999.

———. "A Letter from Huey to the Revolutionary Brothers and Sisters." In *Traps: African American Men on Gender and Sexuality*, edited by Rudolph P. Byrd and Beverly Guy-Sheftall, 281–83. Bloomington and Indiannapolis: Indiana University Press, 2001.

Nicholson, Judy. "Dear Sisters." In *Piece of My Heart*, edited by Makeda Silvera, 281–83. Toronto: Sister Vision Press, 1991.

Norman, Doug. "The Identity Politics of Queer Hip-Hop." Unpublished essay, University of Texas, 2000.

Nugent, Richard Bruce. *Gay Rebel of the Harlem Renaissance*. Edited by Thomas H. Wirth. Durham, NC: Duke University Press, 2002.

Nzegwu, Nkiru. "Cultural Epistemologies of Motherhood: Refining the Concept of Mother." *Jenda: A Journal of Culture and African Women's Studies* 5 (2003). http://www.jendajournal.com/issue5/toc5.htm

Ogundipe, Adoye. "Esu Elegbara, the Yoruba God of Chance and Uncertainty: A Study in Yoruba Mythology." 2 vols. Ph.D. diss., Indiana University, 1978.

Omarr, Sydney. *Day by Day Astrological Guide*. New York: Penguin, 2003.

Omolade, Barbara. "The Silence and the Song: Toward a Black Woman's History through a Language of Her Own." In *Wild Women in the Whirlwind: Afra-American Culture and the Contemporary Literary Renaissance*, edited by Joanne M. Braxton and Andree Nicola McLaughlin, 282–95. New Brunswick, NJ: Rutgers University Press, 1990.

———. *The Rising Song of African American Women*. New York and London: Routledge, 1994.

Oyêwùmí, Oyèrónké. *The Invention of Women: Making an African Sense of Western Gender Discourses*. Minneapolis: University of Minnesota Press, 1997.

———. "Ties That (Un)bind: Feminism, Sisterhood and Other Foreign Relations." *Jenda: A Journal of Culture and African Women's Studies* #1. 2001. http://www.jendajournal.com/vol1.1/toc1.1-htm

Page, LaWanda. *Mutha' Is Half A Word!* Laff Records, 1970.

———. *Pipe Laying Dan*. Uproar Entertainment, 2001.

———. *Watch It Sucka!* Laff Records, 1971.

Pelton, Robert W. *The Trickster in West Africa: A Study of Mythic Irony and Sacred Delight*. Berkeley and Los Angeles: University of California Press, 1980.

———. "West African Tricksters: Web of Purpose, Dance of Delight." In *Mythical Trickster Figures: Contours, Contexts, and Criticisms*, edited by William Doty and William Hynes, 122–40. Tuscaloosa: University of Alabama Press, 1993.

Penley, Constance. *The Future of an Illusion: Film, Feminism, and Psychoanalysis*. Minneapolis: University of Minnesota Press, 1989.

Porter, Kenneth. "The Flying Africans." In *Primer for White Folks*, edited by Bucklin Moon. Garden City, NY: Doubleday, 1945.

Pough, Gwendolyn D. *Check It While I Wreck It: Black Womanhood, Hip-Hop Culture, and the Public Sphere*. Boston: Northeastern University Press, 2004.

Powell, Alison. "Sybil of Soul." *Interview* 26, no. 7 (July 1996): 48–51.

Quashie, Kevin. *Black Women, Identity, and Cultural Theory: (Un)becoming the Subject*. New Brunswick, NJ: Rutgers University Press, 2004.

Queen Latifah. "U.N.I.T.Y." *Black Reign*. Motown, 1993.

Queen Pen. "Girlfirend." *My Melody*. Interscope Records, 1997.

Queens of Comedy. Paramount Pictures Home Video, 2001.
Raboteau, Albert J. "African American Religion in America." In *Global Dimensions of the African Diaspora*, edited by Joseph Harris, 65–83. Washington, DC: Howard University Press, 1993.
Rattray, R. S. *The Ashanti.* Oxford: Clarendon Press, 1927.
Reed, Ishmeal. *Flight to Canada.* 1989. Reprint. New York: Athenaeum, 1989.
Reed, Lady. "Queens Philosophy." *The Lady Reed Album: Queen Bee Talks.* Rent Records, 1971.
Riley, Denise. *Am I That Name: Feminism and the Category of "Women" in History.* Minneapolis: University of Minnesota Press, 1988.
Roberts, Dorothy. *Killing the Black Body: Race, Reproduction, and the Meaning of Liberty.* New York: Pantheon, 1997.
Roberts, John W. *From Trickster to Badman: The Black Folk Hero in Slavery and Freedom.* Philadelphia: University of Pennsylvania Press, 1989.
Robertson, Pamela. "'The Kinda Comedy That Imitates Me': Mae Wests's Identification with Feminist Camp." *Cinema Journal* 32, no. 2 (Winter 1993): 57–64.
Robinson, Cedric. *Black Marxism: The Making of the Black Radical Tradition.* Chapel Hill: University of North Carolina Press, 1998.
Robinson, Debra (Director). *I Be Done Been Was Is.* Women Make Movies Dist., 1984.
Robinson, Sally. *Engendering Subject: Gender and Self-Representation in Contemporary Women's Fiction.* Albany: SUNY Press, 1991.
Rodgers, Carolyn. "The Last MF." In *Songs of Blackbird.* Chicago: Third World Press, 1969.
Roof, Judith. *A Lure Knowledge: Lesbian Sexuality and Theory.* New York: Columbia University Press, 1991.
Rose, Tricia. *Longing to Tell: Black Women Talk about Sexuality and Intimacy.* New York: Farrar, Strauss, & Giroux, 2003.
———. "Never Trust a Big Butt and a Smile." In *Black Feminist Cultural Criticism*, edited by Jacqueline Bobo, 233–55. Malden, MA: Blackwell, 2001.
Ross, Marlon. "Camping the Dirty Dozens: The Queer Resources of Black Nationalist Invective." *Callaloo* 23, no. 1 (Winter 2000): 290–312.
———. "Some Glances at the Black Fag: Race, Same-Sex Desire, and Cultural Belonging." In *African American Literary Theory: A Reader*, edited by Winston Napier, 498–533. New York: New York University Press.
Rust, Paula. *Bisexuality and the Challenge to Lesbian Politics.* New York: New York University Press, 1995.
Salaam, Kalamu ya. "Searching for the Mother Tongue: An Interview with Toni Cade Bambara." *First World* 2, no. 4 (1980): 48–53.
Satten, Vanessa. "Up Close and Personal." *XXL*, July 2001, 90–96.
Savannah Unit Georgia Writer's Project. *Drums and Shadows: Survival Studies among the Georgia Coastal Negroes.* 1940. Reprint, Athens: Brown-Thrasher, University of Georgia Press, 1986.
Scarry, Elaine. *The Body in Pain: The Making and Unmaking of the World.* New York: Oxford University Press, 1985.
Schwendemann, Glen. "Nicodemus: Negro Haven on the Solomon." *Kansas Historical Quarterly* 34 (Spring 1968): 10–31.
Sedgwick, Eve. *Between Men: English Literature and Male Homosocial Desire.* New York: Columbia University Press, 1985.

———. *Epistemology of the Closet.* Berkeley and Los Angeles: University of California Press, 1990.

Seidman, Steven. "Identity and Politics in a 'Post Modern' Gay Culture: Some Historical and Conceptual Notes." In *Fear of a Queer Planet: Queer Politics and Social Theory,* edited by Michael Warner, 105–42. Minneapolis: University of Minnesota Press, 1993.

Shante, Roxanne. "Roxanne's Revenge." *Fat Beats & Bra Straps: Battle Rhymes & Posse.* Rhino Records, 1998.

Shockley, Ann Allen. *The Black and White of It.* Tallahassee, FL: Naiad Press, 1980.

———. "The Black Lesbian in American Literature: An Overview." In *Home Girls: A Black Feminist Anthology,* edited by Barbara Smith, 83–93. New York: Kitchen Table: Women of Color Press, 1983.

———. *Loving Her.* Tallahassee, FL: Naiad Press, 1974.

"Sign." In *Encyclopedia of Contemporary Literary Theory: Approaches, Scholars, Terms,* edited by Irena R. Makaryk. Toronto and Buffalo: University of Toronto Press, 1993.

Smith, Barbara. "Towards a Black Feminist Criticism." In *The Truth That Never Hurts: Writings in Race, Gender, and Freedom.* New Brunswick, NJ: Rutgers University Press, 1998.

———. "Where's the Revolution?" *In the Truth That Never Hurts,* 174–84.

Smith, Jeanne R. *Writing Tricksters: Mythic Gambols in American Ethnic Literature.* Berkeley and Los Angeles: University of California Press, 1997.

Smith, Sarah. "A Cock of One's Own: Getting a Grip on Feminist Sexual Power." In *Jane Sexes it Up: True Confessions of Feminist Desire,* edited by Merri Lisa Johnson, 293–310. New York and London: Four Walls Eight Windows, 2002.

Smith, Valerie. Introduction to *Incidents in the Life of a Slave Girl* by Harriet Jacobs. New York: Oxford University Press, 1988.

———. *Self-Discovery and Authority in Afro-American Narrative.* Cambridge, MA: Harvard University Press, 1991.

Smitherman, Geneva. *Black Talk: Words and Phrases from the Hood to the Amen Corner.* Boston: Houghton Mifflin, 2000.

———. *Talkin' and Testifyin': The Language of Black America.* Detroit: Wayne State University Press, 1977.

Somerville, Siohban. *Queering the Color Line: Race and the Invention of Homosexuality in American Culture.* Durham, NC, and London: Duke University Press, 2000.

———. "Scientific Racism and the Invention of the Homosexual Body." In *Queer Studies: A Lesbian, Gay, Bisexual, & Transgender Anthology,* edited by Brett Beemyn and Mickey Eliason, 241–61. New York: New York University Press, 1996.

Sontag, Susan. "Notes on 'Camp.'" In *Camp: Queer Aesthetics and the Performing Subject: A Reader,* edited by Fabio Cleto, 53–65. Ann Arbor: University of Michigan Press, 1999.

Sow, Alfâ Ibrâhîm. *Anthropological Structures of Madness in Black Africa.* Translated by Joyce Diamanit. New York: International University Press, 1980.

Spears, Arthur. "African American Language Use: Ideology and So-Called Obscenity." In *African American English: Structure, History and Usage,* edited by Sakikoko S. Mufwene, 226–50. London and New York: Routledge, 1998.

Spillers, Hortense. "Interstices: A Small Drama of Words." In *Pleasure and Danger: Exploring Female Sexuality,* edited by Carole Vance, 73–100. London: Pandora, 1989.

———. "Interview." *Black Cultural Studies* 2, February 4, 1998. http://www.blackcultural studies.org/spillers/spillers-intro.html

———. "Mama's Baby, Papa's Maybe: An American Grammar Book." In *African American Literary Theory: A Reader*, edited by Winston Napier, 257–79. New York: New York University Press, 2000.

Spinks, C. W. "Trickster and Duality." In *Trickster and Ambivalence: The Dance of Differentiation*, edited by C. W. Spinks, 7–20. Madison, WI: Atwood, 2001.

Stepto, Robert. *From behind the Veil: A Study of Afro-American Narrative*. Urbana: University of Illinois Press, 1979.

Street, Brian V. "The Trickster Theme: Winnebago and Azande." In *Zande Themes*, edited by Andre Singer and Brian Street. Totowa, NJ: Rowman and Littlefield, 1972.

Stokes, Mason Boyd. *The Color of Sex: Whiteness, Heterosexuality, and the Fictions of White Supremacy*. Durham, NC: Duke University Press, 2000.

Storey, Olivia Smith. "Flying Words: Contests or Orality and Literacy in Trope of Flying Africans." *Journal of Colonization and Colonial History* 5, no. 3 (Winter 2004): 1–34.

Storr, Merl. "The Sexual Reproduction of 'Race': Bisexuality, History and Racialization." In *The Bisexual Imaginary: Representation, Identity, and Desire*, edited by Phoebe Davidson. London and Washington, DC: Cassell, 1997. 73–88.

Stuckey, Sterling. *Slave Culture: Nationalist Theory and the Foundations of Black America*. New York: Oxford University Press, 1987.

Taha, Kofi. "Interview." *Ice* 178 (January 2002): 23–25.

Truth, Sojourner, and Olive Gilbert. *Narrative of Sojourner Truth, A Bondswoman of Olden Time*. 1850. Edited by Nell Irvin Painter. New York: Penguin, 1998.

Turner, Lorenzo D. *Africanism in the Gullah Dialect*. Chicago: University of Chicago Press, 1949.

Vance, Carole. "Pleasure and Danger: Toward a Politics of Sexuality." In *Pleasure and Danger: Exploring Female Sexuality*, edited by Carole Vance, 1–24. London: Pandora, 1989.

Villarosa, Linda. "The War on Girls: Our Girls in Crisis: What Every Woman Needs to Know about the Challenges of Being Young, Black and Female." *Essence* 32, no. 9 (January 2002): 92–99.

Vizenor, Gerald. "Trickster Discourse." In *Narrative Chance: Post Modern Discourse on Native American Indian Literatures*, edited by Gerald Vizenor. Albuquerque: University of New Mexico Press, 1989.

Vrettos, Athena. "Curative Domains: Women, Healing and History in Black Women's Narratives." *Women's Studies* 16 (1989): 455–73.

Walker, Alice. *The Color Purple*. New York: Harcourt, 1982.

Walker, Rebecca. "Interview with Lil Kim." *One World* 7, no. 6 (December 2002/January 2003): 60–67.

Wall, Cheryl. "Response to Kimberly W. Benston's 'Performing Blackness.'" In *Afro-American Literary Study*, edited by Houston Baker Jr. and Patricia Redmond, 185–89. Chicago: University of Chicago Press, 1989.

Washington, Margaret. "Cultural Transmission and Female Diviners in Gullah Slave Society." Unpublished paper, Cornell University, 1986.

Watkins, Me. *On the Real Side: Laughing, Lying, and Signifying: The Underground Tradition of African American Humour*. New York: Simon and Schuster, 1994.

West, Cornel. "Black Sexuality: The Taboo Subject." In *Traps: African American Men on Gender and Sexuality*, edited by Rudolph P. Byrd and Beverly Guy-Sheftall, 301–307. Bloomington and Indianapolis: Indiana Univewrsity Press, 2001.

White, Deborah Gray. *Too Heavy a Load: Black Women in Defense of Themselves 1894–1994*. New York: Norton, 1998.
Wilentz, Gay. *Healing Narratives: Women Writers Curing Cultural Dis-ease*. New Brunswick, NJ: Rutgers University Press, 2000.
———. "If You Surrender to the Air: Folk Legends and Flight and Resistance in African American Literature." *MELUS* 16, no. 1 (Spring 1989–1990): 21–32.
Williams, Elsie A. *The Humor of Jakcie Moms Mabley*. New York: Garland Publishers, 1995.
Williams, John A. *The Man Who Cried I Am*. 1967. Reprint, New York: Thundermouth Press, 1994.
Wiltz, Teresa. "Meshell Ndegeocello Breaks Step with Pop." *Washington Post*, June 19, 2005, N01.
Wright, Richard. *Native Son*. 1940. Reprint, New York: Chelsea House, 1988.
Wynter, Sylvia. "Novel and History, Plot and Plantation." *Savacour* 5 (June 1971): 99–100.
Yellin, Jean Fagan. "Introduction to *Incidents in the Life of a Slave Girl: Written by Herself* by Harriet A. Jacobs. Cambridge, MA: Harvard University Press, 1987.
Young, Robert J. C. *Colonial Desire: Hybridity in Theory, Culture, and Race*. London: Routledge, 1995.

Index

Abrahams, Roger, 18, 20, 59, 74, 159, 167
Afrekete, 76, 77, 78, 79, 80, 81, 125, 186. *See also* Lorde, Audre; *Zami*
Africanisms, 13–14. *See also* Turner, Lorenzo Dow
All the Women Are White, All the Blacks Are Men (Hull, Scott, Smith), 8. *See also* Combahee River Collective
allegorical strap-on, 65–66
Amadiume, Ifi, 156, 297n19
Anansi, 15, 17
Andrews, William, 68, 69
Angelou, Maya, 190
animal tales, 20, 44–47, 161, 165, 262, 296n16; signifying monkey, 58
anti-vernacular criticism, 7, 20, 296n7
Arobateau, Red Jordan, 32, 282–83, 287, 303n8
Asante, Molefi, 153, 158
Aunt Esther, 129, 130, 132. *See also* Page, LaWanda; *Sanford and Son*

Bad Man/Bad Nigga, 152, 160, 247; characteristics, 165–67; homoerotics, 167–69. *See also* Stackolee
Bakhtin, Mikhail, 136–37, 147
Bambara, Toni Cade, xv, 2, 41, 42; English language, 90; on gender roles, 79. *See also* *The Black Woman*; *Salteaters*
Beam, Joseph, 288, 289. *See also* in the life
being, 53–54
Benston, Kimberly, 20, 38, 39, 40. *See also* (un)naming
bisexuality, 17, 223–25, 238, 239, 241, 243–44, 249, 254–55, 307n18; in Black America, 239; as narrative, 242. *See also* Cornerly, Gregory; Daumer, E.D.; Storr, Merl
bitch, 258–61
Black and White of It, The (Shockley), 11, 31, 184, 186–87; "Meeting of the Sapphic Sisters," 188–94; "The Mistress and the Slave Girl," 202–220; "Play It, But Don't Say It," 194–202; "Women in a Southern Time," 202, 305n4. *See also* Shockley, Ann Allen
black folklore research, 12–20
black middle-class fears, 151, 154, 257, 267. *See also* Frazier, E. Franklin
Black nationalism, 151, 153, 157, 296n6, 298n6, 303n2
"Black Unicorn" (Lorde), 99–100
"Black (W)holes" (Hammonds), 1, 4, 184, 186, 216, 222
Black Woman, The (Bambara), xv. *See also* Covington, Francee
black women's language practices, 119, 242. *See also* bitch; Morgan, Marcyliena; signifyin(g)
blue material, definition, 113; reasons for use, 115–16; use by comediennes, 134
blues women, 130, 178, 175, 180, 183
Bodies That Matter (Butler), 34, 183, 195, 210–11, 246, 247, 251,

329

253–54, 309. *See also* Butler, Judith
Bogan, Lucille, 178, 183, 305n20. *See also* blues women
Bogus, Sdiane, 179, 304n18. *See also* Queen B
Bontemps, Arna, 48, 50, 51, 52
Bornstein, Kate, 115
Bost, Suzanne, 266. *See also* female rap
Br'er Rabbit, 20, 45, 47, 122, 123. *See also* animal tales
bringing wreck, 257. *See also* Pough, Gwendolyn
Brooks, Sara, 42
Brown, William Wells, 62–67. *See also* allegorical strap-on; *Clotel*
bulldagger, 179
butch, 203, 210, 211, 212, 214, 216, 218. *See also* femme
Butler, Judith, 29, 35, 37, 124, 130, 157, 183, 195, 210, 246, 249–51, 253–54, 302n5, n12, 308n21; on desire, 28, 29; performative power, 195, 246. *See also Bodies that Matter; Gender Trouble*

camp, 115, 118, 125, 127, 136, 142; in trickster tales, 123. *See also* Newton, Esther; Sontag, Susan
Carby, Hazel, 7, 8, 21–22. *See also Reconstructing Womanhood*
Charles, RuPaul, 115, 118, 125–27, 129, 138–39, 169, 302n3,
chitlinality, 127
chitlin' circuit, 127
chitlinfyin(g) drag, 127
Chinn, Sarah E., 28, 109, 110, 184
Christian, Barbara, 21
Christmas, Annie, 46–52, 78, 81, 173. *See also* Henry, John; levee culture
Clarke, Cheryl, 12–13, 32, 281, 283–293
Coffy, 176–77. *See also* Grier, Pam
Cohen, Cathy, 303n6
Collins, Patricia Hill, 21, 42–43
closet, the, 189, 190, 191, 200, 201, 289. *See also* Sedgwick, Eve
Clotel, 62–67. *See also* Brown, William Wells

Combahee River Collective, 37
Comfort Woman (Ndegeocello), 231–37. *See also* Ndegeocello, Meshell
conjuring, 85–86, 107
Conerly, Gregory, 188, 239. *See also* bisexuality
Cooper, Anna Julia, 296n6
Covington, Francee, 259, 261. *See also The Black Woman*
Cox, Ida, xiv. *See also* blues women
Craft, Ellen, 63–65, 224. *See* Craft, William; *Running a Thousand Miles for Freedom*
Craft, William, 299n18. *See also* Craft, Ellen; *Running a Thousand Miles for Freedom*
Crenshsaw, Kimberle, 297n8
cult of womanhood, 21–22, 69–70

Dahomey (Herskovits), 246, 308n19. *See also* Fa; Fon
Dance, Daryl C., 119–21, 161, 306. *See also Honey Hush; Shuckin' and Jivin'*
Daumer, E. D., 224, 238. *See also* bisexuality
Davies, Carole Boyce, x, 84. *See also* migratory subjects
Davis, Angela, 35–36
Davis, Erik, 9
deconstruction, 6
Def Comedy Jam, 144, 147–48, 302n9
Delany, Samuel, 27, 29. *See also* desire
deLauretis, Teresa, 306n13
D'Emilio, John, 155, 188
Derrida, Jacques, 6, 37, 78, 296n15. *See also* différance
desire, 27–29, 217. *See also* Butler, Judith; Delany, Samuel; Grosz, Elizabeth
différance, 6, 78–79, 296n10. *See also* Derrida, Jacques
difference, 5–6. *See also* Lorde, Audre
divination, 77, 105; importance of touch, 107–8
Dolemite (Moore), 170, 176
dos Santos, J. E. and D. M., 16
Doty, Alexander, 217
Doty, William, 121
Doueihi, Anne, 58, 62, 293

Dove, Rita, 283
drag, 115, 118, 124, 130. *See also* camp; Charles, RuPaul; chiltinality; chitlinfyin(g) drag; Newton, Esther
drag king, 128, 137. *See also* Halberstam, Judith
Dreger, Alice, 186
DuBois, W. E. B., 1, 79
DuCille, Ann, 7, 62

Ellison, Ralph, 40, 244
erotic, the, 80–81, 102–3, 106, 110–11. *See also* Lorde, Audre
erotic priestess, 229, 231
Essence, 224, 256–57, 267–68
Esu Elegbara, 16–17. *See also* Legba
Eva's Man (Jones), 172, 182–83, 301n5
Experimental Love (Clarke), 281, 283–84, 286, 287, 291

Fa, the, 77. *See also* Dahomey; Fon
Favor, J. Martin, 7
female ejaculation, 277; in Lil' Kim's music, 275–78
female rap, 258, 263–67. *See also* bringing wreck; Kim, Lil'; Queen Pen; "Roxanne, Roxanne"
femme, 210, 211, 212, 214. *See also* butch
Ferguson, Roderick A., 155, 158, 220
flying trope, 225, 226; Africans, 227–28; in music, 226, 307–8n6
Fon, the, 77; *See* Dahomey; Fa
Frazier, E. Franklin, 154, 257, 267. *See also* black-middle class fears
From Trickster to Badman (Roberts), 19–20; *See also* Bad Man/ Bad Nigga

Gates, Henry Louis, 18; writing and slave narratives, 53. See also *The Signifying Monkey*
Gender Trouble, 35, 124, 130, 157; definition of gender, 36; drag, 129. *See also* Butler, Judith
Gilroy, Paul, 222, 235, 237
girlfriend subjectivity, 89, 91. *See also* Kevin Quashie

Givens, Adele, 135, 144–48. See also *Queens of Comedy*
go-go music, 249, 250, 252
Gomez, Jewell, 287, 305n6
Grier, Pam, 176–77. See also *Coffy*
Grosz, Elizabeth, 28, 29, 217. *See also* desire
Halberstam, Judith, 128, 130, 137, 216, 245. *See also* drag king
Halperin, David, 182
Hamilton, Virginia, 49, 51. See also *Herstories*
Hammonds, Evelyn, 1, 4, 184, 186, 216, 222. *See also* "Black (W)holes"
Hansome, Rhonda, 134. See also *I Be Done Been Was Is*
Harris, Trudier, x, 24, 43, 86, 297n20, 302n2
Hayes, Laura, 135–37. See also *Queens of Comedy*
healing, acts, 92, 105, 107–8; in Black literature, 85–86, 94; language, 87
Healing, The (Jones), 82–112
Hemphill, Essex, 153
Henderson, Mae Gwendolyn, 300n27
Henry, John, 46, 47. *See also* Christmas, Annie
hero, 15; folk hero, 17–18, 19
Herskovits, Frances, 77
Herskovits, Melville, 13, 77
Herstories, 49, 50, 51. *See also* Hamilton, Virginia
heterosexualization of desire, 157
Holliday, Billie, 211
Holloway, Karla F. C., 24–25, 61, 93. *See also* myth and memory
homosexual folkore, 162–64, 304n12. *See also* Bad Man/Nigga,
Honey, Hush, 119–21, 172, 173. *See also* Dance, Daryl C.
hooks, bell, 3, 9, 26, 29, 82, 295n2, 296nn8–9
Hughes, Langston, 48, 50, 51, 52
humor, 117, 120, 132. *See also* blue material
Hurston, Zora Neale, 33; "Characteristics of Negro Expression," 159, 262; *I Love Myself*, 113; *Mules and Men*, 84,

85; *Their Eyes Were Watching God*, 33, 41
Hyde, Lewis, 46–47. *See also* folkore research; trickster
Hynes, William, 10, 47, 63, 85, 117, 169, 186, 229, 243, 261, 266, 275. *See also* trickster traits

I Be Done Been Was Is (Robinson), 130–35. *See also* Hansom, Rhonda; Robinson, Debra; Warfield, Marsha

Incidents in the Life of a Slave Girl, 67–75. *See also* Jacobs, Harriet
in the life, 288–89. *See also* Beam, Joseph
Irigaray, Luce, 181, 234

Jacobs, Harriet, 67–75. *See also Incidents in the Life of a Slave Girl*
Jackson, Millie, 262–63
Jagose, Annamarie, 160, 305n9, 309n2. *See also* queer theory
James, Joy, 176
Jamison, Laura, 260
JanMohamed, Abdul R., 156–57. *See also* racialized sexuality
Johnson, E. Patrick, 9, 194–95, 196, 289
Jones, Gayl, on oral traditions, 90. *See also Eva's Man; The Healing*
Jordan, June, 2, 17, 295n1(preface), 307n16. *See also* politics of sexuality
Joyce, Joyce A., 306n1
Judy, Ronald T., 53–54
Jung, Carl C., 11, 27, 237–38; parapsychology and trickster, 83; psychology of trickster, 181, 208

Kelley, Robin D. G., 8

Labelle, Patti, 124
Lacan, Jacques, 27; on desire, 28
Lady Reed Album, 175–76
laying on hands, 108
Lee, Valerie, 24
Legba, 16, 77, 246–47, 308n19; phallus, 246–47. *See also* Esu Elegbara
lesbian phallus, 223–24, 244–46, 249, 251–255, 272, 308n21; in Ndegeocello's music, 244–55. *See also Bodies That Matter;* Butler, Judith
lesbian subject, 214, 220
Lester, Julius, 228
levee culture, 48. *See also* Christmas, Annie
Levine, Lawrence, 43, 57, 96, 168, 261, 262
Lil' Kim (Kimberly Jones), 223, 256; ritualized sexual violence, 272–79; sexual militancy 267–70; signifyin' pose, 270, 309n4. *See also* female rap
liminality, 88, 90; subjectivity 89, 91, 94, 112, 226. *See also* Quashie, Kevin
Living as a Lesbian (Clarke), 288, 289–91
Longing to Tell, 4, 8. *See also* Rose, Tricia
Lorde, Audre, 87, 99, 185, 198; "Age, Race, Class, and Sex," 5–7, 43, 57; "Black Unicorn," 99–100; "Uses of the Erotic," 80–81, 102–3, 106, 110–11; *Zami*, 66, 77, 78, 81, 179
Lubiano, Wahneema, 54, 153

Mabley, Jackie "Moms" (Loretta Mary Aiken), 131, 143. *See also* Williams, Elise
Marshall, Paule, 228
Mawu-Lisa, 76–78, 80, 97, 233, 247–48. *See also Dahomey;* Lorde, Audre
McDowell, Deborah, x, 60–61, 299n16
migratory subjects, 84. *See also* Davies, Carol Boyce
Mitchell Kernan, Claudia, 18, 58, 302n11. *See also* signifying
Moore, Rudy Ray, 176. *See also* Dolemite
Morgan, Marcyliena, 119, 242. *See also* black women's language practices; signifying
Morrison, Toni, 33, 185; tar baby, 123
Mosse, George L., 154
Muñoz, José Esteban, 57, 139
Muthafucka, 25–26
myth and memory, 61, 93, 94. *See also* Holloway, Karla
Myth of the Negro Past, 13. *See also* Herskovits, Melville

naming, 37–41

nationalism, 152–56
Ndegeocello, MeShell (Michelle Johnson), 223–55
Newton, Esther, 118. *See also* camp; drag
Newton, Huey P., 152, 303n2
Nicholson, Judy, 185
Nugent, Bruce, 200. *See also* the closet

Ogundipe, Adoye, 16
Omolade, Barbara, 161, 295n1 (introduction)
oral tradition, 90
Oyêwùmí, Oyèrónké, 39, 300n26, 300n28

Page, LaWanda, 25, 114, 126–30, 139–43. *See also* Aunt Esther; *Sanford and Son*; "Whores in Church"
Pelton, Robert, 15, 142, 227, 240, 247
performative power, 195. *See also* Butler, Judith
policing, 153
politics of sexuality, 2. *See also* Jordan, June
Pough, Gwendolyn, 257. *See also* bringing wreck
pregeneric myths, 52, 70. *See also* Stepto, Robert

Quashie, Kevin, 88, 89, 91, 94, 112, 226. *See also* liminality
Queen B (?), 169; function, 170–72, 180–82
Queen Bee, 172–75. See also *Eva's Man*
Queen Bitch, 175–78, 261. *See also* Lil' Kim
Queen Bulldagger, 179–80. *See also* Bogus, SDiane; bulldagger
Queens of Comedy, 131, 145. *See also* Givens, Adele; Hayes, Laura
Queen Pen (Lynise Walters), 239–40, 242, 243, 249, 256. *See also* female rap
queer theory, 160, 182, 217. *See also* Jagose, Annamarie

racialized sexuality, 156–58. *See also* Jan-

Mohammed, Abdul R.
Reconstructing Womanhood (Carby), 21–22
ring-shout, 15. See also *Slave Culture*
Roberts, John W., 19–20, 28, 29, 74, 122, 159, 165, 296n11, 296n16, 298n7, 303n10. See also *From Trickster to Badman*
Robinson, Cedric, 154, 303n3
Robinson, Debra, 131,132. See also *I Be Done Been Was Is*
Roof, Judith, 203, 214. *See also* butch
Rose, Tricia, 4, 8, 263, 265. See also *Longing to Tell*
Ross, Marlon B., 113, 303n9
"Roxanne, Roxanne" (UTFO), 264–65, 268. *See also* female rap; Shante, Roxanne
Running a Thousand Miles for Freedom, 63–64. *See also* Craft, Ellen; Craft, William

sacred/lewd bricoleur, 138–39, 270, 275. *See also* trickster traits
Salteaters, The (Bambara), 2, 85, 86.
Sanford and Son, 125, 129. *See also* Aunt Esther; Page, Lawanda
Sankofa (Gerima), 225
Scarry, Elaine, 110
Sedgwick, Eve, 150, 190, 191, 194. *See also* closet, the
shamans, 83, 95, 226
Shante, Roxanne, 264. *See* female rap; "Roxanne, Roxanne"
shape-shifting, 63, 187
Shockley, Ann Allen, 185. See also *The Black and White of It*
Shuckin' and Jivin', 161, 166, 167, 173, 175, 178. *See also* Dance, Daryl C.
signifyin(g), 18, 58, 59, 90, 251; directive, 241; indirectness, 242. *See also* Gates, Henry Louis; Mitchell-Kernan, Claudia; Morgan, Marcyliena
Signifying Monkey, The (Gates), 18, 53, 251. *See also* signifyin(g)
situation-inversion, 203, 270
Slave Culture (Stuckey), 15, 16. *See also* ring-shout

slave narrative, 52, 68; narrative devices, 68, 69
Smith, Barbara, 23, 185, 289
Smith, Jeanne, 116
Smitherman, Geneva, 16, 147, 195
Sommerville, Siobahan, 209
Sontag, Susan, 118, 133, 136–37. *See also* camp
soul, 230–31, 235, 237
Spears, Arthur K., 146. *See also* uncensored mode
Spillers, Hortense, x, 5, 10, 22–23, 34, 39–40, 116, 174, 204, 210, 298n3
Spinks, C.W., 284
Stackolee, 167–68. *See also* Bad Man/Bad Nigga
Stepto, Robert, 52. *See also* pregeneric myths
Stokes, Mason Boyd, 192
Storey, Olivia Smith, 225
Storr, Merl, 222. *See also* bisexuality
Stuckey, Sterling, 15; on naming and unnaming, 38–39, 298n4. See also *Slave Culture*

Tar Baby, 121–22
Tar Lady, 123
Their Eyes Were Watching God (Hurston), 33, 41
tortoise, 95–97
trickster, 121; as comic holotrope, 30; as cultural transformer, 283; definition of, 9; gender and gendering of, 12–21, 46–47; phallus, 246–47, 266; queerness of, 11; trickster as hero, 15–16, 19–20; violence, 261–62, 273
trickster traits, 9–10, 12, 30, 47, 85, 169, 261
trickster-troping, 10, 12, 34–35, 41, 113
Truth, Sojourner, 55–61
Turner, Lorenzo Dow, 13
turtle myths, 95–96

unnaming, 34–41, 76–77, 81, 120, 184, 191 216, 218, 220, 298n4
(un)naming, 38–39. *See also* Benston, Kimberly
uncensored mode, 146. *See also* Spears, Arthur

Vizenor, Gerald, 30, 90

Wall, Cheryl, 20
Warfield, Marsha, 131, 133, 134. See also *I Be Done Been Was Is*
Watkins, Mel, 117, 127, 131
West, Cornell, 230, 262
White, Deborah Gray, 295n5
"Whores in Church," 140, 141–42. *See also* Page, LaWanda
wild, 3
Wilentz, Gay, 94, 232, 307n13
Williams, Elsie, 117; *See also* Mabley, Moms
Wynter, Sylvia, 42, 187

Zami (Lorde), 66, 77, 78, 81, 179

www.ingramcontent.com/pod-product-compliance
Lightning Source LLC
Chambersburg PA
CBHW030127240426
43672CB00005B/54